MW00528247

GUJARAT RIOTS:
THE TRUE STORY

GUJARAT RIOTS:
THE TRUE STORY

THE TRUTH OF THE 2002 RIOTS

राजेश्री ...... ஐ

SENTHILVEL S

14 जून 2019

M D DESHPANDE

PARTRIDGE

A Penguin Random House Company

Copyright © 2014 by M D Deshpande.

ISBN:	Hardcover	978-1-4828-4165-7
	Softcover	978-1-4828-4164-0
	eBook	978-1-4828-4163-3

All rights reserved. No part of this book may be used or reproduced by any means, graphic, electronic, or mechanical, including photocopying, recording, taping or by any information storage retrieval system without the written permission of the publisher except in the case of brief quotations embodied in critical articles and reviews.

Because of the dynamic nature of the Internet, any web addresses or links contained in this book may have changed since publication and may no longer be valid. The views expressed in this work are solely those of the author and do not necessarily reflect the views of the publisher, and the publisher hereby disclaims any responsibility for them.

To order additional copies of this book, contact
Partridge India
000 800 10062 62
orders.india@partridgepublishing.com

www.partridgepublishing.com/india

CONTENTS

CHAPTER 1

HISTORY OF ATTACKS ON INDIA

Wounds of the past continue to haunt the people. Without understanding the past, one can never fully understand the present. Therefore, we make an attempt to see a brief history of attacks on India- all done by foreigners. The aggressive design against India initiated in 636-37 AD by the Arabs and later on carried further by the groups from the Middle East, has been continuing intermittently for centuries. These attacks started within 14 years of the birth of Islam in AD 622, and within 4 years of the death of the Prophet of Islam in AD 632.

The Godhra carnage of 27th February, 2002 is not a product of the Ayodhya movement, or the Babri mosque demolition on 6th December, 1992. There may be more Godhras in store. India has been bleeding from a thousand wounds. Belgium based world famous scholar, Dr. Koenraad Elst (b. 1959) has written: "You wouldn't guess it from their polished convent-school English, their trendy terminology, or their sanctimoniousness, but the likes of Romila Thapar, Irfan Habib or Gyanendra Pandey have blood on their hands. The wave of Muslim violence after the Ayodhya demolition (and the boomerang of police repression and Shiv Sena retaliation) was at least partly due to the disinformation by supposed experts, who denied that the disputed building had a violent iconoclastic prehistory, and implied that Hindus can get away with concocted history in their attacks on innocent mosques. This disinformation gave Muslim militants the sense of justification needed to mount a 'revenge' operation and to mobilize decent Muslims for acts of violence, which they

7

never would have committed if they had known the truth about Islam's guilt in Ayodhya". (*Source*: *"BJP vis-à-vis Hindu Resurgence"* by Dr. Koenraad Elst, Voice of India, 1997).

Many Muslims genuinely believe that Islam spread in India due to Sufi saints and that Muslim rulers were tolerant or else the whole of India would have converted to Islam. Of course, this is wrong. Swami Vivekananda (1863-1902) said: "Hindu population as quoted by Farishta, one of the earliest Muslim historians, was 60 crores (i.e. 600 million) and today we are only 20 crores (i.e. 200 million)". (*Complete Works*, Vol. 5, p. 233). Former editor of *The Indian Express*, Magsaysay award winner, and ex-Disinvestment Minister of India, Arun Shourie (1941-) also quoted Swami Vivekananda as saying this in an article written on 31 January 1993 which can be read today at http://www.hindunet.org/hvk/articles/1206/156.html

According to *Wikisource* this is also mentioned in a letter written by Swami Vivekananda to Miss Mary Hale on 30th October, 1899 recorded in his *Complete Works, Volume 8, Epistles- Fourth Series CXLV.*

URL:http://en.wikisource.org/wiki/The_Complete_Works_of_Swami_Vivekananda/Volume_8/Epistles_-_Fourth_Series/CXLV_Optimist

Well-known historian, Dr. K. S. Lal (1920-2002) has written in his book *Growth of Muslim Population in India* that according to his calculations, the Hindu population in India declined by 80 million from AD 1000 to AD 1525, perhaps the biggest ever holocaust in human history. This does not mean a mere 80 million killings. Some estimates put the number of Hindus killed in India as 280 million while Swami Vivekananda opined that the number was more than 400 million (Hindus reducing from 60 crores to 20 crores). The point is, many Muslims even today believe themselves as victims and deny the crimes committed by Muslims against others. For example, a shockingly large number of Muslims including well-educated, well-to-do people genuinely believe that 9/11 attacks on USA were done by Jews to make USA target Muslims, or by the USA Government itself. Same is the case with Godhra and many other cases like 26/11, where many simply deny that Islamic fanatics did these crimes and genuinely believe it.

We must quote only authentic sources to make our point clear. Bharatiya Vidya Bhavan has compiled Indian history in 11 volumes and the project was financed by the Jawaharlal Nehru Government (who no one can ever accuse of being 'communal'). The chief editor is world- famous historian, the late R.C. Majumdar (1888-1980), who was Vice-President of the International Commission set up by UNESCO for the history of mankind and is one of the most respected historians. The Volumes on Indian history are contributed by many eminent historians, including those from the then East Pakistan (Bangladesh) and West Pakistan. To see the past, we simply quote Bharatiya Vidya Bhavan's *The History and Culture of the Indian People*. It is hoped that these authentic quotes make everyone (Indian Muslims included) realize the truth of Islam's spread and atrocities on Hindus.

The chronology that follows is incomplete but indicative-

636 AD	- Arabs attacked Thane, near Mumbai [1]
c. 643	- Arabs invaded Debol at the mouth of the Sindhu[2]
c. 660	- Arabs invaded Sindh[3]
c. 661-680	- Arabs sent six expeditions against Sindh[4]
661-680	- Arabs sent expeditions against Kabul and Zabul[5]
685	- The Arabs killed the king of Zabul[6]
699	- The Arabs ravaged Zabul[7]
712	- Muhammad-bin-Qasim slaughtered many Hindus, killed King Dahir and captured Sindh and gave settlement to 4000 Muslims[8]
724-738	- The Arabs sent several expeditions against Gujarat, Jaisalmer, Jodhpur, Broach, Malava, Vallamandal, Ujjain[9]
c. 739	- The Arabs invaded Kathiawar[10]
776	- The Arabs sent expedition against Barda, near Porbandar[11]
c. 948 to 963	- Alptigin of Ghazni plundered Punjab several times[12]
977-997	- Subuktigin of Ghazni plundered Punjab several times & carried immense wealth and killed many Hindus and converted many Hindus of Peshawar. [13]Jaipal was the King at that time.
998-1030	- Mahmud of Ghazni carried out several invasions, looted immense treasure, killed many Hindus and converted many Hindus [14]

1000	- Mahmud of Ghazni seized some parts near Peshawar[15]
1001	- Mahmud of Ghazni attacked the kingdom of Jaipal, slaughtered many Hindus, captured Jaipal and collected 250000 dinars and 25 elephants as ransom[16]
1004	- Mahmud of Ghazni invaded Bagi Ray's kingdom Bhatiya, plundered Bhatiya and converted many Hindus[17]
1005-06	- Mahmud of Ghazni attacked Anandapal; in a battle near Peshawar, Anandapal was defeated[18]
1007	- Mahmud of Ghazni attacked Sukhapal and plundered 400000 dirhams[19]
1008	- Mahmud of Ghazni attacked Anandapal. 20000 Hindus were killed. Bhimnagar (=Nagarkot=Kot Kangra) was laid waste and[20] its treasury looted which consisted of 70,000,000 royal dirhams, 700400 mands of gold and jewellery & precious stones; clothes and garments[21]
1009	- Mahmud of Ghazni attacked Narayanpur in Rajputana, broke many idols, killed many Hindus and took booty[22]
1010	- Mahmud of Ghazni attacked Multan and killed a large number of Hindus[23]
1010	- Anandapal had to agree to send Mahmud of Ghazni annually 50 big elephants laden with valuables and 2000 men to serve the court of Ghazni[24]
1011	- Mahmud of Ghazni invaded Thaneswar, broke a large number of idols and plundered[25]
1013	- Mahmud of Ghazni attacked Nandana, killed many Hindus, captured booty and a host of elephants[26]
1014	- Mahmud of Ghazni attacked Kashmir, took many Hindus as prisoners and converted many Hindus to Islam[27]
1015	- Mahmud of Ghazni attacked Lokhot, a hill-fort in Kashmir[28]
1018	- Mahmud of Ghazni crossed the five rivers of Punjab and crossed Yamuna on 2 December 1018. The king of Baran (Bulandshahar) surrendered and paid 1,00,000 dirhams and 30 elephants.[29] Mahmud of Ghazni attacked Mahaban in Mathura and killed nearly 5000 Hindus. The king

Kulachand killed his wife first and then himself.[30] Mahmud of Ghazni plundered Mathura and captured idols of pure Gold weighing 98,300 miskals. The idols of silver numbered 200. He ordered to burn all temples and the houses. Mathura was pillaged for 20 days.[31] Mahmud of Ghazni plundered Kanauj. King Rajyapal fled. The Hindus were slaughtered. Kanauj had 10,000 temples. The idols were destroyed.[32] Mahmud of Ghazni attacked and devastated Mung, near Kanpur. Many Hindus were killed and all valuables taken.[33] Mahmud of Ghazni attacked Asni, near Fatehpur. Its ruler, Chandrapal, fled. The Hindus were slaughtered.[34]

1019   - Mahmud of Ghazni attacked & plundered Sharva, near Saharanpur. Its ruler, Chand Rai, fled. The booty of gold, silver and pearls worth 30,00,000 dirhams and many elephants were captured. A large number of Hindus were taken as slaves and sold at Iraq's Khurasan. In January 1019 Mahmud of Ghazni returned to Ghazni with 20,000,000 dirhams, 53,000 prisoners and 350 elephants.[35]

1020   - Mahmud of Ghazni attacked the Chandella kingdom of Vidyadhar near Yamuna. The Hindu Sahi kingdom was completely ravaged. Vidyadhar & Trilochanpal fled.[36] Mahmud of Ghazni attacked and plundered Bari, the Pratihar capital. Bari was razed to the ground.[37] Mahmud of Ghazni chased the Chandella King Vidyadhar. Vidyadhar fled. Mahmud of Ghazni captured a huge booty and 580 elephants.[38]

1021   - Mahmud of Ghazni attacked Qirat & Nur and forced the Hindu rulers to embrace Islam. Their temples and idols were destroyed.[39] Mahmud of Ghazni attacked Lohkot, in Kashmir.[40]

1021-22   - Mahmud of Ghazni again launched an attack on the Chandella Vidyadhar. Mahmud of Ghazni attacked Gwalior and Lakangara.[41]

11

1024	- Mahmud of Ghazni started to attack the Somnath temple. On the way he ravaged Ludrava, Anahillapataka, Mundur, Dewalwara etc. The Chalukya king Bhim I fled. [42]
1025	- He reached Somnath in January 1025. More than 50000 Hindus were killed. The booty was worth 20,000,000 dirhams. The temple was razed to the ground.[43]
1027	- Mahmud of Ghazni attacked Jats, killed thousands of Jats, plundered their wealth.[44] He died in AD 1030.
1034	- Ahmad Niyaltigin plundered Banaras and carried away immense booty[45]
1036	- Mahmud's son Masud attacked Hansi, Sonpat and the kingdom of Ram Rai.[46]
1178	- Muhammad Ghuri attacked Gujarat and plundered Nadol[47]
1191	- Battle of Tarain. Ghuri attacked Prithviraj- and was routed[48]
1192	- Second battle of Tarain. He again attacked Prithviraj. One lakh Hindu soldiers lost their lives. Prithviraj was killed. Temples were demolished. Ghuri left behind his fanatic general Qutubuddin Aibak to look after the affairs of India.[49]
1193	- The battle of Chandawar. Muhammad Ghuri killed Jayachandra; plundered Asni and Banaras.[50]
1194	- Qutubuddin Aibak ousted Hari Raj and captured Ajmer, demolished 27 temples[51]
1195	- Muhammad Ghori attacked Bayana and Gwalior[52]
1196	- Qutubuddin slaughtered 50,000 Rajputs and enslaved 20,000[53]
1197	- Qutubuddin invaded Gujarat[54]
1200	- Muhammad Khalji plundered Magadha; slaughtered Buddhist monks of Odantapuri Vihar[55]
1205	- Qutubuddin and Muizzuddin in the battle between Jhelum and Chenab killed Khokars and enslaved many others[56]
1233	- Iltutmish captured Bhilsa and plundered Ujjain[57]
1296	- Alauddin Khalji invaded Devagiri of Maharashtra[58]
1296 to 1316	- His discriminatory regulations ruined the Hindus[59]
1305	- Alauddin invaded Malava[60]

1309	- His general Malik Kafur invaded Warangal[61]
1310	- Pandya kingdom invaded immense booty and 250 elephants were captured[62]
1325 to 1351	- Muhammad Tughlaq ruined Kakatiya, Yadava, Hoysala and Pandya dynasties of the South [63] Nagaya Gauna, Harihar, Bukka were forced to embrace Islam[64]
1361	- Firoz Tughlaq slaughtered nearly one lakh Hindus near the Chilka lake[65]
1362	- Muhammad Shah defeated Telangana king Vinayaka Deva and killed him with barbarous cruelty[66]
1458 to 1511	- Mahmud Begarha held Hindus of Gujarat in thrall[67]
1467	- He invaded and plundered Girnar[68]
1469	- He attacked Junagadh and forced Mandalika to embrace Islam[69]
1482	- Malik Sudha killed many Hindus of Champaner[70]
1483	- Mahmud Begarha plundered Champaner and killed and converted Hindus[71]
1527	- Babur defeated Rana Sangram and killed him and Rajputs[72]
1528	- Babur defeated Medini Rai, killed Hindus in Chanderi [73]
1565	- In Talikota, alliance of 4 Muslim kings defeated Vijaynagar king Rama Raya and thousands of Hindus were killed[74]
1568	- The battle of Chitor: Akbar defeated the Rajputs and ordered massacre of 30,000 non-combatant Hindus[75]
1663	- The Bijapur Sultan plundered Tirucherapalli[76]
1665	- Aurangazeb imposed taxes on Hindu traders[77]
1669	- He ordered demolition of schools and temples of Hindus. Many temples were demolished-including Kashi, Mathura and Patan Somnath[78]
1679	- Aurangazeb reimposed jizyah tax on Hindus. Unable to pay this tax many Hindus converted to Islam[79]
1704	- Fifth attack on Anandpur by Vazir Khan. Guru Govind Singh's mother, brothers, followers were killed; his two sons bricked up alive in a fort wall and then beheaded because they refused to embrace Islam on 27 December 1704[80]

1708	- Two Pathan Muslims stabbed Guru Govind Singh- he died soon[81]
1715	- On Farukh-Siyar's orders Abdur Samad Khan geared up to vanquish Sikh leader Banda. Many Sikhs were massacred[82]
1716	- Banda was brutally killed (Details too horrific)[83]
1739	- Nadir Shah of Persia entered Delhi. People of Delhi suffered terrible horrors. Their property looted, houses burnt, womenfolk raped, the men slaughtered. Three to four lakhs were killed, treasure worth 50 crores was plundered[84]
1748	- Ahmad Shah Abdali's first invasion of India[85]
1750	- His second invasion of India [86]
1751	- His third invasion of India[87]
1756	- His fourth invasion of India[88]
1759	- His fifth invasion of India[89]
1761	- His sixth invasion of India and the Third Battle of Panipat (on 14 Jan 1761) –in which the Hindus were crushed[90]
1764	- His seventh invasion of India[91]
1767	- His eighth invasion of India[92]

All these were foreigners' attacks on India. But even after the end of the foreign Muslim rule and during the British rule there were numerous riots between Hindus and Muslims in India. In many of these riots before 1947 Hindus suffered far more than Muslims. Even Mahatma Gandhi had to acknowledge this. He is reported to have said:

"There is no doubt in my mind that in the majority of quarrels the Hindus come out second best. But my own experience confirms the opinion that the Mussalman as a rule is a bully, and the Hindu as a rule is a coward. I have noticed this in railway trains, on public roads, and in the quarrels which I had the privilege of settling. Need the Hindu blame the Mussalman for his cowardice? Where there are cowards, there will always be bullies...But I, as a Hindu, am more ashamed of Hindu cowardice than I am angry at the Mussalman bullying..."

The source quoted is "Hindu-Muslim Tension: Its Cause and Cure", *Young India*, 29/5/1924; reproduced in M.K. Gandhi: *The Hindu-Muslim Unity*, p.35-36.

In 1921, in Malabar, Moplahs committed horrible atrocities on Hindus, thousands were killed and thousands converted.[93]

In 1926 Swami Shraddhananda was murdered by a man named Abdul Rashid.[94]

And in 1946, on 16 August was the Direct Action Day of the Muslim League, and this saw the great Calcutta killings.[95]

At the same time, horrible Naokhali riots were also seen.

The past is, never ever, far from the present. Hindus suffered horribly at the hands of foreigners for many centuries. This is just a brief summary. The horrid, lurid details of these events will make one's hair stand on end.

[handwritten note: Arab vroshu & Indians or Hindu vs muslins!]

CHAPTER 2

THE GODHRA CARNAGE

"Godhra". The word is more than just the name of a town located in Panchmahal district in the western Indian state of Gujarat. The word used also indicates an event. A mind-numbing one. A horrifying one. An unimaginable one. A barbaric one. The word "Godhra" records the gruesome killing of some 59 innocent people, including 25 women and 15 children and injuries to 40. Independent India saw many horrors. This was one of the worst of them.

This mind-numbing horror was also the cause of many more horrors, many more events, many more riots, many more political changes. It was also the immediate cause of rioting, which left some 1169 people dead (including those killed in police firing).

But this was not the first time, nor the last time, that the town witnessed communal vandalism. The town had a long history of bloody communalism. It was well-known for it. Let us take a brief look at the town's long history of bloody communal riots.

Communal History of Godhra for the Record

Godhra is the main centre of Panchmahal district, which is considered to be communally very sensitive. Chronology of a few communal riots/atrocities, as reported by *Vishwa Samvad Kendra*, Gujarat is appended below:

1927-28: Murder of P.M. Shah, a leading local representative of Hindus.

→ There was no country called Pakistan.

1946: Mr. Sadva Hazi and Mr. Chudighar, pro-Pakistani Muslim leaders were responsible for attack on a Parsi Solapuri Fozdar during communal riots. After partition, Mr. Chudighar left for Pakistan.

1948: Mr. Sadva Hazi conspired an attack on the District Collector, Mr. Pimputkar in 1948 but his bodyguard saved him at the cost of his own life. After that, Mr. Sadva Hazi also left for Pakistan in 1948.

On 24th March, 1948, one Hindu was stabbed to death near a mosque in Jahurpur area. Around 2,000 houses of Hindus were burnt, besides Hindu temples. District Collector Pimputkar could save the remaining areas belonging to Hindus by imposing curfew, which lasted for six months.

1965: Shops belonging to the Hindus were set ablaze near police chowki No. 7 by throwing incendiary material from the nearby two Muslim houses, viz. Bidani and Bhopa. It could be possible allegedly because of the Congress MLA belonging to the minority community. PSI of this police chowki, which was near the Railway Station, was also attacked by anti-social elements.

1980: A similar attack was made on the Hindus on 29th October, 1980, which started from the Bus Station of Godhra. This attack was planned by Muslim miscreants who were involved in anti-social activities near the Station Road area.

Five Hindus including two children of five and seven years of age were burnt alive. A Gurudwara was also set on fire, in Shikari Chal of this area. Forty shops belonging to the Hindus were also set on fire in station area. Due to these communal riots, Godhra was put under curfew for a year, which severely affected the business and industries.

1990: Four Hindu teachers, including two women teachers, were murdered (cut into pieces) by miscreants in Saifia Madarsa in Vhorvada area of Godhra on 20th November, 1990 in front of children. One Hindu tailor was also stabbed to death in this area. All this was done by anti-social elements allegedly at the instance of the Congress MLA of the area.

1992: More than 100 houses belonging to the Hindus were set on fire near the Railway Station in the year 1992 to snatch away this area from Hindus. This area in 2002 was lying vacant as most of the Hindu families had shifted elsewhere.

2002: The bogies of Ahmedabad-bound Sabarmati Express were set on fire on 27th February, 2002 by Muslim miscreants. S-6 coach carrying *karsewaks* returning from Ayodhya was targeted as a pre-meditated plan/ conspiracy. 59 innocent men, women and children died and 40 sustained injuries. The attackers had a plan to set on fire the entire train but could not do so because the train was late for four hours and they could not take the advantage of darkness of night.

(*Source*: *Vishwa Samwad Kendra,* Gujarat and *The Indian Express* dated 30th April, 2002: http://www.indianexpress.com/storyOld.php? storyId=1822, quoting Gujarat's then MoS for Home Gordhan Zadaphiya)

2003 September, Ganesh idol immersion saw stone pelting and conflicts between Hindus and Muslims. This was reported by rediff.com and *The Times of India,* but was forgotten by everyone, including the Sangh Parivar leadership. (*Source:* http://articles.timesofindia.indiatimes.com/2003-09-05/india/ 27208741_1_tear-gas-shells-stone-_pelting-railway-station).

All the above details of Godhra (except the 2003 stone pelting) are also mentioned in an article titled "Godhra in Ferment even before Independence" in the *Milli Gazette* magazine on 16 March, 2002. (*Source*: http://www. milligazette.com/Archives/15042002/1504200276.htm).

This magazine is considered as a voice of Muslims in India. **This is the Indian Muslims' leading English newspaper and it has also published these details about Godhra.**

After the 2002 Godhra carnage, the Nanavati Commission was appointed to probe the carnage which was a full-fledged Commission of Inquiry under the Commission of Inquiry Act, 1952. It submitted its report on the Godhra carnage in September 2008. The report said: "Godhra town is a very sensitive place. There is a high percentage of Muslim population in various places in the district. Communal riots had taken place in Godhra in the years 1925, 1928,

1946, 1948, 1950, 1953, 1980, 1981, 1985, 1986, 1988, 1989, 1990, 1991 and 1992. The communal riots that had taken place in 1948 were very serious. Initially, the Muslims had burnt 869 houses of Hindus. Thereafter, the Hindus had burnt 3,071 houses of Muslims".

The whole report can be read at: http://www.home.gujarat.gov.in/homedepart ment/downloads/godharaincident.pdf

Even Mahatma Gandhi (1869-1948) had also written about the Muslim communalism in Godhra. V.P. Bhatia (1928-2003) wrote in *Organiser* weekly dated 21st April, 2002 in his famous column *Cabbages and Kings*:

"The following article from Gandhiji's entitled "What are we to Do?" in *Young India* (11th October, 1928) reveals that the Muslims were ever aggressive against Hindus in that city (as in other areas of Gujarat) in the wake of the Khilafat fiasco. There was virtually a state of war between the two communities in which the non-violent Hindu was the real sufferer. The following are the exact words of Gandhiji in the said article.

"Two weeks ago, I wrote in *Navajivan* a note on the tragedy in Godhra, where Shri Purshottam Shah bravely met his death at the hands of his assailants and gave my note the heading *Hindu-Muslim Fight in Godhra*. Several Hindus did not like the heading and addressed angry letters asking me to correct it (for it was a one sided fight). I found it impossible to accede to their demand. Whether there is one victim or more, whether there is a free fight between the two communities, or whether one assumes the offensive and the other simply suffers, I should describe the event as a fight if the whole series of happenings were the result of a state of war between the two communities. Whether in Godhra or in other places, there is today a state of war between the two communities. Fortunately, the countryside is still free from the war fever (no longer now) which is mainly confined to towns and cities, where, in some form or the other, fighting is continually going on. Even the correspondents, who have written to me about Godhra, do not seem to deny the fact that the happenings arose out of the communal antagonisms that existed there. "If the correspondents had simply addressed themselves to the heading, I should have satisfied myself with writing to them privately and written nothing in

Navajivan about it. But there are other letters in which the correspondents have vented their ire on different counts.

A volunteer from Ahmedabad, who had been to Godhra, writes: You say that you must be silent over these quarrels. Why were you not silent over the Khilafat, and why did you exhort us to join the Muslims? Why are you not silent about your principles of Ahimsa? How can you justify your silence when the two communities are running at each other's throats and Hindus are being crushed to atoms? How does Ahimsa come there? I invite your attention to two cases:

A Hindu shopkeeper, thus, complained to me: Musalmans purchase bags of rice from my shop, often never paying for them. I cannot insist on payment, for fear of their looting my godowns. I have, therefore, to make an involuntary gift of about 50 to 70 maunds of rice every month?

Others complained: Musalmans invade our quarters and insult our women in our presence, and we have to sit still. If we dare to protest, we are done for. We dare not even lodge a complaint against them.

What would you advise in such cases? How would you bring your Ahimsa into play? Or, even here you would prefer to remain silent!

"These and similar other questions have been answered in these pages over and over again, but as they are still being raised, I had better explain my views once more at the risk of repetition. "*Ahimsa* is not the way of the timid or the cowardly. It is the way of the brave ready to face death. He who perishes sword in hand is, no doubt, brave, but he who faces death without raising his little finger, is braver. But he who surrenders his rice bags for fear of being beaten, is a coward and no votary of *Ahimsa*. He is innocent of *Ahimsa*. He, who for fear of being beaten, suffers the women of his household to be insulted, is not manly, but just the reverse. He is fit neither to be a husband nor a father, nor a brother. Such people have no right to complain..." (extract from *To the Hindus and Muslims*, a collection of articles by Gandhiji from *Young India*)."

Thus, it is clear that Gandhiji mentioned the murder of Purshottam Shah, which happened in 1927. He had also once said that 'Hindus are cowards'. Note here that this writing is solely from V P Bhatia's article in *Organiser*.

The Entire Happenings in Godhra—How the Massacre Occurred

We have seen the bloody communal history of the town. Now let us see the exact horrible, lurid details of the massacre of 27th February, 2002 with the background.

The Vishwa Hindu Parishad (VHP) had organized a *'Purnahuti Yagya'* in Ayodhya in February-March 2002. It declared 15th March, 2002 as the date for the beginning of the construction of Ram temple at Ayodhya. People participating in this *'Yagya'* had simply participated and gone home. They did not stay in Ayodhya until 15th March, 2002 for the construction of the Ram temple in Ayodhya **at the undisputed site** (majority of the undisputed land was owned by VHP and affiliated bodies and the Supreme Court of India in its order of 1994 had said that the undisputed land can be given to its owner).

People from all parts of the country went to Ayodhya, participated in this event, i.e. the *Purnahuti Yagya* and returned home from mid-February to 27th February, 2002. A trainload of such people called *'karsevaks'* or *'Ramsevaks'* were returning to Ahmedabad in Gujarat from Ayodhya after participating in the *Purnahuti Yagya*. Whether they were all members of the Vishwa Hindu Parishad or just ordinary people supporting the VHP's stance on the Ram temple in Ayodhya is not known to the author.

The train, the Sabarmati Express was supposed to reach Ahmedabad early in the morning. It was running four hours late (*Source*: *India Today,* dated 11th March, 2002). Shortly after the train left the Godhra railway station at 7: 48 a.m., a mob (the estimates of the numbers of which have ranged from 500 to 2000) stopped it. This was 500-700 meters away from the Godhra railway station, at Signal Falia area. **The train was not burnt at the railway station, but at Signal Falia.** That is why the attackers could not burn the train from outside. Had it been on a railway platform, they would not have found it too high. **But at Signal Falia, it was too high.** Hence, some of them entered the train cutting the vestibule from the side coach no. S-7 and set it afire from inside and then went out again. The mob was reportedly armed with petrol bombs, acid bombs and swords. The attackers poured petrol into the compartment and then set it afire. Two thousand people were standing on all sides of the compartment to prevent the *karsevaks* from running away and saving their lives from the fire. The *karsevaks* were literally caught between devil and the deep sea. There was fire inside and armed Muslim attackers outside. 59 *karsevaks* were burnt to death in a most horrifying manner. Many of the bodies were charred horrifically. The victims included 15 children, including some toddlers and some old people of above 65. They were all done to death in the most brutal manner.

Account of a 16-year-old Survivor

On 27th February, Gayatri Panchal, a young eleventh class student, was also amongst those who were returning from Ayodhya. She is a surviving witness to the inhuman atrocious cruelty in which right in front of her eyes two of her sisters and parents were burnt alive.

Harshadbhai Panchal, a resident of Ramol in Gujarat, left for *karseva* at Ayodhya on 22nd February, together with his wife, Neetaben and three daughters, Pratiksha, Chhaya and Gayatri. His sister-in-law, her son, her neighbour, Poojaben and her would-be husband were also accompanying him.

All of them were returning to Ahmedabad along with several other *karsevaks*. Harshadbhai and his family, Poojaben and her husband were in one compartment, while his sister-in-law and her husband and their son were in another compartment. The only survivor out of these ten, Gayatri, says about this horrible event that, "On the 27th morning, at around 8 a.m. the train left Godhra Station. The *karsevaks* were loudly chanting the Ram Dhoon. The train had hardly gone a few meters, when it suddenly stopped. Somebody had perhaps pulled the chain to stop the train. Before anybody could know what had happened, we saw a huge mob approaching the train. **People were carrying weapons like *Gupti*, Spears, Swords and such other deadly weapons in their hands and were throwing stones at the train. We all got frightened and somehow closed the windows and the doors of the compartment. People outside were shouting loudly, saying '*Maro, Kato*' and were attacking the train. A loudspeaker from the Masjid (i.e. Mosque) closeby was also very loudly shouting '*Maro, Kato, Laden na dushmano ne Maro.*' ("Cut, kill, kill the enemies of Laden")These attackers were so fierce that they managed to break the windows and close the doors from outside before pouring petrol**

inside and setting the compartment on fire so that nobody could escape alive. A number of attackers entered the compartment and were beating the *karsevaks* and looting their belongings. The compartments were drenched in petrol all over. We were terrified and were shouting for help but who was there to help us? A few policemen were later seen approaching the compartment but they were also whisked away by the furious mob outside. There was so much of smoke in the compartment that we were unable to see each other and also getting suffocated. Going out was too difficult, however, myself and Pooja somehow managed to jump out through the windows. Pooja was hurt in her back and was unable to stand up. People outside were trying to hold us to take us away but we could escape and run under the burning train and succeeded in crawling towards the cabin. **I have seen my parents and sisters being burnt alive right in front of my eyes."** Luckily, Gayatri was not hurt too badly. "We somehow managed to go up to the station and meet our aunty (*Masi*). After the compartments were completely burnt, the crowd started withering. We saw that even amongst them were men, women and youngsters like us, both male and female. I returned here after evacuating the dead bodies of my family members at Godhra Station. Out of 18 of us, ten had laid their lives."

Gayatri's father was a carpenter, whereas, her mother worked in the *Madhyanha Bhojan Yojna* (i.e. Mid-day meal scheme), her elder sister, Pratiksha was serving in the Collectorate.

In spite of what had happened, Gayatri still feels that she would any time once again venture to go for *karseva*. She says, "I shall not allow the sacrifice of my parents to go in vain." (*Source*: VSK, Gujarat and various English dailies such as *The Indian Express* dated 28th February, 2002)

A foreign daily *Portsmouth Herald* reported:

"Sixteen-year-old Gayatri Panchal saw her mother, father and two sisters die before her eyes in the train fire as they returned home after participating in a religious ceremony at Ayodhya.

'We were sleeping and I opened my eyes when I felt the heat. I saw flames everywhere. My mother was in flames, her clothes were on fire,' she said. 'Someone pulled me out of the compartment and then I saw my father's body being taken out. He was covered in black. Then I fainted.'" (URL: http://seacoastauction.com/2002news/2_28_w2.htm).

Among some details of the brutality, an event that reveals the killing of a Dalit *karsevak* in the Godhra massacre is worth reproducing. Umakant Govindbhai of Saijpur was 25 years of age and working in the Collector's Office. Umakant, who was trying to break the closed door and get away, was pelted with stones by the attackers and pushed with the bamboos inside the coach according to an article by Dr. Suvarna Raval in Marathi daily *Tarun Bharat* dated 21st July, 2002.

The Times of India reported 1 year later, on 27 Feb 2003: "For the four Panchal sisters — Komal (20), Avani (19), Gayatri (17) and Priyanka (15) — the last year has been full of tears. Their father Harshad Panchal, mother Mita Panchal, sisters Pratiksha and Chhaya fell prey to the barbarity in Godhra on February 27. And, life was never the same again.

The result. Gayatri, a topper in SSC, today is sickly and struggling with education at grade XII. Lost without their parents the girls often go to bed in tears, as memories of the tragedy come flooding back every day. Said Komal, "We are trying to get on with life but it is difficult. Life seems meaningless without the love and affection of parents."

(Source: http://articles.timesofindia.indiatimes.com/2003-02-27/ahmedabad/27273391_1_godhra-victims-panchal-family-panchal-sisters)

This sort of massacre was not seen anywhere in independent India. Nor could this compare with any other event—such as the murder of Indira Gandhi, or any of the brutal murders of opponents in Kannur district of Kerala state of India, which is known for violent clashes. The terrorist attack on the Akshardham temple in Gandhinagar of 24 September 2002 or various other temples in India or deadly bomb blasts in various places could, in no way, compare with this horrific massacre.

Godhra was by no means an act of sudden eruption of violence or terrorism. Most people say it was terrorism, from the Nanavati Commission, to the Vishwa Hindu Parishad. But terrorism is completely different. The terror is temporary, the pain is momentary. Indira Gandhi (1917-1984) was shot dead by bullets. It was a case of murder, but of a very big leader- the then Prime Minister of India. Murders occurring anywhere are mostly the result of stabbing or bullet shots.

But Godhra was not that. It was much worse. It was an act of a pre-meditated conspiracy of barbarism and not real terrorism. 'Terrorists have no religion' is a statement parroted many times in the media by many people. But Godhra was not done by one or two terrorists. **It was done by a mob, a mass mob of 500+ people, ordinary people, not terrorists undergone training in training camps. Not terrorists armed with AK-47, AK-56 rifles or grenades.** They were locals, not foreigners. The local Muslims did the barbaric, communal and criminal act of Godhra to further a premeditated plan.

The Reaction of the English Media

The rioting in Gujarat in the first three days after Godhra was a result of not just the massacre at Godhra. It was the result of something else. And this something else was the reaction of the Left- liberal-secular media.

The media in general and TV channels like Star News and NDTV (who then had a partnership) in particular, almost all English newspaper editors of the print media, and almost all non-BJP, non-Shiv Sena politicians belong to this Left-liberal-secular brigade. And almost every non-BJP leader, who came on TV on 27 February 2002 in India, rubbed salt into the wounds of the anguished people. This was done by rationalizing or justifying the Godhra carnage. The foreign papers were worse than the Indian media, as we will see later.

At that time, Vir Sanghvi was the Chief Editor of *The Hindustan Times*. He wrote an article entitled "One Way Ticket" in *The Hindustan Times* on 28th February, 2002. He must have written it on 27th February itself, the day of the massacre in Godhra. This is the full text of his article:

"There is something profoundly worrying in the response of what might be called the secular establishment to the massacre in Godhra. Though there is some dispute over the details, we now know what happened on the railway track. A mob of 2,000 people stopped the Sabarmati Express shortly after it pulled out of Godhra station. The train contained several bogeys full of *kar sewaks* who were on their way back to Ahmedabad after participating in the *Poorna Ahuti Yagya* at Ayodhya. The mob attacked the train with petrol and acid bombs. According to some witnesses, explosives were also used. Four bogies were gutted and at least 57 people, including over a dozen children, were burnt alive.

Some versions have it that the *kar sewaks* shouted anti-Muslim slogans; others that they taunted and harassed Muslim passengers. According to these versions, the Muslim passengers got off at Godhra and appealed to members of their community for help. Others say that the slogans were enough to enrage the local Muslims and that the attack was revenge.

It will be some time before we can establish the veracity of these versions, but some things seem clear. There is no suggestion that the *kar sewaks* started the violence. The worst that has been said is that they misbehaved with a few passengers. **Equally, it does seem extraordinary that slogans shouted from a moving train or at a railway platform should have been enough to enrage local Muslims, enough for 2,000 of them to have quickly assembled at eight in the morning, having already managed to procure petrol bombs and acid bombs.**

Even if you dispute the version of some of the *kar sewaks* - that the attack was premeditated and that the mob was ready and waiting - **there can be no denying that what happened was indefensible, unforgivable and impossible to explain away as a consequence of great provocation.**

And yet, this is precisely how the secular establishment has reacted.

Nearly every non-BJP leader who appeared on TV on Wednesday and almost all of the media have treated the massacre as a response to the Ayodhya movement. This is fair enough in so far as the victims were *kar sewaks*.

But almost nobody has bothered to make the obvious follow-up point: this was not something the *kar sewaks* brought on themselves. If a trainload of VHP volunteers had been attacked while returning after the demolition of the Babri Masjid in December 1992, this would still have been wrong, but at least one could have understood the provocation.

This time, however, there has been no real provocation at all. It is possible that the VHP may defy the government and the courts and go ahead with the temple construction eventually. But, as of now, this has not happened. Nor has there been any real confrontation at Ayodhya - as yet.

And yet, the sub-text to all secular commentary is the same: the *kar sewaks* had it coming to them.

26

Basically, they condemn the crime; but blame the victims.

Try and take the incident out of the secular construct that we, in India, have perfected and see how bizarre such an attitude sounds in other contexts. Did we say that New York had it coming when the Twin Towers were attacked last year? Then too, there was enormous resentment among fundamentalist Muslims about America's policies, but we didn't even consider whether this resentment was justified or not.

Instead we took the line that all sensible people must take: any massacre is bad and deserves to be condemned.

When Graham Staines and his children were burnt alive, did we say that Christian missionaries had made themselves unpopular by engaging in conversion and so, they had it coming? No, of course, we didn't.

Why then are these poor *kar sewaks* an exception? **Why have we dehumanised them to the extent that we don't even see the incident as the human tragedy that it undoubtedly was and treat it as just another consequence of the VHP's fundamentalist policies?**

The answer, I suspect, is that **we are programmed to see Hindu-Muslim relations in simplistic terms: Hindus provoke, Muslims suffer.**

When this formula does not work- it is clear now that a well-armed Muslim mob murdered unarmed Hindus - **we simply do not know how to cope. We shy away from the truth - that some Muslims committed an act that is indefensible - and resort to blaming the victims.**

Of course, there are always 'rational reasons' offered for this stand. Muslims are in a minority and therefore, they deserve special consideration. Muslims already face discrimination so why make it harder for them? If you report the truth then you will inflame Hindu sentiments and this would be irresponsible. And so on. I know the arguments well because - like most journalists - I have used them myself. And I still argue that they are often valid and necessary.

But there comes a time when this kind of rigidly 'secularist' construct not only goes too far; it also becomes counter-productive. When everybody can see that a trainload of Hindus was massacred by a Muslim mob, you gain nothing by blaming the murders on the VHP or arguing that the dead men and women had it coming to them.

Not only does this insult the dead (What about the children? Did they also have it coming?), but it also insults the intelligence of the reader. Even moderate Hindus, of the sort that loathe the VHP, are appalled by the stories that are now coming out of Gujarat: stories with uncomfortable reminders of 1947 with details about how the bogies were first locked from outside and then set on fire and how the women's compartment suffered the most damage.

Any media - indeed, any secular establishment - that fails to take into account the genuine concerns of people risks losing its own credibility. Something like that happened in the mid-Eighties when an aggressive hard secularism on the part of the press and government led even moderate Hindus to believe that they had become second class citizens in their own country. It was this Hindu backlash that brought the Ayodhya movement - till then a fringe activity - to the forefront and fuelled the rise of L.K. Advani's BJP.

My fear is that something similar will happen once again. The VHP will ask the obvious question of Hindus: why is it a tragedy when Staines is burnt alive and merely an 'inevitable political development' when the same fate befalls 57 *kar sewaks*?

Because, as secularists, we can provide no good answer, it is the VHP's responses that will be believed. Once again, Hindus will believe that their suffering is of no consequence and will be tempted to see the building of a temple at Ayodhya as an expression of Hindu pride in the face of secular indifference.

But even if this were not to happen, even if there was no danger of a Hindu backlash, I still think that the secular establishment should pause for thought. **There is one question we need to ask ourselves: have we become such prisoners of our own rhetoric that even a horrific massacre becomes nothing more than occasion for *Sangh Parivar*-bashing?"**

Source: http://www.hvk.org/specialreports/guild/1.html

Today it can also be read on Vir Sanghvi's personal website at http://www. virsanghvi.com/Article-Details.aspx?key=611

As we see, when he had written it, no riots had taken place in Gujarat at all. But a close observation of his article indicates that he knew that a backlash would take place in Gujarat, after the inhuman response of the self-styled secularist brigade to the inhuman massacre in Godhra. See his two sentences:

"Even moderate Hindus, of the sort that loathe the VHP, are appalled by the stories that are now coming out of Gujarat: stories with uncomfortable reminders of 1947 with details about how the bogies were first locked from outside and then set on fire and how the women's compartment suffered the most damage" and "My fear is that something similar will happen once again".

What Vir Sanghvi wrote in that article really explains everything, not just about Godhra, but everything that followed after Godhra too. And not just that, but the behavior of the newspaper editors, who call themselves 'secularists' on all major issues too is explained and exposed by this self-confessed article (such as their response to all major communal riots in India and all clashes between the Hindus and other minorities).

Let us see his statement: "We are programmed to see Hindu-Muslim relations in the simplistic terms: Hindus provoke, Muslims suffer."

This is the first and biggest admission of pseudo-secularism from Vir Sanghvi, not just for himself, but also for his entire fellow self-styled secularists.

When any person views any happenings in a biased way, i.e. one person suffers and the other provokes, it also shows his moral and mental bankruptcy. Irrespective of whether a VHP member thrashes a Muslim or whether Muslims thrash or burn alive a trainload of VHP members, the self-styled secularist newspaper editors will continue to bash the VHP and hold it responsible for all the troubles. **They will not even bother to see who has suffered, and try to investigate who is at fault, but simply close their eyes and blame one group, i.e. the Hindu group during the Hindu-Muslim conflicts.**

Something similar was said by the great Congress leader, Kanhaiyalal Munshi (1887-1971): "**If every time there is an inter-communal conflict, the majority is blamed regardless of the merits of the question… the springs of traditional tolerance will dry up.**" (*Source*: *Pilgrimage to Freedom* by K.M. Munshi, p. 312 published by Bharatiya Vidya Bhavan).

He also wrote on the same page: "While the majority exercises patience and tolerance, the minorities should learn to adjust themselves to the majority. Otherwise the future is uncertain and **an explosion cannot be avoided**".

Inability to judge any situation on merits, whether XYZ person attacked ABC person and killed him, or it was the other way round but simply judge it on the names of the persons, i.e. ABC or XYZ or the identities of the persons, Hindu or Muslim, i.e. ABC provokes and XYZ suffers, shows that the 'neutral' observer (in this case, the self-styled secularists) is partial with prejudice and jaundiced vision.

In reality, the Hindu-Muslim relations in India have been different. It is, in fact, often a case of the minority community starting the riots. Ganesh Kanate, a staunch anti-BJP and anti-*Sangh Parivar* journalist with Communist leanings, wrote in his weekly column in the Nagpur-based English daily *The Hitavada* dated 15th August, 2003, "The Muslims start riots and then suffer heavily because of the riots which they themselves start." Even a 'secularist' like Ganesh Kanate said that Muslims start most of the riots. The report of the Congress' Home Ministry blamed Muslims for starting 23 out of 24 riots between 1968 and 1970. This was quoted by Atal Bihari Vajpayee in Parliament on 14 May 1970. This writer would like to make it clear that he feels that every case should be judged on merit, on who is at fault, without any prejudice against any community.

Belgium-based world famous scholar Dr Koenraad Elst also wrote in his book "BJP Vis-à-vis Hindu resurgence" (Published by Voice of India in January 1997): "Another example is riot reporting. Riots, though mostly started by Muslims (e.g. the Mumbai riots of December 1992 and of January 1993), are systematically reported in the world media as "pogroms" committed by well-prepared and well-armed Hindu death squads against poor defenceless Muslims. In journalistic and scholarly references, Advani's peaceful 1990 Rath Yatra has become a proverbially violent "blood yatra"."

How that Mentality Affected Their Reporting on Godhra

This one-sided vision in seeing Hindu-Muslim relations is amply clear by Sanghvi's as well as all other self-styled secularists' reaction to Godhra. Almost all the media rationalized Godhra. After rationalizing Godhra, all of them added that they are by no means 'justifying' it (for token). To say that **they all** justified Godhra will be a bit too harsh. But there is absolutely no doubt that they rationalized Godhra and, some of them, partially justified it.

The Concocted 'Provocations'

As Vir Sanghvi says, some versions have it that *karsevaks* shouted anti-Muslim slogans, others that they taunted and harassed Muslim passengers. In the first place, this too is completely wrong, since there is not an iota of evidence to support any of these claims. But despite this, the TV channels and most of the print media concocted such myths. This was only the detailed part of the provocations. Most of them treated the Godhra massacre as a response to the VHP's Ram temple agitation. **The Ayodhya movement itself was held as a provocation for this massacre.**

Weeklies like *India Today, The Week, Outlook* and fortnightly *Frontline* also published stark lies on this subject by concocting imaginary provocations such as altercations between *karsevaks* and the Muslim tea-vendors on the Godhra railway station, or kidnapping of a Muslim girl by the *karsevaks* at the station, or any number of imaginary details.

Despite knowing fully well that Godhra was a well-planned conspiracy, a large section of the Indian media forcibly did seeking of provocations to defend it as deed done on the spur of the moment. Vir Sanghvi's *The Hindustan Times* carried a front-page headline on Godhra on 28th February, 2002 titled "Gujarat Hit by Ayodhya Backlash", i.e. it held that the Ayodhya movement was the main and the biggest cause of the Godhra massacre. So much so that the headline ignored the act and simply reported the 'provocation', which too was altogether imaginary. *The Hindustan Times* did not even bother to have the headline like: *"58* karsevaks burnt to death in a ghastly attack in Godhra" or something of the sort.

In its editorial on this issue, *The Hindu*, the largest circulated English daily from South India said in its issue dated 1st March, 2002:

"Deadly spiral

THE GRISLY GODHRA (Gujarat) episode of arson on Wednesday that left 50-odd passengers of the Sabarmati Express dead—most of them Karsevaks returning from Ayodhya—and the backlash of mindless violence it had triggered elsewhere in the State, as rampaging mobs have in a series of reprisals hit back at the minority community and its properties, are clear, disturbing pointers to the explosive communal build-up across the country as **a direct consequence of the VHP's provocative and destructive campaign for the construction of a Ram temple in Ayodhya. What happened in Godhra, about which there are different and conflicting versions**, is a dastardly act and it deserves to be condemned unequivocally and in the strongest of terms, and no provocation can even remotely be brought in to justify the slaughter of innocent people. No effort should be spared by the government to track down the culprits and bring them to justice at the earliest, even as quick measures are taken to ensure that the vicious spiral of violence does not get out of hand and a sense of security is restored among the people.

This said, one cannot but pinpoint the harsh reality that events such as the horrors of Godhra were tragically predictable as a result of the wounding and aggressive communal campaign of the VHP. It has been ruthlessly pursuing its agenda of commencing the temple construction on 15th March, 'come-what-may', and whipping up communal passions through mass mobilisation of Ramsevaks—some one million of them—across the country. The whole build-up, which started gaining momentum about a month ago— with the VHP and its *Sangh Parivar* giving an ultimatum to the Vajpayee Government to handover the so-called 'undisputed' part of the acquired land—has been typical of the much-too-familiar strategy of the *Sangh Parivar*, providing an ominous throwback to the run up to the Babri Masjid demolition on 6th December, 1992. As a consequence of the audaciously provocative ways of the Ram temple proponents—as evidenced by their determination to start moving the carved stone pillars to the building site from 15th March and the regular convergence of frenzied karsevak contingents on Ayodhya from different parts of the country daily since 24th February—the situation on the communal front rapidly deteriorated, with sharp polarisation of the majority and minority community, becoming explosive by the day. The dangerous implications of such a trend for a State like Gujarat—known for its high vulnerability to communal riots and its perceived status as a laboratory of Hindutva political doctrines—are alarming. In many respects, the evolving milieu resembles what obtained during L.K. Advani's *rath yatra*, an event that generated communal disturbance all along its route..."

The inhuman massacre in Godhra, unparalleled in human history, was justified by many of the foreign newspapers. *The Independent* insulted the dead *kar sewaks* and leveled baseless allegations. The report written by Peter Popham published on 20 March 2002 was quoted by Madhu Kishwar (Born 1959) in her book "Modi, Muslims and Media" (Manushi Publications, 2014) on pages 205-208. This is widely quoted on the internet. Madhu Kishwar's book quotes the report as saying:

"...What happened in car S/6 was the hideous finale. The story began nearly 36 hours earlier.

... **Many were also drunk or stoned**, or equipped to get that way: flexible, tolerant Hinduism has no hard and fast rules about such things. And they were coming back to Gujarat, the only state in the Indian union that is still "dry". All the more reason to have a bottle or two tucked away.

... The train was late: after a day and a half, it was running four and a half hours behind schedule. That's why it arrived in Godhra not at 2.55am, as scheduled, but at 7.15am. By this time, the *karsevaks* were much the worse for wear.

Trouble had started at Dahod station, nearly one hour and 75km up the tracks. The train had reached Dahod around 6am, and a number of karsevaks got out of compartment S/6 to have tea and snacks at a stall on the platform. **Already they were drunk and unruly.** An argument broke out between the Hindus and the Muslim man running the tea stall – according to one account, they refused to pay unless he chanted "Jai Shri Ram", the chant of Lord Ram's devotees. He refused to oblige, and they started to smash up his stall, before climbing back into the carriage. The stallholder filed a complaint with the railway police.

At Godhra, a similar scene ensued. The *karsevaks*, now noisily drunk, poured on to the platform, ordered more tea and snacks, consumed them, and then made difficulties. Exactly what transpired between the bearded Muslim stallholder and the travellers varies from one account to another. But all witness accounts seen by The Independent agree that there was a row. "They argued with the old man on purpose," one witness said, on condition of anonymity. "They pulled his beard and beat him up... They kept repeating the slogan *'mandir ki nirmaan karo, Babar ki aulad ko bahar karo'*." ("Build the temple and throw out the Muslims...")

Suddenly the row took a dangerous new turn: the *karsevaks* grabbed hold of a Muslim woman. Her identity, and how she became involved, remain ambiguous, but four different witnesses mention this event. One says it was the 16-year-old daughter of the abused tea-seller. She "came forward and tried to save her father". Another mentions a woman washing clothes by the railway line being hauled away. A third describes how a Muslim girl wearing a burqa and taking a shortcut to school through the station platform was pounced on and dragged into the carriage. All agree that a Muslim woman was hauled into the carriage by the *karsevaks*, who slammed the door and would not let her go. Refusing to be quoted by name, a local policeman confirms the story.

And suddenly, what had been just an ugly little fracas, a drunken pantomime of power and subjugation, became something far more explosive.

The *karsevaks* were too drunk for their own good, or they would have chosen a different station at which to pull such a stunt. Because now the social geography of Godhra came into play.

…Godhra station, to the regret of the Hindus, is located in an area that is now entirely Muslim. And a huddle of Muslim-owned businesses sprang up in shacks alongside the tracks, many of them motor-repair yards. This little slum, known as Signal Fadia, has all the material a riot could require: stacks of bricks, petrol, and paraffin and calor gas cylinders. But it also had the necessary human material: a community impoverished and bitter and surviving on the margins of criminality.

The woman seized by the *karsevaks* was dragged into compartment S/6, and word of what had happened began to spread. "The girl began screaming for help," said Ahmed, a wood dealer who was waiting for a train going the other way. "Muslims who were travelling on the train got off. People began pouring on to the platform to try to rescue her. I ran home – I could see trouble was brewing…"

The train moved off, and the gathering crowd began pelting the carriage with bricks. Inside the train, someone pulled the emergency cord; the train stopped, then moved off again; the cord was pulled again 1km out of the station, and this time the train stopped and stayed stopped. "People in the vicinity… started to gather near the train," says one witness. "The mob… requested that the *karsevaks* return the girl. But instead of returning the girl, they started closing their windows. This infuriated the mob…"

The brawl had become a battle, with the *karsevaks* piling in with their swords and sticks, and a crowd now said to be 1,000-strong streaming in from the slum, bringing petrol, gas, rags – anything that would burn. Their gas cylinders broke the bars on the windows and exploded inside; the petrol bombs flew through and set the upholstery and the people trapped inside on fire. By the time that the police arrived in strength one hour later, there was nothing to be saved…"

The reason why *The Independent* stooped to such unimaginable levels was because of the Indian media. The behavior of the Indian media of repeated insults to the dead *karsevaks* and defence of Muslim communalism prompted the foreign authors to write like this. Does this author think that 15 children were also drunk? For this author's information, by that logic Graham Staines (an Australian Christian missionary who was killed in the Indian state of Odisha in January 1999) had it coming because he indulged in conversion of innocent Hindus and ignored repeated warnings to stop conversions. But still, because this insults the dead, we avoid criticizing him. All this nonsense and character assassination of the killed Hindus done by this newspaper is not even worth repudiating.

The then RSS spokesman M.G. Vaidya wrote in Marathi daily *Tarun Bharat* in July 2002:

"The headline in *The Times of India* dated 28th February read: "MOB ATTACKS GUJARAT TRAIN, 55 DIE."

The writer of this report is Sajjad Shaikh. While identifying the reasons for the Godhra massacre, he writes, "*Karsevaks* in the train misbehaved with some washerwomen of Signal Falia". Besides, he also cites: "The rumour of an attack on a religious place in Dahod" as one of the reasons for the Godhra incident. Here, he wants to suggest that though it is not pardonable to burn alive 55 persons, due to the reasons cited by him, it is understandable.

This primary lead news report focused the blame on the *karsevaks* from the very initial stages and did not attempt to investigate how the train was stopped at Signal Falia where a mob of a thousand was already waiting with sticks, petrol bombs, missiles and stones.

In the 1st March issue of *The Times of India*, Siddhartha Varadarajan, a reporter, writes, "While official enquiry will establish the extent to which the attack on the Sabarmati Express was pre- meditated, there can be no doubt about the planned nature of the violence directed against Gujarat's Muslims on Thursday (28th February)". The double standards are evident from his report, which differentiates the incidents of 27th February from the incidents of 28th February. While examining the pre-meditation behind the Godhra attacks on 27th February, he says that it is "official enquiry" which will decide whether the attack on *karsevaks* was pre-meditated or not. But when it comes to violent reaction of Hindus on 28th February, he takes it in his own hands to pass a judgment that the attacks by the Hindus on Gujarat's Muslims were "pre-planned" in nature. Obviously, what had been a heinous crime was rationalized and what had been a spontaneous reaction was condemned as a 'pre-planned' one.

This news report was carried just two days after the Godhra carnage. The gruesome murders of the *karsevaks* is mentioned only once in the 450-plus word report and rest of the report is full of gory descriptions of how the Muslims are being brutally killed in the aftermath." URL: http://www.hindunet.org/hvk/articles/0702/99.html

The Hindu reported the incidents of 27th February as follows in its issue dated 28th February, 2002:

"57 killed as a mob torches train in Gujarat" was the title. The writer of this report, Manas Dasgupta, states that "Eye-witnesses said that about 1,200 *Ramsevaks* were travelling in the train. The local people in the Muslim-dominated Godhra town had been "irritated" by the abusive language used by the *Ramsevaks* while they were going to Ayodhya by the same train a few days ago. They had reportedly raised slogans as the train approached Godhra on the return journey this morning."

The report can be read at http://www.thehindu.com/2002/02/28/stories/2002022803070100.htm

Luckily, the newsmen in India did not go to the extent that *The Independent* went. But *The Independent* report simply showed the true face of the Indian media men. They also reported in much the same way, the difference was only in the extent. Ignoring what the foreign media said, Sanghvi's second observation is equally important. Did any of the 'secularists' of the Indian media bother to give any attention to the 'provocations' after the September 11 episode? As a matter of fact, at that time, many warnings were given before September 11 to the Americans by Osama bin Laden's Al Qaeda to change its policy towards Muslims or face the consequences. But nobody bothered to even remember the warnings given by Al Qaeda or question the USA's policies on Muslims, after the September 11 attack. It was, in fact, only a condemnation of the Islamic terrorism of the Al Qaeda and a concern about the danger the world faces because of it.

After Godhra, however, the VHP and the *Sangh Parivar* were bashed continuously and held responsible for the Godhra carnage **even after Godhra**. This tirade against the *Sangh Parivar* was noticed by Vir Sanghvi in his article's last paragraph: **"Have we become such prisoners of our own rhetoric that even a horrific massacre becomes nothing more than an occasion for Sangh Parivar bashing?"** Another of Vir Sanghvi's statement is equally important, **"Why have we dehumanized these karsevaks to such an extent that we don't even see the incident as a tragedy which it undoubtedly was and treat it as just another consequence of the VHP's fundamentalist policies?"**

This is the most important revelation. Dehumanization. This approach of the media of dehumanizing the dead *karsevaks* including 15 children angered the entire nation. More so Gujarat, in which is Godhra situated.

Even if the *karsevaks* had indeed misbehaved with anyone, or refused to pay for tea and snacks, or shouted anti-Muslim slogans, or taunted or harassed Muslim passengers, or done any of the numerous things which have been charged (all charges are inconsistent and varying, which shows that the aim was to forcibly concoct 'provocations'), still there should have been no mention of it, or even if it was mentioned, the blame should not have been put on the dead. This is because no one insults the dead. Graham Staines really indulged in conversion and ignored all warnings given to him to stop conversion but nobody blamed him for his death because nobody insults the dead.

But, in this case, even though the *karsevaks* did nothing, baseless and absolutely wrong allegations were made to blame the dead for their own death. Even if they had indulged in any sort of misbehavior, such a massacre and brutal roasting cannot be rationalized. And here instead of blaming the Muslims who roasted the train, much of the media— the TV channels in particular—and the politicians made such allegations on people who were not even alive to refute the charges. And all the charges were absolutely wrong. **The people who lost their lives in a human tragedy, in a gruesome massacre, a well- planned attack, were unfairly accused and blamed for something which they did not do.**

The people of Gujarat were used to this policy of the TV channels and the print media. They were used to the continuous bashing of the Hindutva ideology, of the *karsevaks*, of the Ayodhya movement, of the VHP and the continuous defence of the Muslims. But the people thought that the Godhra massacre was just a bit too much. At least, such a horrifying massacre of innocent people including 15 children will make the hearts of the self-styled secularists bleed. At least, in such a huge tragedy, will the media stop insulting the *karsevaks* and condemning the VHP and the *Ramjanmabhoomi* movement? At least now, will the media condemn the fundamentalist Muslims and call them *Jehadis* and criticize them for the unprovoked massacre?

But nothing of the sort happened. The media continued its usual ways. And Vir Sanghvi's fear of a Hindu backlash became a terrifying reality on 28th February, 2002, which was Thursday.

But after the backlash of the first three days, Vir Sanghvi forgot his own words which he uttered before the Hindu retaliation. He himself had warned his 'secularist' brothers that their attitude was aggravating the Hindus. He himself indirectly warned of a retaliation and anger in the Hindus but forgot it while condemning the post-Godhra riots and calling Narendra Modi a 'mass murderer' many times in his newspaper's editorial page.

This Hindu anger continued not just until the riots but until much later. This continued until at least December 2002. On 12th December 2002 were held the Gujarat Assembly elections. The BJP won a huge majority of 127 out of the 182 seats with the Indian National Congress (INC) winning just 51. Not only that, the BJP's popular vote reached a massive 50 per cent, a huge 11 per cent more than the Congress' 39 per cent. Saurashtra and Kutch, which did not see any riots even in the first three days after Godhra, also saw the BJP winning, and not just winning, but winning 'hands down'. As per weekly *India Today* dated 30th December, 2002, out of the 102 riot-affected seats, the BJP won 79 seats. These numbers are also dubious. But let us assume that they are true. That means the BJP won 48 out of the remaining 80 non-riot affected seats, which is still a majority with 60 per cent of the seats. Sixty per cent is still a huge majority considering that the BJP was in power in the state from 1995, with two terms. Despite anti-incumbency, this performance of the party was due to the Hindu anger after Godhra and the 'secularist' brigade's reaction to it.

This Left-liberal-secular brigade also did another wrong. They tried to keep the number of attackers, i.e. Muslims at Godhra as less as they could. Kuldip Nayar gave it as 500 in an article in the *Deccan Herald* dated 3 April 2002. *India Today* weekly, in its issue dated 11th March, 2002, also gave the number of attackers as over 500. On Godhra, Kuldip Nayar wrote in an article published on 6 July 2002: "Narendra Modi would have created a Godhra train incident if it had not happened. The tragedy is that some Muslims played into his hands". Others kept reducing the figure to 1,000, while some gave it 1,500. But the true figure seems to be 2,000 as given by Vir Sanghvi and the Justice Tewatia Committee. Alok Tiwari, another 'secularist' editor, also gave the number of Hindus killed in Godhra as 56 while saying: "Just because 56 Hindus were killed doesn't mean that they should kill hundreds of Muslims...". This figure of the attackers is not important in the sense that it does not really matter whether it is 2,000 or 1,500 who attacked the train. **But it simply discloses the attitude of the self-styled secularists in dealing with the situation. And the attitude is—keep the Hindu suffering as low as possible, Muslim atrocities as low as possible and inflate and exaggerate Muslim sufferings as much as possible.**

And they try to keep increasing the number of Muslims killed in the Gujarat riots, ignoring, of course, the hundreds of Hindus also killed in the riots. When the UPA Government (with Sonia Gandhi as its chairperson and Leftists as outside supporters), which was staunchly anti-BJP, anti-RSS and anti-Narendra Modi gave the figures of 790 Muslims and 254 Hindus killed in the riots (see details later in Chapter 7), what do they get by increasing the number of Muslims killed to 1,000 or 2,000 or 3,000 and saying that "Thousands of Muslims were killed in a 'genocide', 'pogrom' or 'massacre' sponsored by the state government"?

Godhra was Planned, Post-Godhra was a Result of Provocation

Godhra was clearly a planned, unprovoked attack. It is impossible for it to have been the result of petty quarrels at the Godhra railway station. Vir Sanghvi has already said it in his article. As he says, slogans shouted from a moving train or a railway platform cannot enrage local Muslims, and 2,000 Muslims cannot assemble near the railway station in five minutes' time already having managed to procure petrol bombs and acid bombs. And the time was also 8 a.m. in the morning. Some 140 liters of petrol was reportedly bought in cans a day before the massacre. VSK, Gujarat said that:

> "1. Travellers of a particular religion were asked to get down at the previous station of Dahod.
> 2. The patients of a particular community were discharged from the civil hospital of Godhra one day before 27th. Not a single case from a particular community was registered on 27th February.
> 3. Not a single student or a teacher of a particular community was present in the schools of Godhra on 27th February.
> 4. It clearly shows that not only it was a pre-planned attack but many others were aware that something is likely to happen on that day."

Disclaimer: Not independently verified, just what was reported by VSK, Gujarat Weeklies like *India Today* gave imaginary provocations with graphics. But all these people forgot one thing. For the train to have been attacked, the attackers (Muslims) had to surround in on at least two sides. **If it was on the spur of the moment, it would have been very difficult for the Muslims to surround the train on both sides.** How could at least 500 Muslims reach the other side of the train? **If that was the case, then the *karsevaks* would have ran out of the train and saved their lives, by running from the second side before Muslims reached there.** In any case, all these provocations are purely fabricated and a figment of imagination. Something which was done with absolutely no provocation and full planning was rationalized by the media.

Even Kuldip Nayar (born 1923), known for his extreme anti-RSS, anti-BJP and anti-Narendra Modi and pro-Muslim and pro-Pakistani views, wrote in an article published on 3 April 2002: "I have no doubt that the (Godhra) attack was a well-planned one. Otherwise, it is not possible for a mob of 500 carrying petrol and kerosene to assemble in three minutes in an area that can only be reached by running through prickly bushes."

As a matter of fact, such a horrible crime should not be committed even against animals. If 59 animals had been locked in a train, pushed back into the fire as they tried to come out and then roasted to death with bodies charred, it too would have been considered as a gruesome tragedy by all right-thinking sensible people. But because these 59 were *karsevaks* returning from Ayodhya, false charges were made on them—the incident was condemned merely for token with the blame put on the roasted women and children and men, and the VHP. Vir Sanghvi said that the *karsevaks* had been dehumanized. They were actually treated even worse than animals.

And when the things were really a result of provocation, the media largely just ignored it. The post-Godhra riots were reported completely ignoring Godhra. At that time, the Godhra attack faded into the background and the Hindu retaliation of the first three days was decried. And even after so many years, whenever the post-Godhra riots are mentioned, Godhra is completely ignored and it is made to sound as if the BJP Government of the state indulged in ruthless, unprovoked killings of Muslims in alliance with the VHP and the Bajrang Dal.

The big 'provocation' which was far more than a provocation but **the cause** of the retaliation by the Hindus in the first three days was completely ignored and the subsequent riots were reported, that too completely one-sided and magnified and inflated. The difference on the media's attitude is revealed from its reactions. After Godhra, it was said: "The government must bring the culprits to justice. The crime deserves to be condemned. But it is inevitable and predictable because of VHP's Ayodhya movement...VHP bashing..." and after post-Godhra, it was said: "Holocaust...pogrom...genocide...massacre... Modi must quit... international shame...are we like Rwanda...Hitler..."

Vir Sanghvi really gave the game up when he said, "If you report the truth, then you will inflame Hindu sentiments and this would be irresponsible. And so on." **That is to say, Vir Sanghvi admitted that the self-styled secularists utter 'stark lies', no matter what interest in mind.** They lied not only during Godhra but also for some three months after Godhra. They also did so during the Gujarat

Assembly elections of December 2002. In fact, they have repeated their lies so often that by now they themselves may have started believing their concocted lies.

On 27th February, 2002, senior Congress leader and former Gujarat Chief Minister, the late Amarsinh Chaudhary (1941-2004) came on TV at night and **while condemning the attack, also blamed *karsevaks* for provoking it by alleging that they refused to pay for tea at the station.** (Again following Vir Sanghvi's observation—basically, they condemn the crime, but blame the victims.)

The RSS weekly *Organiser* reported the incident in its issue dated 10th March, 2002, which covered events in full till 27th February. While reporting on this issue, *Organiser* also reported in a news item—**"RSS condemns the killings and calls for restraint"** and this report carries the statement of the then RSS Joint General Secretary, Madan Das Devi that RSS urges Hindu society to exercise restraint after the Godhra attack. RSS had asked the Hindu society to observe restraint and not retaliate after Godhra even before the riots had started.

RSS condemns the killings and calls for restraint

RASHTRIYA Swayamsevak Sangh (RSS) has condemned the Godhra carnage and appealed to the Hindu society not to take law into their hands. In a statement issued in New Delhi, Sahsarkaryavah, Shri Madan Das said, "This is the moment of the test of tolerance of the Hindu society. We appeal to the Hindus not to take law into their hands and thus play in the hands of Muslim terrorists. We should help wholeheartedly the Gujarat Government handle the situation effectively," the statement said, adding: "The RSS expects the leaders of the Muslim community to come forward and do their best to control the violent and terrorist elements in their society, so that such extremely provocative incidents are not repeated." The statement also says, "It has been made known to us that this was a planned attack of about 2000 Muslim anti-social elements at Godhra. The RSS is extremely grieved by this heinous act and condemns it in the strongest possible terms."

This is the scanned copy of the report of *Organiser* weekly dated 10 March 2002. On the same page of the same issue was another appeal issued by the then General Secretary of RSS, Mohan Bhagwat (1950-). Mohan Bhagwat urged people to shun acts like even sloganeering, apart from stone pelting and anything that would violate peace. The scanned copy of the report of Mohan Bhagwat's appeal of 27 Feb, as reported by *Organiser*, is seen below.

Ensure security of Ayodhya-bound pilgrims

—Mohan Bhagwat, *Sarkaryavah, RSS*

I appeal to all Sangh swayamsevaks, sympathisers and friends who have faith in Hindutva to do the utmost in preventing any activity that would disrupt peace, like, sloganeering, stone-pelting, keeping in view the disturbed situation in the country for it would only strengthen the hands of anti-national terrorist elements.

I also urge our fellow followers of other faiths not to fall prey to the instigation of terrorist elements and to conduct themselves as children of motherland along with their Hindu brethren.

It is my firm belief that all the volunteers who are going to Ayodhya following an appeal from the Vishwa Hindu Parishad would, in keeping with the Bhakti tradition, preserve the spiritual atmosphere in Ayodhya while keeping their pilgrimage.

At the end, I earnestly appeal to the Central and Sate Governments to provide due security to the thousands of Ayodhya-bound pilgrims and ensure that they do not encounter any hurdles in Ayodhya.

India Today weekly dated 11 March 2002, carrying events till 28th February 2002, reported on the last page of the cover story:

"The mood in the state is militant. A procession of 10,000 marched with the bodies of 11 people from Ramol village near Ahmedabad, who had died in the train. They were shouting slogans like: *'Tumhari shahidi bekar nahi jayegi, Mandir bana kar hi rahenge'* (Your sacrifice will not go in vain, we will build the temple)... This incident drew mixed reactions from the Congress, the main opposition party in the state. **While senior party leader Amarsinh Chaudhary condemned the attack, he also blamed** *Ramsevaks* **for provoking the incident.** Senior AICC member, Ahmed Patel condemned it strongly. They will have time to react. **The bloody cycle of violence so familiar with Gujarat may just have begun."**

So, *India Today* knew on 28th February itself that a bloody cycle of violence had begun in Gujarat and could continue in Gujarat for several days. But, in fact, it stopped only after three days, though petty and stray rioting continued subsequently in Ahmedabad, Vadodara and some places near Godhra. And, in fact, even weekly *Outlook* (a well known diehard anti-BJP, anti-Narendra Modi weekly) in its issue dated 11th March, 2002 (i.e. on 28th February) also reported:

"Gujarat has always been a communal tinderbox and even a small spark ignites big trouble. The ghost of Godhra looks set to walk its streets for months." (*URL*: http://www.outlookindia.com/article/200-On-The --Human-Richter/214849).

Difference between Godhra and Other Tragic Incidents

Several people, unable to understand the sufferings of the Hindu society, have asked: "Why did riots occur only after Godhra? Why was nobody targeted after the Akshardham temple attack (of 24 September 2002)—or after the attacks on Mumbai on 26th November, 2008?"

Well, the answers are many. The terrorist attacks in many parts of India such as Mumbai, Jammu, New Delhi, etc. are done by terrorists and they are acts of terrorism, whereas Godhra was not terrorism, but communalism and barbarism. It was the brutal roasting of 59 people whose bodies were charred to death beyond recognition.

The attackers also differed. Terrorists are people who are considered to have no religion. Those who attacked the Akshardham temple were called 'terrorists' by the media, and rightly so. Two foreign terrorists killed more than 30 people in the attack. It was not done by local Muslims. Nobody said in the media "Muslims kill 30 Hindus in Akshardham". It was said, "Terrorists attack the Akshardham temple". Had the Indian media, the TV channels in particular, and the non-BJP politicians, who came on TV on 27th February, 2002, called the incident as a 'human tragedy' and reacted exactly like they did after terrorist attacks in Mumbai or Akshardham, maybe the riots which occurred, could have been avoided.

Also the mob in Godhra numbered well over 1,000 and as per the report of the Tewatia Committee, the mob was 2,000 in strength. Since only 35 people were arrested for the attack on 27th February, as reported by various English newspapers the next day, it was found to be grossly inadequate by the masses. M.M. Singh—one of the finest police officers Gujarat has ever produced—also said that the police should have cordoned off the area in Godhra after the massacre. This, in his opinion, would have pacified Hindu sentiments to some extent at the very outset. And even a weekly like *India Today* reported in its issue dated 18th March, 2002 that the blame for the riots was being put on the Modi Government for its failure to nab the culprits of the Godhra carnage. Had the culprits not been allowed to flee, the people would not have directed their anger at all Muslims, according to the weekly. The weekly reports:

"The blame for the initial explosion on 28th February is being pinned on the Modi government for its failure to arrest those responsible for the Godhra massacre. The slum from where the train attack was launched was illegally constructed on Railways land and each of the 10 main suspects involved in the attack has a criminal background. Some even enjoyed political patronage. Haji Billal, one of the main accused, was known for his links with smugglers and traffickers. Such was his notoriety, claims a BJP MLA, that 'a few months ago the authorities had difficulty pasting a notice on his door'. On 27th February, the VHP asked the State government to act against them and when it failed, the public anger was directed against all Muslims" (*Source:* http://archives.digitaltoday.in/indiatoday/20020318/cover3.html).

Since it was done by local Muslims and most of the culprits went scot-free and the media kept insulting the dead *karsevaks* and condemning the VHP and the *Sangh Parivar,* the angered masses exploded in Ahmedabad on 28th February.

"After pelting stones, they started pouring kerosene in our compartments and set them afire. Only a few of us managed to come out of the broken windows. The adults and the old people were stuck inside. The old women were pleading, 'don't kill us' but they just didn't listen," says Gayatri Panchal (16), who says 3-4 people ran after her as soon as she jumped off the train (*The Indian Express*, 28th February, 2002).

Sixty-five-year-old Devika Luhana was trembling with anger as she alighted from the ill-fated train. "It was vandalism at its worst. They did not even spare old people like me and pelted stones indiscriminately. They will all go to hell for this act of malice," said Devika, who could not even retrieve her bag as she ran for her life.

"They stormed inside the women's bogie, and before we could react, they set the entire bogie on fire. Some of us managed to escape, but a number of our sisters got trapped...it was horrifying," said Hetal Patel, a member of Durga Vahini.

Terror still haunts 13-year-old Gyanprakash as he bursts into tears from time to time. "I cannot forget the sight of people burning in front of me," he says while recuperating at the Ahmedabad city hospital. Gyanprakash was on the S2 coach of the Sabarmati Express when it was set ablaze in Godhra on Wednesday. His family was returning to Ahmedabad after attending a relative's funeral. They had boarded the train at Kanpur. Gyanprakash recalls the horror: "The train had just left Godhra but stopped a little way away from the station. Suddenly, stones were being thrown at the train. The pelting continued for almost an hour. Then something was hurled into our coach and there was smoke everywhere.

"It was so suffocating I could hardly breathe. I heard my father telling me to get off the train. I went to the door but saw that people trying to get off were being stabbed. I went to the other side and jumped off" (*Mid-Day*, 6th March, 2002).

46

That is, old women were pleading: "Don't kill us" but the attackers did not spare anyone, neither children nor old people, and certainly not the women. Most horrific was the attackers' act of not allowing anyone to escape and watching with their eyes 59 Hindus roasting to death, crying with pain, pleading for mercy. (Those who did come out like Gayatri Panchal were also tried to be pushed back.) Had the 2,000 attackers shot dead these 59 people with bullets, it would not have been so horrific. Had they set afire the train and ran away, it would not have angered the masses so much. But these attackers were indescribable barbarians. They watched and pushed back into fire the victims including 15 children and roasted to death in a horrific manner 59 Hindus returning from Godhra.

Can anyone imagine 2,000 Hindus burning to death 59 Muslims at Karachi Railway Station in Pakistan? If Hindus had mustered courage to do that, each and every Hindu in Pakistan would have been killed after horrible tortures.

To know why the masses retaliated, look at the photos of the victims. **It is necessary to see these pictures to understand this issue fully.**

A simple search saying "Godhra photos" on the Internet will show these images. They can be seen at http://www.gujaratriots.com/index.php/2011/10/godhra-photos/

WARNING: Gruesome pictures.

Anyone who understands human sufferings will realize the cause of the retaliation in Gujarat after looking at these pictures. However, some politicians and media people are blind to Hindu suffering. For some people, Hindus in general and VHP supporters in particular, are not even considered human beings. These gruesome killings also were not enough to melt the hearts of the so-called secularists. One wonders then, what will ever make them condemn Muslims for any act, if they defend Muslims for Godhra and blame the children, who were roasted.

CHAPTER 3

ROLE OF GOVERNMENT
IN CONTROLLING VIOLENCE

•

The much-hyped, much-repeated allegations of a large section of the Indian & global media, both electronic and print, that the post-Godhra riots of 2002 in Gujarat were "sponsored" by the state BJP Government, or at least, "the state government turned a blind eye to the rioting" are nothing but a figment of their imagination, stemming out from their biased and prejudiced vision, as explained and admitted by Vir Sanghvi.

Before going into the details, let us first see the opinion poll done by ORG MARG for *India Today* weekly and *Aaj Tak* TV channel, published in *India Today* in its issue dated 25th November, 2002 on the Gujarat Assembly elections. The poll gave the BJP 120-130 seats with a dizzying 55 per cent vote share, and gave the Congress 45-55 seats with 42 per cent of the vote share. In that poll, the weekly also asked a question: "How did the Modi government handle the riots?" The answer to that question was:

a)   - Fairly and effectively- 61 %
b)   - In a partisan manner- 21 %
c)   - Incompetently- 15 %

The same weekly also did another opinion poll on the same subject in December 2002. That poll gave the BJP 100-110 seats with 52 per cent of the votes and the Congress 70-80 seats with 45 per cent of the votes. The magazine published results of the poll in its issue dated 16th December, 2002. The same question asked earlier gave the results:

a)   - Fairly and effectively –62 %
b)   - In a partisan manner- 20 %
c)   -Incompetently- 15 %

Both these polls also carried a question- "What caused the March riots?" The answer given to that question in the November poll was:

a)   - Godhra incident- 56 %
b)   - Muslim extremists- 20 %
c)   - State sponsored riots - 10 %
d)   - Miscreants on both sides -9 %
e)   - Hindu extremist groups – 3 %

This same question gave the following results in the December 2002 poll:

a)   - Godhra incident- 64 %
b)   - Muslim extremists- 18 %
c)   - State sponsored riots - 7 %
d)   - Miscreants on both sides -7 %
e)   - Hindu extremist groups – 3 %

URL: http://www.india-today.com/itoday/20021216/poll.shtml

This was a survey done of the Gujarati people, much closer in time to the actual happening of the riots. Both the polls gave more or less the same results. Even among the Congress voters, many agreed to the fact that the Modi government handled the riots fairly and effectively. This is what the people of Gujarat felt. **And this was completely different from what some of the newspaper editors said sitting in air-conditioned rooms in New Delhi, miles away from the place where the actual riots happened.**

Analyzing the second question, it would seem clear that hardly 10 % of the people (who had a large proportion of Muslims) considered the riots to be state-sponsored. And hardly 3 % named the Hindu fundamentalists for the riots. Most of the people agreed that the post-Godhra riots were caused by the gruesome massacre at Godhra. And close to 20 % blamed Muslim fundamentalists for the riots.

India Today also did an opinion poll called "Mood of the Nation" in August 2002. In its issue dated 26 August 2002, the weekly also asked the question- "Who is responsible for the Gujarat riots?" The answers were:

a) -Muslim fundamentalists – 26 %
b) -Godhra attackers- 19 %
c) – State government- 14 %
d) -Local miscreants – 13 %
e) -Hindu militants- 5 %
f) -Don't know/ Can't say –23 %

URL: http://www.indiatoday.com/itoday/20020826/cover.shtml

This was a nation-wide survey, done all over the country. This was also before the election results of the Gujarat Assembly polls, which significantly changed the view of the masses towards the Gujarat riots. Even before that, the single largest view was that Muslim fundamentalists were responsible for the Gujarat riots. And so also was the Godhra incident.

What the Government had to Face

The Gujarat Government had to face the most difficult situation in trying to control the post-Godhra riots. That's because Gujarat is an extremely communally sensitive state and often even minor things like kite flying and cricket matches are enough to cause riots.

To understand this issue fully, we have already seen the horrific massacre in Godhra carried out on 27th February. Gujarat has a long history of communal violence, dating from 1714 AD and in the recent past, saw horrible riots in the pre-Independence period of the 1940s and then again riots after Independence.

The Times of India in its issue dated 13th April, 2002 carried a report saying: "Trivial reasons sparked earlier riots" and begins with the sentence:

"If it took a shocking massacre like Godhra to trigger off massive communal riots in the state (Gujarat) in the 21st century, history shows that trivial incidents caused most riots in the 20th century...."

Now the situation was far worse in February 2002 after the gruesome killings in Godhra. But the Godhra killings were not the only cause. At that time in 2002, there were war clouds between India and Pakistan following the attack on India's Parliament (on 13th December, 2001). There was great anger in Gujarat over terrorism and anti-national activity. *India Today* weekly reported in its issue dated 18th March, 2002 in an article by V. Shankar Aiyar:

"The immediate provocation for the riots may have been the Godhra inferno, but the savagery of retaliation belies a resentment spanning years. The Hindu-Muslim gulf has been widening since the 1969 Ahmedabad riots, the 1989 *rath yatra* on the Ayodhya *Ram Mandir* issue and has been fuelled by the Kashmir conflict. The heightening Indo-Pakistan tension and Islamic terrorism in the past two years—from cross-border terrorist attacks in Kashmir to the December 13 Parliament attack—have given Hindu militancy both momentum and respectability.... The past few months have seen mounting public opinion on the lack of action against Pakistan— over Kargil and more recently the Parliament attack. In fact, during his attempts last week to pacify Gujarat, Union Defence Minister, George Fernandes was not only pummelled by stones, but also queries like, 'Why isn't India attacking Pakistan?'

Indifference to or perhaps ignorance of global compulsions has fuelled hostility and the state's Muslim population is being held responsible for Pakistan's *jehadi* policies.

Another aggravation has been the mushrooming of Deobandi *madarsas* in the border state over the past two years. The lackadaisical attitude of the Keshubhai Patel and Narendra Modi governments in curbing their growth has widened the gulf between the communities. In fact, police officials attribute the ferocity of attack at the Gulmarga Society and former MP, Ehsan Jafri's house to the presence of one such *madarsa* in the complex...."

Last week, what marked the slaughter of people was the unprecedented intensity as well as societal sanction. The underclass was supported in the looting by the middle and upper middle classes, including women. They not only indulged in pillaging but openly celebrated the destruction and mounting death toll. Residents from posh localities in Ahmedabad didn't balk at taking to the streets at the slightest hint of an approaching mob. By the chief minister's own admission, the pattern of rioting didn't correspond at all to Gujarat's 100 most sensitive localities. New areas joined the sectarian frenzy." *(URL:* http://archives.digitaltoday.in/indiatoday/20020318/cover3.html)

So, in short, the state had a bloody history of communal violence and was extremely communally sensitive, there was great anger over Islamic terrorism in India, attack on Parliament and over the growth of *madarsas* in Gujarat. Added to that was the Godhra incident and the rubbing of salt into people's wounds after Godhra by the self-styled secularists, particularly the TV channels, and politicians.

The Telegraph published from Kolkata also reported on 1st March 2002: "(On Thursday, 28th February) The Vajpayee government, alarmed that law and order were spiralling out of control, ordered deployment of the army in the state. The army has already begun pre-deployment drills in violence-scarred areas and will be out latest by tomorrow (Friday, 1 March) morning. Defence minister, George Fernandes is travelling to Gujarat tomorrow...Curfew was clamped in 26 towns...**'There is a fire inside us. Our blood is boiling,' Mangalben, a woman from Dariapur, said. 'What is the fault of those children who died? There is a volcano of anger.'"**

In other words, there was a volcano of anger among the masses, whose blood was boiling after the Muslims brutally roasted 59 *karsevaks* including 15 children in Godhra. On the events of 1st March, 2002, *The Telegraph* reported in its issue dated 2 nd March: **"Despite the presence of the army—some 3,500 soldiers have arrived in the state—in Ahmedabad, Surat, Vadodara and Rajkot, the rioting has not stopped."**

That is, so angry were the masses, that even a newspaper like *The Telegraph* published from Kolkata (which was the capital of the then Marxist fort West Bengal) and staunchly anti-RSS in ideology had to publish a report in which a woman said "Our blood is boiling".

Gujarat is a state which can see riots even if cricket batsman Sachin Tendulkar gets out on 90 against Pakistan. Here it saw the most horrific massacre ever known in Independent India. Even in medieval India, when the Turkish rulers committed horrible atrocities on Hindus, an incident where 15 children were roasted to death after being locked and surrounded from both sides, not allowed to escape and the attackers watching the 15 children cry with pain and die in front of their eyes and roast to coal is not on records available to this writer. And this happened in a state which can see riots even on minor things like kite flying and cricket matches.

Even *The Indian Express* in its issue dated 1st March, 2002 said that: **"In a state so polarised as Gujarat, such a violent backlash** (which occurred on 28th February, 2002) **was expected ever since yesterday morning's Godhra massacre..."**

We saw earlier that on 28 Feb 2002 *India Today* and *Outlook* both predicted weeks of violence in Gujarat in their issues dated 11 March 2002.

And the situation was terrible. In Ahmedabad, all 6,000 policemen were deployed and only 1,500 were armed. At one point of time, there were at least 25,000 people targeting Muslims in Ahmedabad alone on 28th February. Police received at least 3,500 calls instead of the normal average of 200 that day. Ahmedabad Fire Brigade received 400 calls as against its capacity of handling 100 calls at once. In fact, the report "Godhra and After" (published by the "Council for International Affairs and Human Rights") of the team headed by Justice D.S. Tewatia, a retired Chief Justice of Punjab and Haryana High Court, after its study of the situation there in the first week of April 2002, said that on many occasions, the rioters had better weapons than the police.

Steps Taken by the Government to Control Violence

To know the steps taken by the Gujarat Government to control violence, we must first also know the background of the political situation at that time. The fact is that at that time, the BJP was running a coalition government at the Centre with around 22 parties who were different in ideology (the parties called themselves 'secular parties') and was following the NDA agenda.

In its 18th March, 2002 issue, *India Today* reported: "Says another party worker alluding to the fact that Modi was, until last fortnight, unwilling to take action on issues relating to *Hindutva* for fear of jeopardising the future of the BJP-led NDA government at the centre: 'Ever since he took over Modi was hell bent upon becoming a Vajpayee but the people have swept him in the direction of Sardar Patel.'"

(*Source*: http://www.indiatoday.com/ itoday/20020318/cover2.shtml)

And that is why we should understand that Modi, who a BJP man claimed, wanted to become another Vajpayee, took firm action against the rioters and quelled the violence as quickly as possible. With a hostile media, NDA allies at stake, Central Government at stake, it was very necessary for the BJP Government to prevent riots in Gujarat.

Steps Taken on 27th February (Wednesday)

Now let us see the steps taken by the Government of Gujarat to control the violence. The Godhra massacre occurred on 27th February at around 8:00 a.m. At 8:30 a.m. to 9:00 a.m., Chief Minister, Narendra Modi, then in Ahmedabad/Gandhinagar, was informed about the carnage. Modi then went to visit Godhra in the evening. Modi imposed curfew in Godhra at 9:45 a.m. from Ahmedabad / Gandhinagar itself.

That is, in a Hindu country, after the partition in 1947 carving out a separate Muslim state, Muslims attacked and roasted 59 Hindus in Godhra in a state ruled by a Hindu party like the BJP and even after that, the BJP Chief Minister issued 'shoot-at-sight' orders in Godhra, primarily aimed at Hindus, who could have retaliated in Godhra. The leading English daily from South India and a staunch anti-BJP newspaper, *The Hindu* in its issue dated 28th February 2002 reported that: "The Chief Minister, Narendra Modi gave shoot-at-sight orders in Godhra".

On 27 Feb itself, *The Times of India* reported in a report titled **"Shoot-at-sight orders, curfew in Godhra"**:

"The Gujarat government imposed an indefinite curfew and issued shoot-at-sight orders in Godhra after 57 people were killed and several injured when a mob set the Sabarmati Express on fire. Four bogies of the train were set on fire by miscreants at the Godhra station…" (*Source*: http://timesofindia.indiatimes.com/articleshow/2256789.cms)

This report was posted at 1:37 p.m. This shows that Modi's claim of imposing curfew at 9:45 a.m. was absolutely true. The same day *The Tribune* (published from Chandigarh) gave a report titled: "Sabarmati Express set ablaze**,** 57 dead, 'Ramsevaks' among victims, shoot-at-sight orders in Godhra" and the report said**: "Indefinite curfew was clamped and the shoot-at-sight orders issued in Godhra town IMMEDIATELY AFTER the incident…"** (Notice the words 'immediately after'). (*Source:* http://www. tribuneindia. com/2002/20020228/main1.htm)

It was not merely them. All English dailies the next day reported this along with websites like rediff.com and so did many foreign newspapers. *San Francisco Chronicle*, a US newspaper, reported on 27th February online:

"Fearing the attack would ignite sectarian riots, Indian officials immediately stepped up security across this vast, religiously divided nation. The prime minister urged Hindus not to retaliate… "It is clear from the statements of survivors that the attack was carried out by local people belonging to the Muslim community and, for this reason, because of chances of retaliation, we have already instructed our police officers to arrange special security cover for the Muslim population" (Gujarat's MoS for Home) Zadaphia said.

Police also deployed extra patrols in cities where Muslims and Hindus live in close quarters. In Old Delhi, the Muslim section of India's capital, security was tightened in the congested lanes of the ancient walled city". (*Source:* http://www.sfgate.com/cgi-bin/ article.cgi?f=/c/a/2002/02/28/MN11171.DTL).

Even Xinhua news agency also reported this online on 27th February, 2002 that the then Prime Minister of India, Atal Bihari Vajpayee appealed for peace. **The same day the website rediff.com also reported that the State Government had taken precautions and tightened security to prevent riots.** These reports of rediff.com are given in Chapter 7, Myth 15, "Narendra Modi gave free hand for three days".

After this, Narendra Modi returned to Ahmedabad in the evening. **On his return to Ahmedabad/Gandhinagar, 827 people were arrested as a preventive measure on his orders.** Narendra Modi said this in an interview to *India Today* weekly dated 18th March, 2002 and this is on official records.

India Today weekly dated 18th March 2002 also admitted that pre-emptive arrests were made without specifying the number.

The same day, on 27th February, **the Gujarat Government deployed the entire police force of 70,000 in Gujarat as per the report of** *The Hindustan Times* **dated 28th February, 2002,** in view of the apprehension that riots may break out in retaliation of burning down of Hindu pilgrims at Godhra. *The Telegraph* **of UK, in its issue of 28th February, also reported that more than 70,000 security men had been deployed in Gujarat on 27th February. These foreign dailies also reported that security had not only been tightened in Gujarat but also in all places with sizeable Muslim population in India on 27th February.** (*Source*:http://www.telegraph.co.uk/news/worldnews/asia/india/138631/ Hindus-massacred-on-blazing- train.html)

The same day, on 27th February, the Gujarat Government deployed the Rapid Action Force in Ahmedabad and other sensitive areas and the Centre sent in the CRPF personnel. This was reported by *The Indian Express* **and also** *Mid-Day* **in their reports on 28th February, 2002** (*Source*: http://www.mid-day.com/news/2002/feb/21232.htm). *The Times of India* reported online on 27 Feb that the Gujarat Government asked the Centre to send 10 companies of CRPF.

These reports were published even before a single large-scale retaliatory riot had taken place.

The Hindu also reported on 28th February that: "(On 27th February) **The state government has appealed to the people to maintain peace…. The Home Minister said the government was taking necessary steps to ensure that the disturbances did not spread during the bandh tomorrow (i.e. 28th February)."** This was reported by many newspapers on 28th February. (*Source*:http://www.hinduonnet.com/thehindu/2002/02/28/ stories/2002022803070100.html)

The VHP also appealed for peace. *The Times of India* reported on 28th February, 2002 even before a single major riot had taken place: "VHP International Vice-President, Acharya Giriraj Kishore told reporters here at Sola Civil Hospital, where 54 out of the 58 bodies of the train attack victims were brought, that 'Hindus **should maintain calm and keep patience.** I appeal to the Muslim brethren to condemn the attack and ask them not to put Hindus' patience to test. Hindus are keeping a restraint but if such incidents do not stop, there can be a counter-reaction, which may be uncontrollable'." (*Source*: http://www.timesofindia.com/articleshow.asp?art_ID=2347298)

The Indian Express dated 28th February, 2002 also reported that the Centre had announced a nationwide alert in the evening of 27th February.

In Godhra on 27th February evening, Narendra Modi, while talking to the media, urged people to maintain calm (and not retaliate). **Narendra Modi himself made an appeal to the people to maintain peace in an appeal broadcast on National TV (Doordarshan) on 28th February. This video was got recorded by him earlier. This video was broadcast for many days on National TV after 28th February, everyday. Luckily, this is also available today on YouTube.**
(*Source*: http://www.youtube.com/watch?v=_BIRMR8zW0iI).

Thus, in brief, the steps taken on 27th February (Wednesday) were:

1. The Gujarat Chief Minister, Mr. Narendra Modi issued shoot-at-sight orders and rushed from Ahmedabad to Godhra.
2. The entire police force was deployed in Gujarat.
3. All the companies of Rapid Action Force in the state were deployed in Ahmedabad, Godhra and other sensitive areas by the State Government.
4. The Central Government rushed CRPF personnel to Gujarat.
5. The State Government imposed curfew in Godhra and other sensitive areas.
6. 827 preventive arrests were made.
7. The Prime Minister, Mr. Atal Bihari Vajpayee and the Gujarat Government urged the Hindus not to retaliate and maintain peace.
8. The RSS and VHP also appealed to Hindus to maintain peace and not retaliate.
9. CISF (Central Industrial Security Force) units were also deployed.
10. The Centre sounded a nationwide alert in the evening.

Also, bodies of the *karsevaks* killed in Godhra were brought to Ahmedabad. This was necessary, because most of the killed *karsevaks* were from Ahmedabad and keeping the bodies in Godhra could have inflamed the situation there and Godhra was also under curfew. So, it was necessary to get the bodies out of Godhra as soon as possible. The bodies were brought to Western Ahmedabad's isolated Sola Civil Hospital, where the Muslim population was negligible. Had the government wanted to instigate Hindus, it would have brought the bodies to Eastern Ahmedabad's main civil hospital from where most of the killed *karsevaks* resided and from where it would have been ideal to instigate the violence against the Muslims. The bodies were brought at 3:30 a.m. of 28th February in a sombre atmosphere (as reported by *India Today* dated 18th March, 2002 and *Times of India* online on 28th February). The time 3:30 a.m. is very difficult to instigate riots with most people asleep and is also very inconvenient for the relatives. Had the government wanted to, it would have brought the bodies at 2 p.m. or 12 noon, which would have been convenient for relatives and easy to instigate riots. The government, thus, seems to have done 4 things right which are:

1. **Bringing the bodies to Ahmedabad instead of keeping them in Godhra so as to calm the matters in Godhra and for relatives' convenience.**
2. **Bringing them to Ahmedabad at 3:30 am instead of in day-time so that chances of retaliation were very low.**
3. Bringing them in a sober atmosphere instead of ceremonial procession.
4. **Bringing them to Western Ahmedabad's hospital where the Muslim population was negligible instead of Eastern Ahmedabad.**

The transport of these bodies was done inside trucks, and no one could see them, and it was also done from 11:30 pm – 12 midnight to 3:30 am, from Godhra to Ahmedabad. Even after coming to Western Ahmedabad's isolated hospital, care was taken to send the bodies to the crematoriums (those which were not cremated at the hospital itself, some had been cremated at the hospital itself) in vehicles, not visible to anyone, while this could have been done on foot as well. This shows the sincerity of the government in preventing display of the bodies. The SIT appointed by the Supreme Court has said all this in its closure report on page 63 as well. The SIT has also said that the decision to bring the bodies was a collective one, taken by many Ministers, and with knowledge and consent of officials like the then Collector of Godhra, the Police Commissioner of Ahmedabad, the DGP of Gujarat, etc. Despite this, several people have tried to spread outrageous lies that 'the dead bodies were paraded by the Government'. The media has not told the truth of all the above facts to clarify things. As a result, many infuriated people continue to believe the lie that the bodies were 'paraded'.

These were the steps taken by the Gujarat Government on 27th February itself to quell the violence, or prevent the violence. But on 28th February, large scale riots happened. That was due to the extreme anger of the masses over Godhra, the reaction from 'secularists' on it, in particular, the TV channels like Star News/NDTV (who then had an alliance), and great anger over terrorism and anti-national activity.

On 28th February (Thursday)

Now the government faced genuine difficulties in controlling the anger of the masses in view of the limited police force. Again let us see what Uday Mahurkar wrote for the weekly *India Today* dated 18th March, 2002:

"That the police was ineffective is clear (on 28th February). But was this intentional? Ahmedabad has a police force of 6,000, including 1,500 armed personnel. In addition, the entire state has just four companies (530 jawans) of the Rapid Action Force (RAF), of which only one company could be spared for Ahmedabad. Considering that the mobs that simultaneously surfaced at nearly half-a-dozen places numbered from 2,000 to 10,000, the forces proved woefully inadequate. At one point on 28th February there were at least 25,000 people targetting the Muslim localities in Ahmedabad alone.

What's more, the police was expecting trouble in Ahmedabad's walled city, which has been the scene of communal violence in every riot in the past two decades. This time, however, it wasn't the walled city where the troubles began. (This was also reported by *The Times of India* online on 28th February, 2002.) At Naroda Patia, the scene of the worst carnage, there was no police presence worth the name to prevent the mobs from grouping in the morning and going on a rampage. There were at least three mobs of 4,000 to 5,000 each attacking Muslims. Among them were members of a tribe called the Chara, who have a township not very far from Naroda. Till now, the Charas were known for thefts and bootlegging. Last Thursday (i.e. 28th February), they earned a reputation for rioting too.

In Chamanpura area, where nearly 40 persons, including former Congress MP, Ehsan Jafri and his family members were killed, there were just a few armed guards when the crowd began assembling. Reinforcements did arrive but by that time, the mob had swelled to 10,000 and **even though police firing killed at least five persons on the spot—in all police firing led to 40 deaths in Ahmedabad alone—it didn't stop the carnage. The situation was aggravated further by Jafri firing from his revolver on the mob injuring seven. Others in the housing complex are said to have thrown acid bulbs too.**

Last Thursday (i.e. 28th February), the Ahmedabad police received at least 3,500 calls for help from the fear-stricken residents, mostly Muslims, against the normal average of 200. The fire brigade, which has the capacity to handle 100 fire calls, received 400 calls on 28th February. Says Ahmedabad Police Commissioner, P.C. Pandey: '**In my 32-year career, I have never seen something like this. It was an upsurge, unstoppable and unprecedented. A stage came when it became physically impossible for the police to tackle mobs running into thousands.**'

Elsewhere in Gujarat, the problem was broadly similar. The state police force is about 43,000 strong, though only 12,000 of them are armed. The SRP numbers 14,000. The mobs which targetted the Muslims in rural areas, ranged in strength from 500 to 10,000. In Sardarpura, where 29 people were burnt to death, the mob was over 500-strong while in Pandarwada, where more than 50 were burnt to death in their homes, the mob, drawn from people of nearby villages, numbered over 5,000. Gujarat Minister of State for Home, Gordhan Jhadaphiya says, 'There is ample evidence to show that the police resorted to effective firing against the rioters'. **Union Law Minister, Arun Jaitley stated in the Rajya Sabha that the police fired 2,000 rounds, which killed 98**

rioters. In addition, 4,000 people were arrested for rioting in the past week....

...there's also much criticism over the delay in calling for the army's help. According to Modi, he had officially called for the army by 4 p.m. on 28th February. By 6:30 p.m., a formal request had landed in Delhi. **By 1 a.m. on 1st March, George Fernandes had landed in Ahmedabad at Modi's behest. At great personal risk, he bravely took to the streets next morning to check the violence. At 11:30 a.m. the army was staging a flag march in Ahmedabad.**

Significantly, Modi tried to ensure that the bodies of the victims were cremated near the hospital, where they were brought for post- mortem at 3:30 a.m. on 28th February from Godhra. The Sola Civil Hospital is on the western outskirts of Ahmedabad, where the Muslim population is negligible. Cremating the bodies there, Modi thought, would have helped contain the anger.

Some VHP leaders present at the spot were also under instructions to convince the relatives of the victims to agree to the proposal. But the moment the proposal was floated, the kin of the dead flared up and accused the BJP 'of acting in a manner worse than the Congress'. Vishnu Sathwara, a VHP worker shouted: 'After using us to climb to the top, the BJP leaders have now left us at the mercy of the wolves....'

...says political analyst, Arvind Bosmia: 'It is beyond the means of the *Sangh Parivar* to lead such an upsurge. **It was largely a spontaneous reaction to the Godhra killings.** And not just Modi but the entire *Sangh Parivar* has been put on this strident path. In fact Modi has been swept up in this militancy.'"

(*Source*: http://www.indiatoday.com/itoday/20020318/cover.shtml)

What does this report from *India Today* reveal? That the Gujarat police had an easy task in dealing with the situation? That is, we must note the vital points here:

1. Entire police force of Ahmedabad was deployed, total 6,000, out of which only 1,500 were armed. The size of the mobs was unprecedented on 28th February and the police forces were woefully short.

2. Even though Rapid Action Force was deployed, it too could not prevent the violence.

3. Ahmedabad police received at least 3,500 calls on 28th February, against an average of 200.

4. Ahmedabad Fire Brigade, which has the capacity to handle 100 calls, received 400 calls on that day.

5. The statement of the then Ahmedabad Police Commissioner, P.C. Pandey also shows that the situation was out of control.

6. *The Hindu* also reported the next day that mob fury reached its crescendo on 28th February, 2002 and the situation slipped out of hand.

The most leading English daily from South India, *The Hindu* reported on 1st March, 2002, covering events of 28th February:

"The Army units, frantically called by the Chief Minister, Narendra Modi, as the situation seemed to slip out of hand, started arriving in Ahmedabad and are likely to be deployed in the city on Friday" (*Source*:http:// www.hinduonnet.com/2002/03/01/stories/2002030103030100.htm).

The Times of India reported on 2nd March, 2002: "Neither the Army nor the shoot-at-sight orders given to the Gujarat police could control the mob frenzy in Ahmedabad on Friday (1st March, 2002) as the city witnessed a total collapse of the law and order machinery for the second straight day, taking a heavy toll of human lives...."

And this was on 1st March when the violence was much less as compared to 28th February. **If even the Army and shoot-at-sight orders could not control the violence when it was much less, what must have been the situation on 28th February when the Army was not present during the day and the violence was far more?**

Even in its infamous article misquoting the Chief Minister, Narendra Modi as saying, "Every action has equal and opposite reaction" (which he never said), *The Times of India* reported on 2nd March, 2002 that: "...the mobs had swelled to enormous proportions. **The sparse police presence looked like a drop in the ocean of violence**". This was despite the deployment of the entire police force, State Reserve Police, Rapid Action Force and CRPF personnel.

The Times of India dated 1st March, 2002 also said that the situation was out of control in Rajkot, and that the fire brigade received 175 calls and was out of water. Police fired two rounds and imposed curfew on half the city— according to this report. The *India Today* report also gave figures of police strength. The state police force was 43,000 strong, the SRP was 14,000 which gives a total of 57,000. In Ahmedabad the police was 6000 strong giving us 63,000. Whether these 6000 include SRP or not is not known. CRPF jawans, RAF, CISF units etc were all deployed making the number of security personnel 70,000. Since we have the reports of *The Telegraph* (UK) and *Hindustan Times* which say that 70,000 security men were deployed, the above figures giving strength of the personnel clearly prove that the 70,000 personnel deployed was the entire strength plus all possible additions like CRPF, CISF and the statement that the entire force had been deployed is absolutely true.

We have also seen the report of *The Telegraph* dated 1st March, 2002 that the Vajpayee Government ordered deployment of the Army (On Modi's request) **as law and order were out of control and protestors slipped out of hand**. This shows that the situation in Ahmedabad had slipped out of hand and no administration, be it of Narendra Modi or of Sonia Gandhi, could have controlled it. What Acharya Giriraj Kishore had warned, reported by *The Times of India* on 28th February, 2002, that the anger of the Hindus could be uncontrollable, became true.

But the state Government dealt with the situation firmly and harshly and, of course, effectively.

India Today in its issue of 11th March (which reported events till 28th February) reported that, "Gujarat Chief Minister, Narendra Modi, an RSS pracharak-turned-BJP politician says, 'The culprits of the gruesome incident will be brought to book, come what may.' He is in a difficult situation. Though Modi had the Army called into Ahmedabad, he said, 'The anger of five crore people of Gujarat is impossible to control with our limited police force. We have done our utmost to prevent the violence from spreading'".
(*URL*: http://www.indiatoday.com/itoday/20020311/cover2.shtml)

India Today reported on 28th February itself that **the Army had been called into Gujarat and that the Chief Minister was caught in a difficult situation.**

The riots began in Ahmedabad on 28th February, 2002 at around 11:00 a.m. At 12:00 p.m. the Chief Minister Narendra Modi called on the Central Government and requested for deployment of the Army, informally. This was reported by weekly *India Today* dated 18th March, 2002 in an article "Chronology of a Crisis". The Army, which was then posted at the border in view of the war clouds between India and Pakistan, sent some of its units immediately. The troops left for Ahmedabad immediately. They did not even take 1-2 days to leave the border areas. Some troops arrived in Ahmedabad before 1:30 a.m. in the morning on 1st March itself. By the 2nd of March, the Army had taken complete control of Ahmedabad. And this was in a record time. In the past, it had often taken three to five days for the Army to arrive in Gujarat to control the riots.

Now we have seen the statement of *The Hindu* in its issue of 1st March that on 28th February (Thursday) Narendra Modi frantically called the Army units to Ahmedabad. Despite this, many anti-BJP, anti-RSS people in the media have spread canards that: "Modi did not call the Army for three days". The Gujarat police were overwhelmingly outnumbered on that day in Ahmedabad. **Despite this, the police fired 1496 rounds on that day. A total of 11 Hindus were shot dead in police firing and 16 were injured.** These are official government figures and also can be seen from the report of *The Hindu* dated 1st March, 2002 (Friday):

"(On Thursday, 28th February) **At least 30 others were killed in police firing, stabbing and other incidents in different parts of the city** while the casualty in other cities and towns in the State was put at over 50.... **Till evening, police fired 46 rounds in Ahmedabad, in which at least 10 persons were believed to have been killed.**"

Now in its earlier statement, it says at least 30 were killed in police firing, stabbing and other incidents in Ahmedabad without specifying how many were killed in police firing. And at another place, it states that at least 10 were believed to have been killed in police firing in Ahmedabad alone by evening. This clearly shows that the official figures of 11 Hindus being shot dead and 16 being injured are absolutely true. Total 17 were killed in police firing on 28 February.

The Portsmouth Herald reported online on 28th February, 2002: "In the state's commercial centre, Ahmedabad, officers fired tear gas at a Hindu mob descending on the Muslim houses. The crowd wouldn't stop, so police fired rifles, injuring six people, three of them seriously, officials at the Civil Hospital told The Associated Press".
(*Source*: http://seacoastauction.com/2002news/2_28_w2.htm).

In fact, the BBC reported online on 28th February when the death toll reported by it was a mere 40 for the entire state of Gujarat, i.e. when violence was going on: "**The army has been deployed there (Ahmedabad)** to counter Hindu youths…. **They included six people, who were shot dead by police in Ahmedabad as they tried to restore calm.** (Final figure was 17 for the state)" (*Source*: http://news.bbc.co.uk/2/hi/south_asia/1845996.stm).

No allegations of police inaction, or police joining rioters, instead it said: "The police tried to restore calm".

The Telegraph dated 1st March, 2002, also reported: "Authorities said police were forced to open fire and lob tear gas shells at several places **as protesters got out of hand** during today's VHP bandh (28th February, Thursday). **Two persons died in police firing in Nadiad and Godhra.**"

The Army units were frantically called to Ahmedabad. *The Hindu* reported in its issue dated 1st March: "**The Army units started arriving in Ahmedabad and are likely to be deployed in the city on Friday (i.e., 1st March)". This shows that the Army units reached Ahmedabad so quickly on 28th February— past midnight—that *The Hindu* had time to report their arrival and publish it in its issue dated 1st March.**

The same day *The Indian Express* also reported: "This pushed the toll, by 1.30 am, to at least 70 out of which 60 was for Ahmedabad alone. **By this time, Defence Minister George Fernandes was in town meeting Chief Minister Narendra Modi and the Army's Gandhinagar-based 11 Division had begun to send out reconnaissance patrols. The news of the Army's arrival came as a glimmer of hope to residents of the city …**"

That is, *The Indian Express* also had time to report the arrival of the Army and also of George Fernandes in its issue of 1st March 2002. So did *The Telegraph* (Kolkata edition) which said: "The Army has begun pre-deployment drills and will be out latest by tomorrow (Friday, 1 March) morning".

The report on the online edition of *The Indian Express* on Feb 28 was:

"1,000 para-military personnel rushed to Gujarat

Press Trust of India

Posted online: Thursday, February 28, 2002 at 1629 hours IST

New Delhi, February 28: Home Minister L K Advani on Thursday directed despatch of about 1,000 personnel of para-military forces to trouble-hit Gujarat following a request by Chief Minister Narendra Modi.

"Eleven companies of para-military forces have been despatched to Gujarat and they will be reaching there by tonight," a Home Ministry official said.

Modi had telephoned Advani to apprise him of the situation in Gujarat in the wake of Wednesday's attack on Sabarmati Express and requested for additional forces to deal with law and order problem."

This clearly indicates how quickly and frantically Narendra Modi called the Army to Ahmedabad. The link for the above report is http://www.expressindia. com/news/fullstory.php?newsid=7922

The time of this report's posting is 4:29 PM. Take into consideration time required for preparing the report, editing, proof reading and posting and it becomes clear that the decision was taken much earlier. It was done so quickly that by 4:30 PM of 28 February, the report was published online.

Among another step taken was the request made to the then Defence Minister George Fernandes by the Gujarat Chief Minister, Narendra Modi himself to come to Ahmedabad. He came immediately on 1st March at 1:00 a.m.

The Tribune (which editorially fully supported the claim of U.C. Banerjee that the Godhra train burning was an accident, absolving Muslim attackers of their heinous crime in January 2005) reported on 1st March, 2002:

"(On 28th February) The police complained they were outnumbered and the rampaging mobs had set up road blocks hindering their movement. Chief Minister, Narendra Modi told a crowded press conference here **700 arrests had been made throughout the state** (BBC report quoted earlier also admitted 700 arrests), including 80 in Godhra, where the train was set ablaze killing

58 persons.... Mr. Modi had telephoned Mr. Advani to apprise him of the situation in Gujarat in the wake of yesterday's attack on Sabarmati Express and **requested for additional paramilitary forces to deal with law and order. The Centre today issued a fresh direction to the state governments and Union Territories to deploy security forces in sensitive areas while arranging logistics for implementation of contingency plans** .... The police opened fire in Kalol town to disperse unruly mobs..."
(*Source:* http://www.tribuneindia.com/2002/20020301/main7.htm).

The staunchly anti-RSS, anti-BJP newspaper, *The Hindu* also reported the next day that on 28th February, the police were outnumbered and discarded tyres were used to create road blockades. **Nowhere is it alleged that the police deliberately turned a blind eye to the rioting**. No mention of police being involved in the violence or giving a free hand to the rioters. No mention of any delay in calling the Army. These charges of "police turning a blind eye, allowing killings for three days, not calling Army until three days had passed... etc." were made after the riots. If these charges were true, the newspapers would have screamed and gone downtown on the very next day. Nothing like this happened. And, of course, no charge that the riots were being 'sponsored' by the Gujarat Government!

The Hindu also reported on 1st March that on 28th February: **"An indefinite curfew has been clamped in 26 cities and towns in the State, including parts of Ahmedabad, Surat, Baroda (i.e. Vadodara), Rajkot, Nadiad, Anand and Kaira in addition to the indefinite curfew in force in Godhra since Wednesday (27th February)."**

Not merely *The Hindu*, almost every newspaper reported this the next day, and so did the weeklies *India Today* and *Outlook* in their issue dated 11th March, 2002, covering events till 28th February.

Perhaps the only newspaper that accused the police of deliberately turning a blind eye to the rioting was *The Indian Express* in its issue dated 1st March, 2002, on the events of 28th February. After that not even *The Indian Express* made any allegations during the actual time of the riots. And *The Indian Express'* allegations too were out of ideological bias. That day newspapers like *The Hindu* did not report anything against the police as such. Now no one can deny that the stray policeman may be lethargic in his duty or sympathetic towards the rioters but does that mean that the government ordered the police to turn a blind eye? **Also when the policemen are overwhelmingly outnumbered by the rioters, if they try to intervene in a hopeless situation, will they not lose their own lives and that too without any gain? Despite this, there are occasions in Gujarat where police officers have saved the Muslims at a great risk to personal life like in Viramgam, Bodeli.** The bias of *The Indian Express* can be seen from the fact that it did not report that the police shot dead 10 rioters in Ahmedabad alone by evening which was reported by *The Hindu* nor did it report that: "Narendra Modi frantically called the Army to Ahmedabad and requested George Fernandes to come", but it did report both of their arrival. Nor did it report that the police fired about 600+ rounds in Ahmedabad and 1,000+ in the whole state. The official records show that 1496 i.e. almost 1500 rounds were fired on 28 February.

The Times of India reported on 1st March in a report titled, "Six Burnt Alive near Godhra":

"...Kalol has been the worst-affected, with nearly 5,000 people descending on it after rumours that the town had been attacked by miscreants**... The police have been grossly outnumbered** on the highway as villagers attacked the passing vehicles... Arad road was one of the worst-affected, with a mob of at least 200 people on the street at any given point of time. Many have armed themselves with knives and sticks. Violence from these two towns has spilled on to the highway, where villagers are having a field day. **They have created roadblocks using boulders, burning tyres, large drainage pipes and leftovers of unfinished engineering projects. Every once in a while a police van arrives and disperses the crowds** from the highway but they are back again the moment the van moves ahead to the next trouble-spot. As one policeman puts it, "They will lynch me if I try to stop them. It is better I turn a blind eye" (*The Times of India* justifies this).

(*Source*: http://timesofindia.indiatimes.com//india/Six-burnt-alive-near-Godhra/articleshow/2472761.cms).

The Indian Express reported on 2nd March, 2002: "(On 1st March) In Vadodara, three persons were burnt alive and one person succumbed to Police bullets when police fired to disperse a violent mob that gheraoed a Deputy

Superintendent of police and an inspector in Manjalpur. Police Commissioner, D.D. Tuteja said additional forces had to rush in to save the policemen."

According to *The Times of India* **in its online edition of 1st March, 2002, police escorted 400 Muslims to safety in Naroda Patiya, after succeeding in dispersing the mob** (*Source*: http:// timesofindia.indiatimes. com/india/Mob-burns-to-death-65-at- Naroda-Patia/articleshow/2473565. cms).

Even before any riots had taken place, *The Times of India* reported: "Vadodara: Five companies of paramilitary forces will be stationed in Vadodara to take care of any untoward incident. **A company of RAF is also scheduled to arrive in the city.** These will be in addition to five companies of SRP already present in the city. One company of recruits from the police training school will also be deployed in the city. Five additional mobiles equipped with communication equipment will also be given to each police station". (*Source*: http://timesofindia.indiatimes.com//city/Ahmedabad/Security-beefed-in-Vadodara/articleshow/2308509.cms).

On 28th February, former Lok Sabha member from Ahmedabad, Ehsan Jafri was killed by a Hindu mob in Gulberg Society in Ahmedabad. Now, in this case, there were around 250 people in the complex. Ehsan Jafri fired on the Hindu crowd with his revolver, injuring 15 and killing one according to the SIT (Special Investigation Team appointed by the Supreme Court of India). His firing was also mentioned by *India Today* (dated 18th March, 2002), *Outlook* and *The Times of India*. This drove the crowd mad and they killed Jafri and 68 others. Here *India Today* weekly clearly states that the police reinforcements arrived outside Jafri's house despite the fact that the police forces were inadequate in the city but, by that time, the mob had swelled to 10,000. **Police shot dead five persons outside his house and saved the lives of 180 Muslims in this episode.** *India Today* **weekly clearly states that the police shot dead five people outside his house.** Narendra Modi in an interview, which we will read later, said that police saved 200 Muslims in this episode. This claim seems to be completely true going by the fact that there were 250 people in the complex and 69 were killed (after all missing were declared dead). When Jafri fired on the Hindu crowd, the situation was further aggravated and the people went crazy and planned to kill each and every person in the complex but the police saved 180 Muslims in this episode. *The Times of India* in its online edition on 28th February, 2002 reported:

"…Meanwhile, fire tenders which rushed to the spot were turned back by the irate mob, which disallowed the Ahmedabad Fire Brigade (AFB) personnel and the district police from rushing to rescue…. Sources in the Congress Party said that the former MP (Ehsan Jafri) after waiting in vain till 12:30 p.m. for official help to arrive **had opened fire on the mob in self-defense**, injuring four (actually 15 were injured and one killed, as per the SIT report, page 1). **Thereafter mayhem ruled the roost**…. The mayor, Himmatsinh Patel appealed to the residents to maintain peace…. The situation remained volatile and an inferno raged till 8:00 p.m., till which time the police forces could not gain entry into the colony".

(*Source:* http://articles.timesofindia.indiatimes.com/2002-02-28/india/27143338_1_gulbarg-society-commissioner-of-police-mk-colony).

The Times of India in its online edition on 28th February, 2002, reported at 2:34 p.m.: "Ahmedabad: **At least six persons were injured when police opened fire to disperse a rampaging mob in Meghaninagar** (Chamanpura, Ehsan Jafri case) **area of the city on Thursday afternoon.** The injured were brought to the civil hospital where the condition of at least three is stated to be serious…the incident took place at Chamanpura area under Meghaninagar police station. Meanwhile, one person was stabbed to death in Kalupur area of Ahmedabad **which is placed under curfew.** The incident took place at Ghadiali-na-Khancho area in the afternoon. With this, the death toll in the post-Godhra aftermath in the state has risen to eight, with four deaths recorded in stabbings in Ahmedabad. The toll is expected to go up higher as reports of more violence are trickling in."

(*Source:* http://timesofindia.indiatimes.com//india/police-open-fire-in-Ahmedabad-6-hurt/articleshow/2360713.cms).

That is, much before 2:34 p.m. itself, police had injured six outside Ehsan Jafri's house and actually five were killed in their firing (considering the time taken to get news, prepare report, edit, proof read and post it online, this must have happened much before 2:34 pm). This despite the hopeless situation which is clear from reading *The Times'* report that the Fire Brigade and police were not allowed to be reached by the mob. **Though police gained control only after 8:00 p.m., they fired much before that, before 2:00 p.m. and saved 200 Muslims.** Kalupur was already under curfew before 2:34 p.m. In fact, reading the online reports of *The Times of India,* one knows that almost all the places where violence was being reported were under curfew, which must have been imposed immediately as violence occurred. Another report posted at 11:31 a.m. on 28th February titled "VHP Bandh Turns Violent; Eight Stabbed to Death" also mentions imposing of curfew at many places. And in its report titled "Indefinite Curfew in Ahmedabad, Vadodara" posted on 28th February, it says:

"Gandhinagar: Curfew was imposed in many areas of old Ahmedabad on Thursday (i.e. 28 Feb) afternoon following unprecedented acts of violence and arson. The district collector of Ahmedabad has requested for more forces to be brought in as violence and arson threatens to spread into rural Ahmedabad. Fires have been reported in more than 80 places in Ahmedabad. According to the government sources, the situation in rural Ahmedabad **could turn grim as enough forces are not available to impose curfew.** Police Commissioner P.C. Pandey said at 12:30 p.m. that he was imposing curfew in the police station areas of Shahpur, Dariapur, Karanj, Kalupur, Bapunagar, Gomtipur and Rakhial and the police chowky areas of Saraspur and Isanpur. **Police burst tear gas shells on C.G. Road to control mobs which were setting on fire shops belonging to a particular community.** Curfew has also been imposed in the towns of Bharuch and Ankaleshwar following acts of arson on Thursday morning (28th February). Curfew was imposed earlier in areas of Vadodara city following deaths of two persons in stabbings. **Curfew in Vadodara:** Indefinite curfew has been imposed in the city from 8 a.m. on Thursday morning (28th February) following two cases of stabbing reported from Salatwada and another from the highway after Wednesday night, a senior police official said. Curfew had been imposed in the six police station areas of the walled city and RAF and CISF (Central Industrial Security Force) companies have been deployed in sensitive areas, city Police Commissioner, Deen Dayal Tuteja said. Indefinite curfew has also been imposed in Lunawada town of Panchmahal district after 2 a.m. on Wednesday night (27th February) following incidents of arson and looting, he said" (*Source*: http://timesofindia.indiatimes.com// india/Indefinite-curfew-in-Ahmedabad-Vadodara/ articleshow/2340805.cms).

No allegations of any inaction! *The Times of India's* report, in its online edition of 1st March titled "Gujarat Violence Hits Industries", also says that police were totally outnumbered in the town of Halol and unable to stop the mobs. The same was the case in other industrial areas like Shapar, Veraval and Latiplot, according to the report. (*Source*: http://timesofindia.indiatimes.com//india/Gujarat-violence-hits- industries/articleshow/2483562.cms).

The Times of India also reported in its online edition on 1st March that rich men in cars became looters, just like *India Today* in its issue of 18th March, 2002 reported.

As per information put up on the site www.indianembassy.org (the official site of the Indian embassy in USA), the state also requested for additional forces from Madhya Pradesh, Maharashtra and Rajasthan. Two companies of Maharashtra Reserve Police Force arrived and were deployed in Surat. The SIT appointed by the Supreme Court has also said this.

The SIT has also said on page 210 of its report that enquiries revealed that on 28 February 151 Muslims and 31 Hindus were killed in Ahmedabad. 17 people were killed in police firing (whether in Ahmedabad alone or in the whole state is not told, but most likely whole state) out of whom 11 were Hindus and 6 Muslims. Since 31 Hindus were also killed on 28 February (assuming 11 in police firing, 20 in riots) it is clear that some Hindus were also attacked. As we will see in the chapter on "Attacks on Hindus", on 28 Feb Hindus were attacked in Ahmedabad's Bapunagar and Jamalpur areas, at least. Hence 6 Muslims were also killed in police firing. And besides, the police cannot generally know the religion of the rioters while firing, in many cases.

Thus, in brief, the steps taken on 28th February were:

1. The riots began in Ahmedabad at 11:00 a.m. The Chief Minister, Narendra Modi informally contacted the Central Government to send Army at 12 noon, i.e. within one hour. Curfew was imposed by 12:20 p.m. at all places in Ahmedabad. In many places, it was imposed much earlier.

2. As per the report of *The Hindu*, Narendra Modi "frantically" called the Army units.

3. Narendra Modi requested the Union Defence Minister, George Fernandes to come to Gujarat.

4. Curfew was imposed in 26 towns and cities in Gujarat.

5. There were around 250 people in the housing complex of Ehsan Jafri and the mob killed 69 with the police saving about 200 Muslims despite being overwhelmingly outnumbered by the mob, and the crowd going mad by Jafri's firing. Police shot dead five rioters outside his house.

6. The police fired 1496 rounds in the state, including at least 600 in Ahmedabad.

7. The police shot dead 11 Hindus and injured 16. At least two were shot dead outside Ahmedabad in Nadiad and Godhra. Total 17 were killed in police firing.

8. The Gujarat Government requested Army deployment within one hour. At 4:00 p.m., a press conference was held, in which this decision was publicly announced. All procedures needed for this were done very quickly. The meeting of the Cabinet Committee on Security of the Central Government was held at 6:45 P.M. under the Prime Minister's chairmanship, it approved Army deployment immediately and Army units reached Ahmedabad after midnight.

9. The Army units reached Ahmedabad so quickly that newspapers like *The Hindu*, *The Indian Express* had time to report their arrival on 28th February, 2002 (Thursday) itself and publish it on 1st March, 2002 (Friday)!

10. Defence Minister, George Fernandes reached Ahmedabad so quickly that newspapers like *The Indian Express* reported his arrival the next day!

11. Police escorted 400 Muslims to safety in Naroda-Patiya after dispersing the mob in Naroda-Patiya. Total of 95 people were killed, at least 900 Muslims were saved, since *The Times of India* reports that 1,000 Muslims lived in the attacked area in Naroda-Patiya.

12. The Gujarat Government requested neighbouring states of Maharashtra, Rajasthan and Madhya Pradesh to send additional police force. All these states were ruled by the Congress. Only Maharashtra sent 2

columns (less than 500 personnel). Madhya Pradesh & Rajasthan did not send at all.

13. **700 people were arrested by the police in the state, including around 80 in Godhra on the very first day of the violence when the situation was out of control.** Tear gas shells were also burst. This writer has been able to find out the exact number of tear gas shells burst on 28 Feb which is 4297 in the whole state. The total number of tear gas shells burst is over 15,000 and it is 6,500 in the first three days.

On 1st March (Friday)

On the next day, i.e. 1st March, 2002, the Army staged a flag march in Ahmedabad at 11:30 a.m. *The Hindu* reported on 2nd March, 2002 (Saturday): **"The Army began flag marches in the worst-affected areas of Ahmedabad, Baroda, Rajkot and Godhra cities and the 'shoot at sight' order was extended to all 34 curfew-bound cities and towns in Gujarat".** The title of the report itself was: **"Shoot Orders in Many Gujarat Towns, toll over 200".** Now, on this day, the Army had arrived, but even the Army could not prevent the riots, nor the shoot-at-sight orders given to Gujarat police, according to *The Times of India.* As mentioned earlier, no newspaper accused the administration of being involved in the riots from this day onward. *The Indian Express* reported on 2nd March: **"The police, its credibility lowest than ever, tried to salvage its reputation intervening in some clashes by opening fire. Twenty were killed in police firing across the state, 12 in Ahmedabad."**

There are two things to be noted from this very vital statement. **First, the police did their best to control the violence and could not be accused by anyone, even *The Indian Express,* of negligence from this day onward, the second day of the riots, i.e. 1st March, 2002. And second, there were "clashes" going on between Hindus and Muslims, and not one-sided massacres of Muslims.**

Direct evidence of the fact that Muslims were also on the offensive is available from the report of a newspaper as anti-BJP as *The Hindu* dated 2

March, 2002: **"But unlike Thursday (28 February) when one community was entirely at the receiving end, the minority backlash (on Friday, 1 March) caused further worsening of the situation.** Police presence had little impact on the two communities pelting stones at each other in Bapunagar, Gomtipur, Dariapur, Shahpur, Naroda (all areas with high Muslim population) and other areas, from where incidents of firing had been reported.... Pitched battle was continuing between the two communities late in the evening. The official sources said timely arrival of the police foiled a retaliatory attempt to break into a prominent temple in Jamalpur locality in the walled city". (*Source*: http://www. hindu.com/thehindu/2002/03/02/stories/2002030203050100.htm).

The Indian Express reported on 2 March, 2002: "(On 1st March) Tension escalated in the walled city areas just before the Friday prayers. There were **violent clashes between mobs in Jamalpur, Bapunagar and Rakhial (all Muslim concentrated areas of Ahmedabad)." Clearly Muslims were on the offensive.** And *The Times of India* also reported the same day: "(On 1st March) There were signs of retaliation in areas like Juhapura, Kalupur, Dariapur and Shahpur (all Muslim-dominated areas)...." This clears all possible doubts.

The bias of *The Indian Express* can be seen from the fact that though it reported that George Fernandes appealed to the citizens for peace in Ahmedabad and later left for Vadodara, it did not bother to mention that he was bravely on the streets of Ahmedabad at a great risk to personal life! **This was mentioned by *India Today* weekly. *The Times of India* also reported this in its online edition on 2 March, 2002 and praised George Fernandes.**

The Hindu reported on 2nd March, 2002 that at least 17 were killed in police firing in Ahmedabad until the second day of the riots. *The Telegraph* (Kolkata) reported on 2nd March, 2002 that "(On 1st March) **Despite the presence of the army—some 3,500 soldiers have arrived in the state—in Ahmedabad, Surat, Vadodara and Rajkot, the rioting has not stopped."**

On the second day, i.e., 1st March, additional 24 Hindus were shot dead and 40 were injured. These are figures given to B.P. Singhal—former Director General of Police, by official government sources. *The Indian Express* reported that 20 were killed in police firing on 1st March. It could be that at that time, many injured were alive when *The Indian Express* wrote the report, and died later, so the number of people killed in police firing on 1st March was more than what *The Indian Express* reported that day. And, of course, due to terrible anti- BJP bias, *The Indian Express* could also have deliberately reported lesser number of people killed in police firing than the correct number, but that seems unlikely in this case to me.

27 Muslims were also killed in police firing on this day throughout the state. Since there was a minority backlash (as reported by *The Hindu*), and shoot-at-sight orders were on, it was natural that Muslims would also be killed in police firing. The SIT's closure report quotes the then Ahmedabad Police Commissioner P C Pandey as saying (on page 217) that the police cannot know the religion of the rioters on whom firing is being done. On 1st March, the police saved 2,500 Muslims from certain death when they were attacked by 8,000 armed tribals in Sanjeli, a town in North Gujarat. This was reported by *India Today*.

And the shoot-at-sight orders were extended on 1ˢᵗ March, 2002 to Ahmedabad and 33 other places as reported by *The Hindu* the next day.

The website www.indianembassy.org reports: "The next brigade of the Army was also deployed in Rajkot and Vadodara on 1ˢᵗ March, 2002 itself. Three columns allotted to Godhra reached in Godhra, Lunawada and Halol on the early morning of 2ⁿᵈ March 2002. Thereafter, the Army has been shifted in Surat and Bhavnagar as and when the situation warranted such a shift." (*Source*: http://www.indianembassy.org/new/gujarat_02/index.htm).

1st March, 2002 was Friday. **On this day the violence was much less as compared to 28th February (Thursday)** and there was a minority backlash. In short, the steps taken were:

1. On the morning of 1st March, George Fernandes bravely took to streets to check violence in Ahmedabad, at a great risk to personal life. He was pummeled with stones. Later, he left for Vadodara.
2. 24 Hindus were shot dead by police and 40 injured. 27 Muslims were also killed in police firing, according to official records.
3. The Army staged flag marches in Ahmedabad, Vadodara, Surat and Rajkot's worst-affected areas.

4. Shoot-at-sight orders were extended to all 34 curfew-bound cities and towns in the state.

5. 2,500 Muslims were saved in Sanjeli, a town in North Gujarat from a crowd of 8,000 armed tribals by the police.

6. The police fired 2167 rounds and 1969 tear gas shells were also burst, according to official records.

7. 568 more preventive arrests were made, 443 Hindus and 125 Muslims and 695 arrests were made for offences. (Official figures)

On 2nd March (Saturday)

2nd March, 2002 was Saturday. On this day also Muslims were aggressive. Ahmedabad was almost completely peaceful on this day with major violence occurring in other parts of Gujarat. The police brought the situation under control there and fired on pitched battles between Hindus and Muslims. *The Tribune* reported on 3rd March, 2002 that: "(On 2nd March) Ahmedabad, the worst hit by the communal flare-up in the wake of Godhra train killings, was virtually back to normal…."

That is, the Gujarat Government managed to control riots in the communally sensitive state in three days after Godhra and in only two days in a communally ultra-sensitive place like Ahmedabad! Reports of *The Hindu* and *The Telegraph* of 3rd March, 2002 also prove that Ahmedabad was virtually back to normal on 2nd March, 2002 itself. *The Hindu* reported that 'the situation improved in Ahmedabad with no major incidents of arson reported' and *The Telegraph* reported that 'Riot spins out of Ahmedabad'.

From the night of the second day till the third day of the riots, i.e. 2nd March, 2002, the police shot dead at least 47 people in Gujarat including 19 in Ahmedabad, as per the report of *The Hindu* dated 3rd March, 2002. *The Hindu* reported: "Even while claiming that the situation was improving, Mr. Modi said the police fired at least 1,031 rounds in different parts of the State since last night (i.e. Friday, 1st March night) besides bursting 1,614 tear gas shells to disperse violent mobs. **While 19 people were killed in police firing in Ahmedabad and eight in Godhra, six people were killed in police firing**

GUJARAT RIOTS: THE TRUE STORY

**in Baroda, five in Anand, three each in Mehsana and Gandhinagar, two
in Kaira and one in Bhavnagar."**

The same day i.e. 3rd March 2002, *The Indian Express* reported: "The toll
went up to over 450 as police recovered more bodies and **77 more people were
killed either in police or Army firing**".

Thus, in brief, the steps taken on 2nd March, 2002 were:

1. The police fired more than 1,031 rounds and burst 1,614 tear gas
    shells. More than this, because these were the figures till Modi's press
    conference in the evening after which more were fired.
2. As per the report of *The Hindu,* at least 47 people were shot dead by the
    police in Gujarat: 19 in Ahmedabad, eight in Godhra, six in Vadodara,
    five in Anand, three each in Mehsana and Gandhinagar, two in Kaira
    and one in Bhavnagar since 1st March night.
3. Curfew was imposed in 40 places in Gujarat.
4. Border Security Force units were dispatched to Surat.
5. 2,000 Muslims were saved in Dahod by the police.
6. 573 preventive arrests (477 Hindus, 96 Muslims) and 711 arrests for
    offences (482 Hindus, 229 Muslims) were made.

The efforts of Narendra Modi to control violence can be clearly seen from
the report in *India Today* weekly dated 18 March 2002 in an article titled
"Chronology of a Crisis".

"27th FEBRUARY, 2002

8:03 a.m.: Incident at Godhra claims lives of 57 *karsevaks.*

8:30 a.m.: Modi is informed of the carnage. (This could be at 9 am)

4:30 p.m.: Gujarat Assembly adjourned and Modi visits Godhra where he
holds a meeting, giving shoot-at-sight orders to the police.

10:30 p.m.: CM holds meeting with senior government officials at
Gandhinagar; (This meeting was simply a law and order review
meeting) orders curfew in sensitive places and pre-emptive arrests

(These orders of curfew and preventive arrests had nothing to do with that meeting).

28ᵗʰ FEBRUARY, 2002

8:00 a.m.: Special control room set up in CM's house to monitor the situation during VHP bandh.

12:00 p.m.: Modi informally contacts Centre for calling in Army. Cabinet Secretary, T.R. Prasad tells Defence Secretary, Y. Narain that army is to be mobilised.

12:30 p.m.: Vice-Chief of Army Staff, Lt. General N.C. Vij tells Narain that only two columns are available as the rest are deployed on the border.

12:35 p.m.: Prasad directs Narain to advise Chief of Army Staff, Gen. Padmanabhan to have troops ready due to the rapidly deteriorating situation in Ahmedabad.

12:45 p.m.: Narain tells Vij to arrange immediate movement of troops to Gujarat.

4:00 p.m.: Modi requests army deployment following consultations with Advani (the then Home Minister of India).

6:45 p.m.: Cabinet Committee on Security meets under the Prime minister's chairmanship; approves the immediate movement of troops to Ahmedabad and other parts of Gujarat. Vajpayee (the then Prime Minister) deputes Fernandes (Defence Minister) to supervise the deployment of troops.

7:00 p.m.: The Gujarat Government's formal request for Army deployment is received in Delhi.

11:30 p.m.: Airlifting of troops begins.

1st MARCH, 2002

2:30 a.m.: A brigade reaches Ahmedabad. The 54th Division's General Officer Commanding contacts acting Chief Secretary.

9:00 a.m.: Discussions between representatives of the Army and the state take place, followed by troop flag march in Ahmedabad." (*URL*: http://www.indiatoday.com/itoday/20020318/cover2.shtml).

Just a couple of clarifications here. Curfew was imposed in Godhra not at 4:30 p.m. in the evening of 27th February when Narendra Modi visited it, but at 9:45 a.m. itself. And second, the Army brigade reached Ahmedabad before 1:30 a.m. of 1st March and not at 2:30 a.m. as reported by *The Indian Express* the next day.

Reports from the Indian English media which was biased against BJP also proved that the real riots had stopped in the first three days. The following report from *The Hindu* dated 4th March, 2002 will make it clear:

"Ahmedabad, 3rd March. The orgy of violence in Gujarat appears to have ended. Today only two deaths were reported, one from Godhra. Officially the death toll is 431, more than half of them in Ahmedabad. Ahmedabad was quiet, apart from two major arson attacks on a Muslim-owned petrol station and warehouse.

Curfew has been lifted in most areas of the 40 towns and cities where clashes were reported, including Naroda and Meghnaninagar (i.e. Gulberg Society case, i.e. Chamanpura, Ehsan Jafri case) in Ahmedabad, where hundreds were killed. The state administration says that curfew will be relaxed in more areas tomorrow. There was a 'sense of normality in the State' today.

But the smouldering remains of burnt-out buildings and the acrid smell of burning rubber, five days after the violence began, are a reminder that 'normality' in Ahmedabad is a very long way off". (*URL:* http://www.thehindu.com/2002/03/04/stories/2002030403090100.htm).

This newspaper report clearly proves that the government's claim of controlling the riots in 72 hours was absolutely true.

We also need to see a few newspaper reports to see what happened after 3rd March, 2002. By and large, reading issues of *The Hindu* of March and April 2002 will give clear indications about the nature of violence. The following was the report of *The Hindu* dated 6th March, 2002:

"Peace Marches, Prayer Meetings Held in Gujarat

By Our Special Correspondent

Ahmedabad, 5th March. The Gujarat Government, voluntary organisations and prominent citizens organised a peace march here today as the situation in the State showed signs of returning to normality.

Hundreds of prominent citizens, Sarvodaya leaders and others marched from the Kocharab Ashram to the Sabarmati Ashram, both set up by Mahatma Gandhi, and held an all-religion prayer meeting. Peace marches and prayer meetings were also held in Surat, Porbandar, the birth-place of the Mahatma, and several other cities and towns.

State-owned transport corporations resumed partial operations. Municipal buses in Ahmedabad are expected to start services from tomorrow, at least in some areas. According to the State Transport Corporation chairman, Kamlesh Patel, the loss to the body due to the violence is more than 15 crores (i.e. 150 million rupees).

Schools have reopened in many parts of the State. The Education Minister, Anandiben Patel, said the remaining schools would be reopened tomorrow.

Board examinations for the secondary and higher secondary classes had been postponed by a week to 18th March.

Even as the police rounded up more than 1,000 people for the violence following the Godhra carnage, opposition parties complained that the Government was shying away from arresting Vishwa Hindu Parishad, Bajrang Dal and BJP leaders named in the *suo motu* complaints filed by the police.

No known VHP or Bajrang Dal leader has been arrested though the Chief Minister, Narendra Modi, has maintained that action would be taken against all those guilty of the "heinous crimes" without any discrimination." (*URL*:http://www.hinduonnet.com/thehindu/2002/03/06/stories/2002030603221100.htm).

The following report from *The Hindu* dated 7th March, 2002 will make things absolutely clear:

"Gujarat Limping Back to Normality

By Our Special Correspondent

Ahmedabad, 6th March. No untoward incident has been reported from any part of Gujarat for the second consecutive day today. The Home Secretary, K. Nityanandam, said the curfew had been relaxed in most areas.

For the first time since the Sabarmati Express was torched on 27th February, curfew was relaxed for six hours in Godhra today. Though the situation was tense, no incidents were reported.

The Chief Minister, Narendra Modi, has announced a judicial inquiry into the post-Godhra violence. But a spokesman of the Chief Minister's Office said that the Government was yet to decide on whether or not to club the inquiry with the one into the train carnage. He said since the 'nature' of the two incidents was different, it was possible that separate commissions would be constituted to go into them.

The Union Home Minister, L.K. Advani, had also preferred separate probes. His view—that while the Godhra carnage was a 'pre-planned act of terrorism', what followed afterwards were 'natural outbursts of revulsion and communal violence'—has been echoed by the State Government.

…**Mr. Modi visited relief camps housing the minorities and instructed the officials concerned to ensure supply of essential commodities. Doctors visited the camps to treat the injured** for the first time today since the beginning of the violence. Some 30,000 people are being sheltered in 18 relief camps…" (*Source*: http://www.hinduonnet.com/thehindu/2002/03/07/stories/2002030702801300.htm).

The Times of India dated 10th March, 2002 also carries a similar report, which makes it absolutely clear that the riots stopped in the state in 72 hours, though stray riots started again later.

After these three days, retaliatory riots were started by Muslims and stray rioting continued. But the above were not the only steps taken by the administration to control violence. Some quotations of the weekly *India Today* blast these myths about the government or the police force turning a blind eye to the riots. The Gujarat police, far from turning a blind eye to the killings or participating in the killings, saved as many as 2,500

Muslims at a single place on a single day, in Sanjeli, which is more than thrice the total number of Muslims killed in the state in the entire period of rioting of two-and-a-half months. **If, at a single place, at a single time, 2,500 Muslims were saved, surely many more must have been saved at other places on the same day, and many thousands in the first three days in total.**

However, it is not merely this act that is on record. Like in Sanjeli, 5,000 Muslims were saved in Bodeli, a town in Vadodara district, from a crowd of over 7,000. The following is another report quoted from *India Today* dated 8th April, 2002: "When a Muslim woman was burnt alive by Hindu zealots (in Viramgam, not far from Ahmedabad), the minorities, who constitute almost 30% of the 70,000- odd population went on the rampage. Soon, nearly 15,000 Hindus from nearby villages encircled Viramgam and targetted the Muslim localities in the town. It took some deft handling by the police and the Army to save the day."

And in the 22nd April issue, *India Today* says: "...take Sanjeli. In the carnage that ensued after the February 27 Godhra killings, 8,000 armed tribals descended on the town of 8,000 in the tribal heartland of Dahod district. Bows, stones and gunshots rained on the fleeing Muslims, killing 15. Police intervention meant another 2,500 were spared a savage death.... In an identical display of insanity, around 7,000 armed tribals marched into Bodeli town in Chotte- Udepur tribal area of Vadodara district intent on massacring the Muslims, who had taken shelter there after being driven out of the neighbouring villages. **While hundreds were saved by the police, Vadodara District Collector, Bhagyesh Jha and other senior officers were fired upon by tribals as they tried to rescue the trapped Muslims.** (A total of 5,000 were saved here).

Tragedy was also averted by the police and army at Viramgam town near Ahmedabad where over 15,000 Hindus, mostly armed OBC Thakores, burnt 250 Muslim houses..." (*Source*: http:// www.india-today.com/itoday/ 20020422/states.shtml).

That is to say, the Gujarat police and the Indian Army together saved thousands of Muslims, of the 21,000-odd of the town- Viramgam. If we assume that there was no police or Army presence, 10,000 Muslims of the town may have been killed. **On the basis of records available to this writer,**

we can conclusively say that the Gujarat police saved at least 17,500 Muslims in Gujarat. As a matter of fact, many sources have told this writer that the Gujarat police saved 24,000 Muslims in the state in the first three days alone.

The website www.indianembassy.org seems to be an official site of the Indian Embassy in USA. It says:

"In the Mora village of Panchmahal district, SDM, Mamlatdar and police rushed to the spot where the crowd was gathered, dispersed the crowd and **saved the lives of 400 people by shifting them to a safe place**.

On receipt of information on 3rd March, 2002, a *madarsa* in Asoj, in Vagodia, Vadodara district was likely to be attacked, nearly 40 persons including 22 children were evacuated to a safe place.

On the night of 2nd /3rd March, 2002, in Dahod, the police escorted over 2000 persons belonging to the minority community to a safe place, rescuing them from the mob that had gathered from surrounding 28 villages.

In the Surat city, protection was provided to about 60 persons and the mosque in Nana Varacha area.

On receipt of information that some women and children were trapped in a mosque, the Surat police escorted them to a safe place.

On receipt of information that 100 persons were trapped near Rita Society opposite Yateem Khana Jain Mandir, the police immediately rushed there and dispersed the mob, but found no persons trapped inside. The Surat police immediately provided protection requested for by 12-15 houses of Muslims near the Khoja Masjid. (*URL:* http://www.indianembassy.org/new/gujarat_02/index.htm).

As we have seen, *The Times of India's* report implied that 900 were saved in Naroda Patiya. 180 were saved in Gulberg Society in Chamanpura. There are many other instances as well. Some of them are:

a) 5,000 people from the Noorani Mosque area were saved by Ahmedabad Police

b) 240 people were saved at Sardarpura of Mehsana district and shifted to safer places

c) 450 were saved in Pore and Nardipur villages of Gandhinagar district, and shifted to safer places

d) 400 were saved in a Madrasa at Bhavnagar

e) 1,500 people were saved from Fatehpura village of Vadodara district

f) 3,000 people were saved and shifted from Kwant village of Vadodara district

Police records and figures given by the Union Home Ministry as well as figures given by weekly *India Today* in its issue dated 18th March, 2002 as well as *The Times of India* dated 7th March 2002 reveal that as many as 98 people were killed in the first three days in police firing. **We have already looked at the reports in *The Indian Express* and *The Hindu* to know that the figure of 98 people being shot dead in the first three days is indeed true. This was a record of sorts. Never before were so many people shot dead in police firing for rioting in so few days** in the entire history of communal riots in India, and certainly not in Gujarat, which saw far worse riots in 1969 and 1985. Of the 98 people killed in police firing, majority are Hindus (60 Hindus). Out of these 98, 40 were killed in Ahmedabad alone. In Ahmedabad, 17 Hindus and 23 Muslims were killed in police firing.

The reason for Muslims also being killed in police firing was that they were on the offensive as well on 1st and 2nd March, 2002. (And no one alleged at the time of the riots, not even the worst critics like *Indian Express*, that the police killed Muslims ruthlessly in firing!) This was natural since *The Indian Express* and *The Hindu* reported that the police tried its best intervening in clashes by opening fire. Truly since 'clashes' were going on between Hindus and Muslims, it is natural that Muslims too would be killed in police firing, and more so when they attacked a prominent temple in Jamalpur locality, as reported by *The Hindu* the next day. **Outside Ahmedabad, out of the 58 killed in police firing, 43 were Hindus. This includes Vadodara as well, where Muslims were almost as on the offensive as in Ahmedabad.** And despite the fact that Vadodara is included here, in 'outside Ahmedabad' category, the proportion of Hindus killed in police firing is very high—43 out of 58. According to ex-Vadodara Police Commissioner D.D.Tuteja, quoted in the SIT report on page 364, in

Vadodara 4 Hindus and 7 Muslims were killed in police firing, which will give us the figure of 39 Hindus out of the 47 killed in police firing outside Ahmedabad and Vadodara.

This clearly nails the lie that the police was lethargic or turned a blind eye to the rioting.

Riots did not Affect the Entire State, Only Parts of It

That the whole of Gujarat was burning is a figment of imagination of the biased and prejudiced people in the media. The riots did not spread to Saurashtra and Kutch, both of which are border areas. Saurashtra (52) and Kutch (6) accounted for as many as 58 out of the Gujarat assembly's 182 seats at that time. That is, they are nearly one-third of Gujarat. Riots simply did not spread to the western and the south- western part of the State of Gujarat. **This is clear indication that the State Government had absolutely no hand in instigating the riots and it by no means wanted to encourage the riots.** The BJP undoubtedly gained in the riot affected areas. It also gained because of the Hindu anger after Godhra. But that by no means indicates that the State Government wanted to instigate the riots. Hindus did not retaliate in one-third of the state even for the first three days. If the State Government wanted to instigate riots, it could have easily done so in Saurashtra and Kutch. It was reported that a section of the Patels were unhappy with Keshubhai Patel's replacement as Chief Minister, and that Narendra Modi was a bit unpopular in them. Since Saurashtra was the home turf of Keshubhai Patel, instigating riots there would have polarized the Hindus there and helped the BJP in general and Narendra Modi in particular. But this region was peaceful!

In the rest of the state of Gujarat too the riots stopped just after the first three days. After the first three days, **Muslims started many of the riots,** directly or indirectly. Northern and southern Gujarat were peaceful after 2nd March, 2002 and only some places in central Gujarat saw riots. Basically, after 2nd March, 2002, riots were limited only to Ahmedabad, Vadodara, and a few places in Panchmahal district near Godhra-by and large.

All TV channels and almost the entire print media admitted at some point or the other that Saurashtra and Kutch remained peaceful throughout the two-and-a-half months of rioting and saw no riots. But this admission was more pronounced not during the time of riots in Gujarat, but many months later, during the coverage of the Gujarat Assembly elections of December 2002.

Around 6th December, 2002, Narendra Modi was invited on Star News/ NDTV's programme *Hotline*. In that programme, the anchor Pankaj Pachouri asked Narendra Modi this question. He said, "Your party always gains because of the riots. But no riots took place in Saurashtra and Kutch, so you are all set to lose there. How will you respond to this?" To that question, Narendra Modi replied,

"When 2% of Gujarat was burning, you were saying that the whole of Gujarat is burning. Now you are saying that no riots took place in Saurashtra and Kutch. So, first you apologize for lying that the entire state was burning when only 2% of the state was burning." **In the entire State of Gujarat, there are 18,600 villages, 240 municipal towns and 25 district headquarters. The riots occurred in no more than 90 places. If one includes the two big cities of Ahmedabad and Vadodara, by the maximum stretch of imagination, it can be said that 2 per cent of the state was affected by riots, or was in flames.**

In this regard, some people quote a report of R Sreekumar, a police officer, of August 2002 and claim that 154 Assembly seats, with 151 towns and 993 villages were affected by riots. Of course this does not mean that all these places saw riots. On page 153 of SIT closure report, Ashok Narayan, ACS (Home) is quoted as saying that Sreekumar arrived at this figure by including all places where food grains and other items of relief had been provided in relief camps or other places by the government. Ashok Narayan is quoted as saying that the actual places seeing violence were lesser. Naturally, there is a vast difference in the places where the foodgrain was provided and places which actually saw violence.

Diehard anti-Sangh Parivar magazine, fortnightly *Frontline* also reported after the December 2002 Gujarat polls: "The Bharatiya Janata Party made its greatest gains in the riot-affected areas — it captured 50 of the 65 riot-affected constituencies…**In places untouched by riots**, the BJP lost ground. **In Kutch**, it got only two out of the six seats, compared with the four seats that it had won in the previous election…**In Saurashtra**, where the water crisis is acute, the BJP slipped from its 48-seat tally in 1998 to just 37 seats this time." http://www.frontline.in/static/html/fl1926/stories/20030103005900400.htm

If Frontline itself claimed 65 riot-affected seats out of 182, (this includes places like Ahmedabad district and Vadodara district which had 19 and 13 Assembly seats at that time, and also 2 other cities of Rajkot and Surat), then it shows that it is absolutely impossible for riots to have occurred in 993 villages and the correct number of places of violence must indeed be close to 90, since Ahmedabad and Vadodara districts themselves account for 32 Assembly seats. And *Frontline* also admitted that Saurashtra and Kutch were untouched by riots.

On the 1st day of the riots, 26 places needed to be placed under curfew as reported by all major dailies the next day, e.g. *The Hindu*. On the 2nd day, 34 places needed to be under curfew as reported the next day by dailies (these include most if not all of the 26 already under curfew). And on the 3rd day 40 places were under curfew (Mostly already under curfew from 1 or 2 days). Since the violence was controlled in 3 days, and after the 3 days, violence was limited mainly to Ahmedabad, **Vadodara and some places near Godhra, we can clearly see that it is absolutely impossible for riots to have occurred in 993 villages, and that the figures of maximum 50 villages and maximum 90 places seeing riots are absolutely true.**

98 people were killed in police firing in the initial violence. No opponent of the BJP and the *Sangh Parivar* has ever challenged these figures. Balbir Punj, then a Rajya Sabha MP of the BJP, a senior functionary and also a spokesman at a time, wrote in an article in *The Pioneer* dated 25th April, 2002, "Out of 31,000 arrests made throughout the State in connection of riots, 80 per cent are Hindus. Out of approximately 800 killed in Gujarat, one-fourth are Hindus. Out of 140 killed in police firing, 80 were Hindus…."

The Times of India reported on 7th March, 2002: "The official statistics say **that 99 persons have been killed in police firing**. The security forces have fired 5,176 rounds of ammunition at the mobs as well as 7,276 tear gas shells" (*Source*: http://timesofindia. indiatimes.com/city/ahmedabad/

Toll-now-677-due-to-recovery-of- more-bodies/articleshow/3055362.cms). Since real riots stopped on 2nd March itself, it clearly proves that in the first three days, the police fired more than 3,900 rounds and burst 6,500 tear gas shells.

Mobs of both communities indulged in fierce, bloody rioting, at least after 28th February.

As for violence after the first three days, *India Today* weekly dated 20th May, 2002 reported:

"Week 1	March 3-9	17 dead
Week 2	March 10-16	32 dead
Week 3	March 17-23	43 dead
Week 4	March 24-30	54 dead
Week 5	March 31-April 6	149 dead
Week 6	April 6-12	51 dead
Week 7	April 13-19	6 dead
Week 8	April 20-26	17 dead
Week 9	April 27- May 3	35 dead
Week 10	May 4-10	30 dead
		Total dead 972"

This shows that around 550 were killed in the first three days in the real large scale riots and 400 in 70 days, average of six killings a day. This shows that these were full-fledged Hindu-Muslim riots and not one-sided riots. As per the police records, Muslims started some 157 riots after 3rd March, 2002. No violence worth the name took place in Gujarat from 11th May, 2002 to 20th May, 2002 and the Army began leaving Ahmedabad on 21st May, 2002.

The following are the excerpts of the interview given by Narendra Modi to weekly *India Today* dated 18th March, 2002:

"A composed Gujarat chief minister, Narendra Modi spoke to Senior Editor, V. Shankar Aiyar and Special Correspondent Uday Mahurkar. Excerpts:

Q. Nearly 600 people have died in the Gujarat riots. Was there a complete breakdown of the official machinery? Are you responsible?

A. It's a false and baseless charge. Let's go by the official records. I was in Godhra on the evening of 27th March (this is a mistake, it should be 27th February) and on my return to Ahmedabad, 827 people were arrested as a preventive measure the same night. I immediately issued shoot-at-sight orders in Godhra. The riots began on 28th February at around 11:00 a.m. and I had requested the Army's presence by 4:00 p.m. On my request, Defence Minister, George Fernandes was in Ahmedabad by 2 a.m. on 1st March.

Q. But all the measures proved ineffective.

A. Only in the minds of those who don't know the state's history of riots. In the early 1980s, some parts of Godhra remained under curfew for a whole year. In 1985, curfew was imposed in Ahmedabad's Kalupur-Dariapur for six months. I have controlled the riots faster than any of my predecessors.

Q. The Muslims allege that the police not only took no action but even collaborated in the killings, arson and looting on 28th February and even later.

A. I don't agree. The police fired 1,000 rounds on the first day. But you must not forget that what happened was a reaction to the brutal killings (in Godhra). The size of the angry mobs on Thursday (28 Feb) was something unprecedented. The police must have been overwhelmed at some places because of this but still it did its best. **Five persons were killed in police firing at the spot where Ehsan Jafri was killed and police saved lives of 200 Muslims in the episode.**

Q. Why do you think the rioting had such a brutal tinge to it?

A. It wasn't a communal riot but something like a mass agitation. There was already great anger against terrorism and anti-national activity. The Godhra episode symbolised that.

Q. Does the spectre of backlash worry you?

A. My perception is that they will try and do something. So in the coming months, Gujarat will have to be very alert.

Q. How do you react to Shabana Azmi's statement calling you a mass killer?

A. There are two types of violence, one communal and another secular. And secular violence being perpetrated by the leftist lobby is equally detrimental for the society. But some continue to perpetrate it. In fact, there's a leftist conspiracy against me". (*URL*: http://www.indiatoday.com/itoday/20020318/cover-box.shtml).

Now, let us see the interview given by Narendra Modi to *Outlook* magazine in its issue dated 18th March, 2002:

"Q. Were you playing the fiddle while Gujarat burned?

A. No. Contrary to what is now being projected, I brought sanity within 72 hours of the violent outbreak. **It would take months before communal rioting during the previous Congress governments could be brought under control and a semblance of normalcy could be restored.** This is for the first time that a communal riot has been controlled in record time.

Q. Your government stands accused of aiding and abetting the Bajrang Dal and the VHP. Their cadre ran amok for a full 48 hours while your police force stood and watched—in some places, it even joined in with the rioters.

A. How can that be? You have to realise that when violent rioting breaks out on such a scale, the police force is under great stress. Resources are limited. More than 70 people have been killed in police firing, so where is the question of the state administration taking sides against one or the other community?

Q. Was the Army deliberately called in late so that the police could play out its passive role?

A. The Godhra massacre took place on 27th February. The next day I declared that Army help had been requisitioned. The Prime Minister called a meeting of the Cabinet Committee on Security on 28th February to take the Army's help. But that was not easy. There was no Army presence in Ahmedabad because of the deployment on the borders. **Next day, on 1st March, shoot-at-sight orders were issued. I spoke to George Fernandes and within 16 hours, the Army was called in. So where is the question of any delay?**

Q. What precisely is your government's connection with the VHP and the Bajrang Dal?

A. I have worked hard to raise the BJP in the state. Can I be accused of improving my party's prospects?

Q. Does that mean that you have played the Hindu card in an effort to boost your party's sagging prospects in the assembly elections which is less than a year away?

A. There are no cards to be played. As the head of this government, I am impartial. I will not play the appeasement card. Everyone involved in the rioting and violence, irrespective of whichever community he belongs to, will be taken to task. A judicial inquiry is looking into the incidents and its verdict will definitely be respected.

Q. Your impartiality was not exactly in evidence over the past few days?

A. In a democracy, anyone can say anything. You have to remember that communalism runs high in Gujarat. If Sachin Tendulkar gets out on 90 against the Pakistani team, riots break out here. Even a small provocation can lead to violence and Godhra was a very big incident. **In the 1969 riots, under the then Congress regime, curfew was imposed for 65 days in a row.**

Q. You speak about previous Congress regimes but what about your party's claim to better governance?

A. We are providing better governance. But can we ignore facts? Of the 80-odd arrests so far, 65 have Congress backgrounds. The Congress is misusing the sentiments. They are alleging that the independent corporators involved in Godhra were backed by the BJP. Until now, the media has been saying that there are no Muslims with the BJP. But when it comes to this incident, my party is supposed to have backed Muslim corporators. There is a limit to double standards. In any case, corporators are not members of any party.

Q. You put a ban on a section of the media. People see this as an authoritarian step designed to muzzle the press....

A. There was no ban on the media. I blacked out just one channel because of the provocative reporting methods used. Traditionally, the print media has used its own methods of self-censorship, taking care not to mention the name of communities while reporting riots. If every half-an-hour the names of communities are going to be mentioned, without any substantiation or any attribution, it inflames the situation instead of allaying it. It is not difficult to see what impact it will have. I must also tell you that since then the channel has rendered an apology and made amends." (*Source*: http://www. outlookindia.com/article.aspx?214916).

Note how *Outlook* increases the time in which police were accused of allowing rioters to run amok to 48 hours. "No police action for 48 hours" but even the worst critic, *The Indian Express* admitted that the police did its best from day 2, i.e. from 24 hours only! Also note that police did not allow rioters to run amok even for 24 hours and did its best firing 1,000+ rounds, saving thousands in Naroda- Patiya, Chamanpura, etc.

Note Narendra Modi's sentence "No. Contrary to what is **now being projected**, I brought sanity within 72 hours of the violent outbreak." In other words, the projection against Modi started AFTER the riots. We have already seen the reports of the newspapers like *The Hindu*, *The Telegraph* to note that there were no allegations against Narendra Modi or the Gujarat Government at the time of the actual riots. They started much later. *Doordarshan* news reported on 3rd March, 2002 (Sunday) at night in the English bulletin: "Violence has ended in a record time in Ahmedabad…Only 3 days… In the past, it would take many weeks…. Today (Sunday) curfew was relaxed, people bought items from bazaar…". No allegation against the State Government but praise of controlling violence in just 3 days! **All accusations on Narendra Modi and demands for his resignation, dismissal started AFTER the riots.** This was because, the media wanted some scapegoat to be made for the riots. It wanted Modi to sack a few police officers, drop a minister or two. But Modi did nothing of the sort. He did not blame anyone, did not make anyone a scapegoat. In an interview to NDTV (*Walk the Talk* program), broadcast in March/April 2004, Narendra Modi said to Shekhar Gupta (Editor of *The Indian Express*): "You all wanted that someone be made scapegoat. I did not do that. I allowed you to break all pots on my head alone. You have all decided, all these riots happened under this man (Narendra Modi). Until this man is removed from the Chief Minister's post, we will not rest in peace. My best wishes to you in your mission." Narendra Modi did not resign, and the BJP did not dismiss him, so the media was livid.

And following are the excerpts from an interview with *The Hindustan Times* dated 10th March, 2002:

"Q. …There is a wide gap between your claims (of prompt action) and eye-witness accounts of the government being a mute spectator for a good 48 to 72 hours after violence erupted during the VHP-sponsored bandh on 28th February. What's your defense?

A. The situation was brought under control in 72 hours. There is no truth also in the charge that we delayed calling in the Army. The Godhra incident took place at 8:00 a.m. At 9:45 a.m, I imposed curfew there. My government opened fire at the Railway Station. **If our purpose was to target a community, we had an opportunity at Godhra. But we did not do that. The challenge before us was the safety of the surviving passengers. To keep the violence from spreading, I gave shoot-at-sight orders before leaving Godhra.** On 27th February night, nearly 800 people (its 827) were rounded up all over Gujarat. The February 28 (VHP) bandh was spontaneous. There weren't any reports of people being forced to join it. Tensions started rising at 11:00 a.m. and at 12:20 p.m. curfew was imposed in Ahmedabad.

Q. You mean you imposed curfew during the VHP bandh.

A. Yes, the very first day. The police strategy to quell violence was based on the past experience. We concentrated on hyper-sensitive areas. **But this time, these areas remained calm and violence erupted in new pockets on the western banks of Sabarmati.** (*Times of India* also said this like *India Today*.) Five people were killed in 600 rounds of police firing in Ahmedabad on 28th February itself. (Actually, 10 were killed, five at Jafri's place.) At 2:00 p.m., I spoke to the Prime Minister. I told him that people in the middle and upper middle class colonies were out on the streets and I needed the Army and para-military forces to control them. In fact, at 4:30 p.m. that day, I told the media that I have sought the Army's help. The troops were withdrawn from the borders and deployed within 16 hours (actually 14 hours). In similar situations earlier, their arrival took between three and five days.

Q. But till now (March 5 morning), neither you nor any of your ministers has cared to visit the devastated localities. Only Defence Minister, George Fernandes touched the trouble-spots, which even Advani avoided during his March 3 visit to Ahmedabad.

A. This is not true. Advaniji took a round of the city covering all sensitive areas. I went with him. The Leader of the Opposition here (Naresh Raval of the Congress) went to his Sardarpur constituency after 72 hours yesterday. But a Cabinet colleague of mine was there within six hours. Now, the government machinery is focusing on the relief work. For the first time, my administration has raised from the Rs 5 to Rs 15, the daily cash-doles for riot victims....

Q. More than material help, what the Muslims need is a sense of security. Are you capable of delivering on that front?

A. This task will have to be accomplished jointly by people and the government. To build confidence and trust between communities, the social, political and religious leaderships will have to combine their efforts.

Q. It is believed that your March 1 statement justifying the backlash to the Godhra killings emboldened the VHP-Bajrang Dal cadres, who went on the rampage in Ahmedabad and elsewhere. What do you have to say about it?

A. I made no statement of that kind. One big newspaper reported that I quoted Newton's law of every action having an equal and opposite reaction. I have never quoted Newton since I left school. I cannot help if people allow themselves to be guided by their predilections and fantasies. I'm willing to suffer if that helps the society. I plead with those opposed to me to wait till normalcy is restored in Gujarat.

Q. What's your personal assurance to the Muslim community?

A. Security and social harmony, that's my assurance to them. This Government is as much theirs as it is of anybody else….

Q. Opposition parties do not believe you and have sought your dismissal.

A. …in the US, nobody sought President Bush's resignation after the WTC bombings. But in India, each calamity is followed by demands of resignation, be it an earthquake or the attack on the Parliament…. Gujarat is a border state and the internal security problems here could acquire an external dimension. Our biggest worry is the *madarsas*. Godhra has a large number of such institutions.

In Bhavnagar, a *madarsa* became the cause of tension when a TV channel reported that an associate of Aftab Ansari had been a student there. To defuse the situation, we had to move 400 students and some Maulvis to safer places."

Now, notice how the time on which the government is being accused of being a mute spectator suddenly jumps to "48 to 72 hours"! Did we see anything like this at the time of the actual riots from the reports of the papers?

As on 25th April, 2002, 77 to 80 Hindus were shot dead by the police in police firing and 207 were injured. Mr. B.P. Singhal (1932-2012), former Rajya Sabha MP, and former Director General of Police wrote in the weekly *Organiser* dated 9th October, 2005:

"...the police had fired over 10,500 rounds.... In addition, in all, 15,000 tear gas shells had also been burst during the Gujarat riots.... The 1984 riots escaped the media glare because TV was barely in its infancy. On the other hand, a lot of mischief was played by the electronic media, which went on repeating some of the gory incidents of riots day after day. One channel repeated a particularly gory scene as many as 21 times. An image was, thus, created by the collaborating media that the massacre of Muslims was continuing unabated in Gujarat, day after day. **The truth is that the total number of riot- related accused that came to light in the entire Gujarat was 25,486 (17,489 Hindus and 7,997 Muslims). The efficiency of the police can be gauged from the fact that out of the above-mentioned number, as many as 25,204 accused were arrested, out of which 17,348 were Hindus and 7,856 were Muslims.** The police in Gujarat was, therefore, not sleeping at any time.

The maximum number of relief camps opened up during riots was 159. At a given point of time, the figure varied as certain camps were closed down and certain new camps were opened up. **As on 5th March, 2002, out of the 98 refugee/relief camps opened, 85 were for Muslims while 13 were for Hindus...** On the other hand, **there was a contrast of night and day in the versions of riots as projected by the national English media as against the sharply contrasting versions appearing in the local Gujarati papers of all hues....**"

Thus, it can be seen that on 5th March, 2002 itself, so early in the riots as many as 13 out of the 98 relief/refugee camps were for the Hindus. Since 3rd March, 2002 was a riot-free day, it is safe to assume that the camps set on 5th March, 2002 were for the victims of the riots in the first three days, i.e. until 2nd March, 2002. That even after the first three days of rioting, more than 13 per cent of the relief/refugee camps were for the Hindus, indicates that at least in 13 per cent of the events even in the first three days, the Hindus also suffered just as much as the Muslims suffered in other incidents of the state.

The following is the report of rediff.com dated 7th November, 2003:

"Ehsan Jafri Fired at the Mob: Witness

At least five Hindus on Thursday told the Nanavati Commission, which is probing the Gujarat riots, that they saw the Congress leader and the ex-member of the Parliament, Ehsan Jafri open fire at a mob outside the Gulbarg Society in Ahmedabad on 28th February, 2002.

...the five Hindu witnesses said it was Jafri who opened fire at the mob. **Three persons had died in the firing**, they added.

Vasu Patel, a resident of Chamanpura, held Jafri, the media and police responsible for the massacre.

He said the media had showed the footage of those who had died in the Sabarmati Express carnage in Godhra, and this had incited people. He added that action should be taken against the media, which acted in a biased manner.

Instead of restraining Jafri, the police beat up locals and opened fire at them, he added.

Another witness, Madansinh Rajput, told the Commission that the Muslims used to misbehave with the Hindus of the area before the riots.

He condemned the English dailies, saying their reports were anti-Hindu.

In all, 15 riot victims/witnesses deposed before the commission (*Source*: http://www.rediff.com/news/2003/nov/06godhra.htm).

This report can be an indication of what happened in the Ehsan Jafri case.

Naroda-Patiya Case

Naroda-Patiya was a case of real anti-Muslim violence. A total of around 95 Muslims were killed by a Hindu mob here on 28th February, 2002, the first day of the riots. The number was revised to 95 from 83 after all missing were declared dead with the 7-year period being over.

Here the attackers included members of the Chara tribe and the police presence was not adequate. In fact, there was no police presence worth the name as per the report of *India Today* weekly. The police were grossly inadequate throughout Ahmedabad that day because the size of the mobs was unprecedented. Years later, *The Hindu* reported on 20ᵗʰ August, 2004:

"Ahmedabad, 19ᵗʰ August. … (Former Police Inspector of Naroda) **Mr. Mysorewala blamed the attack in Naroda Patiya on the 'brutal killing' of a Hindu youth, Ranjit Vanjhara, behind a mosque and the reckless driving of a Muslim truck driver in which a Hindu was killed and two others were injured. (*The Telegraph* of Kolkata also reported this** on 2ⁿᵈ March, 2002).

Rumours were spread in connection with the two incidents that added fuel to the communal fire. Hindus attacked a mosque and later the Muslim houses in the locality.

Inadequate Police Force

According to Mr. Mysorewala, the Naroda police station with 80 policemen was adequate in normal times but the situation on 28ᵗʰ February was unprecedented and was quickly going out of control.

He said he had asked for police reinforcement and was given 24 additional SRP men but even that was inadequate, considering the size of the attacking mob, about 17,000 people." URL: http://www.hindu.com/2004/08/20/stories/2004082012831200.htm

That is, 80 policemen were insufficient to deal with a 17,000 strong crowd and additional 24 SRP men too were woefully inadequate. Despite the fact that the police were overwhelmingly outnumbered in a ratio of 17,000:100 odd, the police saved the lives of more than 900 Muslims in this episode.

Among the other details, it is absolutely clear that the Government deployed the Indian Army as soon as possible despite the fact that the Army was located far away in border areas and there were hardly any reserve battalions available, since almost the entire military strength was posted at the border at that time. But even after the Army was rushed to Ahmedabad, the tensions did not subside and the killings continued. **The fact is, after the first three days, riots continued largely only in those places where the Indian Army was present, i.e. in Ahmedabad and Vadodara.** To accuse the BJP and the Gujarat Government of allowing killings (of Hindus?) would be accusing the

Indian Army of partisanship. Some people would never want to know and accept this.

The Times of India, in a report dated 28th April, 2002, reported that "Of the total substantive arrests made by the police, 9,954 are Hindus and 4,035 are Muslims. However, in the preventive arrests column, the statistics show that the number of Hindus arrested is much higher—17,947 as against 3,616 Muslims."

To quell the violence:

1. Not only did the Gujarat government call the Army as early as possible but also declared this decision publicly on 28th February evening.
2. The Gujarat police arrested nearly 25,204 out of the 25,486 accused as of October 2005.
3. More than 17,000 of the 25,000 arrested were Hindus.
4. Police fired over 10,500 rounds of bullets, including around 5450 in the first three days, though the Army was present for 73 out of 74 days.
5. Police fired over 15,000 tear gas shells, including 6,500 in the first three days.
6. 101 people were killed in police firing in the first week, and 199 for the entire period of the riots.
7. The police arrested 35,552 people as on 28th April, 2002, out of whom 27,901 were Hindus. About 20,000 were preventive arrests.

Note: The figures of 25,204 accused being arrested and religion-wise details are official government figures, given to B.P. Singhal.

Thus, in brief, it can be seen that the Gujarat Government handled the riots extremely efficiently. Just to summarize:

1. *The Indian Express* and *Mid-Day* dated 28th February, 2002 reported that the State Government had deployed the Rapid Action Force in Ahmedabad and other sensitive areas and the Centre sent in CRPF personnel on 27th February itself even before a single riot had taken place.
2. *The Hindu* reported in its issue dated 28th February, 2002 that "shoot-at-sight" orders had been given in Godhra and Rapid Action Force was

deployed on 27th February and so did many other papers, like *The Times of India, The Telegraph, The Indian Express, The Tribune*, etc.

3. *The Hindustan Times* reported in its issue dated 28th February, 2002 that the entire police force of 70,000 was deployed in Gujarat on 27th February itself after the shocking massacre in Godhra in view of apprehensions that riots might break out. *The Telegraph* (UK) also reported this.

4. 827 preventive arrests were made on the evening of 27th February itself on Chief Minister, Narendra Modi's orders on his return to Ahmedabad from Godhra.

5. On 28th February, despite the deployment of the entire police force, the CRPF personnel and the Rapid Action Force, the situation slipped out of control, according to *The Hindu* dated 1st March, 2002.

6. Despite the fact that the situation slipped out of control, the mob sizes were unprecedented and the police were overwhelmingly outnumbered, the police did its best. The police fired more than 1,000 rounds on the first day of the riots, i.e. 28th February including around 600 in Ahmedabad.

7. *The Hindu* reported in its issue dated 1st March, 2002 that at least 10 persons were believed to have been killed in police firing in Ahmedabad alone by evening of 28th February. Five were shot dead outside Ehsan Jafri's house according to *India Today* weekly dated 18th March, 2002. Two were shot dead in Nadiad and Godhra.

8. Curfew was clamped in Godhra on 27th February itself as reported by *The Hindu* dated 28th February, 2002.

9. An indefinite curfew was clamped in 26 cities and towns in the state, including parts of Ahmedabad, Surat, Vadodara, Rajkot, Nadiad, Anand and Kaira on 28th February in addition to the indefinite curfew in force in Godhra since 27th February according to *The Hindu* dated 1st March, 2002.

10. The Chief Minister, Narendra Modi, frantically called the Army units to Ahmedabad on 28th February, as reported by *The Hindu* of 1st March, 2002.

11. *The Indian Express, The Hindu* and *The Telegraph* reported that Army units started arriving in Ahmedabad on the night of 28th February

in their issues the next day, i.e. 1st March, 2002. This shows that the Army units reached Ahmedabad so quickly that the newspapers had the time to report their arrival on 28th February itself and publish it on 1st March!

12. The Army staged a flag march in Ahmedabad on 1st March, 2002 at 11:30 a.m., as reported by *India Today* in its issue dated 18th March, 2002. *The Hindu, The Indian Express* and most dailies also reported that the Army staged flag marches in Ahmedabad and also in Vadodara on 1st March, 2002.

13. The Army began flag marches in the worst-affected areas of Ahmedabad, Vadodara, Rajkot and Godhra cities and the 'shoot-at-sight' order was extended to all 34 curfew-bound cities and towns in Gujarat on 1st March, 2002 as per *The Hindu* dated 2nd March, 2002.

14. The Gujarat police fired a total of around 5450 rounds in the first three days alone. It also burst 6,500 tear gas shells in the first three days.

15. The Gujarat police shot dead 98 people in the first three days, majority of whom are Hindus and 199 for the total period.

16. *The Hindu* reported in its issue dated 4th March, 2002 that only two deaths were reported on 3rd March in the entire state and the violence has ended on 3rd March, 2002. Thus, the Gujarat Government managed to control the situation in three days and in Ahmedabad in only two days even after the shocking massacre in Godhra, while it took the previous Congress governments five-six months to stop the riots in 1985 even without any cause as Godhra and also a longer time on other occasions.

Some people ask: "When magazines like *Outlook, India Today* and papers like *The Times of India, The Hindu* make allegations against Modi now, you don't believe them calling them as biased against Modi. But in case of riots you cite the same papers' reports which you then believe".

The answer is simple. **If papers with a known anti-BJP bias report something in favour of BJP, then it is absolutely impossible that it is false. It has to be true, though it may not be the whole truth.** That is what we have seen- not a single paper or magazine reported all the facts on any day, but only some of the facts. We came to know the whole truth by gathering the facts from all the papers. For example, *The Hindu* reported that on 28 Feb, 10 people were killed in police firing, & the army was called frantically, but it did not report George Fernandes' arrival and call, or 700 arrests. We got to know 700 arrests from other papers. We also don't say that whenever they report anything against BJP it should be called false, it should be judged on merit.

Also, the Gujarat Government spent a lot of money for providing relief to the riot victims. This will be seen in detail in Myth 17 of Chapter 7. In most other cases, no government bothered to do all this. Hitler ordered killing of Jews, not spending money to help them. And yet, some people keep calling the riots as 'state-sponsored' ignoring all relief given by the government.

The then RSS spokesman, M.G. Vaidya, in his weekly column in Marathi daily *'Tarun Bharat'* in July 2002, wrote:

"In a town named Harij in the North Gujarat, the following incident took place: There are only three houses of Muslims in a predominantly Hindu-dominated area. All the inmates of the houses had vacated the houses because of the fear of riots but in one house, there were two 70-year-old women, four kids and four women. These women were virtually shaking with fear. However, the RSS Swayamsevaks reached there. One amongst them was the well-known lawyer of the area, Shri Hargovindbhai Thakkar, who is also the local Sanghachalak of the RSS. He called for his jeep and rescued all the women to a safer place.

In a town called Unza in the Mehsana district, a Muslim woman was an employee in a dispensary of Dr. Maheshbhai Purohit, who is an active worker of the RSS. When the mob came to attack the woman at Dr. Purohit's house, he resisted the mob and saved the woman.

There are many such incidents that reveal the humanitarian approach of the Hindus. But the English newspapers have not published even a single such story." http://www.hvk.org/2002/0702/99.html

Among another of 'many such' incidents is the following one reported in weekly *India Today* in its issue dated 15th April, 2002: "Take Umreth, a little town in Anand district that had practically never witnessed communal violence. **This year it did and when a local BJP leader, Vishnu Patel tried to pacify a Hindu crowd, it turned on him.**"

As another proof of the fact that the real riots stopped in three days, let us take a look at the following facts:

1. In March 2002, both Holi and Moharram were observed with traditional fervour throughout Gujarat. 1,000 Moharram processions including nearly 100 big ones were taken out.
2. 7,000 Haj pilgrims were felicitated in about 800 villages/ cities in 22 districts.
3. 75 per cent of the voters exercised their franchise in the Panchayat polls in almost 1,700 villages.
4. Call for a boycott of the Board exams by the Muslim students flopped with 98 per cent attendance.

In April 2002, as many as 40,000 Hindus were also living in the refugee camps at a time when 1 lakh Muslims were living in the refugee camps.

Thus, Narendra Modi, as the Chief Minister of Gujarat, has an unfortunate image of a "Muslim-killer". In reality, far from being a Muslim-killer, Narendra Modi, if anything was a Muslim-saver, whose administration saved as many as 24,000 Muslims and many Hindus too. If Modi's name ever goes into history, it will be for the effective and efficient handling of the awful riots of 2002 AD.

The violence in the state, post-Godhra, can be briefly divided into three phases:

1. First three days, on 28th February, 1st and 2nd March, 2002
2. From 4th March, 2002 to 12th April, 2002
3. From 21st April, 2002 to 20th May, 2002

The first phase of violence was really the period of Hindu retaliation to the Godhra carnage. Though at places, Muslims were in complete command and they threw out Hindus from their homes and also killed the Hindus, in general, it was the Muslims who suffered. This period saw the real anti-Muslim riots, like when Muslims were attacked and killed in the Gulberg area of Ahmedabad (Ehsan Jafri case) or the Naroda-Patiya killings, where Muslims were the victims.

The second phase was when Muslims started the retaliatory riots in Gujarat, retaliatory, for the first three days of Hindu retaliation. Here Muslims started the riots and attacked the Hindus as will be clear from the next few chapters.

The third phase was after 21st April, 2002, Ramnavmi day. **This was when the riots are alleged to be instigated by the Congress Party as is indicated from the reports of the website rediff.com dated 22 April 2002, *India Today* dated 20 May 2002, *The Hindu* dated 7 May 2002 and the Justice Tewatia Committee report.** At that time, the Parliament was in session and Gujarat was to be debated. The Opposition wanted the Narendra Modi Government to be dismissed. At that time, peace had come to stay in Gujarat. To deliberately attack Narendra Modi, the Congress Party is alleged to have instigated the riots. We will also see this later in detail.

There is a lot of criticism that the Modi Government allowed killings. Newspapers like *The Hindu, The Indian Express, etc.* have been in the forefront of it. But what do these reports quoted earlier show?

The weekly *India Today* itself reported on 28th February: "The bloody cycle of violence so familiar with Gujarat may just have begun." That is, *India Today* expected the violence to last several weeks, if not months. Same was the prediction of *Outlook*. But it was controlled in just three days. Gujarat has seen horrible riots in the past like in 1969 and 1985. That despite such a bloody history of violence, riots could be controlled in such a communally sensitive state in three days, despite magazines like *India Today* and *Outlook* predicting weeks of violence, with Godhra carnage as a huge provocation, shows that the administration did its duties extremely well.

But a section of the media just does not want to listen. It seems to have already crucified its conscience. It has closed its eyes to the evil forces. Reason and truth have taken wings and fled from their journalism. Is it then possible to ensure such constitutional values as fraternity, integrity and unity in a highly complex country, in which, *inter alia,* the media is largely alienated from the truth, biased against a particular party, prejudiced against the centripetal forces, and lenient towards the disruptive forces?

CHAPTER 4

GUJARAT'S BLOODY HISTORY OF VIOLENCE

At times, it is necessary to look into the past to understand any event fully. The same is true for the Gujarat riots. The state undoubtedly saw riots after Godhra, in which about 1,169 people were killed. Had the same number of people been killed in communal riots in, say, Nagpur city of Maharashtra state in India, it would indeed have been considered as 'large-scale riots'. This is because Nagpur region is a region which has hardly seen any communal riots since 1927-28. But since the riots took place in Gujarat, the events have to be viewed in totality, in view of Gujarat's history of communal violence.

If one looks at the past history of communal riots in Gujarat, one would understand that the Gujarat riots of March 2002 were much lesser as compared to the past communal riots in the state. The state saw far worse riots in 1969 and 1985. It also saw riots of a large scale in 1980, 1982, 1990 and 1992.

Hindu-Muslim conflicts have been going on for the past 1,300+ years. But in Gujarat, communal riots between Hindus and Muslims have been going on since as far back as AD 1714, i.e. since the medieval times. This was hundreds of years before the birth of any of the organizations of the *Sangh Parivar*. The Rashtriya Swayamsevak Sangh (RSS) was founded in 1925, the Bharatiya Jana Sangh was founded in 1951, the Vishwa Hindu Parishad (VHP) in 1964, the Bharatiya Janata Party (BJP) in 1980. Even today, conflicts continue between Muslims and Hindus in India, Muslims and Buddhists in China,

Muslims and Christians in Nigeria, in Algeria, in Philippines, in Morocco, in Chechnya, etc. It is not the VHP or the *Sangh Parivar* that is common in all these places.

Hindus and Muslims have clashed in battles, wars and riots since as far back as AD 636, when Arabs invaded Thane (near Mumbai). In AD 712, Mohammad-bin-Qasim invaded Sindh and defeated its king, Raja Dahir. Even before AD 712, the foreign Muslims kept attacking Indian kingdoms since AD 636. The great revolutionary and freedom fighter, Swatantryaveer Savarkar (1883-1966) wrote in his book, *Saha Soneri Pane (Six Golden Pages of Indian History)* that the Hindus kept on defeating and repulsing the invading foreign Muslims at India's western borders for as many as 300 years at a stretch, i.e. from 712 AD to 1001 AD, when Mahmud of Ghazni invaded India. He also wrote about the attack on Thane of AD 636.

Riots are nothing new to India. For the past 125 years, since about 1880 riots have frequently occurred in all parts of India. But among all the Indian states, Gujarat was by far the most communally sensitive state.

Vishwa Samwad Kendra, Gujarat says:

"If we take the history of Ahmedabad for the last five centuries, the city was ruled by the Muslims and the Mughals for about 340 years, the rest by Marathas and the British. Coming to the incidents of communal riots during this era of five centuries, the major incidences are:

1. The 1714 Holi Riots

A Hindu named Hari Ram, while celebrating Holi with his friends at his residence unintentionally sprinkled *Gulal,* a red powder on one Muslim, and the casual frolic was strongly protested by some Muslims. A mob got assembled near Jumma Masjid under the leadership of Sunni Bohra Mullah Abdul Aziz. The Afghan soldiers of the Muslim viceroy also joined the mob seeing the situation. A Kazi interfered for cooling down the angry mob. But the mob set on fire the house of this Kazi. The rioters, thereafter, looted the shops of Hindu Mohalla and set their houses on fire. The rioters could be controlled only by armed guards of a Hindu, Kapurchand Bhanshali.

2. The 1715 Communal Riots

The 1715 communal riots were due to looting of shops of the Hindus by the Muslim soldiers. The riots came to an end with the replacement of the Muslim viceroy, Daudkhan.

3. The 1716 Id Riots

Consequently, during the third year also, communal disturbances broke out during Id in 1716. The Bohra community, a Muslim sect, gathered cows and buffaloes for Id celebration. A Muslim Havaldar just out of pity released one of such gathered cows. Some Muslims protested before the Kazi Khairullakhan, and seeing no outcome to their expectation, they resorted to riots, arson and mass looting of the Hindu establishments. The situation could come to normalcy with Hindu viceroy, Ajitsinh's concerted efforts.

4. The 1750 Temple Demolition

The 1750 riots by Muslims were provoked with a reason cited that their *Namaz* was being disturbed due to the noise of the ringing of bell in an adjoining temple. The Muslims, while returning from the Masjid after *Namaz*, totally destroyed the temple.

5. The September 1927 Ahmedabad Riots

Muslim prayer in a mosque and Hindu song in a temple were the apparent cause of conflict.

6. The 1941 Riots

Communal disturbances broke out on 18th April, 1941. The Muslims diverted to the Muslim League programmes after the incidence of these riots.

7. The 1946 *Rath Yatra* Riots

1ˢᵗ July, 1946 was the *Rath Yatra* day. *Rath Yatra* as usual was passing through Shaher Kotda police station area, on this auspicious day. There took a hot exchange between a Hindu Akhada man and a Muslim watching the procession. The incidence turned into breaking out of communal violence, viz. arson, cudgelling, stone throwing, stabbing, etc. There was also a police firing and curfew was finally imposed to control the situation.

8. The 1953 Ahmedabad Riots

The Ganapati festival and Moharram were the occasions of riots in the city of Ahmedabad.

9. The 1965 Sikh Incidence

The 1965 riots were resulted out of the murder of two Sikh rickshaw drivers by some Muslims. The aggrieved Sikhs took out funeral procession of both these dead bodies. The situation got disturbed at Delhi Darwaja and got converted into a communal riot soon.

10. The 1969 Historic Communal Riots

It was 18th September, 1969, the last day of *Urs*. The violence crept up in the evening time on the ground that Jagannath Mandir cows going back to temple premises disturbed the *Urs*. It may be mentioned that movement of cows was a daily routine irrespective of *Urs* celebration taking place simultaneously. A hot discussion took place that provoked communal tension with a series of violent incidences killing, linking, and soon in various parts of the city.

The riots of 1969 were the biggest of its type in Independent India, having taken lives of thousands of persons.

Among others were the 1985 bloody riots in Gujarat, the 1980, 1982 riots in Ahmedabad and Godhra, the 1990 and 1992 riots."

What follows is a write-up by Hemant Babu published in *Himal* Southasian magazine of May 2002 reproduced by www.countercurrents.org:

... "A sign of this normalcy is the number of incidents of communal violence in the state as recorded officially. Judicial commissions of inquiry, the Justice Reddy Commission and the Justice V.S. Dave Commission, were instituted after two major riots, of 1969 and 1985 respectively. Both commissions referred in some detail to Gujarat's history of communal violence. The Justice Dave Commission traced the history of communal violence in Ahmedabad as far back as 1714, when a bloody riot was sparked off during the Holi celebrations. The city then was still under the Mughal control. Subsequent riots broke out in 1715, 1716 and 1750....**Hindu-Muslim violence continued in the centuries that followed, with the pace and intensity picking up in the second half of the twentieth century**. When communal riots broke out in 1941, curfew had to be imposed for over two-and-a-half months. The Justice Reddy Commission identified as many as 2,938 instances of communal violence in the state between 1960 and 1969, that is, **an average of approximately three riots every four days during this ten-year period**....

During this period, riots began to spread over a much wider geographical area of the state, affecting towns like Veraval, Junagadh, Patan, Godhra, Palanpur, Anjar, Dalkhania, Kodinar and Deesa, all of which have been hit by the ongoing violence.

...but violence of a different, more systematic and sustained order was inaugurated in 1969. The Hindu-Muslim riots of that year mark a major break with the hitherto prevalent pattern of steady, unspectacular social conflict. More than two years of hectic Muslim and Hindu fundamentalist activity preceded the outbreak of these riots. Communal violence in the state acquired a more organised form against the backdrop of the India-Pakistan War of 1965.

...a riot of this magnitude, unprecedented in both scale and duration, had a foundational significance for the politics of the state and the techniques of mobilisation and orchestration that increasingly came into use. The discrete and scattered violence of the preceding period can be presumed to be manifestations of everyday class, caste and community struggles arising from socio-economic conflicts of a more or less local nature. To that extent, their individual histories and repercussions were confined to the respective localities of incidence. The

1969 riots had the critical mass that lent it state- and nation-wide visibility and gave it a prominent place in the historical inventory of community grievances. This riot could now be invoked at will, not just in Gujarat but wherever else tension had to be engineered. In effect, this was the first explicit politicization of both communalism and public violence in the state.

Most importantly, the riots of 1969 took Gujarati society past the psychological threshold of normally tolerable public violence, and this was not just of the communal variety. Once the barrier to the use of violence in inter-party conflicts was crossed, its repeated use acquired a tacit legitimacy as the social conscience became gradually more immune to the incremental doses of it that the polity administered.

...the riots (of 1985) began on 19th March, the day after the newly elected Congress Government assumed office, and was directed against a policy measure declared more than two months ago. In January, the Congress Government had announced an increase in the quota of jobs in government and seats in public educational institutions reserved for backward castes. **The riots lasted six months, much after the policy had been revoked by the government**.... South Gujarat, which had previously been unaffected, now found itself on the riot map of the state. The social base of the violence expanded to include gangsters, bootleggers and professional killers. Various reports of the period quote doctors, who described the stab wounds they attended to as the work of trained hands. The agitation finally degenerated to a point where sections of the state constabulary abandoned their uniforms and relinquished their responsibilities to join the riots.

...Gujarat again witnessed riots in 1992 when the disputed Babri Masjid at Ayodhya was razed to the ground a few hours after the *karsevaks* stormed the monument. **Surat experienced intermittent disturbances over a six-month period. In 1993, more riots followed, after the blasts in Mumbai,** allegedly masterminded by the Muslim underworld D. Ibrahim. Perhaps, these riots were attempts at forging a Hindu unity that, on the face of it, seemed impossible. Whatever the intention, there is no denying that the *rath yatra* precipitated a political crisis in which the existing intra- and inter-party equations began to break down.... Remarkably, for three years following its assumption of office in Gujarat in 1995, the state was free from communal riots. The BJP was clearly living up to its boast of ensuring a riot-free administration, prompting critics to cite this as proof of the party's monopoly of organised public violence...."

A staunch anti-BJP man wrote this article. The website that reproduced it, www.countercurrents.org, is one of the most anti-BJP ones on the entire Internet. Yet, even in its staunchly anti-*Sangh Parivar* article, the writer discloses some very important things. And one of them is Gujarat's bloody history of communal violence.

We already have seen the bloody history of Godhra town of engineering riots since 1927-28. The following is the report of the *Vishwa Samwad Kendra* on the comparisons between the 1969, 1985 and 2002 riots:

"Comparative analysis of the government response to communal riots during 1969, 1985 and 2002:

The communal tension in the State of Gujarat is not an unknown phenomenon. Prior to the present situation, all communal disturbances before Godhra incident, two major communal incidents took place in 1969 and 1985. To inquire into the factors leading to the communal violence in 1969 and 1985, the State Government appointed Judicial Commission to thoroughly inquire into all the aspects leading to communal violence and the response of the State Administration. Both the Commissions have come to specific conclusions and, while coming to the conclusion, they have also made specific observations.

On 18th September, 1969, a major communal riot broke out in the Ahmedabad city and subsequently spread in the other districts of the State. The incident, which sparked the communal violence, took place on 18th September, 1969 at 3.45 p.m. in Ahmedabad near Lord Jagannath Temple. Hon. Justice, Jagmohan Reddy inquired into the violence which broke out during the said communal disturbances. After 1969, a major agitation and communal riots broke out in 1985. Justice Dave Commission inquired into the incidents, which took place during the course of anti-reservation agitation and also communal disturbances during February 1985 to July 1985.

The response of the State Government in the earlier incidents and the recent incident brings to the fore certain important facts which are as under:

In 1969, the incident of violence reported on 18th September at 3:45 p.m. **The Army was pressed into service on 21st September, 1969 at 16:30 hours in limited areas (three police stations only) while the Army was deployed in the entire city on 22nd September, 1969 at 18.00 hrs. In 1985, the riot broke out on 15th April, 1985 and the army was requisitioned on 16th April, 1985. By then, 177 deaths had already been reported.** Compared to this, the Army was requisitioned on the same day, i.e. on 28th February itself. It is very relevant to note that unlike the earlier occasions, the Army at this point of time is deployed on the border. **Therefore, the deployment of Army was difficult at a short notice. However, Hon. Chief Minister (Narendra Modi) impressed upon the Hon. Prime Minister (A B Vajpayee) and the Defence Minister (George Fernandes) to deploy the Army forthwith in view of the prevailing condition in the State. The Central Government also reacted very fast and the Army was airlifted to Ahmedabad the same night.** The Army was in action from the next day of the incident, having completed all the formalities of nominating Executive Magistrates, allocation of vehicles, etc. The incident in 1969 occurred on 18th September, 1969 but the situation was out of control, even on the fifth and sixth day. The violent incidents continued to be reported even after the sixth day. The disturbances in 1985 were spread over a period of five months, from February 1985 to July 1985. However, in the present case, the situation has been brought under control within three to four days only.

In the present case, the curfew was clamped within four hours in Godhra on the same day. (Actually within two hours, at 9:45 a.m.) Compared to this, there was delay in ordering curfew in the earlier incidents. The grievance for such delay was reported before the Inquiry Commission.

The complaint about inaction from the police authorities and the local administration were made before the Inquiry Commission. In the present case in Gujarat, the Law and Order Enforcing Authority has taken a proactive stand to curb the violence effectively. The police authorities have fired more than 3,900 rounds, they have used more than 6,500 rounds of tear gas shells and arrested more than 2,800 people (until 3rd March, 2002). One should also take a note of the fact that 90 people have been killed in police firing (the correct number is 98) which shows that police showed no lenient approach towards the elements spreading violence, arson and looting. It is also very pertinent to note that the geographical area under the grip of such untoward incident was much larger in 2002, compared to the earlier incidents of 1969 and 1985.

The above facts clearly show that the Government had reacted to the situation very quickly, effectively and also with strong political will" (*Source: VSK, Gujarat:* www.vskgujarat.com).

NDTV-Star News had broadcast a programme *The Big Fight* live from Ahmedabad in December 2002, a week or so before the Gujarat Assembly elections held on 12 December. The participants were Harin Pathak of the BJP (BJP MP from Ahmedabad) and Shankersinh Vaghela of the Congress, and a victim of the Gujarat riots, Prof. Bandukwala. In that debate quoting an article from *The Hindustan Times* of 1969, Harin Pathak said that the official death toll in the 1969 riots was around 5,000, but it was actually three to five times the number. At that time, the Congress was in power with the great Gandhian, Hitendra Desai as the Chief Minister. The actual number of people killed in 1969 will thus range from 15,000 to 25,000, if the article quoted by Harin Pathak is correct. Contrast this with the 2002 riots with 790 Muslims and 254 Hindus and a total of 223 people missing, as per the figures given by a Congress Union Minister!

The following is a write-up by Devendra Swarup in the weekly *Organiser* dated 16th May 2004:

"Use of Mahatma Gandhi's name and views certainly makes it emotional but does not seem in accordance with history. Perhaps, the respected judges ignored the fact that Gujarat has a long history of communal violence. During Gandhi's life itself, Gujarat had burnt in such violence. His pain at the 1924 riots of Ahmedabad is visible in his complete works; since Independence, sparks of violence have been spreading in the Muslim-dominated areas of Godhra and Ahmedabad; Mohammad Ghazni was extended invitation to again prevent the reconstruction of Somnath temple, which caused unbearable pain to Gandhi. **Gujarat has had a long history of riots during the Congress regime that called itself the sole inheritor of Gandhi's legacy even after his death. In 1969, during Gandhian Hitendra Desai's rule as Chief Minister, Ahmedabad witnessed communal frenzy, in which more than 3,000 people were killed, i.e. much more than those killed in the riots**

of 2002. Hence, instead of getting caught in the quagmire of ideology, it is necessary to probe into the causes of this endless chain of communal riots in the state" (*Source*: http://www.organiser.org/dynamic/modules.php?name=Content&pa=showpage&page=6&pid=23).

Here, however, Devendra Swarup says only 3,000 people were killed in 1969 in Ahmedabad. He has used this figure out of a sense of moderation and caution, and gives it only for Ahmedabad. The correct official figure could be 5,000 and actual 15 to 25 thousand, as quoted by Harin Pathak, former Union Minister of State for Home, from *The Hindustan Times*.

The Times of India reported in its online issue dated 12th April 2002:

"Trivial Reasons Sparked Earlier Riots

Ahmedabad: **If it took a shocking massacre like Godhra to trigger off massive communal riots in the state in the 21st century, history shows that trivial incidents caused most riots in the 20th century.** An inquiry report prepared by Justice V.S. Dave of Rajasthan High Court, who headed a commission of inquiry to investigate the 1985 anti-reservation and subsequent communal riots, devotes a special chapter to the 'history of riots and agitations in Gujarat'. **Tracing the riots way back from 1714**, the report points out at the causes of riots as festivals and religious celebrations, aggressions and changing of the secular complex of the 'pols', 'khanchas' and 'by-lanes' within the walled city due to migration to areas of greater security. On 18th April, 1941, communal riots broke out and curfew imposed in most localities, was in force for two-and-a-half months. As a result, the civil disobedience movement in the city engineered by the Congress was suspended till October 1941. Both communities suffered in varying degrees in Ahmedabad and elsewhere in the state. Tracing the records, the report observes an important consequence of the riots "after this sad episode, the Muslims of Ahmedabad turned their faces and embraced the programme of the Muslim League". This was followed soon by the communal riots on 1st July, 1946, during the *rath yatra* due to police firing. Curfew was imposed. Records suggest that the communal riots broke out at about 12:30 p.m., in the Sherkotda police station. One Sikandar, who was a well-known Muslim gymnast, accompanied by three or four members of his akhada was watching the performance of a Hindu akhada, which formed the part of a procession. Sikandar allegedly criticized the style of weight lifting adopted by one Chitranjan Chintamani. This led to a scuffle, in which Sikandar and Chintamani were injured; Sikandar and some sadhus, both of whom were excited, were arrested and put in lock-up. This led to riots. This was followed by the 1958 riots and police firing at Khadia. The then district magistrate had eloquently described Khadia locality in connection with a firing on 12th August, in the following words, 'The worst area was as it had invariably been in the previous disturbances, the Khadia ward in Ahmedabad city.' However, it will be wrong to believe that the communal tension has always been between Hindus and Muslims. **In 1965, the city witnessed the first- ever Sikh-Muslim riot in the city, when two Sikh autorickshaw drivers were murdered by some Muslims.** On the following day during the funeral procession, some irate Sikhs broke open some Muslim shops and attacked them. The riots in 1969 have become a history by themselves. The report held '...**that there was never any riot in the state of Gujarat of magnitude as was witnessed in September 1969, which took a heavy toll of human lives and property belonging to both the communities'.** Justice P.J. Reddy commission which inquired into this riot, found that at least 560 people died, while 561 were injured. These riots were sparked by a trivial incident on 18th September, 1969, when a large number of people had gathered for 'Urs' of the Bukhari Saheb's chhila. At about 3:45 p.m., when a herd of the cows accompanied by their keepers had almost reached the temple gates, **some Muslims objected as to why the sadhus of the temple had allowed animals to disturb the fair. An altercation followed between some Muslims and the sadhus in which some sadhus were injured.** Incidents of violence, thereafter, happened in rapid succession in various parts of the city, taking a heavy toll of lives and property. This was followed by 1985 anti-reservation agitation, which took the colour of communal riots and then in 1992 occurred post-Babri riots." (*Source:* http://timesofindia.indiatimes.com/ articleshow/6611833.cms).

An analysis on this article by *The Times of India* really discloses the full story. All these riots happened even without any cause as the Godhra incident. **In these 1969 riots, curfew was imposed for 65 days in a row!** While in 2002, despite the mind-numbing roasting alive of *karsevaks*, a tragedy which has no parallel at least in independent India, riots of far less magnitude took place. And this is a newspaper (*The Times of India*) which no one can ever accuse of having an anti-Muslim bias.

The following is written by V. Gangadhar, a staunch anti-BJP person, in August 1999: "During the 1941 communal riots, **the Hindus took a terrible beating and never forgot it.** Khadia, within the walled city, became a stronghold of Hindus, but there was no militancy in the area. The 1945 communal riots were milder, but when India became free, it was hoped that Hindus and Muslims could live together in peace. This happened for some time.... Yet Hindus and Muslims fought together in the Mahagujarat Movement, which established a separate Gujarat state in 1960...

The year 1969 was a watershed in communal relations. The Hindu-Muslim riots killed more than 5,000 people and Ahmedabad became a vast burial ground. The riots were aggravated because of the conflict between the Congress Government led by Indira Gandhi at the Centre, and the State Government led by Hitendra Desai of the Congress-O...

Congress-O leader Morarji Desai was not personally communal, but he hardly did anything to control the situation. For the first time in the city's history, the labour areas were affected. The killings here were most brutal. Since then, Gujarat has never been the same."

http://www.rediff.com/news/1999/aug/06abd.htm

V. Gangadhar is a known anti-BJP man. But this article helps us to some extent in realizing the history of violence in Gujarat.

Vadodara also saw horrible riots in 1982, just like Ahmedabad and Godhra. According to IPCS Research Papers, Volume 3, March 2004 by B Rajeshwari, the following happened:

"Gujarat also saw riots in 1990, between April and December, which saw nearly 1,400 communal incidences, which left officially 224 people dead and 775 injured. Nearly 120 riots took place in Gujarat in 1991 between January and April, which left at least 38 people dead officially and 170 injured. Ahmedabad again saw riots in October 1990 after L.K. Advani's *Rath Yatra* began, which saw 41 people dead officially. Vadodara again saw riots between April 1991 and July 1991, which was a result of a petty incidence of a boy getting hit by an autorickshaw. Surat saw bloody riots in 1992, which left about 200 people dead, after the demolition of the disputed structure in Ayodhya."

The author B. Rajeshwari is also a professor at the Jawaharlal Nehru University, New Delhi, and is seeped in the vicious anti-BJP, anti-RSS mould, and despite that, she does give some important information to us.

The above instances are enough for anyone to understand Gujarat's history of communal violence. To see some newspaper editors and freelancers writing 'stark lies' on English dailies' editorial pages that, "Narendra Modi is responsible for the worst massacre of Muslims in independent India" or "Modi killed 2,000 Muslims in Gujarat", etc. is all disgusting. **This is not only because of the factual errors, but because these people themselves know Gujarat's history of violence.** Most of the instances mentioned in this book (of Gujarat's past violence) are taken from sources of these people only. And yet, they lie through the skin of their teeth.

Shridhar Patel wrote in weekly *Organiser* dated 22nd December, 2002: "… hardly any newspaper has taken the trouble to understand Gujarat. Strangely enough, the one English-language newspaper to make that effort is the NRI journal published from New York *India Abroad* (May 17, 2002). Sheila Bhat's article "Wounds of History" should be made compulsory reading for our hate-filled columnists. Sheila Bhat recounts how Gujarat's pride was broken and how 'Centuries of being under the exploiters' yoke has left deep scars' on the Gujarati psyche. The last Hindu to rule over Gujarat independently was Karan Vaghelo who fled his kingdom in 1298. 'From then on', writes Sheila, 'there have been small pockets under Hindu kings ruling as vassals of various conquerors but Gujarat was never independent from 1300 to 1947…. The past is never, ever, far from the present….' Our 'intellectual' columnists do not know history, much less Gujarati psychology. They know only hate. The truth is that, in India, Gujarat is a special case. Maharashtra can boast of a Shivaji who stood up to Muslim rule and bears no psychological wounds, Rajasthan has several Hindu heroes like Rana Pratap for one, South India had its great Vijaynagar Empire to be proud of but Gujarat with its open borders has been at the mercy of anyone who has chosen to come in with rape and plunder and pillage. If one does not understand that, one does understand nothing, either about Narendra Modi, or about Gujarat…."

Some newspaper editors are, of course, blind to the historical facts. They are blind to the demolition of the sacred temple at the believed birthplace of the Hindu God Ram in Ayodhya by foreign invader Babur in 1528 and they attach with it no significance. They are also blind to the atrocities committed on Hindus by foreign Muslims in the medieval period, and also the atrocities which the Hindus suffered in Gujarat at the hands of Muslim rulers not only since AD 1298, but also in the communal riots throughout the 1940s.

In 1399, invader Timur killed 100,000 Hindus in a single day. Professor K.S. Lal, in his *Growth of Muslim Population in India*, wrote that according to his calculations, the Hindu population decreased by 80 million between the years 1000 and 1525, probably the biggest holocaust in world history. The Gujarat riots of 1969 were far more serious than the 2002 riots. The death toll, as a proportion of population was far higher.

Godhra (and its twin city of Dahod) is famous in the subcontinent as the birthplace of Aurangzeb (1617-1707, ruled from 1658-1707), the fanatical Mughal emperor. It is also a well-known trouble spot. A large number of people of Godhra have links with the people at violence- prone Karachi in Pakistan, according to www.rediff.com dated 2nd March, 2005 and also *The Times of India* dated 30th May, 2002.

Even a staunch anti-BJP fortnightly like 'Frontline' reports: "The Rath Yatra has often sparked communal violence in Ahmedabad, **including the worst massacre in 1969**" (Frontline, 13-26th March, 2004).

The same fortnightly also reports in an article titled: "The Hindutva Experiment" (written by Dionne Bunsha): "The earliest recorded riot here dates back to 1714 during Mughal rule— it occurred in Ahmedabad. It was sparked by a minor incident— the accidental sprinkling of 'ghulal' during the Holi festival, according to the V.S. Dave Commission report on the 1985 riots. Several riots took place during the Maratha rule, which lasted until 1817. During the British Raj, riots broke out in 1941, following which the Civil Disobedience Movement was suspended. It also marked the time when Ahmedabad's Muslims started supporting the Muslim League. In 1946, trouble broke out in the city again. In post-Independence India, there were riots in Ahmedabad in 1958, 1965 and 1969. The 1969 riots were also sparked by a minor event but led to one of the bloodiest riots in Gujarat" (*Frontline*, 11-24th May, 2002).

That is, a fortnightly as anti-BJP and anti-Narendra Modi as the *Frontline* admits the fact that Gujarat's worst riots were in 1969 under the Congress Party, and not in 2002 under Narendra Modi.

The following is from Rakesh Sinha's article in *The Pioneer* dated 20th April 2002:

"Give a Dog Bad Name and Hang It

It is not for the first time that Gujarat has witnessed communal riots. Its history is replete with communal tension and feuds.

In September 1969, Gujarat plunged into one of the severest riots after Partition. **The immediate reason for the riot was attack on two sadhus of Jagannath Temple by a mob of about 1,000 Muslims, who gathered to celebrate Urs on 18th September, 1969, provoking organised violence in Ahmedabad and many other areas, including Baroda.** The magnitude of riots could be gauged by the figure that 6,000 families lost their houses, properties and belongings. The Sampradayikta Virodhi Committee's report "Gujarat's Riot X-rayed" mentioned the figure of dead people as 3,000.

'Religious-quake' was witnessed during the riots. Incidents were reported but they did not unravel the religious identities of the victims. *The Times of India* reported on its front-page on 20th September, 1969, a father and son being burnt alive when the son was taking his ailing father to hospital. Incidents like these hit our humanitarian sentiment rather than religious or communal feelings, when they are reported with restraint. They do not transcend the communal hatred beyond the boundaries of the communally charged region or the State. This spirit was maintained by the media throughout the riot-span (for a month) in 1969. The 1969 riots were not transformed into a political battle to destabilise the government or to blame the ruling Congress or to settle scores with Hitendra Desai, the then Chief Minister of Gujarat. Prime Minister, Indira Gandhi's short visit on 25th September was both preceded and followed by premeditated violence. Seventeen passengers were killed in the Janata Express near Ahmedabad the same day. But the institution of the Prime Minister was not trivialised or her stature was not questioned due to such horrendous incidents.

During 1969 riots, *The Times of India* reported, 'Sabarmati Harijan Ashram too not spared' as hooligans attacked the Ashramites and damaged the ashram."
http://www.hindunet.org/hvk/articles/0402/171.html

This article also shows that the 1969 riots were far worse than the 2002 riots and that too without any immediate cause as the Godhra incident.

The following is the interview given to *'The Times of India'* by the Gujarat Chief Minister, Narendra Modi dated 30ᵗʰ March, 2002: "Gujarat Chief Minister, Narendra Modi, in an exclusive interview to *The Times of India,* says his state is returning to normalcy. Excerpts from the interview:

Q. In your view, was the burning of 58 *karsevaks* in the Sabarmati Express at Godhra a planned attack or a spontaneous one? Was there an untoward incident on the station platform which sparked the attack?

A. If one looks at the nature of the heinous attack on the Sabarmati Express and the manner in which 58 innocent *karsevaks* were burnt alive in a compartment of the ill-fated train, it would be apparent that it was a deep-rooted conspiracy and a pre-planned, cold-blooded attack.

The train arrived at Godhra at 7:43 a.m. and within five minutes, i.e. at 7:48 a.m., it left Godhra. It was stopped at Signal Falia about 500 metres away and a mob attacked the compartment collectively. How can such an attack be spontaneous? Moreover, the train departed from Faizabad and arrived in Godhra after 36 long hours, and no incident was reported on the behaviour of the *karsevaks en route.* **But the president of the Gujarat unit of the Congress, Amarsinh Chaudhary, has alleged in a television interview that the attack took place because the *karsevaks* did not pay money for a cup of tea at the railway station.** Is it not ridiculous to justify a ghastly incident such as this?

Q. There are reports that the Tableegi Jamiat of the Deobandi School of Islam has been fanning fundamentalist ideology in Godhra and that there were instances of members of the majority community being burnt in the past few years. Are these reports true? If so, on what dates were they

burned and by whom and what is the action taken against the persons concerned?

A. The long history of communal violence in Godhra is not an unknown phenomenon, but it has taken an ugly and serious turn in the last 25-30 years. **Two families have been burnt alive in the same area in the past in a ghastly incident. And ten years ago, four teachers, including two women teachers, were mercilessly cut to death in a school in the presence of children.**

While the then Congress rulers have registered court cases in a routine manner, they have failed miserably to punish the real culprits. Not only this, the main culprit named Asaraf was done to death while in a jail by other accused persons and the whole event was pushed into a corner forever.

Q. Reports of the violence in Ahmedabad give the impression that it was well organised. The reports said armed mobs went around with voting lists targeting Muslims. An IAS officer, Harsh Mander, has given a chilling account of the violence in Ahmedabad. Why has the state not been able to tackle the situation? There are allegations that the police was partisan. Please comment.

A. Those who are acquainted with Gujarat know that this state is very sensitive to communal violence. **There have been serious communal disturbances triggered by petty and minor incidents relating to kite flying or a cricket match. In the past, communal violence has broken out in 200 places at a time and curfew has been imposed in about 300 villages and towns for months together.** Compared to this, the Godhra massacre was unparalleled in history, but we took all proactive measures to curb the violence within 72 hours. The police fired more than 3,900 rounds initially and the Army was airlifted from the border area and deployed within 16 hours in the disturbed areas. There was no complacency on the part of the government or the police...."

Imagine a state where communal riots take place at 200 places at the same time, and many more villages and towns affected by violence, and curfew in 300 places for many months together! The Godhra town also remained in curfew throughout the year in 1980. As compared to that, the violence in 2002 was nothing.

But despite knowing this, a large section of the media just does not want to know. It has exhausted all its resources to attack and target one man—Narendra Modi, one party—the BJP. Instead of thinking objectively and appreciating the spirited work of the Gujarat Government in controlling the communal violence, this section of the media has irrationally and irresponsibly accused the BJP Government of turning a blind eye to the riots. But someone who does not want to see the truth cannot see it. We will see the reason for this Ostrich approach in another chapter.

CHAPTER 5

ATTACKS ON HINDUS

The post-Godhra riots were projected as anti-Muslim riots by the Indian national English media and the electronic media, akin to the anti-Sikh riots witnessed in 1984 in New Delhi and elsewhere. It was reported as if the riots were nothing but a systematic targetting of the Muslims, in which only Muslims were attacked and killed. That is to say, a large section of the media reported as if the riots were one-sided with only the Muslims suffering. This was *deliberate* (mind the word *deliberate*) mischief on the part of the biased people in the English media. In this chapter, let us see the truth of the Gujarat riots, the other side of the coin— attacks on Hindus. As per the police records, some 157 riots in Gujarat after 3rd March, 2002 were started by Muslims. (*Source*: Article by Francis Gautier on www.rediff.com dated 11 March 2003). http://www.rediff.com/news/2003/mar/11franc.htm

As per figures given by the UPA Government comprising anti-BJP parties, anti-Narendra Modi people, **inside India's Parliament** on 11th May, 2005 and that too in a WRITTEN REPLY a total of 790 Muslims and 254 Hindus were killed in the riots of 2002 in Gujarat. Naturally, the question arises, who killed these 254 Hindus in Gujarat?

When this writer talked to some people who call themselves secularists, on the attacks by Muslims on Hindus and Dalits in particular, he got interesting answers. In Muslim-dominated areas of Ahmedabad and other places, the Hindus living in minority (often microscopic minority), many of whom were Dalits, suffered horribly, were thrown out of their homes, attacked and killed by

Muslims. Not only that, even in other areas like Sindhi market and Bhanderi Pole areas of Ahmedabad the Muslims attacked the Hindus. The Muslim backlash started on 1 March 2002, 1 day after 28 February when the Hindus attacked Muslims in Ahmedabad's Naroda Patiya, Gulberga Society and other areas. The people calling themselves as secularists, after listening to these facts of Muslim attacks said to me: **"It is natural and inevitable. If Hindus attack and kill them in Naroda Patiya, they will obviously attack, kill, render homeless the Hindus living in minority in their dominated areas in the next days".** This response has 2 important implications:

1   - When Muslims attack Hindus, they think it is 'natural' and 'inevitable' because of attacks by Hindus on 28 Feb in Naroda Patiya. But the Naroda Patiya attacks were not 'inevitable' and 'natural' because of Godhra killings of Hindus!

2   - They know and admit that Muslims attacked Hindus even after Godhra, when they say its 'natural' and 'inevitable'. If they know that its 'inevitable' that Muslims will attack Hindus in their areas and also other areas if riots last for weeks, then why do they lie that Muslims were massacred in one-sided attacks ignoring attacks on Hindus, in particular, Dalits?

Godhra happened on 27th February. On 28th February was retaliation from the Hindus. On 1st March, the second day of the riots, the Muslim counterattack began. As we saw in the 3rd chapter, *The Hindu* reported on 2nd March, 2002: **"But unlike Thursday (i.e. 28th February) when one community was entirely at the receiving end, the minority backlash (on 1st March) caused further worsening of the situation. Police presence had little impact on the two communities pelting stones at each other in Bapunagar, Gomtipur, Dariapur, Shahpur, Naroda** (Muslim concentrated areas) and other areas from where incidents of firing had been reported. But there were no reports of casualty. **Pitched battle** was continuing between the two communities late in the evening. **The official sources said timely arrival of the police foiled a retaliatory attempt to break into a prominent temple in Jamalpur locality in the walled city."**

The Indian Express reported on 2nd March, 2002: "(On 1st March) Tension escalated in the walled city areas just before the Friday prayers. There were violent clashes between mobs in Jamalpur, Bapunagar and Rakhial." Clearly, Muslims were on the offensive. And *The Times of India* also reported the same day: "There were signs of retaliation in areas like Juhapura, Kalupur, Dariapur and Shahpur…." This clears all possible doubts.

This clearly shows that there was a Muslim backlash. What happened on the second day of the riots in Ahmedabad was 'pitched battles' between Hindus and Muslims, and Muslims were also pelting stones at Hindus. Muslims attacked a prominent temple at Jamalpur in Ahmedabad. Even many awakened people believe that the Hindus were in control for three days. Even S.K. Modi in his excellent book *"Godhra: The Missing Rage"* (Prabhat Prakashan, New Delhi) has written that "Hindus went berserk for 72 hours, though violence on 1st March was much less as compared to 28th February". But the truth is that Hindus went berserk only for one day, i.e. 28th February. The next two days also they attacked Muslims, but Muslims too attacked Hindus.

The *India Today* magazine also says in its issue of 11th March, 2002, "(On 28th February) **In Ahmedabad's Bapunagar area, a township named after Mahatma Gandhi, two groups of over two thousand each fought with each other. Both were armed with swords, sticks and firearms. The casualty is not known.**" This was on 28th February, just one day after Godhra. When the media was painting pictures of one-sided atrocities against Muslims, *India Today* recorded that as many as two thousand Muslims were fighting with equal number of Hindus in Bapunagar area.

Months later, www.rediff.com (16th September, 2003) reported in an article by PTI titled, **"Gujarat Riots Probe: 'Muslims Attacked Hindus'"** that:

"A woman on Tuesday alleged before the two-member Nanavati Commission that an armed mob of Muslims, led by a Congress councillor, attacked Hindus in Bapunagar area in Ahmedabad during the post-Godhra riots. 'On the day of the VHP-sponsored bandh (i.e. 28th February, 2002), armed Muslim men had stormed our locality and some of them even stripped and said: Kill the Hindu eunuchs. Send your mothers and sisters,' Sudha Patel, a resident of Patelnagar, told the panel probing the post-Godhra violence in Gujarat. 'They gorged the eyes of a youth with swords and repeatedly crushed him under their truck till he died, they then stripped and made obscene gestures at Hindus,' she alleged.

Patel told Justice G.T. Nanavati (retd.) and Justice K.G. Shah (retd.) that though all persons in the mob had masked their faces, she managed to recognise the councillor, Taufeeq Khan Pathan, and his son, Zulfi, on 1st March. She alleged that the mob beheaded a local mendicant, who tried to pacify them, in front of her. 'They later hung his head displaying it to the locals, saying: We have chopped off your mendicant,' she alleged. She said terror still reigns in the minds of children in Patelnagar and sought protection from anti-social elements.

Two other majority community members alleged that Muslims of the area were trying to purchase their properties. 'I had to sell my house on two occasions,' one Mulji Patel told the commission" (*Source*: http://us.rediff.com/news/2003/sep/16godhra.htm).

What does this indicate? *India Today*'s report in its issue of 11th March, 2002 gave enough indications of the role of Muslims in rioting. **In Bapunagar, it appears from** the testimony of these witnesses that **Muslims instigated the riots and attacked Hindus as early as 28 February 2002.**

Another report of rediff.com on 19th September, 2003 titled: "Gujarat Riot Probe: 'Muslims Spread Fear in Vatva'" said: "A witness on Friday alleged before the two-member Gujarat riot probe panel that his son was whisked away by a mob of armed people of the minority community and killed.

Deposing before Justice G.T. Nanavati (retd.) and Justice K.G. Shah (retd.), Dahyalal Raval, a resident of Vatva area in Ahmedabad, said his son Mehul had gone to check on his house in Dharmabhumi Society on 1st March. Since then, there has been no news about him. 'Mehul was whisked away by a Muslim mob near Burhani Society and as per my information, they (the mob) might have killed him,' he said.

Another person, Dashrath Patel, told the Commission that a Muslim mob had attacked his housing society on 28th February last year, torched and damaged nearly 26 houses and also resorted to firing from the top of a masjid, resulting in the death of two persons— Satish and Amit Patel. He said Mehul was forcibly taken away by the mob and is unlikely to have fled.

Another person, Kishan Thakkar, alleged that a mob of Muslims had spread terror and fear among Hindus by openly brandishing pistols and other weapons. The witnesses, mostly Hindus, alleged that Muslims from the Vatva area had resorted to heavy violence and slogans like *Kafiron ko kaat dalo* were heard from the masjid in the area" (*Source*: http:// www.rediff.com/news/2003/ sep/19godhra1.htm).

But after the first three days, majority of the riots which occurred were instigated by Muslims in which Hindus and Muslims both suffered.

The following is the report of *Human Rights Watch,* an organization that anyone can accuse of having a bias against the Hindus. But even such an allegedly biased organization gave the following report:

"Mahajan No Vando, Jamalpur

Human Rights Watch visited Mahajan No Vando, a fortified Hindu residential area situated within the Muslim-dominated area of Jamalpur, on 23rd March. Mahajan No Vando was the site of a retaliatory attack by Muslims on 1st March.

According to the residents, approximately twenty-five people were injured in the attacks and at least five homes were completely destroyed. Residents closer to the periphery of the fortified compound and its entrance also suffered extensive property damage. **Muslim residents attacked the compound from the higher Muslim-owned buildings that surrounded it using light bulbs filled with acid, petrol and crude bombs, and bottles filled with kerosene and set some Hindu-owned houses on fire.** According to the residents, who had collected and saved the remnants of what was thrown in and showed them to Human Rights Watch, 'There was acid in the glass bottles and in the light bulbs that were thrown in. They used solvent petrol, kerosene and acid. They filled some Pepsi bottles with them.'

Like many Muslim victims of attacks, the Hindu residents of Mahajan No Vando were surprised at the overnight animosity of their neighbours. One resident told Human Rights Watch: 'There were no problems before 27th February. On the 28th, the VHP declared all of Gujarat closed. We didn't attack anyone. We are all poor people, we live on our labour.'

The appointed head of the community described the method of attack:

"On 1ˢᵗ March, at around 2:15 p.m. they surrounded us. There were so many people, you couldn't count them. They attacked us from all sides. There was a row of twenty-four houses on the periphery of the vando [courtyard] and they burnt them all using petrol. Five or six were completely destroyed but we saved some using water. They also burned other homes and tried to break down the houses and enter. This went on for three-and-a-half hours. The police were few and couldn't really do much, so they left. We are trapped here. We haven't left here since then. Some organizations are helping us. The VHP and RSS have helped us a bit as well. We are worried that once the protection lifts at the end of the month, what will happen to us? We cannot leave for work because it is difficult to come back after 6:30 p.m. No one was killed in this area but some were injured. NGO doctors also came.

A resident named Harki Bhen added:

Kerosene bottles were thrown in through the roof. They threw it through the windows and the openings in the walls. We called the police thousands of times but they told us, 'Sir is out'. In the morning, the mosques began announcing that Islam was in danger, that there was poison in the milk. This is their code word. **We are the only Hindus here, poison here means us.** The rioting lasted between 2:15 p.m. and 5:30 p.m. First they destroyed the police stall outside. At 11:00 p.m., two police people too came to us. We had to give them security.

Kankubhen Kanjibhai lives in the first home on the left next to the colony gates, where the attackers first started to force their way into the area. 'Everything was burned, clothes, dishes, everything. I only have left what I am wearing.' Her one-room house was completely charred. A few houses down, a Hindu shrine had also been destroyed.

A very elderly and frail woman called Ukibhen Sawaji told us: 'I was sitting inside my home and everything started burning. They jumped in; they looted us also. They took our dishes and our bedding that we had kept for the dowry.' Seven-year-old Bharat Rameshbhai showed us the raw exposed skin that covered his right arm: 'They threw bottles down into our home, I was inside the house. The house started burning.' Resident D.R. Rathod, whose home was partly damaged in the attacks said, 'Just like the train was burning, that same way our homes burned too.'

When asked about police response during the attacks, Human Rights Watch was told: "After 5:30 p.m., the brigadier came in. The Rapid Action Force and the military said, 'We got no message to come here. We have been close by for seven hours but got no message that there was any problem here.' The police said, 'We are on our way.' They cut off our phones from the outside. When the police arrived, they threw tear gas inside here."

A strong police presence outside the colony that included several members of the Border Security Force (BSF) was helping to prevent further attacks. But residents feared what would happen once the BSF protection was lifted. While they were frustrated with the pace of police investigations, they noted that the police filed the complaints and even sent an acid bottle to be lab tested. One resident told us:

There are twelve to thirteen people stationed outside. But they will leave on 30th March. We don't know what will happen after that. After the first incident, another acid bottle was thrown in around 15th March. Nothing has happened since then. The police took the acid bottle and sent it to the lab. We are working with the Gaikwaud police station. We have filed complaints with the police. The police noted everything down but there is no combing of the areas.

Two members of the Ahmedabad Home Guard, who were stationed at Jamalpur even prior to the attacks, entered the colony during Human Rights Watch's investigation. They encouraged us to take more photos, carefully note down all the damage and visit each and every damaged home to talk to the resident. Their behaviour stood in sharp contrast to that of police stationed near sites of destruction of Muslim homes, such as Naroda Patia, where a member of Gujarat intelligence worked diligently to note the comings and goings of those viewing the damage interviewing remaining residents.

When asked where they were during the attack one noted: 'The whole city was in a storm, but this incident was the worst incident of Jamalpur. Everywhere else there was just a little bit of stone throwing. These people cannot sleep, they are afraid that someone will come again.'

On 6th March, Chief Minister, Narendra Modi visited Mahajan No Vando and, according to the residents, told them, 'You will be taken care of.' Still, the residents claim that no arrests have been made." (*Source*: http://www.hrw.org/reports/2002/india/India0402-04.htm)

And this was on 1st March, 2002, when the anti-Muslim riots were supposed to be going on in the state. They were. **But this incident, quoted by an organization as anti-BJP as the *Human Rights Watch*, really blasts all the myths created by the media.** HRW has in this report mentioned tales of Muslim girls throwing themselves in fire to prevent rape (as Hindu women used to do in the foreign Islamic rule) and other details which are obviously concocted. Nowhere was any specific instance of any Muslim female immolating herself to escape rape ever mentioned.

India Today's reports on this issue help to some extent to blast these media-concocted myths of the Gujarat riots. That *India Today* too rationalized Godhra on some grounds of flimsy 'provocations' in its issue dated 11th March, 2002 is another thing. It called the Gujarat Chief Minister, Narendra Modi as an 'Untouchable'. It too targeted Narendra Modi for the Gujarat riots and has called the Gujarat riots as a 'massacre of Muslims' ever after the riots. Its issue of 18th March, 2002 dealing with the riots reported as if Muslims were 'slaughtered' in Gujarat in the first three days, ignoring all attacks on Hindus by Muslims on 1st and 2nd March. It also falsely reported the 'pregnant woman womb' story. But many of its reports at the time of the riots really help us to understand the media's lies on the issue.

In between, national English newspapers with a mass circulation, such as *The Times of India* and *The Indian Express*, who were in the forefront of attacks on BJP and Narendra Modi during the riots and have continued their tirade ever since, and continue to publish articles and editorials on the Gujarat riots with complete lies, also let slip in bits and pieces of the truth, during the time of the riots in Gujarat.

The following is what *India Today* reported in the weekly's issue dated 15th April, 2002:

"On 13th March, the Supreme Court's ruling banning any religious activity in Ayodhya proved a psychological setback to the Vishwa Hindu Parishad and its affiliates. It was also the day when some people in the walled city of Ahmedabad burst crackers in celebration and unfurled banners saying: **'You darkened our skies. We will spill your blood on the streets.'**

...the next few days saw mayhem. **In Ahmedabad, violence broke out on 17th March when Dalits in the Danilimda area were attacked by Muslims.** On 19th March, it was Modasa, a town in Sabarkantha district. A police officer's son was stabbed and two communities went berserk. A local LIC building was attacked during office hours.

The stories only got more macabre. **In Himmatnagar, a young man, who went to a Muslim-dominated area to do business, was found dead, with his eyes gauged out.** In Bharuch, the murder of a Muslim youth led to mass violence. Next, the Sindhi market and Bhanderi Pole areas of Ahmedabad, hitherto calm, were attacked by mobs.

This phase, really, was one of Muslim mobs attacking Hindus.

...take Umreth, a little town in the Anand district that had practically never witnessed communal violence. This year it did and when a local BJP leader, Vishnu Patel tried to pacify a Hindu crowd, it turned on him.

...other than inefficiency, the authorities face some genuine problems in trying to arrest the culprits. Combing operations in Muslim-dominated areas have been rendered difficult. **In Juhapura, just outside Ahmedabad, residents (i.e. Muslims) cut the power lines and gathered mobs of human obstacles when the Army arrived to conduct search operations at night.** This experience was by no means unique, it was repeated in areas like Kalupur and Gomtipur (all Muslim areas). Locals explained it as 'spontaneous', police officials said it only provided cover for criminals to remove arms and immunition." (*Source:* http://www.indiatoday.com/itoday/20020415/states.shtml).

This is what some Muslims in these areas did to the Indian Army, not just the Gujarat police. And the Gujarat police, for fear of being labelled anti-Muslim, was slow in dealing with the Muslim extremists. See what happened in Ahmedabad on 13th March, 2002. **Muslims unfurled banners saying, 'We will spill your blood on the streets'.** These things have been largely ignored by the English media.

Now let us come to the most important detail. **Muslims in Gujarat killed a Hindu in Himmatnagar after gouging out his eyes. Surely, this was a case worth noticing by the English media.** The Best Bakery case (in which three out of the 14 killed are Hindus), which was raised by the national media should also have been raised. The causes of the minority communities too should be raised. The media should not become an anti-Muslim institution also. But it should also not be anti-Hindu to the hilt. This case of a young Hindu's eyes being gouged out and his subsequent murder deserves much more publicity than the Best Bakery case. This habit of gouging out eyes and subsequent murder is a medieval practice.

To understand the media's bias as well as details of Muslim aggression, let us see *The Times of India*'s report on this issue dated 18th March, 2002. Let us remember that *India Today* weekly told that on 17th March, Muslims attacked Dalits in Danilimda area of Ahmedabad.

"Mobs Attack Police Post, Combing Operations On

Ahmedabad: Police have carried out massive combing operations in the city following attacks by violent mobs on the security personnel on Friday night. During the combing operations, a 65-year-old man died of shock after he was arrested by an Army contingent from Dariapur for possessing a revolver. A youth was killed in police firing when a **5,000-strong mob tried to attack Dudheshwar police chowky in Madhavpura area.** According to police sources, an Army contingent, which was confronted by a 700-strong mob, identified the accused, a resident of Char Musa Ni Pole in Dariapur, who was brandishing a revolver and a big knife. The mob was dispersed by the Army. In the combing operation that followed, the Army men traced the accused at Char Musa Ni Pole in Dariapur. He was arrested and taken to Dariapur police station where he complained of uneasiness. The accused was taken to the civil hospital where he was declared brought dead. A few hours later, a 23-year-old fell victim to police firing, while eight persons were injured in Dudheshwar area, when police tried to disperse a violent mob. 'Our men braved heavy stone-pelting and petrol bombs but the mob swelled beyond 5,000 around 3 a.m., forcing us to open fire in self-defence,' says G.C. Ravat, senior Police Inspector at Madhavpura police station. **The police and State Reserve Police personnel fired 21 rounds to disperse the mob and prevent it from advancing to the majority community-dominated areas.** Madhavpura police has registered a case against 38 persons for murderous assault on police chowky and clamped curfew in its police station area. **Police recovered crude bombs, sharp-edged weapons, slings and crates of petrol bombs.**

'We have recovered a lot of substances which could be possibly used for fuelling violence,' says M.T. Mehta, Assistant Commissioner of Police, Ahmedabad. **Madhavpura police also opened fire in the Idgah area to control violence unleashed by a 500-strong mob.** Three people were injured. Police fired three rounds and lobbed three tear gas shells to disperse a mob at Rakhial cross-roads. Meanwhile, indefinite curfew continued in the areas of Kalupur, Shahpur and Karanj. Madhavpura and Dariapur were put under curfew since 3 a.m. on Saturday. Police arrested 112 persons from six police commissionerate zones. Reports of crowds assembling at various places in Amraiwadi, Rakhial, Khadia, Karanj and Kalupur areas kept pouring in at the police control room". (*Source*: http://timesofindia.indiatimes.com/articleshow/4006360.cms).

See the sentence: "The police and State Reserve Police personnel fired 21 rounds to disperse the mob and prevent it from advancing to the majority community-dominated areas." This shows that it was a Muslim mob. The Muslims attacked the police and see how *The Times of India* reported it.

The following is another report from weekly *India Today* written by Uday Mahurkar in the weekly's issue dated 20th May, 2002:

"On the morning of May 7, Amrit Chagganlal, a camel cart owner, was passing by the Sarkhej area on Ahmedabad's outskirts. It was the 70th day since communal riots had engulfed Gujarat following the killing of 57 *Ramsevaks* at Godhra on 27th February. It was a difficult and dangerous time but Chagganlal ventured out in a bid to eke out a living. **A mob suddenly appeared as if out of nowhere, surrounded him and hacked him to death before throwing his body into a well.** Chagganlal was the 933rd victim of the continuing communal violence in Gujarat that shows no signs of ebbing....

By nightfall, the death toll had crossed the 940-mark when a group of Muslims in Ahmedabad's Shah Alam area drew Hindus out by throwing bombs at their homes in the Maninagar area and then launched a fierce attack with country-made weapons and crude bombs. BSF jawans who intervened were fired upon before they killed five of the attackers and

arrested several others with a huge quantity of weapons including a country-made cannon....

... True, since the last round of violence began on Ramnavmi day on April 21, violence has been restricted to Ahmedabad, Vadodara and Lunawada, a small town in Panchmahal district....

... The concern is understandable. Unlike the first phase of riots, now Hindus too have begun to suffer thanks to a new belligerence of Muslims who have been under siege for the past ten weeks. The repeated recovery of huge catches from Muslim pockets forced some of the ministers to ask Modi about the steps the police was taking to flush out the armouries...

...says Dharmesh Vyas, 26, an employee of a private company, who is recovering from bullet wounds sustained in firing by Muslim mobs: 'If Modi is removed, the violence will increase because there is a feeling among the Hindus that the riots are now engineered by Modi's rivals to get rid of him. It is Modi's presence that is keeping Hindus in check. Once he is gone, things will become uncontrollable'....

...in Ahmedabad, riots continue despite the two peace meetings between religious leaders of both Muslims and the RSS-VHP combine and joint statements calling for peace. It took the VHP less than two days to consider backtracking from peace initiatives following attacks on Hindu localities....

...among the factors which kept the communal pot boiling in Ahmedabad are the 40-odd relief camps in the city in which over 50,000 Muslims are lodged.... There is pressure on the government to close down some of these relief camps amid unconfirmed reports that at least some of these camps have become sanctuaries for Muslim trouble-makers..." (*Source*: http://www.indiatoday.com/itoday/20020520/states.shtml).

Another report in the same issue of the same weekly says:

"... A series of attacks by Muslims on policemen during the riots have further added to the mutual lack of faith. Now strapped with the anti-Muslim label, the police has been slow in acting against Muslim fanatics..."

This report shatters many of the myths. Far from being anti-Muslim, the Gujarat police was slow to act against Muslim fanatics for fear of being called anti-Muslim. Does the English media not owe a share of responsibility to the society? It is the media, electronic and print, in reality, which prevented the Gujarat police from taking action against the Muslim fanatics.

This report also indicates that it was the Muslims who started many of the riots after 3rd March, 2002. Hindus also rioted in retaliation for Muslim attacks, or in self-defence. Some Muslims attacked Hindus in Ahmedabad's Shah Alam area and not only that, they also attacked the BSF jawans. The Army and also the Gujarat police recovered huge catches of weapons from the Muslim areas. But the media turned a blind eye to this. These were not isolated incidents. Many of the events were similar to them after 3rd March, 2002.

We have seen the week-wise details of people killed as given by *India Today* dated 20th May, 2002 earlier in the chapter "Role of the Government in Controlling Violence". That gives us figures of 550 odd people killed in the first three days, and 400-odd in 70 days. This goes to show that after the first three days, average of about six killings a day took place, which was a result of bloody Hindu-Muslim riots and not one-sided rioting.

Out of the 563 people mentioned by *India Today* who died in the first three days, 57 were killed in Godhra, who were Hindus. (Actually, 59 were killed in Godhra, but at that time, it was reported 57 in most of the media.) Hence, as per the weekly *India Today*, 506 people were killed in the first three days, out of whom, 98 people were shot dead in police firing. Contrast 506 people killed in three days and 409 in more than 70 days.

The same weekly in the same issue also reported: "What is adding to the knife-edge tension is the growing evidence that the violence has a deliberate pattern and there's a motive to keep the flames from being doused. Violence seemed to have been brought under control by the second week of March until sporadic **attacks on Hindus** in Ahmedabad, Bharuch and Modasa in the midst of state school board examinations reignited the embers. **But it escalated on Ramnavmi day (i.e. 21 April 2002) when a police constable was killed in Ahmedabad's Gomtipur (Muslim) area. The sudden spurt of violence followed after a call given by local Muslim leaders to students from the community to boycott the rescheduled state school examinations failed....**"

136

This clearly shows that it was the Muslims who kept the rioting alive. It was they who instigated the violence, at least after 13th March, 2002. After 21st April, 2002, the Congress Party is alleged to have instigated riots.

Now let us read the report of PTI dated 19th September, 2003:

"Pak Flag was Hoisted After Godhra Carnage: Witness

A witness, deposing before the two-member commission inquiring into the Gujarat riots, said today that Muslims in the sensitive Amraiwadi area unfurled the Pakistani flag and raised pro-Pakistan slogans ten days after the Godhra riots. He also claimed that Hindus are still being tormented in the area.

'A large group of Hindus, who were returning after completing the final rites of 15 from Amraiwadi killed in the Godhra train carnage, found a mob of Muslims gathered near Khanwadi locality and heard statements like '*kafeeron ko kaat dalo, makan khali karao* (kill the infidels and empty their houses)',' said Ashok Patel, Bharatiya Janata Party member and municipal corporator from Bagh-e-Firdaus ward. Patel told Justice G.T. Nanavati (retired) and Justice K.G. Shah (retired), 'After nearly 10 days of the train carnage, Pakistani flags were unfurled on top of a public tank in the Ramol area and Muslims shouted slogans like 'Pakistan zindabad [*Long live Pakistan*]'.'

He claimed that though Hindus had observed restraint and averted any major clash on the day of cremation of the Godhra victims, riots were triggered after Muslims instigated them "with an intention of spreading fear".

Patel alleged that after the riots, a large number of Hindu families vacated their houses and moved elsewhere. During cross-examination, the corporator said no Hindu had ever made a representation to him about confiscation of property by Muslims.

At least 15 persons from Ramol and Jantanagar, under the Amraiwadi police station, were among the 59 *karsevaks* charred to death when a coach of the Sabarmati Express was set ablaze near the Godhra railway station on 27th February last year....

A riot victim produced a video-cassette reportedly showing the damage to his shop and urged the police to form a 'committee' of both Hindus and Muslims so that "people can come closer". He said he had given the same cassette to the National Human Rights Commission..." (*Source*: http://www.rediff.com/news/2003/sep/18godh.htm).

We already have seen the report of an organization as anti-BJP as the *Human Rights Watch* to see how Hindus were attacked by Muslims as early as 1st March, 2002 in Ahmedabad. This is what *The Times of India* reported (Sanjay Pandey was the reporter) dated 18th March, 2002:

"Riots Hit all Classes, People of All Faith

Ahmedabad: With great effort, Harish Parmar limps forward to greet you. His right leg was hit with a bullet above his right knee joint when he was running away from the mobsters involved in torching his house. Like Harish, three other youngsters are also limping their way to future at a relief camp allegedly shot at by some bad elements involved in bootlegging business when riots were in full swing in Jamalpur. Their woes, worries and plight is similar to one faced by any other riot-victim clustered at various relief camps. **Contrary to popular belief that only Muslims have been affected during recent riots more than 10,000 persons belonging to Hindu community have also become homeless.** The last batch of refugees in fact came in on Friday night from the Shahpur area when they tried to take shelter in the civil hospital as they had nowhere else to go. Volunteers later took them to a relief camp set up in a school in the Pritampura area on Saturday morning. 'There seems to (be) some confusion about the people affected in recent riots. You will not find them in government roles because they never registered with District Collectorate,' says Narendra Patel, a local relief worker revealing that most of them have taken refuge at various community-sponsored camps. He added that rather than approaching the state government-aided camps, the riot-affected Hindu families got shelter and support from their own community members and relatives. **Most of these affected families were living as micro-minority in some of the Muslim- dominated areas around the city.** Hiralal Ni Chali in Jamalpur, Nagarvel Hanuman in Bapunagar, Mangal Park in Amraiwadi, Saryudasji Mandir at Prem Darwaja and Municipal School, Kankaria are some of the few **relief camps filled with members of majority community. 'Hindus, who have been blamed more often for actively supporting**

hooliganism and triggering post-Godhra riots, have actually found themselves at the receiving end,' says Kalpesh Jha, another relief worker at Hiralal Ni Chali in Jamalpur, complaining that other side of the story was never heard. **'Attack on us was completely unprovoked on the bandh day despite the fact that no-first-attack truce was arrived between both the communities earlier in the day,'** says Babubhai Borisa, 42, resident of new municipal labour quarters at Jamalpur. He narrated that **they were attacked with acid bulbs, petrol and crude bombs and were also fired at (by) local bootleggers belonging to minority community.** Around 600 people from the municipal quarters have taken refuge in Hiralal Ni Chali near Geeta Mandir, Laati Bazaar and refused to go back to their homes unless government makes some arrangement for their safety. 'You are asking me to venture into lion's den,' retorts Paljibhai Muljibhai Parmar when asked whether he would like to go to his original place. **Another 106 families belonging to the Vaghri community were forced to leave their homes when a 2,000-strong crowd torched 70 *pucca* houses in Vaghariwas near Prem Darwaja.**

'They looted our property, torched houses, desecrated our temples and later tried to kill us but we escaped somehow,' says Rameshbhai Dantania camping at Saryudasji Mandir near Prem Darwaja, a stone's throw away from his own house. Dantania alleged that since 1969, there was an SRP point to prevent any untoward incident between both the communities but this time it was removed at the behest of Dariapur police station and incident occurred." (URL: http://timesofindia.indiatimes.com/city/ahmedabad/Riots-hit-all-classes-all-faiths/articleshow/4193006.cms).

It can also be read at http://hindunet.org/hvk/articles/0302/81.html

Need we explain the truth of the Gujarat riots in any further detail? This is a report not from any of the Gujarati newspapers or weekly *Organiser* but from *The Times of India!* This same daily had launched some of the worst hate-campaign against Narendra Modi and the BJP at the time of the riots in Gujarat, and has continued the tirade ever since. It also continues to publish a bunch of lies on the Gujarat riots on its editorial pages and had launched a virtual 'Modi- *hatao*' (i.e. 'Remove Modi') campaign after he won a huge majority in the December 2002 elections in Gujarat. This can be understood by simply reading some of its reports of 2004-05, which were very anti-Modi.

See the statement, "Contrary to popular belief that only Muslims have been affected during recent riots more than 10,000 persons belonging to Hindu community have also become homeless". It should be noticed that this daily does not seem to realize that it itself was responsible for the worst kind of lies on the subject, which resulted in the 'popular belief' that only Muslims were affected by the riots.

Unfortunately, some parts of this story seem unclear. See the statement "Attack on us was completely unprovoked on the bandh day despite the fact that no-first-attack truce was arrived between both the communities earlier in the day." **This statement indicates that Hindus were attacked by Muslims, completely unprovoked, at Jamalpur on 28th February just like in Bapunagar**, since 28th February was the day of the bandh called in Gujarat by the VHP to protest against the Godhra killings, while 1st March, 2002 was the day of the bandh in the rest of India, from which Gujarat was exempted. The SIT also said on page 210 of its report that 31 Hindus were killed on 28 February 2002; even if 11 were killed in police firing, 20 were killed in riots. This must have been in such attacks by Muslims in Jamalpur and Bapunagar.

This article by Sanjay Pandey for *The Times of India* clearly proves that Hindus were also homeless and had to live in refugee camps in Gujarat.

On 21st April, 2002, *The Telegraph* (Kolkata) reported:

"Bad PR Charge on Atal, Modi

New Delhi, April 20: High-profile member of the National Commission for Minorities, John Joseph, today said he had asked the Gujarat Government to publish the names of those killed in police firing in various parts of the state, but the Narendra Modi Government had not bothered to do so.

The commission had summoned the Gujarat Chief Secretary and Home Secretary to Delhi on 6th April. 'We grilled them for two- and-a-half hours and I suggested that they publish the names of Hindus killed in police firing. But the government declined, saying that it would create problems,' Joseph said.

'As on 6th April, 126 persons were killed in police firing, of which 77 were Hindus. There is no doubt, Muslims suffered a lot. If the real list was published, it would have shocking revelations,' he added.

'The Government of India and Gujarat Government's PR work is bad. It is a major lapse. **A good number of Hindus were also killed.** But I do not know why they are not disclosing the names,' Joseph said....."

Even a Christian member of the National Commission for Minorities said that a good number of Hindus were also killed and accused the Atal Bihari Vajpayee Government as well as the Gujarat government of having poor Public Relations work.

B.P. Singhal wrote: "As on 5.3.2002, of the 98 relief/ refugee camps opened, 85 were for the Muslims and 13 were for the Hindus." These 13 refugee camps for the Hindus, as early as 5th March, 2002, must have been for these Hindus rendered homeless in the riot cases in Bapunagar, Mahajan Na Vando and this case in Jamalpur, where Hindus were attacked by Muslims as early as 28th February or 1st March, 2002, just a day or two after Godhra.

India Today reported in its issue dated 18th March, 2002: "At a relief camp where the displaced Hindus were lodged in Ahmedabad, Modi's visit (before 7th March) drew an enthusiastic response." This is another clear admission by *India Today* that Hindus were living in refugee camps in Gujarat as early as 5-6 March, 2002.

Among another crucial thing, let us see the following report of *The Times of India* dated 11th April, 2002:

"Docs Told to Stay Off Minority Areas

Ahmedabad: 'All Hindu doctors are warned that they are not safe practising in Muslim-dominated areas. They are, thus, requested to stop practising in such areas and also in minority trust-run hospitals with immediate effect'. This message issued by the Ahmedabad Doctors' Forum, which has about 100 active members in the city, came as a direct fallout of the attack on Dr. Amit Mehta, who was repeatedly stabbed in his clinic in Juhapura (which is a Muslim area) on Tuesday (9 April 2002).

The incident has sent shock waves through the medical fraternity.

'In the past too, Hindu doctors practising in Muslim-dominated areas like Jamalpur and Gomtipur, have been fatally attacked. And yesterday's attack on

Dr. Mehta should serve as a warning to the Hindu doctors to quit practising in Muslim areas,' ADF founder- member, Dr. Bharat Amin told TNN. Already, Hindu doctors are reluctant to go to Muslim areas where their hospitals and clinics are located and this attack on one of their colleagues has only compounded their fears. 'The uncertainty and insecurity is becoming too much. I have been practising in Shahpur for the past 30 years, but will I be able to trust my patients now?' asks Dr. K.R. Sanghvi. Sanghvi had resumed seeing patients only a few days ago after having stayed away from his clinic for the better part of the month.

Dr. Amit Mehta has understandably decided to give up his practice of 23 years and shut shop. 'I have treated Muslim patients for more than two decades and this is what I got. I have escaped once, but my family does not want me to risk my life again,' Mehta told TNN from the hospital bed, where he is recuperating.

While Mehta stresses that his case should not be generalised, an example is already being made of him. 'Fear is looming large that we will be similarly attacked. In such a situation, we urge the government to provide us security for practising in such sensitive areas,' says president of the 200-member strong Vejalpur-Jivraj Medical Circle, Naresh Shah.

Shah said more than 50 doctors practising on the Vejalpur-Juhapura border have been forced to shut shop due to unprecedented tension.

It needs mention here that it is Hindu doctors who are mostly practising in Muslim areas with Muslim doctors constituting a mere 2-3 per cent of the 5,000-odd medical practitioners in the city.

'Our job is the most difficult. In emergencies, we have to work at nights. If we go, we run the risk of being soft targets and if we don't, we tend to incur the wrath of locals. The situation is getting more precarious by the day,' says a gynaecologist couple practising in Dariapur and Shahpur.

Meanwhile, the Ahmedabad Medical Association too met on Wednesday to discuss the fallout of the attack on the doctor. 'We condemn this communal attack on a doctor, who was giving selfless service to the society without discriminating between Hindu and Muslim patients and stress that government provide security to doctors,' said the AMA president, Bipin Patel.

To this, the health minister, Ashok Bhatt said, 'The attack on the doctor should be treated as an attack on humanity. The respective communities should take responsibility and ensure that doctors, who have been serving the society without discrimination, are safe. The request for security by any doctor will be considered by the government and addressed.'

Even doctors from the minority community have condemned the attack and said this would result in a negative fallout for the community. 'Such assaults may result in a negative impact for a community that is largely dependent on Hindu doctors for treatment,' said the Al Amin Hospital medical superintendent, Dr. Siddiqi Kazi.

Significantly, there are 82 Hindu doctors attached to Al Amin, of which only three have continued their services after the riots broke out. The hospital is reportedly seeking services of doctors from other states now." (*Source*: http://timesofindia.indiatimes.com/articleshow/6512317.cms)

Such attacks were, by and large, ignored by the biased anti- Hindu pro-Muslim Indian English media—just *The Times of India* reported this once. See how communal the attackers were: they were actually attacking the doctors, who were serving members of their own community just because the doctors were of a different community.

Now, let us see one of the biggest evidences of Muslim aggression. The following is the report of NDTV dated 13th.March, 2002:

"Mob Attack in Godhra, 12 Arrested

Wednesday, March 13, 2002 (Godhra): Within a fortnight of the February 27 railway station mayhem and subsequent violent fallout, tension escalated again today with a minority mob allegedly attacking people in the town, leading to police firing.

Police said a '500-people strong mob of minority community' attacked people in the Jahurpura area near the Old Bus Stand. They resorted to stone pelting and also 'opened fire' with private arms, police said. Police opened fire and hurled tear gas shells to disperse the mob. There was no report of any injury or casualty so far.

Additional forces of police, State Reserve Police and anti-riot Rapid Action Force (RAF) personnel led by senior DSP, Raju Bhargava, rushed to the spot and carried out a combing operation. 'Twelve persons including two women were picked up from a nearby place of worship,' police said. The situation was under control but tense, police said" (*Source*: NDTV web).

This was the story carried by NDTV. NDTV, which is similar to CPI (M) as far as anti-BJP ideology is concerned, reported that Muslims attacked Hindus in Godhra again soon after the 27th February carnage. *The Times of India* also reported this PTI news, and it can be read today at http://timesofindia.indiatimes.com/india/Mob-attacks-people-in-Godhra-12-arrested/articleshow/3682215.cms

As another instance of how Hindus were attacked, let us see the report of *The Times of India* dated 23rd March, 2002:

"Rioters Torch 50 Shops at the Revdi Bazaar

Ahmedabad: The Revdi Bazaar in the Panchkuva area of the city transformed into a raging inferno on Thursday (21 March 2002) afternoon, when the manic rioters set shops afire. The market place, which houses wholesale cloth shops, soon erupted in flames that took the Ahmedabad fire brigade more than five hours to bring under control. **Though no casualties were reported, the damage, say local shopkeepers, could well cross Rs. 15 crore**. It all began at 3:54 p.m., when a phone call on '101' reported: 'The Revdi market is on fire.' The first telephone call was followed up with many more SOS at AFB's headquarters in the Danapith area. The calls warned of the biggest instance of arson ever since the days of intense rioting that had gripped Ahmedabad between 28th February and 2nd March. Of the 11 calls that kept the AFB personnel busy, the inferno at the Revdi market proved to be the worst. By the time the first two fire-tenders could reach the vicinity of the Revdi Bazaar, a thick column of smoke told a grim tale that the market area, which houses more than 300 wholesale cloth shops, is characterized by a narrow and intricate network of lanes, prevented fire tenders from reaching the spot of arson, making it doubly difficult for the firemen to douse the raging inferno. Within minutes, 14 fire-tenders and water tankers were called in to control the fire. While senior AFB officials, including the chief fire officer (CFO) Bipin Jadeja, rushed to the spot, the fire-tenders strove hard to bring the blaze under control. The fight had to continue till 9:30 p.m. but by then nearly 50 shops, along with a large stock of garments, were reduced to glowing cinders. Jadeja told TNN: 'We did not make this an all-brigade call in view of the tense situation gripping the city. The other hurdle that we had to encounter was the inaccessibility to the root-cause of the fire. But after this long toil, I am satisfied that my men could stem the loss to property as without prompt action, this inferno could well have engulfed the large number of shops in the market as also the residential quarters behind. We have used nearly three lakh liters of water to douse the flames.' Local residents and shop owners, who have suffered heavy losses due to the arson, said the situation in Panchkuva had been tense soon after daybreak. 'Since morning, there were instances of stone- pelting and abortive attacks on local shopkeepers and their residences. **Matters turned worse after a mob attack on the Sindhi market was foiled by the SRP personnel stationed at the site. The mob then turned its fury on the Revdi Bazaar and started sprinkling acid, oil, petrol and inflammable chemicals on the cloth shops. The next thing we knew, our shops were ablaze,'** said Balram Thavani, a former BJP corporator and a local shop-owner. Thavani, who is also the Vice President of the Revdi Bazaar Salamati Samiti, told TNN: 'Only about 20 per cent of the burnt goods and shops were insured. Thursday's rioting and arson has reduced their life's earnings to ashes. For these middle-class families, earnings of a lifetime were reduced to ashes within moments'" (*Source*: http://timesofindia.indiatimes.com/articleshow/4609603.cms).

See the reporting of *The Times of India* when the Muslims were the attackers! When some 50 Hindu shops were burnt down in the Revdi Bazaar, reducing life-savings of middle-class Hindus to ashes, the media largely ignored the issue. To see the media's inflated reporting of the Muslim suffering in the Gujarat riots, one only needs to look at the weekly *India Today*'s story in its issue dated 25th March, 2002. Very few dailies bothered to report about these losses which the Hindus suffered in Gujarat. But the Gujarati media reported them. And hence, there was a contrast of day and night in the versions of the riots as projected by the 'national' English media, and the local Gujarati newspapers. *The Tribune* reported on 30th April, 2002: "(On 29th

April) Miscreants (Muslims) also reportedly set ablaze more than 36 shops, houses, kiosks, restaurants and godowns in the riot-hit city (Vadodara) in the past 24 hours."

Attacks on Dalits

Let us see the report of the Marathi daily *Tarun Bharat* dated 21st July, 2002 written by Prof. Dr Suvarna Raval:

"Dalits Suffered Heavily during Gujarat Riots

The news of Godhra inferno and the subsequent riots, which erupted in other parts of Gujarat, were highly disturbing events for the minds of any person interested in the welfare of the society. Yet among them, those of fights between Muslims and Dalits and Muslims and Adivasis were very surprising. Generally, the slogan of 'Dalits, Muslims—Bhai Bhai' is raised and given a high pitch. There is also a talk of forming a federation of Dalit and Muslim by alienating Dalits from Hindu society. **On this background, the news of Muslim crowds attacking Dalit localities or Adivasis shattering the Muslim localities was astonishing.** The apprehension, that perhaps, the Dalits are being used as shields in the Hindu-Muslim riots, also came to mind. This was the background in our minds, when we proceeded to visit Gujarat on behalf of the Survey Committee of Samarasata Manch.

But what awaited us was quite different.

…in the group of *Ramsevaks* in the Sabarmati Express, which was burnt to charred remains by Muslim fundamentalists, there were some Dalit youths also. Just as they became martyrs in the carnage, there were many Dalit brothers living in slums of different parts of Ahmedabad, who were victims of the Muslim attacks. We heard a number of heart-rending reports from the relatives and neighbours of the dead persons during our sojourn in Gujarat. I am giving below a few of them by way of samples.

Ramjibhai Parmar was a 24-year-old youth from the Gomatipur area which is inhabited by the Valmiki community. He saw Constable Amarbhai Patil, patrolling near the Masjid, was being attacked with swords by Muslims and went to rescue him but Muslims fired at him and shot him dead. (This was also reported by *India Today* dated 20th May, 2002 and rediff.com quoting the MoS, Gordhan Zadaphiya on 22nd April, 2002.)

Devendrabhai Solanki from Radhanpur, working in the Ahmedabad Sales Tax Office as a Notice Server, had come to the Nanu Wadkar house for Holi. On 30th March, stone-throwing started in the direction of his house. Children were playing in front of the house and to take them inside the home, he came out. **A mob of about 5,000 Muslims rushed on him while Darmesh somehow slipped out, but one of them cut his face with sword. He lost his front teeth. Miss Dipti Solanki, daughter of Devendrabhai Solanki weeping incessantly, told us bitterly that after 13 days, the dead body of Devendrabhai was found cut in 25 pieces. (4 Muslims were convicted for this on 18 May 2006, see the chapter *"Some Court Judgments"*).**

25-year-old Vasantkumar Parmar, earning Rs. 1,000 p.m. by working in a private factory, was looking after his old father and unmarried sister. **After the curfew was withdrawn, bombs were thrown near his house, the lights went out and, by the deafening sound of explosion, Vasantkumar rushed out of house running. The Muslims which were hiding in an ambush on the way-out, attacked him with swords and killed him on the spot.** His death cries shocked his sister-in-law, Gitaben but she had the presence of mind to beat the Dish (Thali) loudly and collected people nearby. **Muslims attacked this locality of 125 families from all four sides.** If we had weapons, we would have fought with them better. Gitaben was sobbing, saying, 'My younger brother-in-law became a victim without any reason'.

Pravinbhai Mooljibhai Solanki, a 25-year-old youth, living in the Ramanpura area, Saatchaali was running a Panpatti shop on lease. On the Ramanavami day (21st April, 2002) while he was returning home after closing his shop, **Muslims attacked and killed him. Mooljibhai told us that Muslims from Daryapur-Kalupur area came in our locality and exploded a bomb.** As the children and women were running away, Muslims fired at them. If Dalits kept arms with them for their protection, the police took action on them, but they take no action on the Muslims when they keep them. He said they had a serious gripe against police for this discrimination.

In the Khariwadi of the Shahpura slum, there are about 220 Hindu and 10-15 Muslim families. To the left of the slum, there is a restaurant, Relief Club. **The Muslim manager of this hotel got together fanatic Muslim youths from the same locality and set the houses in the locality on fire, first taking care to remove all the inhabitants of Muslim houses to a safe place. They burnt houses of 35 Hindu families.** Everywhere there was a desperate cry. Two girls from two houses were burnt alive. Seeing this spectacle, a 10- year Hindu boy, Suresh Mehru, died of the shock. The Sindhi owner of the Hotel Reviera, which is to the right of the slum, gave asylum to all these people and made arrangements for their food. These people of the slum belonging to the Vaghari Community were running the business of selling old clothes.

Behrampura is a Muslim-majority area having a population of 1,20,000. We found that in the minds of the Dalit community, there was a terrible anger against Muslims who had shattered the life of their community. **Yusuf Ajmeri with a 1,000-strong mob and with swords and guptis in their hands, rushed to Hindu locality shouting 'Kill Hindus, Allah is with us'. On 28th February, Kisanbhai Bhikabhai Dantani, who was returning from work, was attacked on his chest with swords and was killed on the spot.** His 70-year-old mother was telling with deep sorrow depicted on her face. She told that this treachery was done by their neighbours, who were living along with them for the last 8-10 years. She said, 'They had come to finish us. My son was killed, my daughter-in- law could not stand it and has left for her village. What will be the fate of my grandson, Sanjay? They have completely made our life desolate and barren.'

Muslims living in Behrampura have houses with 2-3 storeys. They resorted to heavy stone-pelting on the Dalit localities. Jaisinghbhai Shyamjibhai, who had passed the 9th Standard and working in a hosiery shop, was standing near his house. A heavy brick came down spinning at a great speed and hit Jaisinghbhai on the chest. The impact was so disastrous that his chest cage nearly broke open and he died on 1st March. Father of Jaisinghbhai works on daily wages in the Municipality. He was narrating us this history along with his children, all of them were terrified and jittery.

The Dani-Limda area of Ahmedabad has a large population of the weavers community. Piyushkumar, a youngster living in the Annapurna Housing Society, was told by Mustak Kania, Mohamed Rafique, Kasimbhai Ganichiya and Mustak Menon from the Dhruv Society just in the front side, that they were planning to launch a rocket from their building and as the rocket will take off, Mecca and Madina will be visible. Believing this story, he went to see it with curiosity, but on going there, was riddled with bullets in the throat and liver. His father and other youths from the society took him to Lallubhai Govardhandas General Hospital, but before anything was done, he died on 12th April at 6:00 p.m. His parents were unable to speak anything to us and, hence, his grandfather related us this terrible story. (Muslims were convicted for this on 28th March, 2006 and we will see report of *The Indian Express* on this of 13th April, 2002).

Dayabhai Rathod from Nirmalpura had taken Voluntary Retirement and was living along with his wife, three daughters and his only son, Pinakin, 26-years-old. When stone-pelting started, a bullet from the police hit him and he was killed on the spot. We were simply short of any words of consolation for the continuously weeping parents. His maternal uncle was expressing terrible anger against the police.

Ms. Induben Laljibhai Gohil, living in the Municipal Sweepers Colony near Dr. Babasaheb Ambedkar Bridge in Chamunda, died of a police firing. Jitu of the Marwari Community, living in Behrampura locality, also died in police firing.

Dinesh Kantilal Makwana from Damodar Chawl was returning on 3rd March from his work. Near the graveyard, two Muslim youths stabbed him to death. His address was found by the police from some papers in his pocket and his body, which had undergone post- mortem, was handed over to his grandmother, who was the only relative he had.

Soft Target

Generally, the Muslim Community lives close together. In many areas, there are Dalit localities or slums alongside. Around such area, there are many small factories run by Muslims and Dalit labourers working in them, live surrounded by the factories and Muslims. **Those Dalit brothers, who could not go out due to curfew, got caught in the deadly grip of Muslims.** These financially weak people were the soft target for the Muslims. From the terraces of houses, it was easy and safe for Muslims to attack the single-storeyed houses, slums or sometimes two-storeyed houses with stones, and crude bombs. In the closed Muslim locality of Gomatipur, even an electric current was sent, preventing police to enter.

Crooked and Selfish Politicians

These stories are indicative and not exhaustive. Atrocities on Dalits were done on such a vast scale, but no secular politician, from Sonia Gandhi to Ramvilas Paswan, felt like visiting the affected Dalit localities. The reporters of English press or channels did not come at all to these areas. No progressive person wearing the mask of 'anti-fanaticism' felt like wiping the tears of Dalits. Anti-fanaticism means unleashing criticism on Hindus is their equation and they have firm belief in the convictions that the love for Dalits is only a point for propaganda. The Dalits in Gujarat have got the taste of this naked truth in the recent riots. At the same time, Dalits got experience of the people from the so-called anti-Dalit organisations, RSS, VHP, Bajrang Dal, etc. coming to their rescue risking their own lives.

During this survey, we came to know as to how true was the minute analysis of the Muslim mindset done by Dr. Babasaheb Ambedkar." (*Source*: http://www.hvk.org/2002/0702/176.html).

With this report, there is nothing left for me to comment or explain. See the contrasts in the reporting of a large section of the media and the reality! I can only say, the so-called Hindu nationalists of the *Sangh Parivar* have failed to uphold the truth, and save their own skins, and allowed lies to triumph.

Along with this, let us now take a look at the report of *The Indian Express* dated 10th May, 2002, Friday, written by Palak Nandi:

"A Home for Long now Just a Death Trap

Palak Nandi

Posted online: Friday, 10th May, 2002 at 0000 hours IST

Ahmedabad, 9th May: Prem Darwaza in Ahmedabad is another Panwad, **though here Hindus are at the receiving end** unlike the Vadodara village. The locality stands out with its burnt houses, and broken bangles, steel utensils and torn bed-sheets scattered across the streets.

A half damaged wall, full of charcoal scribbles, summarises the Vaghri Vas locality's feelings: 'Mini Pakistan'; 'Miya Vad, Karachi'; 'Don't come back or you'll pay a heavy price'; and 'Hindus not allowed'.

Before the riots, around 800 people lived at Vaghri Vas, mostly Hindu Dalits. In the hate wave that followed, both communities were targetted. While the Dalits fled, some Muslims dared to stay out.

Now things have changed. **Unlike earlier, the minority community now calls the shots.** Jeetendra Datania, an autorickshaw driver, said: 'We were living here for almost 40 years. Though outsiders attacked their (Muslim) homes on 28th February, they avenged it by driving us out on 21st March. Now, not one of us dares to enter the locality.'

A daily wager's wife, Bhavnaben Naranbhai, said: 'We were more in numbers. But we dare not enter our locality now. If we try, they shoo us away saying '*Jo tha, sab khatam ho gaya. Chale jao, varna pachhtaoge*' (Life's no longer the same. Run or you'll regret it).'

The Dalits have put up at a nearby temple for when they returned home about a week back, they found dead animals in their houses. 'The walls were full of warnings,' said Raju, Bhavnaben's younger brother.

Life is much the same at Bhanderi-ni-Pol in Kalupur locality. As many as 518 riot-hit people from Kalupur Darwaza and Kalupur Tower now stay at the Bahuchar Mata nu Mandir. 'We have no choice. My shop was looted, our house pelted with stones and hand- made petrol bombs,' said Jaswantbhai Modi.

The locality of the temple is 'the border' for just across live Muslims. 'A constant flow of stones, petrol bombs and even bullets from across the border is regular,' Nirmalaben Dave said. She lost her house in the riots. 'We avoid going close to the border.'

Though the camps here are registered, the refugees have not been allotted a building to stay in. Refugees in Kalupur sleep on the streets and those in Dariapur spend the days in a building under construction." (This article till recently was available on *The Indian Express'* website at http://www. indianexpress.com/storyOld.php?storyId=2401 but no longer. It can be read at http://www.hvk.org/2002/0502/59.html)

What conclusions can one draw from this report? This report merely confirms the truth, that Hindus were also affected by the Gujarat riots. See the statement, "Unlike earlier, now it is the minority community which calls the shots". As on 25th April, 2002, a total of 40,000 Hindus were living in refugee camps. Far from being poor victims, this is what some Muslims were doing in Ahmedabad.

It is worth reading another article in the same newspaper, i.e. *The Indian Express*, dated 7th May, 2002, also written by Palak Nandi:

"With No Relief, They Turn to Religious Places for Shelter
Palak Nandi

Ahmedabad, **6th May:** These are the 1,000-odd riot victims for whom **relief is an eyewash**. While some have been driven away from their houses, others had no choice but to leave their houses badly damaged in the riots. Relief seems to be a far-fetched idea because since the past fifteen days, they **have been spending their days either on the streets or in a half-constructed building**.

About 550-odd residents of the Prem Darwaja Vagheri Vas, Dariyapur, had no choice but to leave behind their belongings and take shelter in a near by temple, following the violence of 21st March. **These Dalit families claim that they had been attacked by the people belonging to the minority community, who damaged their houses, property and drove them out of the area.**

'We had no choice but to take shelter at this temple. However, the temple cannot accommodate all of us; hence, we are compelled to live in this half-constructed building,' says Gautamiben Dhirabhai, a resident of the Vagheri

Vas. This half-constructed building is right opposite the temple, in the same premises and though it does not have a single fully-built room, it is the 'house' for more than 400 people, while the remaining sleep in the temple.

The situation is no different at a similar relief camp in Kalupur. The Bahuchar-Mata-nu-Madir, located at Bhanderi-ni-Pol at Kalupur, is currently accommodating about 518 riot-affected victims. They are the residents of areas located between Kalupur Darwaja and Kalupur Tower and which witnessed violence on 21st March.

While a few of these people sleep at their neighbour's house, some sleep in the temple while the rest, mainly the men, sleep in the lanes, just outside the temple. The temple area is called as 'border area' by the local residents, as across the temple is the locality of the Muslims. '**There is a continuous flow of stones, petrol bombs and even bullets at times,** from across the border.' All of us avoid even going close to the border,' says Nirmalaben Dave, whose house has been damaged during the riots.

The inmates of both the camps have demanded for a building, but, as yet, none of them have been allotted one. 'We have been demanding for the Kalupur Municipal School numbers 14 and 19, for a long time now, but we have not been allotted the school building. Because of the space shortage, these people have no choice but to eat and sleep in the lanes,' says Paresh Thakkar, organiser of the camp, who lives nearby.

For years, both Hindus and Muslims lived together in the area. Now the mutual trust and faith between the two communities has been replaced by fear, panic and hatred. 'For more than 60 years, we lived peacefully and there was never any problem. However, on 21st March, a few people of my locality came to me and told me that I should leave my house for good and if I return, they will not be responsible for the consequences,' says Badamiben Prajapati, who lives alone with her son.

'It is not safe for these people to live here as one does not know when the stone-pelting and violence will begin. Already, the third floor of my building has been damaged due to the petrol bombs,' says Bhagyovadan Khatri, trustee of the temple. But the refugees are apprehensive about returning to their houses.

'About five of us were injured in a private firing on 21st March. All of us now are very careful and avoid going to their area, except in a group,' says Hitendra Shah, who was injured in the incident."

(This report was available till recently on *The Indian Express'* site at http://cities.expressindia.com/fullstory.php?newsid=16851 but no longer. Today it can be read at http://www.hindunet.org/hvk/articles/0502/53.html)

Some points to be noted here are: Did even the Muslim refugees suffer like this? Even Muslims, who were displaced from their houses, were given refugee camps to live in. But these Hindus had to sleep on the streets or in temples. This is a clear proof of the fact that Dalits suffered heavily in the riots, at the hands of Muslims. But the entire non-Gujarati media generally kept quiet on this issue. But despite this, at times, the media did let slip in the truth. Will the editors of either *The Times of India* or *The Indian Express* remember their stories published in their own newspapers? Of course not. They will lie through the skin of their teeth that only Muslims suffered in the riots. The English media and the electronic media, in particular, NDTV, accused the Gujarati media of being biased. Far from it, it was the English media and the TV channels who were biased. **What the Gujarati media reported about the Hindus suffering at the hands of Muslims was absolutely true; none other than *The Times of India*, *The Indian Express* or *India Today* admitted this on isolated occasions.**

On 30 May, 2002 *The Hindu* reported: "In a chat with *The Hindu*, (CPM Politbureau member) Ms Brinda Karat, who was in Bangalore last week, shared a few thoughts on the hurdles in the rehabilitation of people affected by the riots, both Hindus and Muslims…When she did actually see a cheque for Rs. 22,000, it was at the Kankadia camp, which housed Dalits, and Hindus. There, Karat also came across cheques for Rs. 10,000, Rs. 12,000 and Rs. 22,000. "The government seems to be offering some substantial compensation only to the Dalit community," Ms. Karat observes, emphasising the need to compensate everyone equally." (Source: http://www.hindu.com/thehindu/mp/2002/05/30/stories/2002053000180200.htm)

None other than Marxist leader Brinda Karat also admitted that Hindus and particularly Dalits were also homeless. The compensation provided by the Government was equal for all, just that she 'saw' cheques of different denominations at different relief camps. **While forcibly trying to imply that the Gujarat Government was discriminating Hindu and Muslim victims of riots, she admitted that there were Hindus also rendered homeless.** Note here that Dalits and Hindus are not separate, Dalits are Hindus only, but Brinda Karat tries to separate them.

The Tribune reported on 30th April, 2002: "Ahmedabad, 29th April: The death toll in Gujarat since the February 27 Sabarmati Express carnage reached 900 today, with the fragile peace being shattered repeatedly in Ahmedabad and Vadodara.

The police said of the seven persons seriously injured when the crude bombs they were making exploded in their house in Kalupur this morning, two had died in hospital. **One person was stabbed to death in Gomtipur (Muslim area) within hours of the conclusion of the peace rally led by Defence Minister, George Fernandes and Chief Minister, Narendra Modi.**

Prior to the rally, three persons had died in Chandola Talao area under the Maninagar police station. In Kalupur (also Muslim area), two persons died in police firing late last night as sporadic violence, arson and group clashes continued.

A report from Anand said that two scooter-borne men tried to shoot a man on his morning walk, but he ducked in time. The police later recovered the revolver and cartridge shell from the spot.

Vadodara: Despite imposition of indefinite curfew and heavy security bandobast, sporadic incidents of violence and arson continued unabated in the Vadodara City for the fourth consecutive day.

At least three persons were injured in private firing and another in stone pelting following group clashes at Navidharti in the curfew- bound Karelibaug area, where a rocket launcher was also recovered by the police early today. Reports said at least 15 persons were injured, including five in private firing and as many in acid bomb attacks, during the past 24 hours in the city as mobs engaged in intense fighting.

Miscreants (Muslims) also reportedly set ablaze more than 36 shops, houses, kiosks, restaurants and godowns in the riot-hit city in the past 24 hours. Reports said several families belonging to the majority (Hindu) community had fled from Tandalja following mounting communal tension in the area, where the authorities had provided shelter to nearly 2,000 members of the minority community. **Meanwhile, the police registered a case of attempt to murder against the Congress Councillor, Manzoorkhan Pathan and arrested his brother on the same charge for their alleged murderous attack on a family at Junigadi Harijan Basti on Saturday.**

According to the police, violence also erupted in Savli past night, forcing the police to open two rounds of fire to disperse the warring mobs. UNI" (*Source*: http://www.tribuneindia.com/2002/20020430/main1.htm#3).

This clearly indicates how the aggressor was and who the victim was. Several Hindu families had to flee.

This report quoted from *The Times of India* (dated 18th March, 2002, written by Leena Misra) is also worth reading:

"Ahmedabad: When Union Home Minister, L.K. Advani answered the Rajya Sabha MP, Shabana Azmi's query in the Parliament on Monday, saying that more from the majority community fell to police bullets than the minorities in the recent riots, he was referring to the whole of Gujarat. **Sixty per cent of the people, who died due to police firing, were from the majority community, the state-wide figures show**. But the scene in Ahmedabad is quite the reverse. In the city that is considered communally and politically most volatile, more members of the minority community died in the police firing. According to figures available, 57 per cent (23 out of 40) of the people killed in the police firing belong to the minority community. This figure should be seen with the toll of rioting in Ahmedabad which shows that out of the 286 people killed, some 41 were Hindus killed in about 5,500 rounds of firing by the police. Similarly, in the state, of the 571 people who died in violence, 494 people from the minority community were killed in the riots that followed the Godhra carnage **as compared to 77 from the majority community. But the state figures, as against Ahmedabad, show that of the 100 that succumbed to the police firing, 60 were Hindus**" (*Source*: http://timesofindia.indiatimes.com/articleshow/4002321.cms).

This report shows that until 17th March, 137 Hindus were killed—60 in police firing and 77 by Muslims. And in the state, total number of Hindus killed in police firing was more than Muslims. This was the case till 18th April, 2002 as per Balbir Punj's article in *Outlook*. **This also shows that 43 out**

of the 60 killed in police firing outside Ahmedabad were Hindus. This includes Vadodara as well.

Another report worth reading is the one of *The Times of India* dated 28th April 2002, written by Sanjay Pandey:

"More Fall Prey to Police Firings in Gujarat

Gandhinagar: Two months after the riots began in Gujarat, there is a perceptible change in the type of people falling prey to police bullets. The latest statistics available with the Gujarat police show that more Muslims have been killed in police firing in Gujarat than Hindus.

Statistics made available by top sources in the Police Bhavan here show that out of the 170 persons killed in the state so far, 93 are Muslims and 77 Hindus. According to officials, this was not the case in March when records suggested that 60 out of 100 killed in police firing were Hindus and 40 were Muslims. These damning statistics, which are also being sought by the National Commission for Minorities, clearly show that of the 70 people killed in the second month of violence, an overwhelming 53 are Muslims and only 17 Hindus.

This, police officials would claim, was a result of trying to control the 'Muslim backlash' that was being talked about in the official circles. **Police officials said that the backlash could be especially seen in Ahmedabad, where out of the total number of persons injured in stabbings, 62 are Hindus and 30 Muslims.** The overall figures for Gujarat of those injured in stabbings tell a different story, with 131 Hindus and 179 Muslims. The figures should be seen in the light of the community-wise break-up of total number of riot victims in Gujarat. **The break-up is available for 726 deaths in riots, which show that 552 Muslims and 168 Hindus,** including the 59 Godhra train victims, have been killed so far.

It is significant that the maximum jump in police firing deaths of the two communities has taken place in Ahmedabad, where right from the beginning of the riots, the number of Muslims falling to police bullets is disproportionately high.

About a month back, out of the total of 40 police firing victims in Ahmedabad, 17 were Hindus and 23 Muslims. Today, the Ahmedabad figures show that of the 90 people killed in police firing, 59 are Muslims and 31 Hindus. This means, of the 50 people killed in police firing in Ahmedabad in the second month, 36 are Muslims and only 14 Hindus.

In other words, in the second month of violence, the percentage of Muslims falling to police bullets is a staggering 72 per cent...

The police records also show that of the 523 places of worship damaged in the last two months of riots, 298 were dargahs, 205 mosques, 17 temples and three churches. **Besides, of the total substantive arrests made by the police, 9,954 are Hindus and 4,035 Muslims. However, in the preventive arrests column, the statistics show that the number of Hindus arrested is much higher—17,947 as against 3,616 Muslims.**

The police estimates also put the total property loss in the state at Rs. 682 crore. However, while community-wise break-up of the damage is not available for Gujarat, the figures for Ahmedabad are— Muslims, Rs. 400 crore, and Hindus Rs. 10 crore." (*Source*: http://timesofindia.indiatimes.com/articleshow/8283550.cms).

On 18th March, Leena Misra told us that by 17th March, 137 Hindus had been killed in the riots, 77 in riots and 60 in police firing. That is a total of 137 Hindus. Here Sanjay Pandey gives a figure of 168 Hindus including 59 killed in Godhra. This would mean a total of 109 Hindus killed after Godhra till 27th April, by Muslims. Add 77 Hindus killed in police firing to that, to get 186 Hindus killed after Godhra. And add 59 killed in Godhra, to get 245 Hindus killed since 27 February. The Muslims killed were 552 in riots, and 93 in police firing to get a total of 645, as of 28 April 2002. With missing people declared dead later, and more bodies found, the final figures were revised.

This is just the tip of the iceberg. Quotations and analysis of reports of the newspapers of those days exposing the myths of the Gujarat riots can go on and on. But despite these evidences, a large section of the media is hell-bent on denying the bitter truth, that even after Godhra, the riots that happened were not one-sided.

CHAPTER 6

ATTACKS ON MUSLIMS

Outwardly, it may appear that this book attempts to highlight the attacks on the Hindus and to pinpoint the lies of the political rivals, of the biased people in the English media, and of the so-called social activists. To read it so grossly, to assess it so superficially, is to commit another serious mistake. This is not to suggest that the Hindus alone suffered in the Gujarat riots. The Muslims also suffered in violence in the first three days, i.e. on 28th February, 1st March and 2nd March, 2002 and later also. Let us here deal with the attacks on Muslims in Gujarat riots.

The cause of the retaliatory riots has already been discussed at length in the second and third chapters. But there were also many more causes. The weekly *India Today,* in its issue of 18 March 2002 discusses many of these causes. We have seen some of them earlier in the second chapter, like anger over Parliament attack, mushrooming *madarsas,* etc. One major cause of anger also included reports that three Hindu girls had been kidnapped in Godhra by Muslims, raped and their breasts cut off. According to the Justice Tewatia Committee report, these reports appear to be untrue. But there was no way to confirm this on 28th February. But even weekly *Outlook,* a staunch critic of Narendra Modi, reported in its issue of 11 March 2002 covering events till 28 Feb that though the government denied the rumours, the damage had been done. It shows that the Gujarat Government immediately denied the rumours so quickly that *Outlook* had time to carry it in its issue of 11 March even though it took many days for this fact to be established.

There was unimaginable anger in the people's minds after the mind-numbing Godhra carnage. No *Sangh Parivar* organization alone could be blamed for the riots. If any was involved, it was purely incidental. And incidentally, twenty-five Congress leaders were also accused of attacking Muslims in the post-Godhra riots as per a report in *The Times of India* dated 9th August, 2003.

The Council for International Affairs and Human Rights sent a study team to do field study and submit a report on the communal riots in Gujarat. Justice D.S. Tewatia, Vice-Chairman of the Council and a former Chief Justice of Calcutta and Punjab and Haryana High Courts, was the leader of the team. Other members were: Dr. J.C Batra, senior advocate, Supreme Court of India, Dr. Krishan Singh Arya, Academician, Chandigarh, Shri Jawahar Lal Kaul, former Assistant Editor, *Jansatta*, Delhi, and Prof. B.K. Kuthiala, Dean, Faculty of Media Studies, G.J. University, Hisar. The team left for Gujarat on 1st April and returned on 7th April, 2002.

The report "Godhra and After" of the Council says:

"...3. Hindu mobs, especially during the first week of March, comprised a mix of people belonging to lower, lower middle and upper middle socio-economic strata of the society.

4. Involvement of upper middle class Hindus in arson and looting is a phenomenon seen for the first time in the country.

5. The Hindu mobs appeared to be more interested in destroying the property of selected establishments of Muslims. It was reported that a chain of restaurants with Hindu names and owned by a Muslim family was targetted because of the perception that lot of money from the gulf countries had been invested, thereby putting Hindu competitors at a disadvantage.

6. Another new phenomenon reported to the Study Team was the presence and active participation of women in the mobs."

Attacks on Muslims

Attacks by large mobs began in the districts of Ahmedabad, Vadodara, Sabarkantha and, for the first time in its history, Gandhinagar on 28th February. Violence spread to the then largely rural districts of Panchmahal, Mehsana,

Kheda, Junagadh, Banaskantha, Patan, Anand and Narmada the next day. Over the next two days, Bharuch and Rajkot and later Surat were hit.

To understand exactly the attacks on Muslims, it is necessary to read the English as well as the Gujarati newspapers of that time. *India Today's* report on that in its issue dated 18th March, 2002 is also useful. A report from that issue reads thus:

".... Aware that people would shy away from blatant aggression in their own areas, outsiders were recruited to attack the pre-targetted localities. In most cases, the locals didn't protest and actually egged on the rioters, so intense was the hatred of the 'other'.

There was also a deliberate attempt to mar the economic interests of the Muslim community. Not only were shops and establishments with obvious Muslim names attacked, but in a chilling revelation of the meticulous planning, so were those with names like Aashirwaad or Saffron that were jointly owned by Hindus and Muslims. Armed with information on share-holding and partnerships, they swooped down on establishments that variously included a medical shop near Ellis Bridge, the Honda franchisee on Gandhi Nagar road and the truck operator, who carted Opel cars at Halol. The approximate loss suffered by business in six days of violence: Rs. 500 crore a day." The same report also says: "In a week of a vengeful spree following the February 27 Godhra carnage, more than 600 people have died across the state and 20,000 rendered homeless in Ahmedabad alone. Mosques and *dargahs* have been burnt or damaged, and several have been converted into Hulladiya Hanuman temples or Godhadiya temples in honour of the Godhra victims. Fluttering saffron flags signal a perverse victory. Despite a past pockmarked by communal riots, Gujarat has all but lost its moorings as a tolerant society."(What this issue of *India Today* reported was completely one- sided, ignoring all attacks on Hindus that took place in Gujarat. But this reporting is enough to understand the attacks on Muslims.)

The following was the report of *The Hindu* dated 1st March 2002, on the events of 28th February:

"Ahmedabad, 28th February. At least 140 people were killed, 60 of them burnt alive in two housing colonies here today, as mob frenzy reached its crescendo during the 'Gujarat bandh' called by the Vishwa Hindu Parishad and supported by the ruling BJP in protest against Wednesday's (27 Feb) torching of the Sabarmati Express.

At least 30 others were killed in police firing, stabbing and other incidents in different parts of the city while the casualty in other cities and towns in the State was put at over 50.

Shops and business establishments belonging to Muslims were targetted by mobs. About 40 were feared killed when 15 houses in 'Gulmarg' Society in the Meghaninagar locality here were set afire. At least 20 people were feared trapped in a building set ablaze in Naroda industrial area.

Among the deceased in the Gulmarg Society carnage was the former Congress member of the Lok Sabha, Ehsan Jafri, and his entire family. The Home Secretary, K. Nityanandam, confirmed the torching of the Gulmarg Society, but said he was not sure if Mr. Jafri was among the victims.

Police have recovered some 20 bodies from the Society and at least 15 more are believed to be inside the burning houses. **At Naroda, efforts are being made to put off the fire before the recovery of the bodies could start.**

The authorities said the toll in the day's orgy of violence in Ahmedabad alone could be at least 90. The number of cases of looting and arson, particularly of the minority shops and business establishments, was officially put at 118 in Ahmedabad but the authorities admitted that they had lost count.

The authorities, for obvious reasons, refused to confirm the burning of a mosque in Surat city, the attack on the Islamic Study Centre in Baroda and the torching of the Waqf Board office in the Old Secretariat building in Gandhinagar. But eyewitness accounts confirmed the incidents.

The Army units, frantically called by the Chief Minister, Narendra Modi, as the situation seemed to slip out of hand, started arriving in Ahmedabad and are likely to be deployed in the city on Friday.

At least five people were killed in Viramgam and four in Baroda, where the house of a leading Muslim social activist was attacked. Six were killed in Derol town near Godhra. Till evening, police fired 46 rounds in Ahmedabad, in which at least 10 persons were believed to have been killed. The toll in the torching of the Sabarmati Express, meanwhile, had risen to 58 with the recovery of the body of a child late last night. An indefinite curfew has been clamped in 26 cities and towns in the State, including parts of Ahmedabad, Surat, Baroda, Rajkot, Nadiad, Anand and Kaira in addition to the indefinite curfew in force in Godhra since Wednesday. The skyline of Ahmedabad and Baroda was filled with black smoke emanating from the burnt shops and cabins, discarded **tyres to create road blockades** as well as dozens of State road transport and city municipal service buses set afire by the miscreants.

For the first time in many years, the response to the bandh call was almost total in all the cities with not even a single shop or roadside cabin, petrol pump or commercial establishment open. Hooligans forced the closure of most of the State and Central Government offices in Ahmedabad, Gandhinagar and other cities. All schools and colleges, cinemas and other establishments remained closed. Even the cable television operators, 'under instructions' from the VHP, were forced to suspend telecast of all entertainment and sports channels, allowing only the news channels to function during the day.

The hooligans indulging in looting and arson had a field day with police either conspicuous by their absence or, outnumbered by the attackers, looking the other way. Journalists and cameramen were also attacked at many places and their equipment damaged.

It was also perhaps for the first time that the capital city of Gandhinagar witnessed violence with groups of people attacking even the old secretariat building housing the offices of many of the State Government-owned boards.

Several minority places of worship were made the specific target of the attacks. In Ahmedabad, a mausoleum in the middle of a road in the Shahibagh locality, barely a few metres from the office of the city Police Commissioner, was razed to the ground by the hooligans with the police vehicles passing by but refusing to intervene.

Mr. Modi, who described the train attack as a 'terrorist-type' action, said the Government had ordered a judicial inquiry by a retired judge of the Gujarat High Court. Mr. Modi said 80 people, including two local councillors of Godhra, who were believed to be involved in the train attack and the owners of the two petrol pumps suspected to have supplied fuel to the attackers, had been arrested. Both the pumps have been sealed, he said and added that the Government would not hesitate to invoke POTO or the Prevention of Anti-Social Activities Act (PASA) against the Godhra attackers."

Though this report is from a biased anti-BJP newspaper like *The Hindu* and this report is also biased, its reports on attacks on Muslims were mainly true. However, this report admitted that the Chief Minister, Narendra Modi made frantic calls to get in the Army in Ahmedabad and that some units had started arriving in Ahmedabad as early as night of 28th February itself. This report also admits that the police shot dead at least 10 rioters on 28th February itself. The only place where *The Hindu* accuses the police of inaction was: "In Ahmedabad, a mausoleum in the middle of a road in the Shahibagh locality, barely a few metres from the office of the city police commissioner, was razed to the ground by the hooligans with the police vehicles passing by but refusing to intervene". **Now note that it was far more important to save human lives than a mausoleum.** The police were already overwhelmingly outnumbered (despite the entire force being deployed) and it was necessary to save lives than mausoleums. **So, the vehicles refused to intervene in mausoleum demolishing as they must have been going to an urgent call to save human lives, rather than tombs and mausoleums.** The SIT's closure report quotes Shivananda Jha, the then Additional Commissioner of Police, Sector-I, Ahmedabad (He was till 9 April 2002) on page 347 that in Ahmedabad City, there was an acute shortage in the police force and with the limited resources available, they had to control the riots and therefore, it was considered essential to save lives first and then concentrate on protecting the properties, but the magnitude of the riots was so large that it was not possible to protect each and every property.

Now, let us read the report of this very newspaper dated 2nd March, 2002, covering the events till 1st March:

"Shoot Orders in Many Gujarat Towns, Toll Over 200
By Manas Dasgupta

"There were 2 photos, one of AFP and the other of Reuters given here."

A Hindu mob waves swords at an opposing Muslim mob during street battles in Ahmedabad on Friday. FACE OF FEAR: A Muslim seeks mercy from rioters.—Reuters

Ahmedabad, 1st March. The Army began flag marches in the worst-affected areas of Ahmedabad, Baroda, Rajkot and Godhra cities and the 'shoot-at-sight' order was extended to all 34 curfew-bound cities and towns in Gujarat as the orgy of violence in the aftermath of the Godhra train carnage continued unabated for the second day today.

The toll in the violence has been officially put at 136, including 119 deaths being reported from Ahmedabad city alone, of which at least 17 people were killed in police firing. But unconfirmed reports put the toll at over 200 with more bodies still being extricated from the minority housing colonies set ablaze in Meghaninagar and Naroda localities on Thursday (28th February). Five persons were killed in police firing during fresh incidents of violence in the labour-dominated Bapunagar locality, where at least five persons were burnt alive in a car in one of the gruesome incidents during the day. Eight persons were burnt alive in their car on the outskirts of Juhapura (Muslim) locality. A policeman was stabbed to death and his body set afire by a mob in the Naroda locality. (Who must have done this? Hindus or Muslims?)

The official sources admitted that the casualty in the Meghaninagar (Chamanpura, i.e. Jafri case) and Naroda burning incidents was much higher than originally estimated and so far over 105 bodies had been recovered from the Gulmarg Society in Meghaninagar and Naroda, which alone accounted for at least 65 deaths. But hospital sources said at least 163 burnt bodies had been recovered from the two places in one of the worst-ever mass murder incidents in the history of the state since the 1969 riots.

The entire pandal of the Gujarat-Expo exhibition, where various State Governments and co-operative organisations had their stalls on the Gujarat University ground, was on fire. It, however, was not immediately clear whether the fire was accidental or was caused by some miscreants, who looted the stalls.

The Gujarat Chief Minister, Narendra Modi, however, claimed that the situation was 'improving' and the intensity of violence was 'much less than what it was yesterday'. He was confident that the situation would be brought under control soon.

He claimed that despite the prevailing tension in the walled city and the labour-dominated areas of Ahmedabad, the flag march had a 'salutary effect'. He said one Army brigade, airlifted from the border areas and which arrived early this morning, began the flag march later in the day while another brigade was expected to arrive in the night. He said if the situation demanded, the Army would be deployed in the affected areas to help the civil authorities restore normalcy.

Though Gujarat was 'exempted' from the Vishwa Hindu Parishad's national bandh call for today, life remained paralysed in most parts of the state for the second day today because of the prevailing tension or due to the imposition of indefinite curfew. Even outside the curfew-bound areas in Ahmedabad, none of the shops, cabins and other business establishments were opened today. Banks, schools and colleges, cinema theatres and most other institutions remained closed while only a few private offices functioned with minimum staff.

Despite the imposition of indefinite curfew, sporadic incidents of violence, group clashes and stoning continued throughout the night and during the day today in the walled city and labour-dominated eastern parts of Ahmedabad. But unlike Thursday, when one community was entirely at the receiving end, the minority backlash caused further worsening of the situation.

Police presence had little impact on the two communities pelting stones at each other in Bapunagar, Gomtipur, Dariapur, Shahpur, Naroda (all Muslim dominated) and other areas, from where incidents of firing had been reported. But there were no reports of casualty. Pitched battle was continuing between the two communities late in the evening.

The official sources said timely arrival of the police foiled a retaliatory attempt to break into a prominent temple in Jamalpur locality in the walled city. But at least 15 places of worship of the minority community in Ahmedabad and some other parts of the state were vandalised and were converted overnight into 'temples' during the last two days."

30 Burnt Alive (PTI Reports) "A Baroda report said 30 persons were burnt alive today at the Pandarwal village in the Panchmahal district of Gujarat, official sources said here. Curfew has been imposed in the area and Rapid Action Force personnel have been deployed."

This report does point the true picture of the riots on the second day. What does this say? Unlike the first day, i.e. 28th February, the Muslims had already started retaliatory riots as early as 1st March, 2002. What this newspaper forgets, just like most others of its type, is its own reports during the actual time of the riots. Why did A.G. Noorani in fortnightly *Frontline* (publication of *The Hindu*) and *The Hindu* itself in its various editorials ever after, call the riots a 'pogrom', a 'genocide' and a 'massacre' when its own reporter reported that Muslims too were on the offensive, as early as 1st March, 2002?

Now let us see the report of this same newspaper dated 3rd March, 2002, covering events till 2nd March, 2002:

"Ahmedabad, 2nd March. As many as 86 people were killed in fresh incidents of violence in different parts of Gujarat today with disturbances spreading to newer and remote rural areas, even as the Chief Minister, Narendra Modi, claimed that the situation was 'fast returning to normalcy' in the State.

In yet another incident, 27 persons were burnt alive at Sadarpar village in Vijapur taluka of Mehsana district, while seven persons met a similar fate in a bakery near Dabhoi town in Baroda district. Four persons were also burnt alive at Por village and one was stabbed to death in Kalol town in Gandhinagar district. At least 47 persons have been killed in police firings in different cities and towns since last night, including 19 in Ahmedabad city alone, where the police had to open fire repeatedly to disperse violent mobs engaged in pitched battle. Eight people were killed in police firing in Godhra town.

For the first time, disturbances have spread to the capital district of Gandhinagar and Surat and Bhavnagar, cities where indefinite curfew was clamped after 22 people were killed in stabbing and police firing. Curfew, however, was partially lifted from 14 cities and towns, including Ahmedabad, to give a semblance of normalcy, but at least 40 cities and towns in the state were under indefinite curfew.

The death toll, according to Mr. Modi had reached 289, including 160 in Ahmedabad, but unconfirmed reports put the toll at above 350... Mr. Modi said the incident in Sadarpar was sparked by rumours that the minorities had collected in a building and were preparing to attack and in retaliation, the majority community set fire to the building.

In Surat, two mosques, at least 15 houses of the minorities and a timber market were set ablaze in Pakhinawad. Five people were killed in stabbing in Gopipura and some other parts of the city, following which an indefinite curfew was clamped in five police station areas. In Bhavnagar, one person was killed in police firing and four were stabbed to death, forcing the police to impose indefinite curfew.

Mr. Modi said the Border Security Force units had been dispatched to Surat to assist the civil authorities to maintain law and order and the government would consider sending the Army to the diamond city after the promised second brigade reached Ahmedabad.

The situation, however, has improved in Ahmedabad today where no major incidents of arson were reported since last night, though members of the two communities were engaged in pitched battles pelting stones and acid bulbs necessitating the police to open fire at several places. In the only case of the patrolling Army units opening fire to disperse violent mobs, two persons were injured in the industrial belt of Odhav.

In the interiors of the western suburbs of the city, some shops and other business establishments reopened today after two days.

Even while claiming that the situation was improving, Mr. Modi said the police fired at least 1,031 rounds in different parts of the state since last night, besides bursting 1,614 tear gas shells to disperse violent mobs. While 19 people were killed in police firing in Ahmedabad and eight in Godhra, six people were killed in police firing in Baroda, five in Anand, three each in Mehsana and Gandhinagar, two in Kaira and one in Bhavnagar.

The toll in stabbing and arson was officially put at 242, in which Ahmedabad alone accounted for 131 killings and Mehsana, the home district of the Chief Minister, 40. Even the tribal-dominated districts of Sabarkantha and Dahod accounted for 15 and 10 deaths respectively. Strongly denying that the police had failed to act in time, Mr. Modi claimed that '90 per cent areas' in the state remained incident-free because of the pro-active role played by the police. The presence of the Army had created a 'salutary effect' in bringing the situation under control in Ahmedabad, Baroda and Godhra.

Mr. Modi convened a meeting of the leaders of political parties here this evening to discuss the riot situation but it was boycotted by the Congress."

Let us see some other sources' reporting on attacks on Muslims. This is what the weekly *India Today* reported in its issue dated 25th March 2002 in a report by Uday Mahurkar:

"As smoke starts to lift and flames flicker away from the carcass that was once a community, a structure begins to take shape. That's all there's left of it, a misshapen frame. A splintered psyche jutting ominously, a fractured faith protruding starkly. As for the heaving, throbbing spirit, it has been hacked and burnt, pillaged and plundered, left for dead. Which is perhaps why breathing life into the state's Muslim community seems less of an option, more of an impossibility for now.

It is a minority haunted by visions of burning houses and bodies that followed the killing of 57 *karsevaks* at Godhra on 27th February. It is a community oppressed by figures. Of a death toll numbering 750 according to official records, but probably double that. Of the nearly 1.25 lakh displaced in central and north Gujarat, with nearly 50,000 lodged in makeshift camps in Ahmedabad and another 50,000 reportedly staying with their relatives. Of the Rs. 3,000 crore suffered in losses as estimated by the community's leaders.

This last is the most forbidding. For besides their homes, many thousands have lost their livelihood. The paanshops and bakeries, the barber shops and cycle-repair shops, the hotels and factories have all been razed by mobs, at times 10,000-strong. The insurance claims from the community amount to Rs. 400 crore so far. An estimated Rs. 50 crore has been lost by the destruction of 75 per cent of the state's bakeries, Rs. 200 crore by the demolition of 60 textile and chemical units and powerlooms in Surat and Ahmedabad. Almost 18,000 two- and three-wheelers and 800 trucks have been destroyed. Says Firoze Khan, owner of the Telco service station that was torched along with 22 trucks by a mob of 7,000 at Jetalpur near Ahmedabad: 'God alone knows how we will bear this economic blow.' Though the building and trucks were insured, the spare parts worth lakhs of rupees stocked by the service station were not.

Along the Navsari-Mehsana stretch on the 700-km Mumbai- Mehsana highway and other state highways, most of the restaurants were owned by Muslims; nearly 700 have been burnt. Mohammed Iqbal Kuskiwala, 45, owner of a biscuit factory at Modasa, a small town in north Gujarat, lost Rs. 50 lakh. His factory was ransacked by a crowd before being blown up by dynamite. 'I have decided to shift to Malawi in Africa. The African nations are notorious for their security, but is there any safety in this country any more?' asks Kuskiwala.

Equally grave is the altering demographic profile of the state. Makeshift camps for displaced Muslims dot the state's towns—Dohad, Lunawada, Godhra and Chhotta-Udepur in central Gujarat, Modasa and Khedbrahma in north Gujarat, and in other places.

...For compounding the Muslims' problems is the campaign calling for an economic boycott of the community. As part of the crusade, a large number of leaflets are being circulated in the state. Without any mention of the publisher's name, they urge the Hindus to save their religion and country by severing economic dealings with the Muslims 'in order to teach them a lesson'. They warn against employing Muslims, buying from them or selling to them. Though the Gujarat VHP leaders deny having published the leaflet, they add that the prevailing atmosphere is a natural corollary. More worrisome is the support that the campaign is gaining among the Hindus this time in sharp contrast to the past when calls for a similar boycott were ignored by the majority community. 'The Muslims find themselves at a dead end,' says J.V. Momin, a senior Congress leader.

Says Mohammed Ali, a member of the Shia Chelia community that was seldom attacked in previous Hindu-Muslim riots: 'There is a complete crisis of confidence in the Muslim community.' Ali is one of the fortunate few whose restaurant in Ahmedabad escaped destruction.

A large number of restaurants and hotels that were torched in the riots belonged to Shia Chelias who have traditionally maintained a low profile on controversial issues choosing instead to concentrate on their thriving commercial interests. Much like the Dawoodi Bohras, who too suffered an immense loss of life and property this time.

Speculation is rife on the reason for the attacks on this section of the community. A moderate Muslim leader from the Congress says that activities of the fundamentalist groups, both at the national and the state levels are partially responsible for the intense and widespread reaction...."

This issue was dated 25th March, 2002, covering incidences till 14th March, 2002. But the reporter, Uday Maḥurkar, does not give us the slightest clue as to when all these attacks took place, unlike all his other reports in *India Today* on this issue. There is a strong possibility that he was merely giving details of the anti-Muslim riots that occurred on 28th February, 1st and 2nd March, 2002.

Now, let us see Uday Mahurkar's report in the weekly dated 22nd April, 2002: "...take Sanjeli. In the carnage that ensued after the February 27 Godhra killings, 8,000 armed tribals descended on the town of 8,000 in the tribal heartland of Dahod district. Bows, stones and gunshots rained on the fleeing Muslims, killing 15. The police intervention meant another 2,500 were spared a savage death. Today, all the 450 Muslim houses in Sanjeli are destroyed, the town sanitised of Muslims, almost all of whom were followers of the radical missionary group, Tableeghi Jamaat. The village mosque run by the Jamaat is wrecked; at the nearby *madarsa* torn and burnt books are strewn all over the floor.

In an identical display of insanity, around 7,000 armed tribals marched into Bodeli town in Chhotta-Udepur tribal area of Vadodara district intent on massacring the Muslims who had taken shelter there after being driven out of the neighbouring villages.... Tragedy was also averted by the police and army at Viramgam town near Ahmedabad where over 15,000 Hindus, mostly armed OBC Thakores, burnt 250 Muslim houses. The attack has caused large-scale Muslim migration.

It is an occurrence new to the country. Hundreds of villages in rural areas of central and north Gujarat, particularly in the tribal belt, have been wiped clean of Muslims by the tribals and OBC Hindus.

'Riots have largely been an urban phenomenon in India,' says political analyst, Vidyut Thakar. 'What is intriguing is that for the first time mobs have attacked Muslims in rural areas, particularly in the tribal belt.'

Of the more than 800 people killed in rioting (140 in police firing), nearly 150 people have died in tribal-related violence in the state, over 90 per cent of them Muslims. Combined with the violence unleashed by OBC Thakores in rural areas, the toll is 400. Brutalised Muslims now stationed at camps in Dahod and Jhalod are also bewildered at the unexpected magnitude of reaction in small towns." (*The Times of India* dated 7th March, 2002 also reported the tribals' involvement in the riots).

The report "Godhra and After" of the Justice Tewatia Committee quoted earlier says:

"Earlier in Gujarat, tribals never got involved in the Hindu- Muslim riots. However, their involvement in post-Godhra riots added a new dimension to the communal violence. In rural areas the vanvasis (i.e. tribals) attacked the Muslim moneylenders, shopkeepers and the forest contractors. They used their traditional bows and arrows as also their implements used to cut the trees and grass while attacking Muslims. They moved in groups and used coded signals for communication. Two factors seem to have contributed to this disturbing phenomenon:

1. A delegation of tribals told the Study Team that the Muslim moneylenders, shopkeepers and forest contractors have been exploiting the tribals for decades. They charged exorbitant rate of interest to money loaned to tribals. In certain cases, the rate of interest is as high as 50 per cent per year. Having got into this never-ending vicious circle of loans, the tribals have been reduced to the status of bounded labour. Tribals working as servants are ill-treated by these moneylenders, who happen to be Muslims. The accumulated anger of years of exploitation became explosive when moneylenders sexually exploited their womenfolk. The tribals are no longer allowed to use forest produce that has been their sustenance for centuries. This too fuelled the feelings of anger, hatred and revenge among them.

2. Tribals have, of late, become conscious of their Hindu identity because of the awareness campaign launched by VHP and other Hindu outfits. Burning alive of Hindu pilgrims by a Muslim mob at Godhra provided the spark for the fire of revenge and hatred."

Muslims suffered at the hands of the tribals in Gujarat. There is no doubt that Muslims suffered far more than the Hindus in Gujarat, in the riots of 2002 AD. There were unprovoked (not unprovoked, Godhra was the cause. But unprovoked by Muslim attacks on houses) as well as retaliatory attacks on Muslims. In this report, Uday Mahurkar admits that out of the 800-odd deaths in the Gujarat riots then, as many as 140 were due to police firing. Out of the 1,000-odd deaths (952 at that time), 199 were due to police firing, a record of sorts to see nearly 20 per cent people being killed in police firing.

As one makes a thorough analysis of the Gujarat riots, one finds out that there were two instances of large-scale anti- Muslim riots in Gujarat, after Godhra. Both were in Ahmedabad. One was the killing of former Congress Lok Sabha MP from Ahmedabad, Ehsan Jafri, and the other was the attack on Muslims in Ahmedabad's Naroda-Patiya area.

Ehsan Jafri Case

This was one of the most publicized cases in the Gujarat riots. Many writers have given contrasting and completely different reports on this case. The estimates of the number of the people who attacked Jafri's house have ranged from 3,000 to 20,000. Now the official number of people killed has been given—which is 68 apart from Jafri, after all missing were declared dead (39 were killed and 30 missing were declared dead).

On 28th February Ehsan Jafri fired on the Hindu crowd injuring 15 people in the mob and killing one, according to the SIT closure report on page 1. Whether he should have fired in self-defense or not is a matter of debate. However, after this act of Jafri, the situation rapidly deteriorated and Jafri was done to death along with many others. However, a close analysis of this case will reveal that no rapes of women took place in this case at all. Reports of the then English newspapers like *The Hindu, The Indian Express* and *The Times of India* did not make the slightest mention of anyone being raped. But later, a section of the media concocted imaginary tales of women being raped and killed and the biased writers had the time of their lives in concocting imaginary detailed stories and lies.

One only needs to read English newspapers like *The Indian Express* who reported this incident in the first week of March 2002 to understand the real situation. Here is what *India Today* reports (18th March, 2002):

"I never saw such a huge mob—they burnt alive my husband," Zakia Nasin, wife of a former MP, Ahmedabad

Ehsan Jafri, a former MP, living in Ahmedabad's Gulmarg Society, began calling the police at 8:30 a.m. His wife, Zakia Nasin was worried—they lived in a Hindu area—but Jafri had faith in his neighbours, who had called to warn him of mobs. By noon, a hostile crowd was pelting stones and Jafri's pleas went unheeded. The ex- MP began calling politician friends, but it was of no use. The mob swelled to about 5,000 and began throwing burning tyres. Jafri sent his family upstairs while he stood at the gate. "That was the last time we saw Jafrisaab," says Zakia, **who denies he used his gun.** The police arrived at 5:00 p.m. after the mob had razed the complex. His neighbours showed that they deserved his faith—the mob was not local—and dozens of residents lost their lives with him."

However, there is a factual error here. This same weekly says in this same issue that: "Reinforcements did arrive—but by that time, the mob had swelled to 10,000" and that "Police shot dead five people outside his house". Then how can they say that police arrived at 5:00 p.m.? The police saved 180+ Muslims in this episode. And Zakia Jafri's claim that he did not use his gun reveals her lie, if the report giving her denial is correct. Even a Congress loyalist weekly *Outlook* admitted that Jafri did fire on the crowd. *India Today* and *Times of India* also admitted it, and so did many Muslim witnesses. We have also seen the report of *The Times of India* posted online at 2:34 p.m. which says that the police fired on the Hindu crowd in Chamanpura, injuring six, of whom at least 3 were critical (ultimately five died). The SIT report also says on page 1 that the police lathi-charged the mob, fired 124 rounds and burst 134 tear gas shells, which resulted in death of 4 Hindus and injuries to 11. This is hardly consistent with claims of an 'inactive police force'.

The *Human Rights Watch* in its report says:

"Thirty-eight-year-old Mehboob Mansoori lost eighteen family members in the attack at the Gulmarg Society. He described the day's sequence of events to Human Rights Watch (full testimony in introduction):

They burnt my whole family. At 10:30 a.m. the stone pelting started. First, there were 200 people, then 500 from all over, then more. We were 200-250 people. **We pelted stones in self-defence**.... Early in the day, at 10:30 a.m., the Police Commissioner came over and said not to worry. He spoke to Jafri and said something would work out and then he left. The name of the Commissioner of Police that visited in the morning is P.C. Pandey, Commissioner of Police Ahmedabad...."

Actually, the testimony of this witness is a poorly constructed story. S.K. Modi, in his book *Godhra: The Missing Rage,* had quoted this story and completely dismantled it. But the Police Commissioner P.C.Pandey has denied that he visited Jafri's place in the SIT report. The SIT report says on page 201 that it is conclusively established that P C Pandey did not meet Jafri in the Gulberg Society in the forenoon of 28 February. It also says on the same page that Mr. Ambalal Nadia had come to meet the late Ehsan Jafri at Gulberg Society at about 10 am and he left at 10:30 am. The statement of this witness, Mehboob Mansoori, that "We were 200-250 people" and the fact that 68 were killed along with Jafri, shows that the police did save more than 180 Muslims here.

Uday Mahurkar also writes on the same subject in the same issue of *India Today*: "…In Chamanpura area, where nearly 40 persons, including former Congress MP, Ehsan Jafri and his family members were killed, there were just a few armed guards when the crowd began assembling. Reinforcements did arrive but, by that time, the mob had swelled to 10,000 and even though police firing killed at least five persons on the spot—in all, police firing led to 40 deaths in Ahmedabad alone—it didn't stop the carnage. The situation was aggravated further by Jafri firing from his revolver on the mob, injuring seven. Others in the housing complex are said to have thrown acid bulbs too…"

This was in Gulberga locality. Large-scale killings had also taken place in Ahmedabad's Naroda-Patiya area. But again, Uday Mahurkar admits that out of around 40 deaths in Gulbarga, at least five were shot dead by the police. He also admits that police firing killed as many as 40 people in Ahmedabad alone (also reported by *The Times of India*). And this same weekly ignores these very reports these days and calls the Gujarat riots as a 'pogrom' or a 'massacre' of Muslims.

India Today also reported on the killings at Naroda- Patiya: "…in a siege of untempered hatred, 5,000 mindless marauders bore down on 200 families, undeserving victims of their faith…. That evening, the police in Naroda-Patia counted 27 charred bodies, among the 73 trapped to their deaths in a 60 sq.ft. alley…"

In fact, in this report, *India Today* alleges that a woman's womb was cut open and foetus taken out and then she was killed. But we will see in Chapter 7, Myth 16 that nothing like this happened. ***India Today* too can be sued for defamation and infuriation of Muslims because of this report.** At least, it should have checked the doctor's post-mortem report, which he made on 2nd March, 2002. These two were the major incidents of anti-Muslim riots in Gujarat. This report was also in its issue dated 18-03- 2002.

The Hindu dated 20th August, 2004 reported that while appearing before the G.T. Nanavati and K.G. Shah Judicial Inquiry Commission, probing into the Godhra train carnage and the post-Godhra communal riots (Former

Inspector of Naroda) Mr. K.K. Mysorewala said he had also seen a senior Bajrang Dal leader, Babu Bajrangi, in Naroda- Patiya locality in the afternoon, talking to the people but did not know what role he played.

Mr. Mysorewala blamed the attack in Naroda-Patiya on the "brutal killing" of a Hindu youth, Ranjit Vanjhara, behind a mosque and the reckless driving of a Muslim truck driver in which a Hindu was killed and two others were injured. Rumours were spread in connection with the two incidents that added fuel to the communal fire. Hindus attacked a mosque and later the Muslim houses in the locality.

This report also shows that it may well have been 'provocation', something even in addition to Godhra, responsible for the Naroda- Patiya killings. *The Telegraph* of 2nd March, 2002 also reports that. But no provocation can justify killings of innocent people. But along with 95 killings, 900 Muslims' lives were saved there. Police firing killed 2 people here, according to Mysorewala.

Third Case of Anti-Muslim Riots

In Pandarwada village in Panchmahal district, 27 Muslims were burnt— after rumours that three Hindus had been attacked. *The Hindu's* report was: "A Baroda report said 30 persons were burnt alive today at Pandarwada village in Panchmahal district of Gujarat, official sources said here. Curfew has been imposed in the area and Rapid Action Force personnel have been deployed." *The Telegraph* reported on 2nd March, 2002: "An agency report suggested vengeance for the death of three persons (i.e. Hindus) earlier in the day as the motive for the attack at Pandarwada, 70 km from Godhra."

Similarly, around 30 Muslims were also killed in Sadarpura. *The Telegraph* reported on 3rd March, 2002 on this issue: "Trouble erupted in Sadarpura town in Mehsana district last night after some members of the minority community gathered in a house, apparently out of insecurity. But the word spread that they were planning an attack. Soon a mob surrounded the house. **A police patrol opened fire, killing one person....** At least 27 people were burnt alive and several injured."

Thus, in brief, the suffering of the Muslims can be seen as:

1. A total of 790 Muslims were killed in the riots after Godhra and a total of 223 people were missing as per the UPA Government's figures given on 11 May 2005. But after the 7-year-period expired and all the missing were declared dead in February 2009, the official figure given was 1,180 with 228 missing people assumed dead up from 952 earlier. This was reported by all English newspapers on 1ˢᵗ March, 2009. But, 101 missing people were later found alive and hence the total number of missing people is only 127. **Finally, ex-gratia was paid to 1,169 people by both the Gujarat Government and the UPA Government, which gave a special package for Gujarat riot victims in May 2008.** Let us believe, for the time being, the figures of 790 Muslims and 254 Hindus given by UPA in the Parliament on 11ᵗʰ May, 2005.

2. In Naroda-Patiya, after the revised figures of February 2009, a total of 95 people (mostly Muslims) were declared dead instead of the earlier figure of 84. In Naroda Gram, 11 people were killed—most likely all Muslims except Ghanshyam Patel, the earlier figure was nine.

3. In the Gulbarga Society case, in which Ehsan Jafri was killed, 68 others also lost their lives, perhaps all Muslims.

4. In Pandarwada village, 27 people were burnt alive as per the reports of *The Hindu* and *The Indian Express*.

5. In Ahmedabad, the *dargah* of the Sufi saint-poet, Wali Gujarati in Shahibaug and the 16ᵗʰ century Gumte Masjid mosque in Isanpur were destroyed. The Muhafiz Khan Masjid at Gheekanta was ransacked. The police records list 298 *dargahs*, 205 mosques, 17 temples and three churches as damaged in the months of March and April. This was as per the report of *The Times of India* dated 28ᵗʰ April, 2002, written by Sanjay Pandey.

6. Over 1 lakh Muslims were rendered homeless apart from 40000 Hindus.

7. An estimated loss of 3,000 crores was suffered by the Muslims as per the community leaders' estimates reported by *India Today*.

Thus, after Godhra, Muslims suffered in Gujarat. We have, by and large, seen the real major cases of rioting. The causes of the minority communities too should be raised. And what should be told is the whole truth.

CHAPTER 7

CONCOCTED LIES AND MYTHS BY THE MEDIA

By now, we have seen much of the reality of the post-Godhra riots. The media, by and large, continues to report in the same manner, and does not reveal the truth. In this chapter, let us see some of the malicious lies circulated on this subject for the past many years.

Myth 1: 2,000 Muslims were Killed in the Gujarat Riots

Fact: As per figures given by the then Union Minister of State for Home, Shriprakash Jaiswal, who belongs to the Congress Party, **in Parliament** on 11th May, 2005, that too in a WRITTEN REPLY, 790 Muslims and 254 Hindus were killed in the riots, 2,548 people were injured and 223 people were missing. The report placed the number of riot-affected widows at 919 and the number of children orphaned at 606. The UPA Government, which was a staunch opponent of Narendra Modi gave these figures, and, hence, they themselves could be inflated as there have been many occasions of massive exaggeration by several leaders of the UPA coalition on this issue many times. (*Source*: http://www.expressindia.com/news/fullstory.php?newsid=46538).

Even Indian Muslims' English newspaper *Milli Gazette* also reported this (*Source*: http://www.milligazette.com/Archives/2005/01-15June05-Print-Edition/011506200511.htm).

The editorials of many Indian national English dailies, and the articles published from the freelancers and others on the Indian and global newspapers' editorial pages carried a pack of lies for many years with an exaggerated death toll mentioned. Newspapers like *The Times of India*, *The Hindustan Times*, etc. published articles saying, "Win in Assembly elections of December 2002 does not whitewash Narendra Modi's sins of the Gujarat pogrom of 2002 when 2,000 innocent Muslims were butchered" or "The Gujarat pogrom of killing thousands of Muslims did not help the BJP in the long term", etc.

All these numbers again came into the picture when Narendra Modi was denied a US diplomatic visa in March 2005 by the USA and his earlier tourist visa, issued in 1998 was revoked just one day before his scheduled visit to the USA. Why the USA took as many as three years after the Gujarat riots to revoke Modi's earlier visa was not told. But it shows that Modi had a US visa for as many as 3 years after the 2002 violence.

But these numbers are nothing but a pack of lies. The number of Muslims killed in the post-Godhra riots is inflated and exaggerated to unimaginable levels. Let us see the interview given by the then Gujarat Chief Minister and now the Indian Prime Minister, Narendra Modi to *Aaj Tak*'s Prabhu Chawla, excerpts of which were published in the weekly *India Today*, dated 4th November, 2002:

"Q: Your opponents call you 'Jinnah of the Hindus'.

A: I am hearing this for the first time though I still don't consider you as an enemy.

Q: You are held responsible for the killing of 1,100 innocent people in the riots.

A: In our previous interview, you said 900 people. Now you are saying 1,100. Are you adding all the people killed in other states like Maharashtra and Bengal to Gujarat's account? (Narendra Modi is talking of the Solapur riots of 10th and 11th October, 2002 in Maharashtra and other riots which occurred long after Godhra.)

Q: So what is the correct toll?

A: There would have been no riots in Gujarat if there had been no Godhra.

   ...

Q: Do you accept that you failed to provide security to the people of the state?

A: 98 per cent of Gujarat would not have had peace if we had failed to fulfill our duties. We managed to control the riots within 72 hours.

   ...

Q: Why don't you accept that Gujarat is being defamed because of Narendra Modi?

A: If that is true, give the people of Gujarat a chance to pronounce their verdict through elections." (*Source*: http://www.indiatoday.com/itoday/20021104/conf.shtml#co).

As we see, the number of people killed in the riots jumped from 900 to 1,100 after Narendra Modi's previous interview, i.e. within four months! Now it has jumped from 900 to 2,000. May be after 10 years, at this rate, it will jump to 10,000! Already it is being said that, "Thousands of Muslims were killed in Gujarat" and "3,000 innocent Muslims were butchered in Gujarat".

What These Lies have Done to Well-meaning People

It is generally believed, even in the *Sangh Parivar*, that the post-Godhra riots were one-sided. Even a correspondent of RSS weekly *Organiser* once believed the bluff that 2,000 Muslims were killed in the riots. He actually reported: "Over 2,000 Muslims were killed *in Ahmedabad*". Many leaders of BJP seem to be blatantly ignorant of the truth of the Gujarat riots. Whenever Congress leaders or anti-BJP journalists raise the issue of the Gujarat riots on TV, some BJP leaders often fail to give befitting reply. They falter in speech. They merely try to point out that the Gujarati electorate gave a huge mandate to the BJP and to Narendra Modi in the December 2002 Gujarat Assembly polls, and mention the Godhra incident as a cause of the riots. Many of them don't point out any instance of Muslim aggression, sufferings of the Hindus in the riots, police firing deaths, or the fact that less than 90 places out of 18,600 saw riots. This could be because of ignorance and blind belief on media lies.

After many terrorist attacks, like the bomb blasts in various Indian cities (e.g. Ahmedabad in July 2008), the Indian English media rationalized the deed on grounds of the 'Gujarat riots'. The Gujarat riots were the result of the Godhra massacre. A large section of the English media rationalized Godhra (as a response to the *Ramjanmabhoomi* i.e. the Ayodhya movement), did not justify or rationalize the post-Godhra riots (which were the direct result of Godhra) where Muslims were killed and ignored the killings of the Hindus, and it tried to and tries to de-link post-Godhra and Godhra. And it rationalizes and/or justifies the (so-called) 'reaction' to the post-Godhra riots.

The very fact that some terrorists claim that they "plan to avenge the Gujarat riots" clearly shows the devastating consequences of the media lies. A large section of the media lied about Gujarat riots being a 'pogrom' and instigated innocent Muslims to terrorism. In March 2005, the Pakistan cricket team was on a tour to India. It refused to play a Test match in Ahmedabad on 'political' grounds, i.e. for 'the killings of Muslims' in that city. All this is clearly the result of stark lies concocted in the media for many years. All these lies and myths need to be thoroughly exposed.

That the UPA Government, with Congress President and Italian-born and staunchly anti-BJP Sonia Gandhi (1946-) as the UPA chief, and Communists as outside supporters, gave the figure of 790 Muslims and 254 Hindus killed in the Gujarat riots **inside the Parliament** is something worth pondering about. These figures themselves could be exaggerated given as they are by a staunch opponent of BJP. This was in a WRITTEN REPLY, i.e. the government knew fully well what it was doing. It was in response to a question asked by a Congress member of the Rajya Sabha and Babri Masjid Action Committee lawyer, R.K. Anand. The compensation paid by the Gujarat Government shows 1169 deaths [It is said that these 1169 include 863 Muslims and 306 Hindus but this could not be independently verified by me]. The UPA Government also gave a special additional package of 3.5 lakh rupees to the Gujarat riot victims in 2008, also to the same number- 1169. UPA Government would have given compensation to all those killed in the riots, and there is no way it would not have given to the kin of any dead, so it shows that the correct figure of people killed is around 1169.

India Today reported in its issue dated 20 May 2002, when the riots had almost stopped that "Total dead—972". Out of these 972, *India Today* included 57 people killed in Godhra, i.e. 915 after Godhra. If anyone sees the English newspapers of those days, i.e. between 10 and 21 May, 2002, no riots took place in Gujarat in those 10 days and the Army began leaving Gujarat on 21st May. A maximum of 20 more deaths might have happened in Gujarat after that. The death toll in Gujarat riots would, thus, be 935. I myself recall reading in English daily *The Hitavada* that 936 people were killed in the Gujarat riots after the Army left Ahmedabad on 21st May, 2002. The official figures, before the missing were declared dead were 952. http://www.telegraphindia. com/1090301/jsp/nation/story_10608005.jsp

But let us, for argument's sake, assume that the figures given by the UPA Government are correct. Does that give anyone the reason to believe that more than 790 Muslims were killed in Gujarat? Why should some of the English dailies and the 24-hour news channels lie through the skin of their teeth that 2,000 Muslims were killed in Gujarat? A total of 127 people are said to be missing (After finding 101 people alive). Out of them, how many are Hindus is also not told. The maximum number of people thus killed in Gujarat, assuming that all the missing are dead, would thus amount to 1171 i.e. 790+254+127=1171. There is no scope for anyone in the world, including the human rights organisations and religious freedom groups and the TV channels like NDTV and company to report that one more than 1171 people was killed in the Gujarat riots.

Despite this, Prafull Bidwai, a self-proclaimed secularist wrote in the English daily, *The Hitavada*'s Sunday magazine, *Insight* in July 2006 soon after the Mumbai blasts that killed 187 people in the city, that, "VHP, Bajrang Dal and the BJP butchered 2,000 Muslims in Gujarat". And he was not the only one. NDTV repeated many times during the Lok Sabha elections of April-May 2004 that "2,000 Muslims were killed in Gujarat".

2,000 is the number of Muslims who carried out the massacre and gruesome roasting alive of 59 Hindus, including 25 women and 15

children in Godhra. It is not the number of Muslims who were killed in the subsequent riots. There is no justification for violence and of even a single death, be it in Godhra or after Godhra. But why lie through the skin of your teeth that 2,000 Muslims were killed when 790 were killed? **Who gains by these lies?** And it is everybody's duty to correct the figure. The point is: what should be reported is the truth, the whole truth and nothing but the truth.

Burkha Dutt of NDTV tried to keep the number of Hindus killed as low as possible in 2002. In one of her talk shows, she said: "The *karsevaks* killed in Godhra—-what's the number, 53 or 57....." The correct number is 59, the numbers given by self-proclaimed secularists reveal their attitude which we have seen in the second chapter, which is of trying to reduce Muslims' fanaticism and Hindus' suffering as much as possible. And it is this mentality which is responsible for them exaggerating the number of Muslims killed in the riots to as much as possible. When the total number of people killed in the riots, Hindu as well as Muslim, is 1169, they lie that 2,000 Muslims were killed in the riots like former Pakistan President Pervez Musharraf did in the United Nations in September 2002. Teesta Setalvad increased this number to 2,500 Muslims (as if not a single Hindu was killed) in one of her articles titled "What Ails Gujarat?" published in CPI(M) party weekly *People's Democracy* in its issue of 16th July, 2006.

(*Source*: http:// pd.cpim.org/2006/0716/07162006 teesta.htm).

And *Tehelka* reported in 2007 after its sting operation that 2,500 Muslims were killed in the first three days, impling that many more were killed in the further days of riots! This reveals the mentality of increasing Muslims' suffering as much as possible in reporting.

Myth 2: Muslims were like cattle hiding from the slaughter house

Fact: Of course, Muslims were killed in one-sided attacks in many places in the state like in Naroda-Patiya, Gulberg Society, Naroda Gram, Sadarpura, Pandarwada, Ode and other places but by and large, the riots were not one-sided and Muslims were hardly the cattle hiding from the slaughter house. As we have seen in a couple of earlier chapters, some Muslims were equally on the offensive, at least after the first three days. Muslims attacked Hindus brutally in Himmatnagar, Danilimda, Sindhi Market and other areas of Ahmedabad. Reports of *The Indian Express* and *The Times of India* show that Muslims drove out Hindus from their houses, and started some riots. *India Today's* report on this subject in its issue dated 15th April, 2002 also points out this same thing.

Around 40,000 Hindus were forced to take shelter in the refugee camps. The Dalits suffered horribly in the riots at the hands of Muslims. On 21st March, 2002, 50 Hindu shops were burnt in Ahmedabad's Revdi Bazaar that caused a loss of 15 crore rupees. Some Muslims are on record starting as many as 157 riots in Gujarat after 3rd March, 2002. They did not allow the police and the Army to search for criminals in their areas. They pelted the police and even the Army with bullets and stones, when they arrived to conduct search operations in Muslim areas. The residents formed human chains and cut off power at night so that the criminals could flee with weapons from the Army according to *India Today* weekly report's implication.

Many judgments of different courts in Gujarat have sentenced some Muslims for rioting in Ahmedabad and Vadodara, post-Godhra. On one occasion, seven Muslims and on another occasion, nine Muslims were convicted and punished for rioting and killing post-Godhra. This will be seen in detail later. The conviction of Muslims proves that some Muslims were equally on the offensive.

Myth 3: Whole of Gujarat was burning

Fact: Out of the state's 18,600 villages, 240 municipal towns, and 25 district headquarters, maximum 90 places saw riots. If one includes the two big cities of Ahmedabad and Vadodara, by the wildest stretch of imagination, only 2 per cent of the state can be assumed to have been burning. Had the State Government been involved in the riots, or wanted to encourage the riots, it could have created riots in 10,000 out of Gujarat's 18,600 villages. In the past, curfew has been placed in 300 villages at the same time. As compared to that, very little happened in 2002.

We have seen in Chapter 3 how one-third of Gujarat, i.e. Saurashtra and Kutch were untouched by the riots even in the first 3 days. Also only 7 out of 25 districts of Gujarat saw any major violence. Remaining 18 were less affected or untouched by riots, according to official records. We have seen Narendra Modi's interview to NDTV- Star News' Pankaj Pachouri of around 6 December 2002 to know the reality. These malicious lies were exposed during the Gujarat Assembly elections of December 2002. After the BJP's huge victory in Gujarat in December 2002, the media largely again ignored these facts and implied that the whole of Gujarat was burning.

Myth 4: The Gujarat Police Turned a Blind Eye to the Rioting

Fact: Even though the situation was terrible, the police performed its work extremely efficiently. The police force was woefully insufficient. We have seen *India Today* (18th March 2002) report the strength of the Ahmedabad Police (6000 in all, with 1500 armed) and the size of the mobs on 28 February in the 3rd Chapter. We have also seen *The Times of India* report, "The sparse police presence looked like a drop in the ocean of violence." This was despite the deployment of the entire police force. *The Hindu* also reported the next day that on 28th February **"Mob fury reached its crescendo"** and "**The situation seemed to slip out of hand**" and "**Police were outnumbered by the rioters**". Same was the report of *The Telegraph, The Tribune.* We have also seen *The Times of India* say that neither the Army nor the shoot-at-sight orders could control violence on 1st March, 2002 when it was much less than 28th February (Thursday). If even the Army and shoot-at-sight orders could not stop the violence when it was much less, then what must have been the situation on 28th February when the Army was not present in the day and the violence was much more?

Despite this, 5450 rounds were fired in the first three days alone and 6,500 tear gas shells burst. Official records now show that 5450 rounds and not 4000 rounds were fired in the first 3 days. As many as 98 people were shot dead by the police in the first 3 days, majority of whom are Hindus. For the complete period of rioting, despite the presence of the Army for 73 out of 74 days, as many as 15,369 tear gas shells were burst, and a total of 10,559 rounds were fired. Out of the total people killed in the riots, 199 have been killed in police firing- 101 of them in the first week.

In fact, the encyclopedia Wikipedia reported, based on sound sources that as many as 200 policemen laid their lives trying to quell the violence during the riots. I feel this number is impossible. **Official records show that 83 officers, 419 men and 50 Home Guard were injured- total 552 injured.** The number of deaths is not given.

Out of the 25,486 accused, the Gujarat police arrested as many as 25,204 people as of October 2005. The Gujarat police saved as many as 2,500 Muslims in Sanjeli, a town in North Gujarat, 5,000 Muslims in Bodeli, in Vadodara and at least 10,000 Muslims in Viramgam. A total of at least 24,000 Muslims were saved. Police officials themselves suffered injuries in trying to save the Muslims.

Myth 5: Gujarat Police was Anti-Muslim

Fact: Far from it, the police was slow to act on Muslim fanatics for fear of being called 'anti-Muslim' by the media. Out of the total killed in police firing in Gujarat, majority were Hindus in the first three days (about 60 out of 98). As on 6th April, 2002, out of the 126 people killed in police firing, 77 were Hindus. Until 18th April, 2002, more Hindus were killed in police firing than Muslims. Hindus were on the offensive for perhaps three out of the 74 days while Muslims were on the offensive perhaps for 73 out of the 74 days. On the first day, i.e. 28th February, 2002, 17 people were killed in police firing of whom 11 were Hindus. Muslims attacked Hindus in places like Bapunagar and Jamalpur areas of Ahmedabad on 28 Feb. On the second and third days, both Hindus and Muslims were attacking each other, and, hence, both were killed in police firing. Actually, since there was a large-scale killing of Muslims in 4-5 places—Naroda-Patiya, Ehsan Jafri case, Sadarpura and Pandarwada and the mobs were out of control, police could not kill many in firing in these cases. Since there was a ferocious Muslim backlash from 1st March 2002 and the situation was not out of control when Muslims attacked, they were also killed in police firing. As of 27 April 2002 the figures were 77 to 80 Hindus and 93 Muslims killed in police firing, and the bigger number of Muslims killed is explained above.

On some occasions, some Muslims greeted the police, and also the army, with bullets and turned off the power supply and made life hell, and also started riots and accused the police of being biased, when the police came to search for armories in Muslim areas. For the fear of being labelled anti-Muslim, the police failed to do their duty.

India Today, in its issue dated 20 May, 2002, clearly admits that, far from being anti-Muslim, the Gujarat police did not act speedily against Muslim fanatics and rioters, for fear of being called anti-Muslim by the media. It says: "A series of attacks on policemen by Muslims has further added to the lack of faith. Now, strapped with the anti-Muslim label, the police has been slow in acting against Muslim fanatics". (*Source: http://archives. digitaltoday.in/ indiatoday/20020520/states2.html*).

The police arrested nearly 10,000 Hindus for rioting and nearly 18,000 as preventive arrests as of 28 April 2002, as per *The Times of India.* Finally there were 4274 cases registered, i.e. FIRs and the number of people arrested was 19,200 Hindus and 7,799 Muslims to get a total of 26,999 i.e. almost 27,000 arrests. This is slightly different from October 2005 when 25,204 were arrested. Moreover, the prosecution of the police was so efficient that until September 2012, at least 443 people have been convicted in Gujarat—out of whom at least 332 are Hindus and 111 Muslims in cases of Godhra and rioting as per official records.

Myth 6: Gujarat Riots were the 'Worst-Ever Massacre' in India

Fact: Gujarat riots of 2002 A.D. were far less serious as compared to Gujarat's past riots of 1969 A.D. And they were again far less as compared to pre-Independence riots of the 1940s in Ahmedabad, when the Hindu community took a sound beating. There were also riots of a large scale in Gujarat in 1980, 1982, 1985 (very big ones), 1990 and 1992.

Much worse riots took place in New Delhi in 1984 under the Congress Party's rule. Officially, 3,000 people were killed. Riots were also not limited to New Delhi then. They occurred in far-off places like West Bengal, Tripura as well. Killings of more than 40,000 Indians have happened in Jammu and Kashmir State of India since 1989. As compared to that, less than 1,200 people were killed in Gujarat in 2002 A.D., for the sins of 2,000 attackers of Godhra. Out of them, more than 250 are Hindus. Post-Godhra riots were neither 'pogrom', nor 'genocide', nor 'massacre'. They were not even 'massacre', not to talk of the 'worst-ever massacre in India'. Despite this, self-proclaimed secularists like Teesta Setalvad, Harsh Mander, Amulya Ganguly, Prafull Bidwai and others like *Tehelka*, political opponents, etc. have called the 2002 riots as 'Gujarat massacre' and said that there was "Gujarat massacre of Muslims with the sanction of Narendra Modi". Some people have demanded action against Modi. Far from any action being taken against Modi, action needs to be taken against stark liars—there was no "massacre" in the 2002 riots but plain Hindu-Muslim riots. Hundreds of Hindus were also killed by Muslims even after the gruesome and horrific roasting of 59 Hindus including 25 women and 15 children in Godhra. 40,000 Hindus were thrown out of their homes by Muslims, despite comprising only 11 per cent of the population, and that too in a state ruled by a party like the BJP with a man like Narendra Modi as Chief Minister. That is, Muslims had the strength to **throw out 40,000 Hindus from their homes in a Hindu country like India even after the Partition of India in 1947 and Muslims getting a homeland and that too under Modi's rule.**

The worst-ever massacre was of the Hindus during the medieval times. Timur massacred some 1 lakh Hindus on a single day in Delhi in 1399. Nadirshah, the invader, massacred many people in 1739 in Delhi. The massacres of Hindus in medieval India would have put Hitler's Nazi death-chambers of the 1930s to shame. These massacres happened under all the medieval rulers of India including Akbar (who ruled from 1556-1605 AD), who ordered killing of 30,000 Hindus in February 1568. Mahmud of Ghazni also massacred many Hindus in between 1001 and 1027 A.D. So did all others. The invaders were like a cloud of locusts destroying and devouring everything on their way. We have seen a very very brief and cursory list of Muslim attacks on India in Chapter 1. Swami Vivekananda opined that more than 40 crore (400 million) Hindus were killed in medieval times by Muslims 'since the historian Farishta reported that Hindus are 600 million and today (around 1900)we are only 200 million'.

Pakistan and Bangladesh were also parts of India and the Hindu population in Pakistan has declined from 20 per cent in 1947 to around 1 per cent now—perhaps the biggest unreported genocide, massacre and holocaust in recent times. While in medieval India, Hindus, in the face of extreme cruelty and death, saved Hinduism from onslaughts of foreign invaders, in the modern, progressive age they suffered the worst damage with Hindus thrown 'to the mercy of wolves'. The Indian media and the government did nothing to raise this issue with Pakistan. Similarly, the Hindu population in Bangladesh has declined from 34 per cent in 1901 to 29 per cent in 1947, to just 10 per cent in 2001. Even in India, the Hindu population has declined from 85 per cent in 1951 to 80.5 per cent in 2001. The 'liberals' in the Indian media— human rights activists, and even the Government have never ever raised this near-complete disappearence of Hindus from Pakistan ever in the world. On the contrary, Islamists have exaggerated and inflated the case of Gujarat riots, along with the Indian media, and whitewashed Islamic fanaticism in annihilating Hinduism in Pakistan and Bangladesh, and also Kashmir.

Pakistan's tallest Hindu leader, Sudham Chand Chawla was killed in broad daylight in Jacobabad on 29th January, 2002 while returning from his rice mill. The culprits were not punished. He had, in fact, been complaining to the civil society of Pakistan for years about the threat to his life, to the Human Rights Commission of Pakistan and yet nobody did anything. If this was the case with the biggest Hindu leader, then what must be the story of ordinary Hindus, who have already been reduced from 20 per cent in 1947 to just 1 per cent now? (*Source*: http://www.sudhamchandchawla.com).

Looking at the modern, independent India, these riots were still nothing as compared to many other incidents of violence. The worst-ever massacre in independent India was of the Hindus in Kashmir, which continues till date. Then there were the 1984 riots, when the Sikhs were massacred by the ruling Congress Party's supporters. In Bhagalpur, Bihar, under the Congress rule itself, more than 1,000 people were killed, majority of whom were Muslims, after Muslims allegedly threw bombs on Hindu localities in 1989. There were killings in Assam in 1983 resulting in more than 2100 deaths.

Myth 7: Only Muslims were Rendered Homeless and Suffered Economically

Fact: As early as 5th March, 2002, out of the 98 relief/refugee camps set up in the state, 85 were for the Muslims and 13 were for the Hindus. As on

17th March, 2002, as per the report of *The Times of India,* more than 10,000 Hindus were rendered homeless in Ahmedabad alone. As on 25th April, 2002, out of the 1 lakh 40 thousand refugees, some 1 lakh (i.e. 100 thousand) were Muslims and 40 thousand were Hindus. *The Indian Express* devoted two full reports exclusively to Hindu victims of Ahmedabad. Dalits were attacked by Muslims in Ahmedabad and were rendered homeless. *The Indian Express* dated 7th May, 2002 and 10th May, 2002 gave two reports on the plight of Hindu victims. We have also seen the report titled "Riots Hit All Classes, People of All Faith" of *The Times of India* dated 18 March 2002 which said: "**Contrary to popular belief that only Muslims have been affected in the recent riots, more than 10,000 people belonging to the Hindu community have also become homeless**". This was the case only in Ahmedabad. What happened to Hindus in other cities like Vadodara was not told. This report also indicates that Muslims attacked Hindus unprovoked on 28th February itself in some areas of Ahmedabad. The Hindus who were living in minority in Muslim-dominated areas of Ahmedabad suffered horribly. The Dalits suffered heavily at the hands of Muslims.

The Hindus also suffered economically. *The Tribune* dated 30th April, 2002 reports looting of at least 36 Hindu shops by Muslims in Vadodara. As per the reports of none other than *The Times of India*, as many as 50 Hindu shops were torched in the Revdi Bazaar area of Ahmedabad on 21st March, 2002 by Muslims. The financial loss was as much as 15 crore rupees. Many more Hindu shops were looted in the rest of Gujarat too.

Myth 8: The Gujarat Government was Involved in the Riots

Fact: Gujarat Government of the BJP, headed by Narendra Modi, was blind to the mushrooming of *madrasas* in the state. Not only that, the previous government headed by Keshubhai Patel too was equally blind to the same. From *India Today* we know that it was perhaps because of fear of harming the BJP's newly discovered 'secular' image that the party did nothing to control the *madrasas*. It reported in its issue of 18th March, 2002:

"The general perception is that this was the venting of a latent anti-Muslim sentiment fostered by the unchecked activities of radical Islamic schools in the state. Being debated just as hotly is the question of why the authorities failed to check the blood-letting. Was it because the BJP feared its new-found secular image would suffer if it came down heavily on the fundamentalists? Or was it plain administrative inefficiency?"

So, the BJP did not want to risk losing its 'secular' image. Maybe even if there was no such fear the government would have been neutral and efficient in dealing with riots. But with the NDA allies at stake, 'secular' image at stake, the BJP Government of Gujarat was definitely determined to prevent riots. The government deployed the entire force of 70,000 on 27 Feb itself. Preventive arrests of as many as 827 people were made, shoot-at-sight orders were given in Godhra on 27 Feb, and at other places after 27 Feb. The Rapid Action Force was deployed. We have seen details in Chapter 3.

The Congress Party allegedly instigated riots in the state at least after 21st April, 2002 so as to target Narendra Modi in its *Modi-hatao* campaign as per allegations made which seem to have basis. The Rajya Sabha debated on Gujarat on 6 May 2002. The NDA allies' votes were also going to count. To get NDA allies to vote against the Modi Government, the Congress allegedly wanted the riots on in Gujarat. It perhaps hoped for collapse of the NDA, with allies quitting coalition because of the riots. We will see this in detail later.

Riots in the first three days were all the result of Godhra. But Godhra itself was the brain of some local Muslim Congress leaders. Riots were caused after Godhra by the media and the political leaders' inflammatory response to Godhra. Gujarat Congress chief and former Gujarat Chief Minister (the late) Amarsinh Chaudhary rationalized Godhra on some sort of provocations, i.e. the *karsevaks* not paying for tea and snacks at the Godhra railway platform, which was a figment of imagination. **The Indian Express of 5th March, 2002 reported on Godhra that Congress leaders are accused in Godhra:**

1. **Mehmud Hussain Kalota, convenor of the Congress district minority cell and president of the Godhra municipality.**
2. **Salim Abdul Ghaffar Sheikh, president of the Panchmahal Youth Congress.**
3. **Abdul Rehman Abdul Majid Ghantia, a known Congress worker.**

4. **Faroukh Bhana, secretary of the district Congress committee.**
5. **Haji Bilal, a known Congress worker.**

When 31 people were convicted for the Godhra roasting in February 2011, two Congressmen were given life imprisonment and one was given death penalty out of the above five. Abdul Rehman Abdul Majid Ghantia and Faroukh Bhana got life imprisonment and Haji Bilal got death penalty—three out of these five.

Myth 9: Gujarat Riots Were Like the 1984 Anti-Sikh Riots

Fact: There was a contrast of day and night in these two riots. At times, NDTV, whose owners are close blood relations of top leaders of the CPI (M), and company, and some stark liars misled the nation by equating the two riots. In May- June 2005, NDTV asked a question to its viewers in its programme ***"Khabron ki Khabar"*** (anchored by Vinod Dua):

"Which of these issues are you most bothered about?

1. A question like say-Sachin Tendulkar's injury.
2. A question like say- on films, and
3. The blot on BJP and the Congress for the Gujarat and 1984 riots.

This question's options are typically Marxist. Option 3 belies the reality and equates the 1984 riots with the Gujarat riots, and indirectly accuses the BJP of orchestrating the riots.

The next chapter will comprehensively point out the differences between the Gujarat riots and the 1984 riots. In 1984, riots occurred outside New Delhi, including places like West Bengal, Tripura while not a single riot occurred outside Gujarat in 2002. (The people killed in other states like Maharashtra, as said by Modi in his interview, were killed months after Godhra in other riots.)

Not only was there a huge difference in the nature of the riots, there was also a huge difference in the government handling of the riots. We will see the full details of these contrasts in the next chapter.

Myth 10: Gujarat Became a Dangerous Place to Live in, in 2002

Fact: The opinion poll by the weekly *India Today* in its issue dated 25 November 2002 asked a question to its respondents: "Do you feel secure living in Gujarat today?" in which 68 per cent people including 56 per cent Muslims felt secure. While commenting on the entire poll, *India Today* reported, "Voters have rallied solidly behind the chief minister's aggressive posturing. They have endorsed his view of the riots being a reaction to Godhra. They approve his fulmination against outsiders who have vilified the state. And they contemptuously dismiss all suggestions that Gujarat has become a dangerous place to live in." (*Source*: http://archives.digitaltoday.in/indiatoday/20021125/cover2.html).

Myth 11: In Ehsan Jafri Case, Women were Raped

Fact: The following is some part of Arundhati Roy's article in weekly *Outlook* dated 6 May 2002 on the Ehsan Jafri case:

"Last night, a friend from Baroda called, weeping. It took her fifteen minutes to tell me what the matter was. It wasn't very complicated. Only that Sayeeda, a friend of hers, had been caught by a mob. Only that her stomach had been ripped open and stuffed with burning rags. Only that after she died, someone carved 'OM' on her forehead....

...a mob surrounded the house of former Congress MP, Iqbal Ehsan Jafri. His phone calls to the Director-General of Police, the Police Commissioner, the Chief Secretary, the Additional Chief Secretary (Home) were ignored. (**Note how the allegation of a call to Narendra Modi does not come at all!**) The mobile police vans around his house did not intervene. The mob broke into the house. They stripped his daughters and burned them alive. Then they beheaded Ehsan Jafri and dismembered him. Of course, it's only a coincidence that Jafri was a trenchant critic of Gujarat Chief Minister, Narendra Modi, during his campaign for the Rajkot Assembly by-election in February..." (*Source:* http://www.outlookindia.com/article.aspx?215477).

Outlook had the guts to publish a rebuttal from a senior functionary of the BJP, the then Rajya Sabha MP Balbir Punj. The following was the reply titled **"Fiddling with Facts as Gujarat Burns":**

"Introduction: The Roys in the media are harming India with half-truths and worse. "(Here Balbir Punj quotes some sentences from Roy's article dated 6th May, 2002)....

That was the Goddess of small things, Arundhati Roy, painting the big picture of Gujarat in *Democracy: Who's She When She's at Home?* (*Outlook*, 6th May, 2002). Roy sums here neatly almost all the charges against the *Sangh Parivar*. When a reputed weekly like *Outlook* publishes a Booker Prize winner, it is meant to be serious commentary. **(Our comment:** Here we disagree with Balbir Punj. In our opinion, *Outlook* is not a reputed weekly but a Congress loyalist magazine and Arundhati Roy, though a Booker Prize winner, is considered as an ultra-Left author by some and her writings are not taken seriously by many.) And concomitantly, Roy has put her brilliant linguistic skills to the service of 'truth'. Read her graphic details—'The mob broke into the house. They stripped his daughters and burnt them alive'. Roy speaks with the confidence of an eyewitness. Alternatively, she must've access to an eyewitness. Anyways, it reads heart-rendingly honest.

Heart-rending, yes, but honest, no. **Jafri was killed in the riots but his daughters were neither 'stripped' nor 'burnt alive'. T.A. Jafri, his son, in a front-page interview titled 'Nobody Knew My Father's House was the Target' (*Asian Age,* 2nd May, Delhi edition), says, 'Among my brothers and sisters, I am the only one living in India. And I am the eldest in the family. My sister and brother live in the U.S. I am 40 years old and I have been born and brought up in Ahmedabad.'**

So, Roy is lying—for surely Jafri is not. But what about the hundreds of media lies that haven't been exhumed as yet? Her seven- page long (approx: 6,000 words) hate charter against India and the *Sangh Parivar* is woven around just two specific cases of human tragedy, **one of which—by now, we know for sure—is a piece of fiction**....

...she terms Gujarat the "petri dish" of the *Sangh Parivar*. The fact is that Godhra has been used as a crucible by the secular fundamentalists. No wonder, after the roasting of the *Ramsevaks*, they, while condemning the crime, blamed the victims. Many of them invented events such as a quarrel with hawkers, misbehaviour with women and shouting of provocative slogans to justify the horrendous crime....

...but was what happened in Gujarat a 'pogrom' targeted at Muslims? Loss of 900-odd innocent lives (both Hindus and Muslims) is definitely not a 'genocide' of any one community. Yet it is one more shameful event in the long and unfortunate chain of communal riots in India, since the 1893 Bombay and Azamgarh riots. Beginning from the 1714 Holi riots in the Mughal period, Ahmedabad itself has witnessed no less than 10 major recorded riots.

The *Sangh Parivar* was not there in 1714, nor was it a dominant force during the '69 and '85 riots. So, what explains these riots when Gujarat was not a '*Sangh Parivar* petri dish'?...

...following Godhra, massive spontaneous violence broke out in various parts of Gujarat against the Muslims. Since the rioters were mainly Hindus, they also accounted for about 75 per cent of those who fell to police bullets in the first three days. In fact, till 18th April Hindus accounted for more deaths in police firing than Muslims.

But for almost three weeks now, the violence has been led by Muslims against Hindus and, naturally, a bulk of the casualties are accounted for by them. The police have booked 34,000 rioters, majority of whom are Hindus. Both the communities have suffered heavy loss of business and property in the arson and looting. While rioters are communal in picking their targets, looters are not—and they target at random. One lakh Muslims are struggling in relief camps, **but so are 40,000 Hindus.** This is a horrible riot, which is sad enough, but why call it a genocide? Whom does it help? Not the riot victims, only our enemies across the border.

The country hasn't suffered so much loss of face in the world as it has now, though it is like one of the scores of riots India has seen. Why? The obvious culprits are those who set ablaze a compartment full of innocent *karsevaks* at Godhra and those who indulged in the senseless violence in the following weeks. **But the real villains in tarring India's image are the Roys in the media and a section of public life, who mix half-truths with fiction to settle their ideological or political scores with the *Sangh Parivar*.**

Roy (a role model for several in the secular pack) opens her hate charter with the case of a woman named Sayeeda 'whose stomach was ripped open and stuffed with burning rags'. I heard similar horror stories in the Parliament. The most frequently quoted were the cases of women raped (in some cases, gang-raped), their stomachs ripped open, foetuses taken out and paraded on swords or trishuls. **But no one was able to give me even one specific case with all the particulars**. Roy gave one, but it proved to be a piece of fiction....

.... Blatant myths and fiction have lacerated the facts on Gujarat. *The Times of India* **(3 rd March) reported Modi's much-publicised misquote of Newton's third law—'Every action has an equal and opposite reaction'. In fact, the CM had never said such a thing and no other paper except for** *The Times of India* **had carried the misquote in its original reportage. But later on, numerous editorials were penned on the basis of this canard. All his denials were thrown in the dustbin....**

...the Editor's Guild came down heavily on the Gujarati press and hailed the role of the English press in coverage of the riots. The former might have been guilty of exaggeration but I am sure it has not concocted stories the way the Roys did in the English media. Surprisingly, the Guild has nothing critical to say on the role of the electronic media and of the Roys, guilty of blackening India's name, generating more communal hate at a critical time and demonising a section of citizens through half-truths and complete lies. Some rioters may be guilty of rape and should be punished for their heinous crimes, but what about those who have raped the truth and the country in the last two months?" (*Source:* http://www.outlookindia.com/article.aspx?215755).

This really gave the game up. After this, Arundhati Roy wrote "An Apology" in the *Outlook* dated 27th May, 2002. The full text of that apology titled "To the Jafri Family, An Apology" was:

"In a situation like the one that prevails in Gujarat, when the police are reluctant to register FIRs, when the administration is openly hostile to those trying to gather facts, and when the killings go on unabated—then panic, fear and rumour play a pivotal role. (**Note how she blames others!)** People who have disappeared are presumed dead, people who have been dismembered and burnt cannot be identified, and people who are distraught and traumatised are incoherent.

So, even when those of us who write, try and use the most reliable sources, mistakes can happen. But in an atmosphere so charged with violence, grief and mistrust, it's important to correct mistakes that are pointed out.

There is a factual error in my essay *Democracy: Who's She When She's at Home?* (6th May). In describing the brutal killing of Ehsan Jafri, I have said that his daughters had been killed along with their father. It has subsequently been pointed out to me that this is not correct. Eyewitness accounts say that Ehsan Jafri was killed along with his three brothers and two nephews. **His daughters were not among the 10 women who were raped and killed in Chamanpura that day.**

I apologise to the Jafri family for compounding their anguish. I'm truly sorry.

My information (mis-information, as it turned out) was cross- checked from two sources. *Time* magazine (11th March) in an article by Meenakshi Ganguly and Anthony Spaeth, and "Gujarat Carnage 2002: A Report to the Nation" by an independent fact-finding mission, which included K.S. Subrahmanyam, former I.G.P. Tripura, and S.P. Shukla, former Finance Secretary. I spoke to Mr. Subrahmanyam about the error. He said his information at that time came from a senior police official. (**What was the name of that official? Neither Subrahmanyam nor Arundhati Roy tell it!**) This and other genuine errors in recounting the details of the violence in Gujarat in no way alter the substance of what journalists, fact-finding missions, or writers like myself are saying."

Years later, Balbir Punj wrote in weekly *Organiser* dated 9 July 2006:

"Some four years ago, I had a clash in print with Arundhati Roy. The occasion was the Gujarat riots that had come as a windfall to 'secular' brigade's publicity campaign. Those 'secularists' are nowhere visible, not even with a telescope, when Hindus are killed in Doda...

Roy had begun her charter of hate with another damning description: 'Last night a friend from Baroda called, weeping. It took her fifteen minutes to tell me what the matter was. It wasn't very complicated. Only that Sayeeda, a friend of hers, had been caught by a mob. Only that her stomach had been ripped open and stuffed with burning rags. Only that after she died, someone carved 'OM' on her forehead'.

Shocked by this despicable 'incident', I got in touch with the Gujarat Government. The police investigations revealed that no such case, involving someone called Sayeeda, had been reported either in urban or rural Baroda. **Subsequently, the police sought Roy's help to identify the victim and seek** access to witnesses who could lead them to those guilty of this crime. **But the police got no cooperation. Instead, Roy, through her lawyer, replied that the police had no power to issue summons.** Thus, she hedged behind technical excuses. I took up this incident in my rejoinder published as *Dissimulation in Word and Images* (*The Outlook*, 8th July, 2002)."

However, here it is worth mentioning a couple of things which even Balbir Punj did not mention. This apology is also false, since Roy claims that 10 women were raped and killed that day. In reality, after reading the then English newspapers in the first week of March 2002, one finds no mention of any rapes at all. These stories of rape started coming out in the middle of March 2002, after *Time* magazine concocted lies in its issue of 11th March, 2002, copied by Arundhati Roy. Neither Roy nor the *Time* correspondent can point out any proven rapes in this case. **Roy also apologizes to the Jafri family, not to the BJP or Narendra Modi for defaming them by her incorrect claim. She should also have done that. And she should also have apologized to the country. Note how, while giving the apology, Roy makes sure that it is only "To the Jafri family".**

Second incorrect fact: The police did nothing to stop the mob in Jafri's house. We have seen earlier details of police action.

Also Roy says, "His phone calls to the Director-General of Police, the Police Commissioner, the Chief Secretary, the Additional Chief Secretary (Home) were ignored. The mobile police vans around his house did not intervene." **What rubbish again! Police vans outside his house not only intervened, they shot dead five rioters outside his house and saved the lives of 180 Muslims at a great risk to their own personal life. They fired 124 rounds and burst 134 tear gas shells at the spot.** *The Times of India* also reported online that the police and fire brigade did their best to disperse rioters and nowhere did it allege any inaction on the part of police.

Note here that Roy does not claim that Jafri telephoned the Chief Minister, Narendra Modi as late as May 2002! Now lies are out that Jafri actually phoned Modi and was abused by Modi on phone! The fact is that that day the situation was out of control. Modi frantically called the Army to Ahmedabad and he was very busy handling the situation. **There is no record of any call made by Jafri to Modi.** And yet some liars seem to have paid bribes to witnesses (like Imtiaz Pathan) to falsely claim that Modi had abused Jafri on phone and Jafri told them this fact before he died!!! Imtiaz Pathan lies when he says that Jafri called Modi. There is no record of any call being made to Modi, and though Modi had a mobile phone at that time, he did not use it much. That day, all his official lines were busy and he was very busy handling the riots. Imtiaz Pathan has also said that police did not come till 4:30-5:00 p.m. when everything was over. We have already seen, *Times of India's* online report published at 2:34 p.m. on 28th February, 2002 that the police fired on the Hindu crowd, injuring six at that time and that the police and the fire brigade had come. Before 2:34 p.m. itself, police had injured six outside Ehsan Jafri's house and actually five were killed in their firing and 11 injured. This despite the hopeless situation, which is clear from reading *The Times of India's* report that the Fire Brigade and the police were not allowed to be reached by the mob. Though the police gained control only after 8:00 p.m., they fired much before that.

Some other questions, which can be raised here, are: Why didn't Jafri call any Congress leader and ask the Congress Party to assemble 500 workers outside his house to save his life? He is reported to have done that also. Why couldn't the Congress Party have done anything to save its former MP? A Congress leader, Meghsinh Chaudhary himself is a top accused in this case, who was arrested by the SIT, not the Gujarat Police.

Even the National Commission for Women in its report stated that the media needlessly exaggerated the plight of women victims of the communal carnage. On 22nd April, 2002, *Tehelka's* website said: **"Nafisa Hussain, a member of the NCW, has gone on record, saying that several organisations and the media have needlessly blown out of proportion, the violence suffered by minority women in the communal riots of Gujarat."** This was the statement of a Muslim member of the National Commission for Women (NCW).

Myth 12: The Photo of Qutubuddin Ansari is Genuine

Fact: We do not give this picture again as the victim has repeatedly said that he doesn't want it and wants to be left alone. This photo was carried by *The Hindu* dated 2nd March 2002. This photo has been used repeatedly to tarnish the name of BJP, VHP and the Bajrang Dal throughout India. The victim, Qutubuddin Ansari, is reported often by the media to be pleading for mercy to the rioters. Later, he is shown in Kolkata, living happily on the help given by the West Bengal Government, which was then of the CPI (M) and other Left parties (They ruled West Bengal uninterrupted from 1977 to 2011). Many questions that arise (and some of which were raised by the then RSS chief K.S. Sudarshan (1931-2012) in his speech in Nagpur on 4th October 2003) are:

1. **A massive clue is got on this photo being fake** (means taken when Ansari was genuinely in such a position but definitely after the incident was over, or in an unlikely case, taken after the incident by the photographer asking the victim to pose thus) looking at the bandage on the poor victim's face. This suggests that after the incident was over, bandage was applied to his face, and then the photo was clicked. If this photo was clicked with the mob targetting him and he pleading a blood-thirsty mob for mercy, how did he have the time to apply bandage on his face?

2. Also, it seems scarcely believable that the victim is pleading to rioters to spare his life on the first floor of the building, no rioter is seen in the photo, the photographer, Arko Dutta was present at that very moment in that building to snap this in his camera and the rioters did nothing to either the photographer or the victim and allowed him to snap such a clear photo of the victim. **We have utmost sympathies for the victim, Mr. Qutubuddin Ansari since he was, no doubt, a victim of the riots. But that cannot be a license to concoct a fake photo and circulate it the world over, instigating innocent people to terrorism.**

3. If Mr. Qutubuddin Ansari was seen pleading for mercy to rioters on the first floor of a building, how is it that no rioter is seen in the photo?

4. How and why did the rioters leave him and not attack him?

5. How was the photographer allowed to take the photo by the rioters? Why did they not attack him?

6. How, at least, did the rioters not destroy his camera if they would have left both Ansari and the photographer alive?

7. Can the photographer, Mr. Arko Dutta of the *Reuters,* explain any of the above questions?

8. Can Mr. Ansari answer any of the above questions and other questions, which may be raised on this issue?

Here it must be said that the poor victim, Qutubuddin Ansari is reported to have said, "This photo was taken after the mob had left my house. The police were there and I was very scared and, at this time, the photo was clicked". This is what has been said by a senior journalist of Gujarat to the author. However, we could not get such a newspaper report available today on the web. But to be fair, we also could not get any report in which Ansari claims to be pleading before a mob to spare his life. **So, it is possible that Qutubuddin Ansari himself denies that he was pleading to a blood-thirsty mob.** Someone must now pin-pointedly ask him about this. If Mr. Ansari claims that he indeed was pleading before a blood-thirsty mob, then it must be asked to him as to how he had bandage applied on his face. The poor guy is also fed up of the constant use of his photo and harassments and has urged the media to leave him alone many times, starting from as early as August 2003 (*Source*: http://hindu.com/2003/08/stories/2003080806871100.htm).

We repeat here that we have utmost sympathies for the victim, Mr. Qutubuddin Ansari since he was, no doubt, a victim of the riots.

We have seen the horrific Godhra photos earlier in Chapter 2. The media, especially some TV channels like NDTV and CNN-IBN, will never, in their wildest of dreams, think of showing these photos, which are true, but will circulate the photo of Qutubuddin Ansari worldwide, which is highly inflammatory. The lies of the media have caused many innocent Muslims to turn fanatics. If the Muslims (and also our own liberals) had known the guilt of Muslims in roasting Hindus in Godhra, and seen the gruesome photos of Godhra, a section of them would not have been needlessly so instigated by the post-Godhra riots (which were also not one-sided).

Myth 13: Narendra Modi said: "Every Action has Equal and Opposite Reaction."

Fact: Balbir Punj writes: "Blatant myths and fiction have lacerated the facts on Gujarat. *The Times of India* (3rd March) reported Modi's much-publicised misquote of Newton's third law—"Every action has an equal and opposite reaction". In fact, the CM had never said such a thing and no other paper except for *The Times of India* had carried the misquote in its original reportage. But, later on, numerous editorials were penned on the basis of this canard. All his denials were thrown in the dustbin…."

Virendra Kapoor wrote in *Cybernoon* on 19th March, 2002: "An angry Modi wrote to the English daily, which had first put the quote in his mouth, protesting that he had never met its correspondent nor had he an occasion to say what he had been quoted as having said and that it was only fair that the paper made amends for its wholly 'inventive reportage'. The newspaper editors, however, refused to do so and, two weeks later, were still sitting on Modi's letter. Left to himself, perhaps the paper's senior- most editor may well have published Modi's letter but since his writ does not run and the place is teeming with new-fangled journalists who openly talk of blacking out all news about the *Sangh Parivar*, and the paper's management is only obsessed with packing nothing other than revenue-earning advertisement in its columns, Modi's letter has not been published. Modi, therefore, is not entirely wrong in complaining of the bias of the media and the attempt to tar his image. For, the quote in the said paper was immediately recycled and rehashed by the rest of the print and audio-visual media.

Inquiries reveal that no one from the paper had met the Gujarat Chief Minister on the day he is supposed to have quoted Newton's law to its correspondent to justify the revenge killings of the minority community in Ahmedabad and other places in the state. The paper's editors too have concluded that the said quote was 'invented' by the correspondent to indicate 'the attitude of the Modi government'. Indeed, it was all a cooked up job to justify what the paper's deputy bureau chief in New Delhi said at a gathering of secularist scribes to 'fight the fascist forces and not to give them any space in 'our' papers'.

Time the owner woke up to this little upstart, who seeks to usurp the ownership of their paper for his own brand of fascism. Meanwhile, Modi is contemplating taking his complaint to the Press Council of India."

In an interview to *India Today* published in its issue of 8 April 2002 Narendra Modi said: "After the riots began, I was quoted as saying that every action has an opposite reaction. The fact is I never said anything of that kind but one newspaper had a headline that said I had. I later wrote to the editor of the newspaper asserting that I had never said it. **The electronic media was there at that press conference of mine. You can check the tapes**".URL: http://archives.digitaltoday.in/indiatoday/20020408/cover6.html

And in an interview with *The Hindustan Times* published on 10th March, 2002, Narendra Modi said: "I made no statement of that kind. One big newspaper reported that I quoted Newton's law of every action having an equal and opposite reaction. I have never quoted Newton since I left school. I cannot help if people allow themselves to be guided by their predilections and fantasies. I'm willing to suffer if that helps the society. I plead with those opposed to me to wait till normalcy is restored in Gujarat…"

There are official records available, which show that no one from *The Times of India* had any appointment with Narendra Modi that day. When anyone makes an allegation, he has to prove it. No one has ever been able to prove that Modi ever uttered these words. And these people, far from apologizing, have not even published Modi's denials properly.

Even the Supreme Court-appointed Special Investigation Team (SIT) said in its report that there is no evidence at all of Narendra Modi saying "Every action has equal and opposite reaction" and his statements were quoted out-of-context and twisted. Some people in the media could not digest this and tried to paint the SIT as a team which gave a report which Modi's advocate would do. So if Modi did not say that every action has equal and opposite reaction, should the SIT have forcibly claimed this false charge?

Myth 14: *Sangh Parivar* organisations like the VHP organized the riots

Fact: Out of Gujarat's 18,600 villages, the Vishwa Hindu Parishad (VHP) i.e. the World Council of Hindus, had units in 10,000 villages at the time of the 2002 riots. If it had wanted, it could have easily organized retaliatory riots in many of these 10,000 villages. Instead, only maximum of 50 out of the state's 18,600 villages saw riots. The then VHP General Secretary, Dr. Praveen Togadia is a Patel and hails from Saurashtra region of Gujarat, just like Keshubhai Patel. And yet, no riots happened in Saurashtra at all!

On the other hand, the scale of the riots on 28 February in Ahmedabad was so large that no organization or group of organizations like the *Sangh Parivar* could have done it alone. It was a spontaneous mass reaction to the Godhra killings. Arvind Bosnia, political analyst, said the same.

Many people have asked: "On one hand, you say nothing happened, hardly 40-50 villages saw riots. On the other hand, you say that the riots were so enormous that they could not have been organized by anyone".

Both these things are simultaneously true. On 28 Feb. in Ahmedabad there were 17,000 people attacking Muslims in Naroda-Patiya area as per the report of the then Police Inspector of the area, K.K. Mysorewala. *India Today* also reported in its issue dated 18 March 2002 that the Charas had attacked in Naroda-Patiya leading three mobs of at least four to five thousand each. At one point of time in Ahmedabad, there were at least 25,000 people targetting Muslim localities. The Rapid Action Force and the CRPF jawans could not control the violence. *The Hindu* also reported the next day that the situation seemed to slip out of control. The Ahmedabad police received 3,500 calls instead of the normal 200. And *The Times of India* also said, "The sparse police presence looked like a drop in the ocean of violence", despite the deployment of the entire police force. It was beyond the means of the *Sangh Parivar* or anybody to organize mobs on such a large scale in Ahmedabad within 24 hours.

However, the VHP could have easily organised riots in many of the 10,000 villages in Gujarat where it had units, either on 28 Feb or later.

On 27 February occurred the Godhra massacre. That same day, the RSS gave a statement saying: "RSS condemns the killings and calls for restraint". *The Hindu* also reported in its report on 28 February that the "RSS appealed to the people to exercise restraint". We have seen in the 2nd chapter the scanned image of the report "RSS Condemns the Killings and Calls for Restraint" and of Mohan Bhagwat's appeal in *Organiser* dated 10 March 2002. *The Telegraph* reported on 28 February 2002:

"(On 27 February) **The RSS rallied behind the Prime Minister, pleading for restraint. Joint General Secretary, Madan Das Devi said: 'The tolerance of the Hindu society is a litmus test. Instead of taking the law into their hands, people should cooperate with the State Government in dealing with the serious situation.'"** (*Source:* http://www.telegraphindia. com/1020228/frontpa.htm#head1).

On 2 March 2002 www.rediff.com reported quoting Agencies:

"The RSS, VHP Appeal for Peace in Gujarat

In the wake of mounting violence in Gujarat, the RSS and VHP on Saturday appealed to their volunteers to avoid any action that would disturb peace in the country and expressed hope that 'good sense will prevail'.

"I appeal to all the RSS volunteers, sympathisers and friends, who have faith in Hindutva to do their utmost in preventing any activity, like sloganeering and stone-pelting, that would disrupt peace, keeping in view the disturbed situation in the country, for it would only strengthen the hands of anti-national terrorist elements," the RSS General Secretary, Mohan Bhagwat said in a statement in Delhi.

He urged followers of other faiths not to fall prey to the instigation of terrorist elements and "to conduct themselves as the children of India alongwith their Hindu brethren".

Meanwhile, the VHP also made an appeal to put an end to the ongoing violence in Gujarat, saying 'any kind of violence against anyone' was a matter of concern. Talking to reporters in Delhi, the VHP spokesman, Veereshwar Dwivedi said: "The Godhra incident and the violence that followed was tragic. Any kind of violence against anyone is a matter of concern."

Calling for an end to the ongoing carnage in Gujarat, he said: "Good sense must prevail soon." Dwivedi also condoled the deaths and expressed sympathies for those affected by the violence in the state.

He, however, regretted that opposition parties had decided to send a delegation to Gujarat to assess the situation but did not consider it appropriate to do so after the Godhra killings. Dwivedi said this was being done, taking vote bank politics into consideration—*Agencies*" (*Source*: http://www.rediff. com/news/2002/mar/02train10.htm).

This statement was given by Mohan Bhagwat on 27 February itself and was reported in the weekly *Organiser* in its issue dated 10 March 2002.

The VHP also appealed for peace. *The Times of India* reported on 28 February 2002 even before a single major riot had taken place: "VHP international Vice-President, Acharya Giriraj Kishore told reporters here at the Sola Civil Hospital, where 54 out of the 58 bodies of the train attack victims were brought, that '**Hindus should maintain calm and keep patience**. I appeal to Muslim brethren to condemn the attack and ask them not to put Hindus' patience to test. Hindus are keeping a restraint but if such incidents do not stop, there can be a counter-reaction, which may be uncontrollable'". (*Source*: http://www.timesofindia.com/articleshow.asp? art_ID=2347298).

On 27 Feb, *The Times of India* online reported that the Gujarat VHP appealed to every Hindu to 'stay indoors' the next day, i.e. 28 Feb, the day of the bandh. Naturally this would not make it possible for Hindus to retaliate if they all stayed indoors.

Myth 15: Narendra Modi Gave Free Hand to Rioters for three days

Fact: This allegation is baseless. Narendra Modi frantically called the Army units to Ahmedabad on 28 February as per the report of *The Hindu* the next day. *India Today*'s report 'Chronology of a Crisis' on this topic in its issue dated 18 March 2002 also proves this beyond doubt.

The fact is that the Army staged a flag march in Ahmedabad, Vadodara, Surat and Godhra on March 1, i.e. the second day. So, there was no question of giving anyone a free hand. The blatant lie was repeated many times in the media. The TV channel CNN-IBN on its Hindi channel, reported on 26

October 2007 by writing on TV screens: "There was given three days freedom to kill in Gujarat". The fact is, out of the three days, the Army was present for two days and the extent of violence was far less as compared to the first day. *The Hindu* itself reported on 3 March 2002 that the situation improved in Ahmedabad on March 2, the third day of the riots.

Moreover, there was already a minority backlash on the second day of the riots, i.e. on 1 March as reported by *The Hindu* the next day. The question of the next two days does not arise (as the Army was present) and even on 28 February when the Army was not present, the police shot dead 11 Hindus and 16 were injured. The police fired around 1496 rounds, out of which at least 600 were fired in Ahmedabad alone on 28 February. 4297 tear gas shells were burst and 700 arrests were also made. Police saved 2500 Muslims from certain death in Sanjeli on the second day of the riots.

Narendra Modi did not even give three minutes, not to talk of three days to the rioters. We have seen details of steps taken to prevent and stop the violence. Also the then Defence Minister George Fernandes was in Ahmedabad on 1 March at 1:00 a.m. on Narendra Modi's request. And the next day, he was bravely on Ahmedabad's streets at a great risk to personal life.

On 27 February itself, www.rediff.com reported, "The situation became tense as news of the incident spread to other parts of the state **prompting the state government to initiate precautionary security measures.**

Security has been tightened in Godhra and other parts of Gujarat" (*Source*: http://www.rediff.com/news/2002/feb/27train.htm).

Rediff.com also reported quoting PTI on 28 February evening that: "**The Army has been asked to stand by and the Rapid Action Force and the Central Industrial Security Force have been deployed in Ahmedabad and other places"** (*Source*: http://www.rediff.com/ news/2002/feb/28train15.htm).

Rediff.com reported on 27 February itself after Godhra that: "**Two companies of the Rapid Action Force and one company of the State Reserve Police were deployed at Godhra to guard against further outbreak of violence"** (PTI report). (*Source*: http:// www.rediff.com/news/2002/ feb/27train4.htm).

On 28 February, curfew was imposed in Baroda at 8:00 AM in the morning itself, as reported by rediff.com the same day. The report says:

"Indefinite curfew was imposed in the city from 0800 hours, following the stabbing incidents, a senior police official said. **Curfew had been imposed in the six police station areas of the walled city and RAF and CISF companies have been deployed in sensitive areas, Police Commissioner Deen Dayal Tuteja said. Indefinite curfew has also been imposed in the Lunawada town of Panchmahal district after 0200 hours on Wednesday night following incidents of arson and looting, he said.**

Meanwhile, indefinite curfew, imposed in Godhra town after the attack on the train on Wednesday, continued on Thursday without any relaxation. No untoward incident was reported during the curfew so far, the police said. The situation had remained peaceful and under control in other parts of the state during the night, police said" (PTI report). (*Source*: http://www.rediff.com/news/2002/feb/28train1.htm).

On the second day of the riots, shoot-at-sight orders were extended to 34 places. The report of rediff.com on 1 March 2002 was:

"Alarmed by the unabated incidents of violence in the city, the Gujarat Government on Friday (1st March) issued shoot-at-sight orders to the police against those indulging in arson and violence. The announcement was made by Chief Minister, Narendra Modi in Ahmedabad, official sources said. Modi has issued directives to the police to deal 'strictly with arsonists and if need be, shoot-at- sight any person indulging in rioting', they added.

Meanwhile, the Army staged flag marches in the violence-hit areas of Ahmedabad—Daraipur, Shahpur, Shahibaug and Naroda—to instill confidence among the people as unabated violence has claimed 111 lives in the city alone so far.

The Army personnel were out in different areas like Daraipur, Shahpur, Shahibaug and Naroda, police said". (*Source*: http://www.rediff.com/news/2002/mar/01train4.htm).

And they say that Narendra Modi gave three days to the rioters to kill! They demand that the BJP and Narendra Modi should 'apologize' for the Gujarat riots. They should realize and so also those BJP spokespersons who come on TV and fail to point out the truth, that it is not Narendra Modi who should apologize, but a section of the media, for lying and lying, exaggerating, defaming Narendra Modi. The liars can be tried under Section 153-A (creating enmity between two groups) because of one-sided reporting and infuriating Muslims and Section 500 of IPC (Defaming) for needlessly defaming BJP, *Sangh Parivar* and Narendra Modi and also tarnishing the image of India.

Myth 16: A Pregnant Woman's Womb was Ripped Open and Foetus Taken Out

Fact: Dr. J.S. Kanoria, who carried out the post-mortem of the woman, Kausarbanu, on 2 March 2002 found that her womb was intact, and that she had died of burns suffered in the riots.

Weekly *India Today* dated 5 April 2010 reports: "Significantly, in March 2003, the SC had stalled the trial of nine Gujarat riot cases, thanks to the relentless campaign by the human rights activists seeking justice for the Muslim victims. The riot victims said they won't get justice as long as the Gujarat government had a role in the police probe and the subsequent trial. The SIT is reinvestigating the cases under the virtual supervision of the apex court, with even the judges and public prosecutors being selected under the SC's monitoring.

As the SIT goes about its task, more and more evidence is surfacing that the human rights lobby had, in many cases, spun macabre stories of rape and brutal killings by tutoring witnesses before the SC. In the process, it might have played a significant role in misleading the SC to suit its political objectives against Modi and his government.

Last week (March 2010), one of the most horrible examples of cruelty resurfaced once again as the trial of the Naroda-Patiya case, where 94 persons were killed, began in the SC-monitored special court in Ahmedabad. Soon after the riots, the human rights activists and the Muslim witnesses had alleged that a pregnant woman, Kausarbanu's womb was ripped open by rioters and the foetus was flung out at the point of a sword. The gruesome incident was seen as the worst-possible example of medieval vandalism in the modern age.

Last week, eight years after the alleged incident, Dr. J.S. Kanoria, who conducted the post-mortem on Kausarbanu's body on 2nd March, 2002, denied that any such incident had ever happened. Instead, he told the court: 'After the post-mortem, I found that her foetus was intact and that she had died of burns suffered during the riot.' Later, Kanoria, 40, told

India Today, 'I have told the court what I had already written in my post-mortem report eight years ago. The press should have checked the report before believing that her womb was ripped open. As far as I remember, I did her post-mortem at noon on 2nd March, 2002.'

A careful study of the three police complaints, claiming that Kausarbanu's womb was ripped open by the rioters, shows several loopholes. While one complainant accuses Guddu Chara, one of the main accused in the Naroda-Patiya case, of ripping open Kausarbanu's womb, extracting her foetus and flinging it with a sword, another complainant accuses Babu Bajrangi, yet another accused in the case, of doing the act. A third complainant, on the other hand, does not name the accused but describes the alleged act.

Modi will also have reasons to smile at the affidavits filed by the Muslim witnesses in the SC in 2003 at the behest of Citizens for Justice and Peace (CJP) and Teesta Setalvad, on the basis of which, the trials in nine cases were stalled for six long years. The most glaring hole is in the affidavit of Nanumiya Malek, a key witness in the Naroda Gram case. In his affidavit before the SC filed on 15th November, 2003, Malek stated that a newly married woman called Madina, who lost four of her relatives, including her husband in the riots, had been raped by the rioters.

Malek's affidavit states: 'I was witness to the crimes of murder and rape that took place on Madina and her family. I also saw seven people being burnt alive, including four orphans. I request the SC to keep the details of this rape victim confidential since she is alive and use it only for the purpose of trial and conviction of the rapists.' But on 5th May, 2009, in his statement before the SIT, Malek said:

'I had wrongly claimed that Madina had been raped. I made the charge because of Teesta Setalvad's pressure. I kept on telling her not to include that charge in my affidavit, yet it was included.' In her statement before the SIT on 20th May, 2008, Madina, who has remarried now, said: 'The charge made by Malek claiming that I was raped by a riotous mob is false. I wasn't raped. When the riotous mob put my house on fire, I tried to run but was attacked by a rioter who injured me with a knife. Later, I managed to merge in a Muslim crowd.'

There are six other affidavits filed by different Muslim witnesses on 15th November, 2003, that wantonly allege rape in the Naroda Gram and Naroda-Patiya riot cases, without giving any details. Interestingly, all the affidavits have a uniform language: 'Over 110 persons were not simply killed, but raped and mutilated as well, including young children. We urge the SC to stay the trials and transfer them to a neighbouring state and also order fresh investigation.' The affidavits state that they had been filed at the behest of Setalvad and in the presence of her co-activist, Rais Khan.

If this wasn't enough, other glaring attempts by human rights activists to tutor witnesses have come to the fore. For example, soon after the Gulbarga massacre, in which Ehsan Jafri was killed, nearly a dozen **Muslim witnesses told the police that Jafri had fired in self-defence, killed a rioter and injured 14 others.** They also said that this led the mob to resort to violence and attack Muslims in Gulbarga with vengeance. But almost half of them, who deposed before the special court, have retracted from this statement.

The statement of Imtiaz Pathan in the Gulbarga trial also raises eyebrows. He told the special court that before being killed, Jafri told him that Narendra Modi abused him (Jafri) on phone when he sought protection during a mob attack. **Incidentally, there is no record available of Jafri having made any call to Modi. Pathan didn't name Modi in the first police statement he made soon after the riots.** Interestingly, he has also identified as many as 27 individual attackers from a mob of thousands of rioters.

When the SIT started taking statements of witnesses in the Gulbarga Society case, around 20 witnesses came with typed statements. But the SIT objected to it, citing Section 161 of the CRPC, saying that the police must record the statements of a witness. So when the SIT forced the witnesses to give their statement during the interrogation, there was a vast difference between the 'ready-made typed' statements and the oral evidences that the police had received earlier.

As a senior lawyer defending the accused, puts it: 'The witnesses, under the influence of the human rights activists, didn't allow videotaping of their statements, while they were being recorded. There is an obvious attempt on the part of activists to dictate not just the SIT, but also the courts.' Last week, *India Today* quizzed Setalvad about the charge of tutoring the witnesses and creating false evidence before the courts in the 2002 Gujarat riot cases.

Her response: 'I am under no obligation to respond to your questions.'…"
(*Source*: http://indiatoday.intoday.in/site/Story/89840/States/Inhuman+rights.
htm). Note here that this weekly does not seem to realize that it also reported
this lie, of a pregnant woman's womb being ripped open and foetus being taken
out, in its issue dated 18 March 2002.

It is not merely this report. Even a newspaper as biased against Narendra
Modi as *The Times of India*, which falsely reported that Narendra Modi
had said "Every action has equal and opposite reaction" and did not even
prominently publish the Chief Minister's letter denying having said any such
thing, reported on 18 March 2010 thus:

"Doc's Testimony Nails Lie in Naroda-Patia Fetus Story

Ahmedabad: One of the goriest stories of the Naroda-Patia massacre, of
how a pregnant woman's womb was ripped open and the fetus dangled on the
tip of a sword by the mob, before she was killed, has been busted by a testimony
given by a government doctor.

After 95 persons were killed on 28th February, 2002 at Naroda- Patia,
stories were doing rounds that the killers had cut open eight- month pregnant
Kausarbano Shaikh's womb, pulled out the fetus and killed her.

Dr. J.S. Kanoria, who conducted post-mortem on the woman's body on 2nd
March (2002), told the special court on Wednesday, supported by documents,
that he found the fetus intact. He said he was posted at Nadiad but called to
the Civil Hospital following the emergency, when he conducted the autopsy
on an unidentified body, which was later identified as Kausarbano.

**Kanoria showed his post-mortem report to the court saying he found
the fetus intact in the woman's womb itself.** The fetus weighed 2,500 g and
was 45 cm long. He mentioned about burn injuries in his post-mortem report,
but was quiet on whether there was any other injury on the body.

In April last year, the Gujarat Government argued before the SC on this
case after SIT submitted a report in a sealed cover. The government's claim
was that SIT had refuted charges that Kausarbano's fetus was pulled out of
her womb and killed by sword before her eyes by violent mob. Senior counsel,
Mukul Rohatgi contended that such allegations levelled by an NGO were

proved false by the SIT report. Nearly a year later, the doctor, considered a neutral witness, has deposed the same before the trial court". (*Source*: http://timesofindia.indiatimes.com/india/Docs-testimony-nails-lie-in-Naroda-Patia-fetus-story/articleshow/5696161.cms).

One of the very few other papers to even report Dr. Kanoria's statement in court was *The Hindu*. *The Hindu* too has lied and called the riots a 'pogrom', 'genocide' and 'massacre' of Muslims ever after the riots and published stark lies on this subject on its edit page. But even it reported on 18 March 2010:

"Foetus was Intact in Naroda-Patia Victim: Doctor

MANAS DASGUPTA

Ahmedabad: The doctor, who performed autopsy on the bodies of three victims of the Naroda-Patia massacre during the 2002 communal riots in Gujarat, has denied that the womb of a pregnant woman was slit open by the attackers.

During the cross-examination before the special court judge, Jyotsnaben Yagnik on Wednesday, Dr. J.S. Kanoria said that he found the foetus in place in the womb of Kausarbano Shaikh. **As part of the post-mortem procedure, it was he who took the foetus out of the womb, the doctor said.**

It was widely alleged during the riots that the then State Bajrang Dal convener, Babu Bajrangi, had led a violent mob of activists, some of whom not only burnt alive local Muslims but also raped the pregnant woman, slit open her womb with a sharp-edged weapon and threw both the mother and the foetus into a fire.

Dr. Kanoria admitted that he had found Kausarbano's body 100 per cent burnt. To a question by the public prosecutor, he did not rule out the possibility of her having been thrown alive into a fire by the attackers, resulting in her death, but disagreed with the claim that her womb was slit open.

As a large number of bodies were arriving at the Ahmedabad civil hospital, Dr. Kanoria was specially summoned there from the Nadiad hospital and he conducted post-mortem on three bodies including that of a pregnant woman, who was later identified as Kausarbano…" (*Source*: http://www.hindu.com/2010/03/18/stories/2010031863801300.htm)

Myth 17: Gujarat Government did nothing to help the Victims

Fact: We have already seen the steps taken by the government to quell the violence, and in saving the lives of the victims, for example, in Sanjeli, Bodeli and Viramgam areas of Gujarat. Hindus were also saved by violent Muslims in many places in Gujarat, like in Jamalpur on 1 March 2002 and in Modasa on 19 March 2002 when Muslims attacked. But there has also been a claim by many that the Gujarat Government was like Hitler and have called these plain riots as 'holocaust' and equated them with the killing of Jews in Germany. What a ridiculous comparison!

The Gujarat Government spent a lot of money for providing relief to the riot victims. None other than the UPA Government's MoS for Home, Shriprakash Jaiswal said this in the Rajya Sabha that too in a written reply on 11 May 2005. He said an amount of Rs. 1.5 lakh was paid by the government to the next of kin of each person killed and Rs. 5,000, Rs. 15,000, Rs. 25,000 and Rs. 50,000 to those injured upto 10, 30, 40 and 50 per cent respectively.

In addition, Jaiswal said **relief was also extended by the State Government to the victims of the riots under the heads of cash doles and assistance for household kits, food grains to the Below Poverty Line (BPL) families in the affected areas, housing assistance, rebuilding earning assets, rehabilitation of small business, assistance to industries/shops and hotels and so on.**

The State Government, Jaiswal said, has informed that a total of Rs. 204.62 crore (Rs. 2046.2 million)has been incurred by it towards relief and rehabilitation measures. The Gujarat Government has also informed that they had published the data as recommended by the NHRC, he added. (*Source*: http://www.expressindia.com/news/ fullstory.php? newsid=46538).

And the Gujarat Government, in an advertisement given in weekly *India Today* dated 6 May 2002 said:

"At the rate of Rs. 30 per person **the government is spending Rs. 35 lakh (i.e. Rs 3.5 million, roughly US $ 70,000) a day** on providing food grains to the 1.1 lakh inmates of the 99-odd relief camps in the state, 47 of them in Ahmedabad.

The relief operations at the camps are being directly looked after by the IAS officers of the rank of Secretary to the State government.

The camps in Ahmedabad have been divided into six groups. Each group is being monitored by a bureaucrat of the rank of Secretary. The secretaries have been looking after the minutest problems of the inmates. **Teachers were deputed in each camp to help the children prepare for the exams and the state Health Department has been taking special steps to look after the well being of the inmates. In order to rehabilitate the rural inmates, the government has floated the *Sant Kabir Awas Yojana* as per the directions of the Prime Minister A.B. Vajpayee. The scheme will enable the inmates to build houses.**" (And in these camps were 1 lakh i.e. 100 thousand Muslims and 40,000 Hindus as well).

The SIT also quotes, on page 320, the then Ahmedabad Collector K Srinivas as saying that 71,744 persons were provided relief in the camps between 1 March 2002 and 31 December 2002 and these camps were provided government assistance in the form of essential commodities such as wheat, rice, dal, oil, milk powder, sugar, onions, potatoes, tea, etc for a total amount of Rs 6,89,57,547,50. This comes to 689.57 crore i.e. 6895.7 million Rupees. In addition, to meet miscellaneous expenses, Govt. assistance of 4.10 crore i.e. 41 million was provided, he claimed.

How ridiculous to equate this with Hitler! Did Hitler ever spend crores on helping Jews or other Christian Germans affected by violence? He ordered killing of Jews, not spending of money to help them. Has any government in the world ever cared about minority Hindus who suffered like this? In the 1971 East Pakistan genocide, West Pakistani soldiers killed allegedly around 2 million Hindus (and also other Bangladeshi Muslims, when their leader declared that Bangladeshis are un-Islamic) and also raped at least 2,50,000 Bengali women. **From 1947, Pakistan has constantly reduced the Hindus, reducing their population from 20 per cent in West Pakistan to 1 per cent now. In Bangladesh also the Hindu population has declined from around 29 per cent to just 10 per cent in 2001.** Hindus are regularly killed, women raped, abducted and forcibly converted to Islam, temples attacked, Hindus thrown out of their homes in Bangladesh and Pakistan. In Kashmir, in January 1990, Hindus were given three choices by the local Islamic leaders—convert to Islam, die or leave Kashmir. **Nobody ever reconstructed houses for these Hindus. Nobody gave them financial compensation of crores of rupees. And nobody spent 35 lakhs per day on them. Nobody arrested the culprits and punished them.** Those who order killing of others, or want others to suffer horribly, do not take the pains to do all that the Gujarat Government did. Not only did the Gujarat Government do all this, the police also arrested 35,552 people as of 28 April 2002 out of which 27,901 were Hindus. Around 20,000 people were arrested as a preventive measure. Mass murderers like Stalin, Hitler never carried out preventive arrests to save the victims. And already 443 people have been convicted for the violence—the highest ever in Gujarat.

No Islamic country has punished anyone for the killings of Hindus as much as they would if the victim was Muslim, not even of the tallest Hindu leader of Pakistan, Sudham Chand Chawla, who was killed by the Islamic radicals on 29 January 2002. And the so-called human rights activists have concocted many tales of rapes and killings, like the false claim that Ehsan Jafri's daughters were raped, or Medina was raped, or the outrageous lie that a pregnant woman's womb was ripped open and foetus taken out, when nothing like this happened. Nobody has ever lied and falsely exaggerated the killing of Hindus in Pakistan and Bangladesh at the hands of Muslims, or made fake stories of Hindu women's wombs being ripped open and foetuses taken out. Actually, they have all done exactly the opposite. Killings of lakhs of Hindus in Pakistan and Bangladesh have been ignored, rapes and abductions of Hindu girls have been suppressed ever after 1947. Just like some people deny the holocaust of Jews (like the Iranian President), some people have whitewashed Islamic fanaticism, even of medieval India when crores of Hindus were killed.

The PR work of the Gujarat Government indeed does not seem good. The media is, of course, guilty of ignoring all these facts, and needlessly infuriating Muslims by lying that Narendra Modi is responsible for the harm caused to the community. Far from it, his government actually helped the victims, both Hindu and Muslim, by spending lakhs per day on them. 40,000 Hindus were thrown out of their homes by Muslims in the Gujarat riots and the Gujarat Government gave them relief camps and rehabilitation help too.

Myth 18: Narendra Modi Never Expressed Sadness for the Post-Godhra Riots

Fact: It is not astonishing to see biased people in the media level absolutely false and wrong charges on the then Chief Minister of Gujarat, Narendra Modi. But what is astonishing is the extent to which a large section of the media goes in putting unbelievable factual errors and sticking to them, and believing its own lies. These days, some media people and political parties opposed to Narendra Modi have all made full use of the myths and lies concocted on him. And the much-repeated claim that Narendra Modi never expressed sadness at the Gujarat riots is factually totally incorrect.

Narendra Modi has expressed sadness for the riots and termed the riots as 'unfortunate'. In an interview to *Aaj Tak*'s Prabhu Chawla on its program *Seedhi Baat*, the excerpts of which were published in *India Today* weekly dated 4th November, 2002, Narendra Modi was asked "Prime Minister, Vajpayee and Home Minister, Advani have said that whatever happened in Gujarat was wrong", to which he said, **"I say the same thing. The communal riots in Gujarat were unfortunate and we are sad they took place".** (*Source*: http://www.indiatoday.com/itoday/20021104/conf.shtml#co)

After the 2002 Gujarat riots, Narendra Modi made a statement in the State Assembly (Vidhan Sabha) in March 2002. One paragraph from that statement is "Are we not supposed to soul-search ourselves? **Whether it is Godhra incident or post-Godhra, it does not enhance the prestige of any decent society. The riots are a stigma on humanity** and do not help anyone to hold his head high. Then, why is there a difference of opinion?"

When Narendra Modi went on his "Sadbhavana fast" in Gujarat in 2011, some newspapers said, "In a statement interpreted as his first sign of regret over the 2002 post-Godhra violence, Gujarat Chief Minister, Narendra Modi Friday said the pain of anyone in the state is 'my pain' and he had a duty to do justice for everyone.

'Constitution of India is supreme for us. As a Chief Minister of the state, pain of anybody in the state is my pain. (Delivering) Justice to everyone is the duty of the state,' Modi said on the eve of his three- day fast."

It was not merely this paper (DNA), almost the entire media said the same thing. What a ridiculous interpretation from the media calling this as 'a first sign of regret', and how factually incorrect it reported! Before this fast in 2011, he had directly condemned the riots many times. The entire self-styled secularists and activists have carried on this myth in their hate-campaigns against Modi. Gujarat Congress leaders too have repeated this. How the BJP allowed such a massive lie to crop up without ever bringing out the truth is beyond comprehension.

What is correct is that Narendra Modi has not apologized for the Gujarat riots, and rightly so. Apology is given when someone does something wrong, makes a mistake and asks for forgiveness for a mistake. What wrong has Narendra Modi done? He actually has done an excellent work in controlling the 2002 riots, his administration saved more than 24,000 Muslims and many Hindus also, the riots were controlled in three days, while weeklies like *India Today* and *Outlook* predicted weeks of violence on 28th February, etc. The media's argument often is: "The Congress has apologized for the 1984 riots. Will the BJP apologize for the 2002 Gujarat riots?" This was asked to the BJP leader Nalin Kohli on 16 May 2009 on TV after the BJP's massive debacle in the 2009 Lok Sabha polls.

There is absolutely no need to equate the two. Firstly, there is not a single parallel between the post-Godhra riots of 2002 and the 1984 riots. We will see the contrasts between these two riots in the next chapter. **Secondly, Congress apologizing for the riots is not an action of credit. Apologizing means accepting culpability in the 1984 riots in which 3,000 Sikhs were killed. Is the sin of killing 3,000 people forgivable by merely issuing an apology?** Accepting culpability for the death of 3,000 people means the concerned people deserve severe punishment. **3,000 murders cannot be pardoned and condoned by an apology.** The then Congress Government took no action against the rioters, hardly any arrests were made and according to TV channels CNN-IBN and NDTV 30 people have been convicted in 12 cases (till April 2013). CNN-IBN should be asked to give the list of convictions so as to clear all doubts, since it was claimed by some that the convicted people were 16 in 7 cases and not 30 in 12 cases. The Congress leader and former Prime Minister, Manmohan Singh reportedly said in 1999 before the Lok Sabha polls in Delhi (where he contested and lost from South Delhi to BJP's Vijay Kumar Malhotra) that "1984 riots were done by RSS" and he has not yet apologized to RSS or to anyone for this ridiculous statement. It is this strange charge which was a big reason for his defeat in South Delhi. http://www.rediff.com/election/1999/sep/02man.htm

It took the previous Congress governments far more time to stop riots in 1985 and 1969 even without any cause like Godhra. It should be remembered that not a single English newspaper actually accused the Chief Minister, Narendra Modi of any wrong doing on the actual days of the riots, i.e. 28 Feb 2002 (Thursday), 1 March 2002 (Friday) and 2 March 2002.

Myth 19: Narendra Modi told the Police officers to go slow on Hindus in the 27 February night meeting

Fact: Before getting into the details, let us post one important thing here. **Is Narendra Modi a fool to openly give such orders to so many officials in such a meeting where any of the officers could have secretly recorded such orders or which would have had 9 witnesses against Narendra Modi?** If he did want such orders to be issued, he would have done it through middlemen and other communicators being careful not to come into the picture directly! **It is astonishing to see that no one with an iota of common sense has till now raised this point.** Even if he did want to issue such instructions, there is no way in the world that he would have given them directly in an official meeting.

On 27 February 2002 occurred the Godhra massacre, at around 8:00 a.m. The Chief Minister Narendra Modi was informed about the carnage at 8:30 to 9:00 a.m. He immediately issued shoot-at- sight orders and curfew in Godhra. He visited Godhra on 27 February and returned to Ahmedabad the same day. 827 preventive arrests were made on his orders on his return to Ahmedabad. All these are well-documented facts. In an article titled "Chronology of a Crisis", *India Today* said:

"27th FEBRUARY, 2002

...10:30 p.m.: CM holds meeting with senior government officials at Gandhinagar; orders curfew in sensitive places and **pre-emptive arrests.**"

Now this gives us a crucial piece of information. And that is, that this meeting had indeed taken place on 27 February 2002 late night (not midnight, as claimed by some opponents of Narendra Modi, like *Outlook* once did). Secondly, this meeting was not at all kept secret (and denied having taken place) by the government. But that was to discuss steps to **control the violence** which could possibly break out the next day.

Firstly, let us see the background of that crucial 27 February meeting. In the chapter "Role of the Government in Controlling Violence", we have already seen the steps taken by the government to control the violence. We will just take a brief re-look at them. On 27 Feb the website rediff.com also reported that the State Government had taken all precautions and tightened security to prevent riots. 70,000 security men, RAF, CRPF etc were all deployed. In Godhra on 27 February evening, while talking to the electronic media, Narendra Modi made an appeal asking the people to maintain calm and not retaliate and an appeal was broadcast on National TV the next day.

We saw in the 3rd chapter how the remains of the slain *karsevaks* were brought from Godhra to Western Ahmedabad's isolated hospital at 3:30 a.m. on 28 February (as reported by *India Today* dated 18 March 2002 and *The Times of India* online on 28 February) which is a very inconvenient time to instigate riots, and also for relatives.

Considering all these facts, it would actually be sufficient to conclude that far from asking the administration to 'allow Hindus to vent their anger', what was discussed were the steps to prevent and control the violence the next day in that 27th February meeting. That this indeed was the case is proved by the actual action of the police and the administration. **The police and the administration the next day did not allow Hindus to vent their anger and did their best to control the violence.**

WHO HAS ALLEGED THAT MODI TOLD THE POLICE TO GO SLOW ON HINDUS?

Now, let us come to the point of the 27 February meeting. The weekly *Outlook* magazine, which is extremely anti-Narendra Modi, has alleged that Modi told officials to allow Hindus to take revenge the next day in that crucial

27 February night meeting. It first did this in its issue dated 3 June 2002, following which Narendra Modi sent a defamation notice as reported by *The Indian Express* on **8** June 2002.

(Source: http://www.outlookindia.com/article.aspx?215889)

Now, there was a Concerned Citizens Tribunal headed by Retd. Supreme Court Judge, Justice Krishna Iyer, which conducted its own 'study' and report on the Gujarat riots and, as expected, held the government guilty. **Sadly for it, it also made a fool of itself by trying to absolve Muslims of the crime of Godhra by suggesting that the fire was set 'from inside' (as if it was an inside job!) and denying outrightly that any mob had torched the train.** *Outlook* reported that a certain Gujarat Minister (at that time it did not name him, but after his murder named him as Haren Pandya) was interviewed by this CCT and he revealed that in that 27 February meeting, Modi told officials to allow Hindus to vent their anger.

The *Outlook* reported in that article:

"The minister told *Outlook* that in his deposition (to the CCT), he revealed that on the night of 27th February, Modi summoned DGP (i.e. Director General of Police) K. Chakravarthy, Commissioner of Police, Ahmedabad, P.C. Pandey, Chief Secretary, G. Subarao, Home Secretary, Ashok Narayan, Secretary to the Home Department, K. Nityanand (a serving police officer of IG rank on deputation) and DGP (IB) G.S. Raigar. Also present were officers from the CM's office: P.K. Mishra, Anil Mukhim and A.K. Sharma. The minister also told *Outlook* that the meeting was held at the CM's bungalow. **(Notice that Sanjiv Bhatt comes nowhere in the picture!!!)**

The minister told the tribunal (CCT) that in the **two-hour meeting**, Modi made it clear there would be justice for Godhra the next day, during the VHP-called bandh. He ordered that the police should not come in the way of "the Hindu backlash". At one point in this briefing, according to the minister's statement to the tribunal, DGP Chakravarthy vehemently protested. But he was harshly told by Modi to shut up and obey. Commissioner Pandey, says the minister, would later show remorse in private but, at that meeting, didn't have the guts to object.

According to the deposition, it was a typical Modi meeting: more orders than discussion. By the end of it, the CM ensured that his top officials—especially the police—would stay out of the way of *Sangh Parivar* men. The word was passed on to the mobs. (According to a top IB official, on the morning of 28th February, VHP and Bajrang Dal activists first visited some parts of Ahmedabad and created minor trouble just to check if the police did, in fact, look the other way. Once Modi's word was confirmed, the carnage began.)"

Now there are clear factual errors in this. The *Outlook* report names Chief Secretary, G. Subarao and an officer in the CM's office, A.K. Sharma, as among those at the meeting. **Neither was present in that meeting. That day, Subarao was on leave and instead it was acting Chief Secretary S.K. Varma, who participated in that meeting! This single goof-up alone is enough to dismiss the claims of *Outlook* on that meeting, or, assuming that the late Pandya did make such allegations, his.** *Outlook* realized its terrible goof-up and in the 19th August 2002 issue it acknowledged its error in its claimed interview with Pandya.

Let us assume that the late Minister Haren Pandya did tell *Outlook* that Modi told officials to allow Hindus to vent their anger the next day in that meeting. What credibility does Pandya have when he was not even present in that meeting? **And when he could not even correctly tell the people who were in the meeting, wrongly naming two people as being present there, how can anyone believe that he would know what happened inside the meeting? He also said that it was a 2 hour meeting, while it lasted only 30 to 45 minutes! (SIT report said so).** *Outlook*'s aim is also exposed here. *Outlook* wanted to crucify Narendra Modi by hook or by crook, and in its issue of 3 June 2002 it held Modi guilty without bothering to cross-check if the information provided by the Minister (Pandya) was correct or not, assuming that Pandya did speak to *Outlook*. Was it not *Outlook*'s duty to cross-check the facts before making such a serious allegation against a Chief Minister? Haren Pandya was demoted in the Cabinet, from Home Minister to Revenue Minister. There were reports of his personal grudge against the Chief Minister. It is said that after he became Chief Minister in October 2001, Narendra Modi wanted to contest a bypoll from Ellisbridge (which is one of the safest seats for the BJP in Gujarat and in the country) which was represented by Pandya. It is reported that Pandya refused to vacate this seat for Modi and, hence, Modi had to contest from Rajkot II, which Narendra Modi won.

In all this, *Outlook* relies only on the testimony of Haren Pandya, whom it did not even name at that time. **But neither the tribunal nor *Outlook* have given any evidence that Pandya met them or told them anything of this sort.** *Outlook* claims that it has a taped interview of Haren Pandya of August 2002. In its issue dated 19th August, 2002, *Outlook* reports: "Modi's pet theory was that the man, who went to the tribunal, was his then revenue minister, Haren Pandya. He even asked his intelligence officials to get proof to nail Pandya. But the intelligence wing, *Outlook* learns, gave no conclusive proof to Modi. Yet, he sent Pandya a show-cause notice through the state BJP president, asking him to explain if and why and with whose permission he went to the tribunal. **Pandya, in his sharp reply that unmistakably ridiculed Modi, denied he went to the tribunal.**" So, neither *Outlook* nor the tribunal have any evidence that Pandya told them anything, and Pandya himself denied the charge! Now, in the same issue (19 Aug 2002), they give an interview with a Minister (who, *Outlook* claims after his death was Haren Pandya, and that it has the conversation on record). In that entire interview, there **is not the slightest allegation that Modi ordered the officials to allow Hindus to vent their anger on 27 February night in that crucial meeting. He is simply talking about the meeting, and the officials present in it.** In short, there is no proof in public domain that Haren Pandya ever made any allegations on Modi on that 27th February meeting. There is no evidence in public forum of Pandya ever telling *Outlook* anything before August 2002, or of him deposing before the CCT.

But this writer does think that Pandya could have deposed before the CCT and may have talked to *Outlook* for its 3rd June issue as well. This possibility is not ruled out by us. We are merely saying that till now no evidence has been provided to prove that Pandya ever said this.

The link for *Outlook's* interview with Pandya of August 2002: (Assuming *Outlook's* claim of having taped it is true) http://www.outlookindia.com/article.aspx?216905

In this interview of 19th August, 2002 *Outlook* reports: "**Minister (*continuing*):** See, whatever I told you, it was not as if some disgruntled man was saying it. I didn't say all those things because I was unhappy. **(That exactly was the reason- that he was unhappy!).** There is nobody in my position who can fight him. So, it's important I remain an insider, in power, in position. That's why I want my identity to be protected.

You mentioned Subarao. There was trouble with that. *(The* Outlook *report named chief secretary G. Subarao and an officer in the CM's office, A.K. Sharma, as among those at the meeting. Neither was present.)*

Minister: What happened was that there was a chief secretary- in-charge then. I got my facts mixed up. But listen, their denial was very weak, wasn't it? If they try to make an issue of it, tell them that you want the official denial from all the people mentioned in the story on paper, with their signatures. Leave the two they say weren't there at the meeting but ask the others to say that there was no meeting, no direct or indirect orders. Let them say that on paper with their signatures....

Minister (*continuing*): I made a mistake with the chief secretary's name. **But the rest is all true. The time, the place, everything was correct. If they put pressure, ask them for official denial from the officers.**

Minister (*continuing*): Vijay Rupani (who was supposed to organise the yatra) will give information on the (Gujarat) Gaurav *Rath Yatra*. But be careful when you meet these people. They are such guys that they'll try to extract my name from you. Be careful."

And *Outlook* stuck to its story even after the clear goof-up. See the role of *Outlook*. It admitted that it wrongly named two people as being present in the meeting. That should have been enough to dismiss this charge, when *Outlook* and an alleged Minister cannot even correctly tell the names of the people who were present in the meeting (Haren Pandya was, of course, not present and has never claimed to be present either). How could they know what happened in that meeting? **So what *Outlook* said in effect was: "Though our report wrongly named two people as being present, though we could not even tell correctly who were present, our charge that Modi ordered the police to allow Hindus to vent their anger is 100% true".** A magazine with an iota of honesty would have said: "We relied on a man whose information was incorrect and who had personal grudges. We withdraw our story".

But that's not all! **Even in its 19th August issue, there are blunders. Haren Pandya says (as claimed by *Outlook*) "I made a mistake with the chief secretary's name. But the rest is all true."**

But the rest is also not all true. Not only was the chief secretary not there (he was on leave and it was the acting chief secretary S.K. Varma, who participated), another officer, A.K. Sharma was also not present. This was admitted by *Outlook*, not by the Minister! And sadly for *Outlook*, there was a THIRD BLUNDER in this allegation even in the 19th August issue, which is that DGP (IB) G.C. Raigar was also not present in this meeting! **Neither *Outlook* nor Pandya knew this.** So even in the 19th August issue, when they admitted mistakes in the 3rd June issue, they stuck to their story saying 'rest all information is correct', **but the information in the 19th August issue was also wrong since G.C. Raigar was also wrongly named as being present.** Pandya said: "1 man was wrongly named: Chief Secretary, G. Subarao, rest all was correct". (Actually, a single mistake is enough to dismiss these ridiculous claims.) *Outlook* said: "2 people were wrongly named: Chief Secretary, G. Subarao and A.K. Sharma". **But the fact is that THREE people were wrongly named, G.C. Raigar also was not present!** And the magazine continues to hold Modi guilty in that 27th February meeting, ignoring all its mistakes. Also note that it also mentioned the name wrongly- his name is G.C.Raiger, not G.S.Raiger! And the meeting did not last 2 hours either.

Also, note that the names mentioned by *Outlook*, of the people being present at the meeting do not include Sanjiv Bhatt at all! **He is nowhere in the picture, and wasn't for nine years after that meeting.** Nobody, for nine years after that meeting ever mentioned the name Sanjiv Bhatt. Notice how even a magazine like *Outlook*, which forcibly tried to hold Modi guilty in that 27 February meeting, has never even mentioned Sanjiv Bhatt. Why would Sanjiv Bhatt have taken nine years to claim that he was present at that meeting, if he really was?

The only police officer who has made allegations against Modi apart from Sanjiv Bhatt, is R. Sreekumar. Former Gujarat IPS officer, R.B. Sreekumar told the Nanavati Commission in an affidavit and later also the SIT that the then Director General of Police, V.K. Chakravarthy, who had participated in that crucial February 27 meeting, told him that the CM had directed officers to go slow against Hindu rioters and allow them to give vent to their feelings against the Muslims. **Note that Sreekumar does not even claim that he was present in that meeting and that Modi told officers in front of him to go slow on Hindus. He alleges that the then DGP, Chakravarthy told him so.** There is absolutely no evidence that Chakravarthy told him (Sreekumar) so. If Chakravarthy told Sreekumar so, then he could easily have told some others, like *Outlook* or anyone else, or the other media or the Nanavati Commission in private.

However, what Chakravarthy and many other officials involved with police department at that time told the Nanavati Commission was exactly the opposite. They said Modi had told them to control the riots. Plus, Sreekumar started making anti-Modi charges in the case **only after the government denied him promotion on strong grounds and made a person junior to him as the DGP. What's more he did not make the same charge in his first two affidavits he filed before the Nanavati Commission, which he submitted before he was denied promotion.** Chakravarthy also debunked Sreekumar's claim that he ever told any such thing to Sreekumar and outrightly denied telling this to him. Significantly, Sreekumar sticks to his ground when he says: "The SIT virtually functioned as B-Team of the Gujarat police and ignored the evidence I produced".

That is, Sreekumar admits that the SIT saw through his game and did not fall for his 'evidence' which is absolutely nothing, since he was not present at all in that meeting, and he has no proof at all that Chakravarthy told him anything. And even if Chakravarthy told him anything, that would be no proof, since Chakravarthy has to tell it to the Nanavati Commission or the SIT.

So, in short, let us mention about the people who are supposed to have alleged that Modi told the officials to allow Hindus to vent their anger the next day. They are:

1. **Sanjiv Bhatt.** He has no credibility, was not present at that 27th February, 2002 meeting at all. No one, including Modi's biggest enemies like *Tehelka* and *Outlook,* while trying to crucify Modi, ever claimed for nine years after that meeting that he was present in that meeting. This man has a very terrible past and has cases against him.

He was absent from duty for many many days without any reason and when he was finally suspended, tried to become a 'martyr'. We will see this in detail in the chapter on the SIT report.

2. **R. Sreekumar.** He too was not present at that 27ᵗʰ February meeting. He claims that a man, who was present, told him that Modi ordered the officials to go slow on Hindus the next day. Even if the man did tell him so, this is no proof. Sreekumar has given no proof at all that that man (Chakravarthy) ever told him this. **Chakravarthy has told the Nanavati Commission exactly the opposite.** Sreekumar made these allegations only after he was denied promotion, and not in his first two affidavits.

3. **Haren Pandya.** There is, in fact, no proof in public forum that he ever made any allegations that Modi ordered the officials to go slow in that 27ᵗʰ February meeting. There were alleged differences between Narendra Modi and Haren Pandya. He was first degraded in the ministerial portfolio (and then denied a ticket in assembly polls of December 2002). Owing to these issues, Haren Pandya resigned from the Gujarat Cabinet in August 2002. This clearly shows that there were personal and other matters which could have prompted Pandya to speak against Narendra Modi. **Also, note that many self-styled secular activists had alleged Pandya himself being culpable in the 2002 riots, of being involved in an attack on a *dargah* in the 2002 riots.** But after his murder in March 2003, for which Muslims were convicted, or ever after he started speaking against Narendra Modi in 2002 itself (on personal grudges, since he was demoted from Home Minister to Revenue Minister and ever since the issue of refusing to vacate the Ellisbridge seat for Narendra Modi to contest rose) the media immediately took to him as a 'hero', forgetting its allegations on him! The self- styled liberals were howling against Haren Pandya since March 2002, when it was alleged that Pandya was involved in demolishing a *dargah* on 1ˢᵗ March, 2002. He allegedly took the leadership on the next day of burning of Godhra train, to demolish a *dargah* which was protruding on the main road of Bhathha (Paldi) not far away from his own house. Thereafter, he started double

talking against the government for not protecting the minority. The demolition, he allegedly did, brought him on the top of the hit list, and therefore, he was killed.

But his strategy of targeting Modi worked wonders for him-the media forgot its charges on him and took to him as a 'hero'. This also shows that the biased section of the media will make a hero out of anyone who targets Narendra Modi without judging the case on merits.

That is, not even one person who was actually present at that meeting has alleged that Narendra Modi told them to allow Hindus to vent their anger. All those who were present, like the then DGP Chakravarthy, have reported that Modi told them exactly the opposite, to control the riots. **All those, who have alleged that Modi told officials to go slow at that meeting, were not even present at that meeting, neither Sanjiv Bhatt, nor R. Shreekumar, nor, if he did, the late Haren Pandya.**

Let us say, for argument's sake, that Modi did tell the officials at that crucial meeting on 27th February night to go slow on Hindus. But did they do so the next day? Not at all. We have seen all details of what the police actually did. **If the police had really allowed Hindus to vent their anger, the media would have gone crazy on 28th February itself in its reports of 1st March.**

Myth 20: Zakia Jafri's complaint against Narendra Modi is a genuine one

Fact: First thing to be noted is that Zakia Jafri did not make any complaint against Narendra Modi at all, for as many as 4 years after the 2002 riots, i.e. until 2006! In this time, she made statements before the police, the Nanavati Commission, filed affidavits in the courts as well and never once made any complaint against Narendra Modi! It is only after 2006 that she began speaking against Modi, perhaps tutored by some influential 'activists' when they saw this as a chance to frame and crucify the biggest fish! The complaint, filed against Modi and 61 others including government officials and state ministers by the wife of late Congress leader, Ehsan Jafri, who was killed in the 2002 riots, was a bundle of inexplicable factual errors, legal loopholes and wild allegations and virtually looked like a tutored child's complaint, simply impossible to prove.

Factual Blunders

The complaint alleges that the Anand district police chief B.S. Jebalia was not only witness to unimaginable massacre at Ode village soon after the Godhra carnage but was also an abettor in it through a brazen connivance. **The complainant obviously did not know that the truth is that another police officer, B.D. Vaghela, and not Jebalia, was posted as the Anand district police chief at that time!**

Zakia's complaint also says that Chief Secretary, Subarao participated in the February 27 (2002) night meeting, in which it alleged that the Chief Minister gave orders to the officers to direct law enforcement agencies to allow Hindus to give vent to their feelings in reaction to the Godhra carnage. **But the fact is Subarao was on leave on that day and instead of him, it was the acting Chief Secretary, S.K. Varma, who participated in the meeting.** This blunder has been made by many Narendra Modi-baiters such as weekly *Outlook* in its article dated 3rd June, 2002, trying to nail Modi forcibly. This single blunder is enough to see through the claims of people like Zakia Jafri and magazines like *Outlook*.

But that is not all! Many persons, who had either no direct connection with the 2002 riots or had, in fact, played positive role in controlling the riots, have been named as conspirators and abettors in the complaint. These seriously militate against the established canons of law and justice. For example, former Ahmedabad Police Commissioner, K.R. Kaushik, who was brought on to the post to control the riots has also been named as an accused. How can Kaushik be accused as an abettor or conspirator when he had been brought in to control the riots on 10 May 2002 and after whose arrival there was further improvement in law and order situation in Ahmedabad? Actually, the Commissioner, P.C. Pandey's removal was demanded (despite the fact that he too did a commendable job) and as the controversy escalated in 2002, Kaushik was appointed. **The complaint has been filed by people who either did not know this fact, or did not know the reason behind Kaushik's appointment,** and the fact that after his appointment there was further improvement in law and order in Ahmedabad.

Zakia Jafri has further alleged in her complaint that the remains of the slain *karsevaks* were purposefully brought from Godhra to Ahmedabad "in a ceremonial procession" on 27th February after the carnage at Godhra in order to instigate Hindus to target Muslims. Of course, this is again wrong on facts!

The fact is that the bodies were brought to Ahmedabad after the midnight of 27th February in a very sombre atmosphere and not in a ceremonial procession. We have seen earlier how the bodies were brought at 3:30 am, to an isolated hospital and to Western Ahmedabad, at a time at which most people are asleep and it is almost impossible to instigate riots.

Wild allegations

But the most unimaginable allegation she makes against Modi is that while issuing instructions to his officials in the 27th February night meeting **to give long rope to Hindu rioters, Modi also indicated that Hindus be encouraged to "indulge in sexual violence against Muslim women"**. This whole mischievous and manufactured charge has to be seen in the light of the fact that many Muslim witnesses who claimed to have witnessed, acts of rape on Muslim women in their 2003 affidavit before the Supreme Court, later told the SIT in May 2009 that they had been made to make the false charge by human rights activists (see in Myth 16 and that meeting in Myth 19). Assuming that Narendra Modi did give such instructions in that 27th February meeting, is it believable that he would have told the police officials and other authorities to tell Hindus to 'indulge in sexual violence against Muslim women'? This is an utterly unbelievable and far-fetched allegation. In support of her charge that Modi gave instructions to his officials not to act against Hindu rioters in the 27th February night meeting, she produces only one piece of evidence, namely the deposition of former Gujarat IPS officer, R.B. Sreekumar, who told the Nanavati Commission in an affidavit and later also the SIT that the then Director General of Police, V.K. Chakravarthy told him that the CM had directed officers to go slow against Hindu rioters and allow them to give vent to their feelings against the Muslims.

But we have already dismantled Sreekumar's claims in Myth 19. **We have already seen in Myth 19 the truth of the 27th February meeting.** Also note that Ehsan Jafri fired on the Hindu crowd outside his house in self-defense on 28th February, 2002. It is a well-established fact that Jafri fired on the Hindu crowd in self-defense. But Zakia Jafri once denied even this basic fact. In its 18th March, 2002 issue, *India Today* reported that "Zakia Jafri denies that Ehsan Jafri fired on the mob".

Legal Loopholes

Interestingly, there are several law sections applied in the complaint, which are simply inapplicable in the manner she has done. Like Jafri has asked section 193 of IPC to be applied, which is about giving false evidence in court during judicial proceedings. But this section can be applied only by the court and not an individual. Then Section 6 of the Commission of Inquiry Act has also been slapped on the accused by Jafri, which only a Commission of Inquiry can apply.

Then the Protection of Human Rights Act too is wrongly invoked in the complaint, whose actual prayer is that the complaint should be turned into an FIR for registering cases against Modi and other accused as conspirators and abettors in the 2002 riots.

Interestingly, the many factual and other contradictions in Jafri's complaint show that old complaints of 2002 filed by Muslims and human rights activists with a view to building a case against the Modi Government and having it pulled down under Article 356 of the Indian Constitution, had been put together in a footloose manner for Jafri by some low-level lawyer in a form of one full-fledged complaint.

The role of the media in all this is condemnable. It is simply impossible that the "Gujarat-obsessed" media would not have known these facts. But they did not bother to report them. Not a single paper has ever bothered to publish these facts, so much is their hatred for Narendra Modi. **The media knows that if the truth of Zakia Jafri's complaint comes out, even the most biased judge cannot convict Narendra Modi or entertain the complaint and, hence, it is suppressing all these facts.**

Only the weekly *India Today* has published just some of the few errors, and that too much after the case was settled by the Supreme Court of India, when on 12th September, 2011, the Supreme Court ordered the case to go back to the trial court and end its monitoring, and refused to file an FIR against Narendra Modi. What prevented weekly *India Today* from carrying all the errors, or most of the errors, when the complaint was filed and still in courts, is a question worth asking. Perhaps, it wanted the Supreme Court to entertain such a childish complaint of Jafri so that Modi could be crucified. But when it was no longer possible for the Supreme Court to entertain and monitor such a complaint, it just let slip in bits and pieces of the truth.

India Today did admit that Zakia Jafri's complaint contained some errors when it wrote: "The real reason for the court's ruling perhaps lies in the series of glaring factual errors and misplaced allegations in Zakia's complaint. She alleged that Modi gave instructions to officials in a meeting at his residence on the night of 27th February, 2002, the day 59 Hindus were killed at Godhra, that the community should be allowed to give vent to its anger against Muslims. She also alleged that the State Government "sanctioned sexual violence against women". The list of officials, Zakia has named as being present at the meeting, is also inaccurate. She claims the then Chief Secretary, G. Subarao and Modi's Secretary, A.K. Sharma were present, which was not the case. Zakia also wrongly alleged that the burned bodies of the 59 victims of the Godhra carnage were brought to Ahmedabad in a ceremonial procession to inflame Hindu passions. The bodies were actually brought without any brouhaha to Ahmedabad's western outskirts to be handed over to the relatives" (*Source:* http://indiatoday.intoday.in/story/2002-gujarat-riots-narendra-modi-supreme-court-order/1/151573.html).

There are many more facts of this Zakia Jafri complaint and SIT report which we will see in another chapter.

Myth 21: A B Vajpayee said Narendra Modi is not following *Raj dharma*

FACT: This incident happened on 4th April 2002, when the then Prime Minister Atal Bihari Vajpayee visited Gujarat. When a reporter asked the Prime

Minister in his joint press conference with Narendra Modi what message he will like to give the Gujarat Chief Minister, he said: "A ruler should follow *Rajdharma* (Duty of the ruler). Not differentiate between the subjects on the basis of caste or religion. I always try to do so. I am sure Narendra*bhai* is also doing so."

The latter part of the sentence: "I am sure that Narendra Modi is also following Rajdharma" was completely ignored, not reported and it was made to sound as if Vajpayee had said: "Narendra Modi should follow Rajdharma (Implied that he is not doing so now)".

Luckily, the entire video is today on YouTube and can be viewed by anyone. http://www.youtube.com/watch?v=x5W3RCpOGbQ

The Hindu **reported on 5 April 2002, i.e. the next day, in a report titled "Vajpayee's advice to Modi" that: "The Prime Minister added, "I believe he is performing his Raj dharma properly."**

http://www.hindu.com/thehindu/2002/04/05/stories/2002040509161100.htm

In 2002 itself, just a few days after this, when the media lies went on, the then Prime Minister himself clarified the reality. On 6 May 2002, Vajpayee said the media had only highlighted his remark that the Gujarat chief minister should follow *raj dharma* [ethics of governance], but did not pay much attention to Narendra Modi's response that he was doing the same. He sought to know whether there was no other way to follow *raj dharma* other than seeking the resignation of Modi.

http://www.rediff.com/news/2002/may/06train3.htm

In the days of the domination of the mainstream media with no social media, and terrible PR work from the people who mattered, this lie continued unchallenged for almost 10 years. But now with the social media and YouTube taking away the monopoly of TV channels, the reality came out. Hence, after suppressing the truth for 10 years by not reporting Vajpayee's next line viz. "I am sure Narendra Modi is also following Rajdharma", some biased media people tried to find some excuses. They said: "Modi's body language was uncomfortable", "He made Vajpayee say that" etc. Thus they tried to imply that though Vajpayee said Modi is following Rajdharma, he actually meant that Modi is not!

Such interpretations can be drawn only by the most outrageous liars, dishonest people who indulged in selective reporting to distort the truth, in a cruel and disgusting way to delude people. The journalist who actually asked the question was Priya Sehgal. There were many others also present there at the press conference. When the truth came out, Priya Sehgal raised non-issues like Modi's body language, his discomfort etc. Priya and all others present at that press conference never once apologized for completely twisting Vajpayee's words and blacking out the clear line: "I am sure he is performing *Rajdharma*".

This tale of lies and myths is unending. It can go on and on and on. We will, however, need to conclude this chapter here itself. An enterprising writer would do well to compile an encyclopedia of these media lies on the entire Gujarat scenario. He can start with media lies on Godhra, on concocting imaginary 'provocations' for Godhra, the lies concocted on the post-Godhra riots such as the extent of the riots, the number of people killed, the imaginary tales and stories of unnamed victims, etc. And he can conclude with the media's malicious reporting during the Gujarat Assembly elections of December 2002. The BJP and the Sangh Parivar who suffer the maximum damage from these lies, have unwisely allowed the particular section of the media to escape the courts for one-sided, malicious lies.

CHAPTER 8

CONTRASTS BETWEEN 1984 AND GUJARAT 2002 RIOTS

Some of the stark lies and blatant myths have already been seen in the previous chapters. But it is necessary to remove some more misconceptions. A section of the media has always tried to equate the Gujarat riots of 2002 A.D., and the 1984 anti-Sikh riots in the aftermath of the then Indian Prime Minister Indira Gandhi's assassination on 31 October 1984. Again, well-meaning people have fallen prey to the media myths.

Justice Nanavati, heading the Nanavati Commission of Inquiry probing the 1984 anti-Sikh riots submitted his report to the then Union Home Minister of India, Shivraj Patil on 9th February, 2005. The report was kept under the wraps for six months, and released on the last day of the time limit viz. 8th August, 2005. After the release, a large section of the Indian media equated the 1984 riots and the 2002 riots of Gujarat. NDTV broadcast *The Big Fight* on this issue in August 2005. Vinod Mehta, the then editor of *Outlook* weekly magazine equated both the riots and said, "A lot of things are exactly the same. In 1984, it was the killing of Indira Gandhi, in Gujarat it was Godhra…both the causes served a cause for the massacre…."

Editorial of *The Times of India* dated 12th August, 2005 on this issue was:
"Now for Modi
BJP and Gujarat CM should take a cue from Tytler, Sajjan

We welcome the resignations of Jagdish Tytler from the ministry and Sajjan Kumar from the official post he held in the Delhi government.... People, who are even remotely connected with rioting, can't be allowed to hold office. This is given in a secular democracy. Where does that leave men like Gujarat Chief Minister, Narendra Modi? He has no option but to quit office. The BJP and its allies like the Akali Dal and Janata Dal (United) were unequivocal in demanding Tytler's resignation. The parties invoked the ethics of Parliamentary democracy as well as the morality of public conduct to press the government for action on the Nanavati Commission. Their arguments hold true for Modi as well...."

As a result of this media hype, none other than some leaders of the BJP itself could have started believing that the two riots were similar. In November 2004, on NDTV's *The Big Fight*, when Congress spokesperson Jayanthi Natrajan said, "We don't call you (BJP) communal because of Uniform Civil Code. We call you communal because of Gujarat", the BJP participant said: "I can call you anti-secular because of the 1984 riots. You have no face to show". This was ok. But after that, perhaps he should have tried to explain the truth of the Gujarat riots, and said that the party's secular credentials are strengthened because of the Gujarat Government's handling of the Gujarat riots when the government managed to control the riots in three days, saved more than 24,000 Muslims and many Hindus too. However, he unwittingly conceded, perhaps unknowingly, that the Gujarat riots were similar to the 1984 riots!

NDTV aired *The Big Fight* in March 2005 on the issue of Modi being denied a visa by the USA, which included Digvijay Singh of the Congress, a leader of the BJP and the Jawaharlal Nehru University's Purushottam Agrawal. NDTV also had an American voice with an American woman briefly invited through videophone from Delhi, and it was four against one with the BJP participant not able to counter NDTV. This is because he did not seem to have the knowledge of facts needed to speak in this debate, though he is a good debater, a lawyer and was a BJP spokesman. He did not attack NDTV for putting it four against one. He talked of the 1984 riots, which simply cannot be compared with the Gujarat riots. It is a figment of imagination of some biased people in the media and deliberate attempt to malign opponents that such comparisons are made, and the 1984 riots and the Gujarat riots are equated. The differences are too glaring for the two to be equated. The BJP participant could not mention some true facts of the Gujarat riots, and lost the debate to the Congress-Marxist combine.

B.P. Singhal's article in the weekly *Organiser* dated 9th October, 2005 and in *The Pioneer* dated 28th September, 2005 on this issue is very useful (*Source*: http://www.organiser.org/dynamic/modules.php?name=Content&pa=showp age&pid=99&page=14).

Let us here see the contrasts in detail:

Godhra and Indira Gandhi's Murder

In 1984, Indira Gandhi's assassination on 31 October was the cause of the riots. **Indira Gandhi's murder was terrorism.** It was done by two people, both terrorists, with bullets. It was a big human tragedy. But it was not like Godhra, where the victims were locked and burnt alive, and not allowed to escape.

The entire Sikh community could not, in any way, be blamed for that murder. It was an act done by just two people, both Indira Gandhi's bodyguards. They were not ordinary people, but terrorists. It was not a communal act, but a terrorist one.

The culprits were immediately brought to book. Two Sikhs killed one Congressperson, although she was the country's Prime Minister. It was also more an attack on an individual. It was not an attack on a community, a political party, i.e. the Indian National Congress. The attackers just wanted to kill an individual. And both were given punishment later.

On the contrary, Godhra was not really terrorism, even if Justice Nanavati, Narendra Modi, George Fernandes, L.K. Advani, VHP, BJP, *Organiser, Panchjanya* claim so. Godhra was unparalleled in the history of independent India. The pain that Indira Gandhi suffered was perhaps momentary. But this was not the case with Godhra victims. In Godhra, the train was set on fire and not a single passenger was allowed to escape out, the train being surrounded by Muslims from both sides, armed with petrol bombs, acid bombs and swords. The passengers were burnt to death in a ghastly manner. The pain was not momentary. And even 15 children were burnt to death by the mob, which did not think of letting the children escape the ghastly death.

The attackers in Godhra were not terrorists, who had AK-47 rifles, guns and grenades. They were ordinary local Muslims. Local 2,000 Sikhs did not kill Indira Gandhi. Out of the 2,000 Godhra attackers, even if one had called the police and informed them about such a conspiracy and planned attack much before 7:48 a.m., when the attack took place, the killings could have been prevented. Not even one of the 2,000 attackers did so. The killers were also not brought to book. Only 35 people were arrested for the carnage on that day, i.e. 27 February, in which as many as 2,000 people participated. Nobody seriously expected all 2,000 to be caught, but at least two-three hundred should have been caught. What follows is an excerpt from the weekly *India Today* (18th March, 2002):

"The problem, according to the former Director-General of Police, M.M. Singh, one of the finest officers Gujarat has seen, began in Godhra on 27th February. **He says the police should have immediately cordoned off the area from which the attackers came and taken strong action instead of allowing the culprits to flee. This, he says, would have pacified Hindu feelings to some extent right at the very outset.** 'Where any act is bound to lead to communal violence, the police should always take strong steps against the group, which has committed the act. That invariably has a salutary effect.'… There's another story doing the rounds about which few are keen to talk about. According to it, Modi was given an ultimatum on 27th February itself by the VHP leadership to act against the perpetrators of the Godhra carnage by evening or else face the music. By evening that day, the police had detained two of the six main accused besides 50 others. That was found to be inadequate by the VHP because the number of attackers in Godhra was over 1,000." The culprits went scot-free in Godhra (most of the 2,000 attackers) and this was one reason for the explosion on 28th February.

In Godhra, the attack was on a community, the Hindu community, and not on an individual. It was also not on an organization like the VHP, and certainly not on the individuals killed, as was the case in 1984. As a result, the retaliation was done by the entire community and not by any single organization. Also, after Indira Gandhi's murder, no one rubbed salts into the people's wounds by blaming her for her murder, or the Congress Party for her murder. On the contrary, after Godhra, the media-politician combine in India rubbed salt in the people's wounds by blaming the Godhra killings on the VHP and arguing that the dead men and women and children had it coming to them. Some, like Congress leader the late Amarsinh Chaudhary, accused the *karsewaks* of not paying for tea and snacks at the railway platform and blamed them for the Godhra killings. Many accused the dead *karsewaks* of acts like taunting and harassing Muslim passengers, etc. This angered the people even more and resulted in the initial explosion on 28th February, 2002. Nothing of this sort was done in 1984 after Indiraji's killing to provoke and anger the people.

Difference between the Rioters

In 1984, the riots were not a 'mass uprising'. They were killings by supporters of a single political party with alleged involvement of party leaders and workers. It is alleged that leaders of the Congress like the late Rajiv Gandhi (1944-1991), P.V. Narasimha Rao (1921-2004), Kamal Nath, Sajjan Kumar, Jagdish Tytler were culpable in the 1984 riots, though many of them had no cases against them, and out of those who have, none have as yet been found guilty in any court of law. In 1984, it was a political party that was enraged by the killing of one individual. The nation was also sad and angry, but did not have feelings of revenge. In Gujarat in 2002, it was the entire society that was enraged by the Godhra killings. *India Today* reports (18th March, 2002):

"Says political analyst, Arvind Bosmia: 'It is beyond the means of the *Sangh Parivar* to lead such an upsurge. It was largely a spontaneous reaction to the Godhra killings. And not just Modi but the entire *Sangh Parivar* has been put on this strident path. In fact, Modi has been swept up in this militancy.'"

This clearly proves that the 2002 Gujarat riots were impossible to have been carried out by the *Sangh Parivar* alone. While in 1984, only the Congress supporters were involved in the riots. The RSS cadres protected the Sikhs in 1984. Former National Minorities Commission chairman, Tarlochan Singh is on record saying this. ("Sikhs can never forget how RSS activists protected them in 1984 and in the Partition riots in 1947"— Tarlochan Singh on 26 July, 2003). But in the 2002 Gujarat riots, Congressmen were also involved, not only in Godhra, but also during attacks on Hindus, and also Muslims. *The Times of*

India reported on 9th August, 2003 that 25 Congress leaders were also accused of being involved in killing of Muslims in the post-Godhra riots. (*Source*: http://timesofindia.indiatimes.com//india/Cong-silent-on-cadres-linked-to-Guj-riots/ articleshow/122796.cms).

Past History of Riots

There have been hundreds of Hindu-Muslim riots in India since A.D. 1714. There have been conflicts between Hindus and Muslims right since A.D. 636. The foreign Muslim rulers committed horrible atrocities on the Hindus in the medieval period, some of which we have seen in the first chapter. Muslims were the aggressors in many of the Gujarat riots right since A.D. 1714. In the 1940s, in particular, the Hindus suffered terribly in the Ahmedabad riots. There were also horrible riots in 1969 and 1985 in Gujarat. Wounds of the past haunted the people.

In 1984, the conflicts with Sikhs and the attackers, if at all they can be called 'conflicts' and not 'genocide of the Sikhs', were the first case of clashes between the two communities. Sikhs had not terrorized Congress leaders in the past, right since A.D. 636. **After independence, Hindu-Sikh conflicts were not seen even once, not to talk of twice, under the rule of the BJP (or, for that matter, even the Congress) in New Delhi. While in Gujarat, far worse riots took place at least twice under the Congress rule, as compared to the riots in 2002 under the BJP rule.** The 1984 riots were the only and the bloodiest.

Action against Rioters

In 1984, no action was taken against the rioters. Not many arrests were made, despite the fact that officially close to 3,000 people were killed. According to ex-DGP B P Singhal, **not even one person was shot dead by the police or the Army.** The police was conspicuous by its absence for three full days. The Army, even though available locally, was not called for three full days. But these riots escaped the media glare, because in those days, TV was barely in its infancy. (*Source*: Article by B.P. Singhal in the weekly *Organiser* dated 9th October, 2005).

In Gujarat, as of October 2005 as many as 25,204 out of the 25,486 accused were arrested by the Gujarat police. As of May 2012, 26,999 were arrested. *The Times of India* dated 28 April, 2002 reports that 20,000 people were also arrested as a preventive measure- more than 17,000 of them Hindus. *The Times of India* also reported on 9 August 2003 that nearly 30,000 accused in the riots have been arrested. In Gujarat, the entire police force of 70,000 was deployed on 27 February itself, along with all available units of the Rapid Action Force. The Army was called immediately on 28 February, and newspapers like *The Hindu* and *The Indian Express* reported on 1 March, 2002 that the Army had started arriving in Ahmedabad. We have already seen the details of quick administrative action.

Already, we have at least 443 people (including 111 Muslims) convicted for Godhra & post- Godhra violence in Gujarat in 10-12 years. On the contrary, only perhaps 30 people in 12 cases were convicted till April 2013 for the 1984 riots. In Gujarat, the police arrested more than 35,000 people as on 28 April 2002, the highest ever in its history for rioting. **Not even in 1969 and 1985 were so many people arrested by the then Congress governments**, when at least 5,000 people were killed in riots (according to an article from *The Hindustan Times* of 1969 quoted by Harin Pathak), which lasted as long as five to six months in 1985.

Police/Army Action

In Gujarat in 2002, as many as 98 people were shot dead by the police for rioting in the first three days. Out of the total killed, 199 were killed in police firing as per official records. As many as close to 20 per cent people killed in the state were in police firing. The deployment of the Army, which was then posted on the border (almost the entire military strength was posted on the border in view of war-clouds between India and Pakistan) was in very quick time.

Even on 1st and 2nd March, 2002, riots took place in places where the Indian Army was present, i.e. Ahmedabad and Vadodara. But after 3rd March, 2002, riots took place almost entirely in those places where the Army was posted.

In 1984, despite the army being available locally, it was not called for three days. At that time, there was not even an insurgency in Kashmir. There was no war-like situation between any of the neighbours of India with whom India has had wars before, neither Pakistan (wars in 1947, 1965, 1971 & mini-war in 1999) nor China (war in 1962). The entire military strength was not deployed on the border. Neither were police visible in New Delhi. The police did not kill a single attacker in firing in 1984 according to B P Singhal. Not even a single preventive arrest appears to have been made in 1984, as against 827 made on 27th February itself, even before a single riot had taken place in Gujarat. Many more preventive arrests were made after the riots had begun (20,000). **Narendra Modi gave shoot- at-sight orders in Godhra on 27th February. There were also similar orders in many other towns in Gujarat.** No shoot-at-sight orders were given in 1984 on 31st October or even 1-2 days later.

In 2002, the Gujarat police saved as many as 24,000 Muslims from certain death. Police saved at least 17,500 Muslims in Sanjeli, Bodeli and Viramgam from the rioters and Hindus too in Modasa, Bharuch, etc. There are no such available records for the 1984 riots, where it can be said that Sikhs were saved and rioters were killed. The entire Sikh community was held responsible for the deeds of two Sikhs, in 1984. And the police turned a blind eye to the riots for 3 days at least and no action was taken against the rioters. Hardly any convictions took place in any court of law. A total of 16 or 30 people have been convicted till April 2013.

Versions of the Riots

During the time of the 1984 riots, the versions of the riots were similar and identical in all sections of the press throughout India. Whether it was the national English dailies, the local English dailies, the local Hindi dailies, or the regional language dailies all over the country, the reporting on the riots was exactly the same. The reporting of the TV news, radio news, was also exactly the same. There was not an iota of difference between the reports of any section of the media on a single case.

On the contrary, **there was a contrast of day and night in the versions of the riots as projected by the national English media as against the**

sharply contrasting versions appearing in the local Gujarati newspapers of all hues. This was because the Gujarati media reported the truth, while the English media always took the side of the Muslims, even if they indulged in cold-blooded murder, or were at the receiving end.

There was also a huge difference in the versions of the riots as projected by the same national English media and the electronic media, during the actual time of the riots in March-April 2002, and the reports by the same media months after the actual riots. Anyone reading the English dailies like *The Indian Express, The Hindu,* and the weeklies like *India Today* of March-April 2002, will understand this fully. These same dailies/weeklies ignored their own reports during the time of the riots ever after, and started reporting completely wrong.

The TV channels also played a lot of mischief on the issue of the Gujarat riots. NDTV owners are related to the leaders of CPI (M) – the Communist Party of India (Marxist). **This is because NDTV boss, Radhika Roy, wife of NDTV Chairman, Prannoy Roy, and CPI (M) MP and Politburo member, Brinda Karat, wife of CPI (M) General Secretary, Prakash Karat, are blood sisters.** Not just that, both Prannoy and Radhika Roy are staunch Communists. The CPI (M) party beliefs and ideology are staunchly anti-BJP. The CPI (M) always states publicly that its biggest political opponent is the BJP. CPI (M) has been a staunch opponent and critic of Narendra Modi. B.P. Singhal writes in an article in the weekly *Organiser* dated 9th October, 2005:

"On the other hand, a lot of mischief was played by the electronic media, which went on repeating some of the gory incidents of riots day after day. One channel repeated a particularly gory scene as many as 21 times. An image was, thus, created by the collaborating media that the massacre of Muslims was continuing unabated in Gujarat, day after day."

People Killed in the Riots

In 1984, as many as 3,000 people were killed officially in just a week for the deeds of two people. In actual, the number could be higher. According to the Ranganath Mishra Commission, 3,874 Sikhs were killed, out of which 2,307 Sikhs were killed in Delhi alone. Eminent Indian journalist the late Khushwant

Singh (1915-2014) who was a Sikh, told the Nanavati Commission: "The 1984 bloodbath left me feeling like a Jew in Nazi Germany." The Ranganath Mishra Commission reported: "In the mobs attacking Sikhs, were people with sympathy for the Congress (I) and associated with the party's activities."

On the other hand, in Gujarat in 2002, 790 Muslims (a number given by the UPA Government) were killed for the deeds of 2,000 Muslims in Godhra, in addition to as many as 254 Hindus killed after Godhra, plus the 59 Hindus killed in Godhra. A net result of deaths in Gujarat in 2002 would be 790 Muslims and 313 Hindus. While in 1984, it was at least 3,000 Sikhs and one Congressperson. The sinner-victim ratio (of co-religionists) in 1984 was 2: 3000, while in 2002 in Gujarat, it was 2000: 790 and, in addition, 254 Hindus at least were killed in the post-Godhra riots.

Riots in 2002 A.D. in Gujarat were controlled in just three days, and after 3 March, 2002, the state was almost completely normal except for some violence in Ahmedabad, Vadodara and some places near Godhra. This was in sharp contrast to the Gujarat riots of 1985, which continued for as long as 5-6 months, or even the 1990-91-92 riots in the state.

No Congress members (or for that matter, other attackers) were killed in 1984, while as many as 254 Hindus were killed in Gujarat in 2002, after Godhra. It is on record that Muslims had started 157 riots in Gujarat after 3rd March, 2002. Muslims attacked Hindus in Himmatnagar near Ahmedabad and killed a young Hindu after gouging out his eyes. In 1984, on the contrary, the Sikhs did not start even a single riot. No Congressman was killed after gouging out of eyes. The Sikhs did not attack any Congressman. Sikhs were poor victims in 1984, unlike the Muslims in 2002 in Gujarat, who were equally on the offensive.

Riots' Geographical Areas

In 1984, the riots occurred not just in New Delhi, but also in many other places. Not just that, Sikhs were attacked in as far off places as West Bengal and Tripura. Veteran CPI (M) leader, the late Harkishan Singh Surjeet (1916-2008) in an article in August 2005 accused Mamata Banerjee of being involved in the attacks on Sikhs in West Bengal in the 1984 riots. This prompted Mamata to threaten to file a defamation case against Surjeet. Surjeet's own comrades in West Bengal dissociated themselves from his charge. Anil Biswas, West Bengal secretary of the CPI(M), gave a clean chit to Mamata Banerjee, saying: "I have no knowledge about Mamata Banerjee having played any role in anti-Sikh riots in Kolkata..." (*Source*: http://www.indianexpress.com/oldStory/76644/).

We certainly do not believe this charge against Mamata Banerjee at all, but merely use it to prove that anti-Sikh riots occurred in as far off places as West Bengal, Tripura, etc. In 2002, no one was attacked or killed in any place outside Gujarat, not even in riot- prone Mumbai. As B.P. Singhal (1932-2012) wrote in his article in *Organiser*, "The Hindu community in the country ensured that the riots did not spread beyond Gujarat even though Godhra had severely outraged the Hindus all over the country." If the VHP or the Bajrang Dal were hell-bent on creating riots, as a matter of policy, there could have been mayhem in almost every part of India. However, none of this happened. The riots were limited to Gujarat only.

Even in Gujarat, no riots took place in one-third of the state, i.e. in Saurashtra and Kutch, even in the first three days. VHP had units in 10,000 out of Gujarat's 18,600 villages. Had it wanted to, it could have caused riots in all the 10,000 villages. However, riots were limited only to 50 villages and a total of maximum 90 places.

People Rendered Homeless

In the 2002 Gujarat riots, Hindus were also rendered homeless. We have seen earlier that 40,000 Hindus were in relief camps in Gujarat in April 2002.

In 1984, not a single Congressman or non-Sikh individual was rendered homeless. B.P. Singhal writes in his article, "On the other hand, no attempt was made to open even a single refugee camp for the hounded Sikhs at any point of time anywhere. Actually, as per the Nanavati Commission report, weapons of the Sikhs living in the Sikh localities were withdrawn with the promise of protection by the police, while the same localities were then attacked."

Far from non-Sikh people staying in refugee camps because of attacks by the Sikhs, even the displaced Sikhs were not provided refugee camps to stay. This was in sharp contrast to Gujarat in 2002, when Hindus were forced out of their homes by Muslims and forced to stay in refugee camps. Some Hindus were forced to live in temples, since no relief camps were available for them.

Elections Held

Though this issue is not directly related to the riots, a contrast here too is worth mentioning. After the anti-Sikh riots between 1st November and 7th November, 1984, the general elections of the Lok Sabha were held within 45 days. In these general elections, the Congress Party, riding on a sympathy wave generated by Indira Gandhi's assassination, won as many as 415 out of the 543 Lok Sabha seats. In the Gujarat Assembly elections held in February 1985, the Congress won a staggering 149 out of 182 seats (the last time it won an Assembly election in Gujarat, since then the Congress has lost every election held: in 1990, 1995, 1998, 2002, 2007 & 2012).

While in Gujarat in 2002, the elections were held in December 2002, as many as ten months after Godhra, and a good eight months after the riots. Despite this, the BJP won a huge majority of 127 out of the 182 seats, with a huge 11 per cent difference in the vote share of the Congress (39 per cent) and the BJP (50 per cent). It needs to be remembered that while the entire anti-BJP establishment was baying for Narendra Modi's blood saying "Modi *hatao*" (i.e. "Remove Modi"), they did not want elections to be held in Gujarat. That is, they did not want the people of Gujarat to have a chance to decide who should be the Chief Minister, something which only the people of Gujarat can decide. They got the elections delayed as well (while in 1984, they were held in 45 days), and still lost by a huge margin.

Who is going to awaken the public about the truth of the Gujarat riots? Those who claim to be 'awakened' themselves seem ignorant of the truth of the Gujarat riots. Those who are aware of the truth of the riots seem to do nothing to educate the masses and the well-meaning leaders on this issue, barring exceptions.

From the present situation, it may take nothing less than a miracle to blast the myths on the Gujarat riots, and let the truth triumph.

CHAPTER 9

ROLE OF THE RIVALS AND MEDIA IN INSTIGATING VIOLENCE

The Indian national English media, and the Indian National Congress (INC) were two of the groups that launched horrible attacks on the BJP and Narendra Modi for the Gujarat riots. They both (a section of the media, and the whole Congress Party) held Narendra Modi and the BJP responsible for the post-Godhra riots, and alleged that the post-Godhra riots were 'state-sponsored riots'. The truth is that far from being state-sponsored, some of the riots in Gujarat could have actually been instigated by the rivals of Narendra Modi, so as to target BJP and Narendra Modi.

Reason for this

During the time of the post-Godhra riots, the BJP was in power at the Centre in India. The BJP at that time had 182 seats out of the 543 in the Lok Sabha, the lower house of the Indian Parliament, way short of 272 needed for majority. The ruling National Democratic Alliance (NDA) at that time consisted of more than 22 alliance partners, which included DMK, MDMK, PMK, Lok Janshakti Party (LJP), Trinamool Congress, Telugu Desam Party (TDP), Janata Dal (United), National Conference, Biju Janata Dal, Akali Dal, AGP, INLD, RLD, Samata Party, etc. These parties staunchly followed, or claimed to follow at that time, the same ideology as claimed by the then Opposition Congress on the policy of secularism. These parties were opponents of BJP in the past, and had joined the NDA coalition on condition that the NDA Government will abandon the agenda of Hindutva of the BJP and leave out controversial issues like the construction of Ram Temple in Ayodhya. These parties were strongly opposed to organizations linked to the BJP (like RSS, its ideological parent, or the religious body, the VHP). In fact, the NDA had adopted a resolution on 2 February 1999 that: "Since the BJP is the core of our alliance, it shall make every effort to ensure that the prestige and cohesiveness of the coalition are not diluted by organisations belonging to its ideological fraternity." (Read RSS, VHP). These allies were providing crucial support to the NDA Government.

At that time, some of the allies pressurized the BJP and indulged in severe brinkmanship. The BJP was soundly thrashed in the Assembly elections in four states held in February 2002. The BJP was soundly thrashed in Uttar Pradesh, India's largest and politically most important state, with the party winning just 88 seats out of the 403 in the state assembly- down from 176 it had won in 1996 out of 425 in undivided Uttar Pradesh. The BJP had also lost Uttarakhand (winning 19 out of 70 seats with Congress winning 36, though vote percentage was the same) and won a mere three out of the 23 seats it contested in Punjab in alliance with the Akali Dal, out of a total 117. That had already shaken the NDA.

There was a motion moved in the Parliament by the Congress-led Opposition and backed by the Communists in May 2002 against the Gujarat Government headed by Narendra Modi. Sonia Gandhi had earlier sat on a *dharna* in the Parliament in the first week of March 2002 demanding Narendra Modi's dismissal as the Chief Minister of Gujarat, because of the false reports that only Muslims are being targetted in Gujarat, ignoring Muslim attacks on the Hindus, and, of course, the Godhra incident.

The role of the NDA allies was very crucial. If the allies had voted for the motion, Article 356 (Dismissal of a state government by the Central Government) could well have been implemented. Many of the allies were speaking against Narendra Modi, in particular, TDP (which had a huge 28 MPs in the Lower House, on whose support the government depended), and the Trinamool Congress. The debate on this issue was to start in the Rajya Sabha on 6 May 2002.

The riots in Gujarat had already stopped on 12 April 2002. This was detrimental to the Opposition's intention of the collapse of the NDA with allies like TDP, Trinamool Congress withdrawing support, and dismissal of the State Government. At that time, the Congress had launched a Modi-*hatao* (remove Modi) campaign which had the active support of some NGOs and self-proclaimed secularist organizations like PUCL (People's Union for Civil Liberties). This campaign was also not succeeding in removal of the Chief Minister. Gujarat had become normal as early as 3 March 2002. After that, riots continued only in small pockets. But they had altogether stopped by 12 April. But the Opposition allegedly wanted the riots to continue till at least 5 May 2002, so as to attack Narendra Modi and the BJP, and get the NDA allies like TDP, DMK, etc. to vote against the Narendra Modi Government and set the collapse of the NDA.

As a result, the Congress Party is alleged to have instigated riots in Gujarat after 21ˢᵗ April, 2002, which was *Ramnavami* day.

That despite this, the motion was defeated by a huge margin, 281 versus 194 in the Lok Sabha, is a different matter altogether.

Now let us see the report of *India Today* dated 20 May 2002:

"...True, since the latest round of violence began on *Ramnavami* day on 21ˢᵗ April, violence has been restricted mostly to Ahmedabad, Vadodara and Lunawada, a small town in the Panchmahal district.... The concern is understandable. Unlike the first phase of the riots, now Hindus too have begun to suffer, thanks to a new belligerence of the Muslims, who have been under siege for 10 weeks. The repeated recovery of huge caches of weapons from Muslim pockets forced some of the ministers to ask Modi about the steps the police was taking to flush out these armouries.

Meanwhile, the dangerous divide in Gujarat is getting wider. Chunibhai Vaidya, eminent Gandhian, says, "Any other chief minister would have resigned owing moral responsibility. What stops Vajpayee from replacing Modi now?" But there are an equal number ready to echo Vajpayee's logic. Says Dharmesh Vyas, 26, an employee of a private company, who is recovering from bullet wounds sustained in firing by Muslim mobs: "If Modi is removed, the violence will increase because there is a feeling among Hindus that the riots are now being engineered by Modi's rivals to get rid of him. It is Modi's presence

250

that is keeping the Hindus in check. Once he is gone, things will become uncontrollable."

What is adding to the knife-edge tension is the growing evidence that the violence has a deliberate pattern and there is a motive to keep the flames from being doused. Violence seemed to have been brought under control by the second week of March until sporadic attacks on Hindus in Ahmedabad, Bharuch and Modasa in the midst of the state school board examinations reignited the embers. But it escalated on *Ramnavami* day (21 April) when a police constable (he was a Hindu named Amar Patil) was killed in Ahmedabad's Gomtipur (which is a Muslim) area. The sudden spurt of violence followed after a call given by local Muslim leaders to students from the community to boycott the rescheduled state school board examinations failed. **Significantly, among those who were exhorting the students to boycott the exams, were five local Congress leaders besides members of the radical Islamic movement, the Tableeghi Jamaat.**

Local BJP leaders point to other incidents to suggest there was a method in the mayhem. Hours after Defence Minister, George Fernandes led a peace march in Ahmedabad, violence broke out on the route he had taken. (This was also reported by *The Tribune* dated 30 April, 2002.) The area had not witnessed any riot in the recent past. **Strangely, the rioting stopped a day before (Congress President) Sonia Gandhi's peace rally in Ahmedabad on 1st May.** But on 5th May, a day before the Rajya Sabha debated the censure motion and barely 24 hours after (Super cop, K.P.S. Gill, who had finished militancy in Punjab) Gill took over his Gujarat assignment, violence erupted again. This time Muslim rioters attacked Bhilwas locality in the Shah Alam area. Says political analyst Vidyut Thakar: **"A pattern is visible in the new round of violence. There is an impression that it has to do with the Modi-hatao campaign."**

Gujarat Congress leaders, however, rubbish the BJP and the Hindu leaders' charges that the Congress was instigating the violence. Says state Congress chief, Amarsinh Chaudhary: "How can Modi place his miserable failure to curb the riots at our door? He has the entire state machinery at his command to take whatever steps that are needed to quell the violence." Modi, on whom the pressure is beginning to show, retorts, "Even a blind man can make out that interested sections want to keep the embers burning with a specific objective. Only anti-national forces can be happy in such a situation" (*Source*: http:// www.india-today.com/itoday/20020520/ states.html).

What conclusion can we draw from the above report by *India Today*? However, this issue of *India Today* is not the only source of the alleged Opposition hand in the Gujarat riots. The following is the report of *The Hindu* (23rd April, 2002):

"Toll could rise in Ahmedabad

Manas Dasgupta

Ahmedabad, 22nd April: After the Gujarat bandh day on 28th February, **the first day of the post-Godhra violence, the *Ramnavami* day on Sunday accounted for the highest number of deaths in the city in a single day:** nine persons succumbed to injuries in hospital late in the night, in addition to the nine killed earlier in the day. The casualty figure may go up as the condition of at least 18 injured was still critical.

Indefinite curfew continued in Kadi in Mehsana and Kapadvanj, Mehmadabad and Chhota-Udepur towns, all in central Gujarat, which witnessed violence during the last two days. Curfew was clamped in the Chhota-Udepur town in Baroda district last night, after rival groups pelted stones and set fire to shops and cabins, forcing the police to open fire.

One person was killed in police firing in Mirzapur area late last night, while three persons were stabbed to death in Gheekanta, Jamalpur and Prem Darwaja today. A 19-year-old student, who was going on a motorcycle to appear for the Gujarat University examinations, was stabbed near Raikhad and was admitted in hospital.

Almost the entire walled city areas were tense as sporadic incidents of group clashes and arson were reported. **Timely intervention by police saved the Sarvodaya commercial complex on the busy Relief Road, where a violent group attempted to set the shops on fire.**

At least 30 huts, shops and cabins were set on fire in Shahpur. Some residential areas also came under attack from violent mobs, but no one was injured. The curfew-bound Gomtipur, Bapunagar and Rakhial areas remained tense but peaceful today after the orgy of violence, which started on Sunday afternoon, continued throughout the night.

As the trouble spread to Mirzapur late in the night, one person was killed and three others injured when police opened fire on a group of arsonists. Groups of people in the Gomtipur, Bapunagar and Rakhial areas continued to fight pitched battle throughout the night forcing the police to open fire repeatedly....

...the state Congress president, Amarsinh Chaudhary, favouring continuation of the examinations, took a serious view of some of his party colleagues joining hands with minority leaders to give a call to the students to boycott the examinations. Talking to media persons here today, Mr. Chaudhary said he would seek an explanation from those who were believed to have supported the boycott call" (*Source*: http://www. hinduonnet.com/2002/04/23/02hdline.htm).

It seems that the Opposition instigated these riots and the calls for boycotting of exams with Islamic leaders. And it need not even be mentioned that these were riots and not 'massacre', as one can see from the report of Manas Dasgupta, they were by no means one-sided.

Now let us see another report of *The Hindu* (7th May, 2002):

"The ruling BJP and the Congress indulged in allegations and counter-allegations over 'instigating riots.' While the Chief Minister, Narendra Modi, said at a public function in Surat that the Congress was 'instigating violence' in the state for political gains, the Gujarat Congress president, Amarsinh Chaudhary, said the violence started yesterday was 'clearly sponsored by the State Government'."

The very fact that a newspaper like *The Hindu* reported that the Congress party was being accused of instigating the riots for political gains, shows that that allegation had basis. It is not merely that such an 'allegation' was made. Five local Congress leaders were indeed actively egging on the students to boycott the board examinations, just like the radical Tableeghi Jamaat. The failure of the calls for boycott of the examinations by the students led to more attacks on Hindus by the Muslims.

The website www.rediff.com reported on 22nd April, 2002:

"Gujarat Home Minister Sees Plot to Break NDA

Sheela Bhatt in Mumbai

Gujarat Minister of State for Home, Gordhan Zadaphia has blamed the Congress for the fresh spurt in violence in the state on Sunday (21 April 2002), which cost 21 people their lives, saying the opposition party was trying desperately to break the National Democratic Alliance Government at the Centre.

'Yesterday's (21 April) riots in Ahmedabad's Gomtipur and Rakhiyal area were planned,' Zadaphia told rediff.com: 'The Congress and the minority community do not want peace. **The Congress wants to break the NDA alliance in Delhi by fuelling riots in Gujarat.** Political parties in India are in the race for appeasing the minorities. They will not say a word against the Jama Masjid imam's speech yesterday, where he incited Muslims to break India.'

According to Zadaphia, the Congress plan is **'to continue the rioting, raise the issue in Parliament, force the NDA partners to raise their voices and, in turn, force the Modi Government to resign'.**

Corporators like Badruddin Sheikh and Taufik Pathan and their sons were leading the crowd, he alleged. 'The crowd wanted to attack the colonies and kill as many as they can,' he said. 'It was a serious attack. The railway tracks were full of people with bombs and weapons in their hands.'

Asked about six Muslims being shot by the police at point- blank range, he retorted, 'What do you expect the police to do when Amar Patil, my constable, was stabbed to death just outside the masjid? At another place, six SRP [*State Reserve Police*] men were injured when the minority crowd attacked them? Do you have any idea of the impact on the morale of the police?'

Zadaphia claimed that Pathan and Sheikh were bent upon disrupting the current high school exams. **'They are harassing Muslim students,' he said. 'In relief camps and Muslim areas, they have announced on loudspeakers that Muslim students shall give college exams, but not the 10th and 12th standard exams.'**

The minister said the 'disruptive elements' were upset because 98 per cent of students have appeared in the exams. 'Their supporters are forcing students to get down from buses provided by the government,' he claimed. 'They are tearing away the entry receipts of the students. What does this mean?'

Zadaphia promised that he would arrest the people, who were inciting communal tensions to disrupt the exams. 'We will break the 50-year-old negative psyche of such people,' he said.

Naresh Rawal, leader of the Congress in the assembly, dismissed the minister's allegations. 'The NDA will be dismantled soon for other reasons,' he told rediff.com, 'These are bogus allegations. Modi is failing to maintain law and order. He is the number one villain in India today. People's perception is that Modi connived with the rioters. He should go. Let the BJP get a new CM and stop making such baseless allegations'". (*Source*: http://www.rediff. com/news/2002/apr/22bhatt.htm).

Doesn't this report give an indication of the situation prevailing in Gujarat at that time? Even *The Hindu* reported that five leaders of the Congress were instigating Muslims to boycott the exams along with the radical Muslim organization *Tableeghi Jamaat*.

Moreover, *India Today* reports, "Violence seemed to have been brought under control by the second week of March until sporadic attacks on Hindus in Ahmedabad, Bharuch and Modasa in the midst of the state school board examinations reignited the embers. But it escalated on *Ramnavami* day (21st April, 2002) when a police constable was killed in Ahmedabad's Gomtipur (which is a Muslim) area. The sudden spurt of violence followed after a call given by local Muslim leaders to students from the community to boycott the rescheduled state school board examinations failed."

This indicates that the opponents could have instigated the riots from as early as 13th March, 2002 so as to target the BJP and Narendra Modi, and shake and disintegrate the NDA. The biased people in the media, and some particular TV channels were always going to hold the BJP and Narendra Modi responsible for the riots, closing their eyes, and turning a blind eye to the Muslim instigation and the Opposition's hand. We saw in the second chapter K. M. Munshi warn of the tendency to blame the majority in case of any inter-religious conflict regardless of the merit of the question.

The report of www.rediff.com **dated 2nd April, 2002 titled "Politicians, Gamblers Keep Gujarat's Cycle of Violence Going" also seems to imply**

that the Opposition was instigating riots in Gujarat on 2nd April, 2002. That report says:

"...in a volatile place like Gomtipur, once charged crowds come face to face, clashes are inevitable. Here, like in many other parts of Gujarat, Dalits (Hindus belonging to the so-called lower castes) live in close proximity with Muslims. The crowd in Shanker Ghanchi Lane consisted mostly of Dalits. Both sides were prepared, said social worker, Ashok Shrimali, a resident of the area, who saw the clash. 'A huge fire started when petrol bombs were thrown on a residential area. A few Dalit homes got burnt, tension increased and things became uncontrollable.'

Parikh, who witnessed the entire battle from a police jeep, said, 'People had unusual weapons. Long swords to *gilole* (a handy instrument made of strings and leather) and hand-made sulphate bombs. Bottles of Thums Up filled with petrol were in plenty.'

Shrimali remarked, 'The Muslims were screaming revenge while the Dalits seemed to have been provoked by politicians. In our area, Congress leaders are active again.' Pravin Pandya, a former member of the state scheduled caste board, said, 'Since Dalits have suffered more casualties, the Congress is playing with their insecurity. If Dalits are pitted against Muslims, which is quite an easy game, the Congress stands to gain.'

But Naresh Rawal, Leader of the Opposition in the Gujarat assembly, dismissed this allegation as '*raddi*' (rubbish). Instead, the Congressman, who visited Kadi—which witnessed clashes last week— on Sunday evening, told rediff.com, 'The way riots are spreading to new areas, we can see the BJP pattern emerging'" (*Source*: http:// www.rediff.com/news/2002/apr/02bhatt. htm).

The Justice Tewatia Committee report mentioned earlier also states:

".... Sectarian violence continues even more than a month after Godhra. **This fourth phase of violence has no provocation or justification other than to sustain the 'Remove Modi' campaign.** It is the constitutional duty of the State Government to protect citizens and maintain law and order.

It is also in the partisan interest of the ruling party in the state to put an end to the communal violence as its continuity in office depends on how soon and how effectively it combats violence. **It is, therefore, hard to reject Chief**

Minister's contention that the Congress Party that has a vested interest in getting him sacked is perpetuating the communal violence by provoking stray incidents.

Thus, the Study Team concludes:

… 26. Communal violence in Gujarat has become politicized, and instead of treating it as human tragedy, it is being used to get political mileage by political parties.

27. Loaded statements made by political leaders propounding their action plans, increases the hiatus between Muslims and Hindus.…"

This report was made after a study from 1 to 7 April. This implies that from 1st April and before the Congress could have been instigating riots.

We have seen details on number of people killed weekwise in Gujarat in March-April 2002. Violence from week 9, 10 and 11, after 20th April adds up to 52 people killed. At least, in the last three weeks, violence seems to be instigated by the rivals of Modi, killing 52 people. The opponents could have started instigating the violence from as early as the 3rd week. Adding the deaths from week 3 to week 10, we get a total of 355 people killed. But we can say that it implies from the reports of the Justice Tewatia Committee, *The Hindu*, *India Today* and rediff.com that the Opposition could be responsible for the deaths of 52 people killed in the last 3 weeks.

No less a man than the then Deputy Prime Minister of India, L K Advani (born 1927) said in July 2002 in an interview to a reputed weekly *India Today*: "In Gujarat, the past riots have been caused by very trivial reasons-a cricket match, kite-flying, something of that kind. This time it was a horrendous incident at Godhra which sparked that riot... **Three-four days later it seemed to have been contained considerably but after that it seems that some vested interests kept it alive.**"

http://www.indiatoday.com/itoday/20020722/cover8.shtml

DIRECT EVIDENCE OF OPPOSITION INSTIGATING RIOTS

Members of the Congress party have been declared guilty for rioting and attacking and killing Hindus in Vadodara in March 2002 on 16 October 2003. The accused had stabbed to death Pankaj Chauhan at Resham Wali Gali near

Champaner on March 22, 2002. Former Deputy Mayor of Vadodara and Congress leader Nisar Bapu was acquitted, but his son and son-in-law were convicted. Total 4 Muslims were convicted for this. This is direct evidence of the involvement of the Congress in riots in Gujarat on 22 March 2002. This was reported by at least 3 English dailies, including *The Times of India* on 17 October 2003. This report can be read by opening the link: http://timesofindia.indiatimes.com//india/Four-get-life-imprisonment/articleshow/236376.cms

Role of the Congress Party in Godhra Massacre

The cause of the Gujarat riots was the Godhra massacre. But what the media and even the rivals of the Congress Party ignore is the role of the Congress Party in the Godhra massacre. Some top Congress corporators of Godhra are the accused in the Godhra massacre case. This is what Rajeev Srinivasan reports on www.rediff.com dated 25th March 2002:

"Godhra, 'Secular', 'Progressives' and Politics

As usual, during the bloodbath in Gujarat, the Nehruvian Stalinists in the English-language media showed their cowardice and bigotry by blaming the Hindus for all sorts of real and imagined faults. It never strikes them that the non-Hindus of India could possibly be anything other than victims oppressed by 'cruel, medieval, casteist Hindus'; never mind that such Hindus exist largely in their hyperactive imaginations.

The Nehruvians twisted themselves into pretzel-logic in their eagerness to justify the unjustifiable: the carnage that was set off by the usual suspects, that is, Muslims with links either to Pakistani subversives or to the Congress Party. The difference between the two groups is vanishingly small when it comes to pressing forward Muslim demands. Consider some implicated as suspects in the Godhra incident according to BJP sources, as reported by *The Indian Express* of 5th March:

- Mehmud Hussain Kalota, convener of the Congress district minority cell and president of the Godhra municipality.

- Salim Abdul Ghaffar Sheikh, president of the Panchmahal Youth Congress.
- Abdul Rehman Abdul Majid Ghantia, a known Congress worker.
- Farroukh Bhana, secretary of the district Congress committee.
- Haji Bilal, a known Congress worker."

(*Source*: http://www.rediff.com/news/2002/mar/25rajeev.htm)

When 31 people were convicted for the Godhra carnage, two Congressmen were given life imprisonment and one was given death penalty out of the above five. Abdul Rehman Abdul Majid Ghantia and Farroukh Bhana have got life imprisonment and Haji Bilal has got death penalty—three out of these five.

The following was the report of NDTV dated 3rd March, 2002:

"*Sunday, March 3, 2002 (Godhra)*

The prime suspect in the Godhra train carnage case, Mohammad Hussain Kolota, local Congress leader and president of Godhra Municipality, was today arrested, bringing the total number of arrests in connection with the attack to 27. Kolota, convener of city Congress minority cell, was picked up by personnel of the anti-dacoity squad of the city police from the residence of one Iqbal in Polan Bazar area during a combing operation at about 4 a.m. (IST), Inspector General of Police, Deepak Swaroop said. Kolota, 45, has been evading arrest since the attack on the Sabarmati Express last Wednesday, in which 58 people were killed.

Police have already arrested two municipal councillors and were looking for another two—Bilal Haji and Farookh Bhana—in connection with the mayhem that led to widespread communal violence in several parts of Gujarat, claiming more than 300 lives.

Kolota, who practised law in the town, reportedly joined Congress six years back, informed sources said in Godhra.

Others arrested from different places were identified as Siraj Jamsa, Zabir Kala, Abdul Sheikh and Abdul Rauf Yayman.

With this, the total number of arrests in this connection has gone up to 27. Earlier, police had arrested 22, including two councillors—Salim Shaikh and Abdul Rahim Dantia. Both the councillors had contested the polls on independent symbols (PTI)."

This was the report of the Press Trust of India (PTI) but reported also by NDTV. Even NDTV had to carry this report which exposed the links of the Congress Party to the attackers. Two councillors, who contested as independents, were reported to be Congress rebels. After winning the elections as rebels, they were alleged to have rejoined the Congress Party.

While it will be wrong to suggest that the Congress Party was involved as an organization in the attack or that its Delhi-based leaders ordered the attack to be carried out so as to cause riots in BJP-ruled Gujarat and target the BJP, there can be no denying that those who were behind the attack, belonged to the Congress Party. This may well have been incidental, and there may not have been any involvement of anyone else from the party except those accused. But facts, howsoever bitter, have to be faced.

Media Responsible for Godhra?

Balbir Punj wrote in his counter article in *Outlook* dated 27th May, 2002:

"...The rest is hyperbole, punctuated with venom and vitriol to demonise the *Parivar*. **Precisely this type of demonisation had resulted in the macabre incident at Godhra. The vicious propaganda unleashed by the secularists for over a decade had made ordinary and gullible Muslims see the innocent *Ramsevaks* as demons who deserved to be burnt alive.**

She (Arundhati Roy) terms Gujarat the 'petri dish' of the *Sangh Parivar*. The fact is that Godhra has been used as a crucible by the secular fundamentalists. No wonder, after the roasting of the *Ramsevaks*, they, while condemning the crime, blamed the victims. Many of them invented events such as a quarrel with hawkers, misbehaviour with women and shouting of provocative slogans to justify the horrendous crime...."

The Muslims do not see *karsevaks* as an enemy merely because of the fear-psychosis generated by Mulayam Singh Yadav, and company and the media. But such reporting in the media definitely infuriates them against the *Sangh Parivar*. What can one like to conclude from these comments from Balbir Punj? He may not be far from the truth. However, for fanatics, who don't blink an eye when 15 children are roasted in front of their eyes, media provocation is not needed to commit any deadly crimes.

We have seen Dr. Koenraad Elst say that the likes of Romila Thapar, Gyanendra Pandey and Irfan Habib have blood on their hands.

Role of the Media and the Congress in Post-Godhra Riots

This was because of their irresponsible behaviour on Godhra. Chapter 3 discusses this in detail. The late Amarsinh Chaudhary, the then Gujarat state chief of the Congress Party, came on TV on 27 February 2002 and blamed *Ramsevaks* for 'provoking' the Godhra carnage.

This is what Uday Mahurkar wrote for *India Today* (18 March 2002): "… within Gujarat, it is a completely different story. Here, even the Opposition Congress balks at demanding his dismissal. 'We are not here to play politics in this hour of crisis,' said the Congress observer, Kamal Nath, who was in Ahmedabad three days after the riots began. **Gujarat PCC President, Amarsinh Chaudhary, who accused the *Ramsevaks* of provocation immediately after the Godhra episode, had to modify his stand four days later.** It is a far cry from the Congress that sought the State BJP Government's resignation after the Hindu-Christian clashes in Dangs in 1998-99 in which not a single person died."

This provocative statement from Amarsinh Chaudhary further angered the already anguished masses. Vir Sanghvi in his article in *The Hindustan Times* (mentioned in the second chapter) also said, "Nearly every non-BJP leader, who appeared on TV on Wednesday (27 Feb 2002), treated the massacre as a response to the Ayodhya movement." One look at and complete reading of Vir Sanghvi's article will explain everything about the post-Godhra riots.

Had the media condemned the attack and blamed the attackers instead of the victims, the riots could have been avoided. The insensitive, thoughtless and irresponsible reporting was inflammatory. **Instead of understanding the feelings of sufferings of the masses and the dead victims, the media kept insulting the dead victims by arguing that they had it coming.** To use a metaphor, the media went on kicking the dead dog and kept a safe distance from the mad dog. These people's concocted lies about Hindus 'provoking' the Muslims at Godhra angered the masses.

The masses in Gujarat felt that such a huge tragedy will at last melt the hearts of the English and electronic media and the non-BJP politicians. The non-BJP politicians will at last condemn Muslim communalism. The 'secular brigade' consisting of the media and every non-BJP, non-Shiv Sena politician will at last give up its tirade against the VHP and the *Ramjanmabhoomi* movement and condemn the Muslims who roasted the *karsewaks*. But that did not happen.

When the repeated insults of the dead, of the VHP, of the *Ramjanmabhoomi* i.e. the Ayodhya movement kept on continuing, the masses finally exploded in Ahmedabad on 28th February.

The media further caused violence because of its one-sided and malicious reporting of the riots. The Godhra attack faded into the background while the Hindu retaliation of the first three days was decried. The riots were also projected completely one-sided. There was a contrast of day and night in the versions of the riots as projected by the national English media and the TV channels, and the reality of the riots after the first three days at least.

Despite knowing fully well that the riots had been controlled by the 3rd March 2002, a section of the media went to town implying that the riots were still going on and that the whole of Gujarat was burning, even at a time when riots had stopped everywhere except Ahmedabad, Vadodara and some places near Godhra.

One-sided reports and stark lies on 'Muslims being butchered' ignoring Muslims' attacks caused more and more violence because the Hindus were angry at the lack of attention to their suffering and indifference to their pain. Justice Tewatia's team was alarmed at the anger about the national media among the Hindus. The media largely ignored the factor of Muslim aggression after 3rd March. And the media's infuriation of Muslims by repeatedly keeping Muslims angry about their co-religionists being 'butchered' in Gujarat caused more and more attacks by Muslims. The media's false painting of the Gujarat police as 'anti-Muslim' was one major reason for the numerous attacks on policemen by Muslims. One Muslim resident of Gujarat who was a witness to the riots told this author that the perception of police being anti-Muslim was the main cause behind the attacks on policemen.

The Hindu anger on their suffering and media indifference also led to more and more violence. The media, by and large was indifferent to Hindus being driven out of their houses and rendered homeless. Only in parts and in between, some truth was being reported.

The report "Godhra and After" of the study team headed by Justice Tewatia said: "Repeated telecasts of arson and violence contributed in spreading the tension to unaffected areas. TV channels ignored warning from officials and kept telecasting communal riots like infotainment.

Coverage of Machhipiti in Vadodara is an example. One national news channel went overboard to telecast police firing at Machhipiti as if it had taken place in Ahmedabad....

The code of ethics prescribed by the Press Council of India was violated by the media with impunity. It so enraged the citizens that several concerned citizens in the disturbed areas suggested that peace could return to the state only if some of the TV channels were closed for some weeks."

The same report also says: "English language media, particularly the Delhi Press, is perceived by the Gujaratis to be biased. The information disseminated by it was neither balanced nor impartial.

By converting half-baked news stories into major headlines, print as well as electronic media widened the psychological hiatus between Muslims and Hindus. By disseminating half-truths and lies, the media played no mean role in distorting country's image in the world.

The credibility of the media—both electronic and print—is at dangerously low ebb in Gujarat....

1. Local and regional papers, at times, seemed to be emotionally surcharged and lost sight of objectivity. However, Gujarati newspapers, by and large, were factual in day-to-day reporting.
2. The editorial pages of local and regional newspapers maintained a balance in projecting all viewpoints.
3. **Newspapers published in English from Delhi invariably editorialized the news. Direct and indirect comments in the news writing were so telling that the personal likes and dislikes of the news reporters were too obvious to be missed.**
4. **English language newspapers published from Delhi appeared to have assumed the role of crusaders against the State Government from day one. It coloured the entire operation of news gathering, feature writing and editorials.**

5. The edit pages of English language press carried comments that clearly indicated biases:

    a. against the State Government of Gujarat,
    b. in favour of Congress, leftist parties and the secularist intellectuals,
    c. indifferent to the carnage at Godhra,
    d. against the Hindu organizations, and
    e. against the NDA Government at the Centre.

6. **Most of the national newspapers and news channels played down the intensity of Godhra carnage and projected it as a result of provocation by pilgrims.** Not many reporters were deputed to dig out facts or to do follow-up stories. This resulted in large number of editorials and articles that projected Godhra as a 'reaction to provocation by *karsevaks*' and riots in rest of the state as 'state-sponsored terrorism'.

7. **A distorted image of sectarian violence in the state was projected by the electronic and print media based in Delhi.**

...

12. Media did not help to cool down the tempers. It failed to act as a platform for a dialogue between the Hindus and Muslims on the one hand and between the people and the establishment on the other.

The Study Team is of the considered opinion that the media, in general, failed to perform as conscious and socially responsible gatekeepers of information....

Telecasting images that spread hatred and instigated violence is unhealthy, but their repeated telecast is lethal. The media acted as an interested party in the confrontation, not a neutral reporter of facts.

The team was alarmed at the intensity of hostile attitude among the people of the state for Delhi press and television news channels. This attitude was especially articulated by delegations of intellectuals like lawyers, doctors and businessmen. Even the tribals complained that the media had no time to hear their tale of their agony and was spreading canards against the Hindus...."

This is a report not of any RSS study team but of the Justice Tewatia Committee! A section of the media also attempted to de-link the post- Godhra riots and the Godhra tragedy. The Godhra incident was completely ignored while condemning the post-Godhra riots. And, a section of the media then started lying about Godhra not being done by Muslims at all. Statements such as: "Godhra was done by the VHP to unleash an anti-Muslim wave" or "It is a mystery as to how so many people were burnt in the fire at Godhra" etc. sought to create unnecessary confusion on the train massacre. That section of the media was timid, and is timid, even today of openly admitting that about 2,000 Muslims carried out an unprovoked, pre-planned attack at Godhra.

Vir Sanghvi wrote in the *Sunday Hindustan Times* on 21ˢᵗ April, 2002: "As much as some of us may try and pretend otherwise, nobody with any intellectual honesty can dispute that riots were a response to Godhra."

India Today dated 18 March 2002 said: "…the polarisation along communal lines is total at the moment. **As the secular lobby plays up the anti-Muslim violence more and more while underplaying the Godhra tragedy, which was actually the cause of the violence, Modi and the BJP reap more and more benefits at the ground level from the consolidation of the Hindu vote.** Says Kalpesh Shah, an Ahmedabad businessman: 'How can those, who are demanding the dismissal of Modi, forget that it all began with the Godhra incident? If the anti-Muslim violence was unprecedented, the Godhra incident too was unprecedented in independent India. The more the secularists gun for Modi, the more popular he will become among the Hindus.'

At present, Modi is clearly the unwitting beneficiary of the Hindu backlash…."

This clearly shows that the media hullabaloo on the Gujarat riots caused severe anguish among the Hindus and resulted in riots. Instead of looking at the role of the Opposition in the Godhra massacre, and in instigating violence at least after 21ˢᵗ April, the media focused on blaming the BJP and Modi.

The Times of India's report dated 9 August 2003 said:

"Cong silent on cadres linked to Gujarat riots

NEW DELHI: The Congress has been going to town over Best Bakery and other instances of the Narendra Modi government's complicity in the anti-Muslim violence which shook Gujarat last year. But when it comes to the involvement of its own party cadre in the killings, 10 Janpath maintains a deafening silence. Even when confronted by a long-standing ally from the freedom movement days, the Jamiat Ulama-i-Hind.

According to the JUH, "most Congress corporators" and some Congress leaders of Gujarat had actively participated in last year's riots. Mahmood As'ad Madani, JUH general secretary told The Times of India: "We wrote letters to Congress president Sonia Gandhi, gave a list of Congress leaders involved in the riots, asked her to take action against them but to no avail."

On April 29, 2002, for example, the JUH received a list of 25 Congress leaders from its Gujarat chapter, which was promptly forwarded to her. This included a former Congress minister, a sitting MLA and a former MP. Then on August 20, Madani reminded Gandhi: "Similarly our appeal forwarded to you in respect of involvement of Congress MLAs, corporators and workers in Gujarat carnage along with the list of culpable names remains disregarded."

When contacted by TOI, Ambika Soni, in-charge of Gandhi's office, said she was not aware of the correspondence. Ahmed Patel, Gandhi's political secretary, to whom copies were marked by the JUH was not available for comment.

The JUH insists it had accurate information from the ground. For instance, its Gujarat branch had written to the police commissioner of Vadodara city on March 21 that, "After the Godhra incident an urgent meeting of the activists of the BJP, VHP, RSS and Bajrang Dal was held under the leadership of Yogesh Patel (MLA)... Chinnam Gandhi (Congress corporator)... They had alloted the activists their jobs, they made a plan and instructed the activists to carry out this work without any fear and told them that they would get full support of police officers." The Gujarat JUH had mapped the Congress leadership even at the district level. Mehsana and Patan districts' list has 8 names of Congress leaders including local MP Atmaram Patel as having played a "negative role." A fax message sent on May 1 from Mehsana has this against Patel's column: "Still has not come to help Muslims; taking sides in favour of a criminal person of Sardarpur and Ladoi village."

A list of 15 from Anand is headed by a secretary of Gujarat Youth Congress. But to be fair to the Congress and the JUH, the report is all praise for the "positive role" played by Patan MP Pravin Rashtrapal. JUH secretary N A Farooqui says: "The Congress has committed sins of omission and commission during the riots. Former MP Ehsan Jaffri had called up Sonia Gandhi for help. She didn't take a strong stand in her subsequent visit to Gujarat. The local bodies were mostly headed by the Congress which could have done a lot for relief and rehabilitation, but it was all left to the NGOs."

Though Farooqui maintains that the JUH "has not severed its relationship" with the Congress, the party's ambivalence has led to debates within the Muslim intelligentsia over which political formation is best placed to defend the country from the danger of communal division."

Bhure Lal, former Indian Administrative Services (IAS) officer, who had also served in the Indian Army in Vigilance Commission and is a highly respected expert, wrote in his book *The Monstrous Face of ISI* (published in early 2000 just after Kargil, Siddharth Publications, New Delhi) on pp. 44-45:

"The (Pakistan Intelligence agency) ISI resorts to the following:

...5. **Infiltrate and capture mass media and identify pro-Islamic newspapers and asking them to write pro-Pakistani and pro-Islamic articles.**

6. **Spreading disinformation through media that Indian Muslims are victimized.**

7. Identifying Indian politicians, who thrive on Bangladeshi Muslim vote bank, so that they can be protected against police and other administrative action....

12. **The agency had set up a 'disinformation' cell and planted 'stories' designed to denigrate India. The ISI has funds placed at its disposal to manipulate news....**

15. The ISI employed tens of thousands of agents, 'including at least every other newspaper reporter'....."

Here a couple of things do come to mind. A section of the media keeps on instigating Indian Muslims as 'victims' repeatedly raising the Babri mosque demolition of 6 December 1992, and the post-Godhra riots. It can be seen many times that terrorists like Hafiz Saeed (the alleged mastermind of 26/11) keep saying, "Muslims will avenge Babri demolition, post-Godhra,

Samjhauta killings". A large part of the blame here goes to the Indian media. It is an established fact that before 6 December 1992, at least 75 temples were demolished in (Indian) Kashmir. After 6 December, at least 100 temples were demolished in Kashmir under Indian control. Here we will not even talk about the hundreds of temples demolished in Pakistan and Bangladesh right since 1947, and especially after 6 December 1992. Weren't these 'enough' to avenge one Babri demolition? Had the media repeatedly raised these facts, of 200 temples demolished in Kashmir before and after 6 December, and hundreds in Pakistan and Bangladesh, **the sense of infuriation among the Muslims would never have been there**.

As a matter of fact, after that in March 1993 occurred the terrible Mumbai bomb blasts which killed 257 people, injured many more and inflicted damage worth hundreds of crores of rupees. Since no one was killed in Babri demolition (except the *karsevaks*), a structure that was anyway long abandoned by Muslims in 1934, which was on a sacred Hindu site, wasn't this more than enough revenge? Actually seen in the correct context, Babri demolition itself was absolutely nothing Muslims should have had much infuriation about had they truly known the reality, as Koenraad Elst said. As for the post- Godhra riots, the less said the better. A section of the media truly has blood on its hands because of its one-sided and inflammatory reporting of Godhra and after.

It carried absolute stark lies for years without ever stopping to think what the impact of its lies has been on the nation while serving its narrow- minded short-term goal of maligning Narendra Modi and the *Sangh Parivar*. It carried the outrageous lie that a pregnant woman's womb was ripped open and foetus taken out, while, in reality, the doctor, who did the post-mortem, had found the womb intact and foetus inside it in his post-mortem on 2nd March, 2002. It has all along shown the photo of Qutubuddin Ansari pleading with folded hands, while, in reality, his face shows a bandage, which shows that the photo was clicked after the mob attacked and left.

The self-styled liberals, who have lied and exaggerated sufferings of Muslims, have even rationalized terrorism. After every terrorist attack, they have blamed the "Gujarat riots" for it: for example, after the July 2006 Mumbai blasts. Rajdeep Sardesai in his article dated 2nd April 1993 in *The Times of India* tried to blame Muslim extremism on poverty and economic conditions.

In an article in July 2006, erstwhile torch-bearer of 'secularism', Tavleen Singh wrote, "Now they are blaming it on Gujarat riots. Before that, it was Babri demolition, and before that it was poverty and unemployment". In that article, Tavleen Singh condemns all attempts to rationalize Muslim communalism on some or the other excuse.

The self-styled liberals should do some soul-searching. Instead of forgetting its own sins, this section of the media should do some introspection, and take at least some share of the blame for the riots. The political opponents seem equally guilty. And one cannot but put some of the blame on the so-called Hindu nationalists too who have been unable to blast the myths on Gujarat riots and allowed Muslims to be instigated and infuriated and the image of India lowered in the world.

CHAPTER 10

SOME COURT JUDGMENTS

Let us here see some court judgments on the post-Godhra riots cases. There has been huge media coverage on the Gujarat riots court cases. A vast section of the media has attacked Narendra Modi and has not left him in peace ever after the 2002 Gujarat riots. Even the huge victory in a direct ideology-driven election, which was not an ordinary election but a direct battle between two ideologies: Hindutva and Nehruvianism, has not dented the media's hate campaign one bit.

The Supreme Court of India in its judgment dated 12 April 2004 ordered re-trial of the Best Bakery case outside Gujarat on the petition by the National Human Rights Commission (NHRC). The sessions court of Justice Abhay Thipsay convicted nine out of the 17 accused on 24 February 2006 in Mumbai, Maharashtra state outside Gujarat. These judgments have been given huge publicity in the media. The Mumbai High Court acquitted 5 out of these 9 on 10th July 2012. But there are many other judgments which have remained largely ignored.

Some parts of the ruling of the Supreme Court dated 12th April, 2004 are quoted hereunder:

"When the ghastly killings take place in the land of Mahatma Gandhi it raises a very pertinent question as to whether some people have become so bankrupt in their ideology that they have deviated from everything which was so dear to him...

The little drops of humanness, which jointly make humanity a cherished desire of mankind, had seemingly dried up when the perpetrators of the crime had burnt alive helpless women and innocent children. Was it their fault that they were born in the houses of persons belonging to a particular community? The still, said music of humanity had become silent, when it was forsaken by those who were responsible for the killings....

...Judicial Criminal Administration System must be kept clean and beyond the reach of whimsical political wills or agendas and properly insulated from discriminatory standards or yardsticks of the type prohibited by the mandate of the Constitution.

Those who are responsible for protecting life and properties and ensuring that investigation is fair and proper, seem to have shown no real anxiety. Large number of people had lost their lives. Whether the accused persons were really assailants or not, could have been established by a fair and impartial investigation. The modern day 'Neros' were looking elsewhere when Best Bakery and innocent children and women were burning, and were probably deliberating how the perpetrators of the crime can be saved or protected. Law and justice become flies in the hands of these 'wanton boys'. When fences start to swallow the crops, no scope will be left for the survival of law and order or truth and justice..."

What follows are parts of an article by Devendra Swarup in the weekly *Organiser* dated 16 May, 2004:

"A two-member Bench of Supreme Court delivered an important verdict on 12th April in the widely publicised Best Bakery case of Vadodara (Gujarat). The 69-page verdict delivered by Justice Doraiswamy Raju and Justice Arijit Pasayat was written and read out by the latter.....

...decision becomes a weapon.

The Supreme Court accepted these petitions on 13th January and completed the hearings on 24th March, before delivering its verdict on 12th April. Those people, who complain about the lakhs of cases pending with the Supreme Court and the delay in justice, should rejoice at the speed with which the apex court delivered its decision. The Supreme Court has ruled that the hearing in the Best Bakery case should be held afresh, and that too in the neighbouring state of Maharashtra, and not in Gujarat....

...did it not occur to Justice Pasayat that the Gujarat riots of 2002 have not only a humanitarian but a political aspect too? **It is clear like the sun that if Muslims had not committed the gruesome act of killing 59 innocent women, children and the old at Godhra on 27ᵗʰ February, 2002, out of religious intolerance, then whatever happened as a reaction would never have occurred.** Whatever took place was unfortunate and highly condemnable. Any civilised society would have been embarrassed in its heart of hearts at such retaliatory frenzy in time of peace. But what justice is this to turn a blind eye to an incident that fans the fire of frenzy and centres all its attention on the undesirable reaction only? Why don't Teesta Setalvad, Father Cedric Prakash, Shabnam Hashmi and supporters of human rights raise the question of the perpetrators of the Godhra crime?

Why is no campaign launched to bring them to the witness stand of justice? **Why don't they express sympathy for the hundreds of Hindus killed in Gujarat riots?** Why do they portray the one- sided picture of the attack of the Hindus over the Muslims and as killers in the Gujarat riots? When in reality the culprits are those who through their atrocities pushed a peace loving and sympathetic society to adopt a cruel posture.

Who Stands to Benefit?

...even if Teesta had not been physically present in the Gujarat High Court and has been manipulating the strings from behind the curtain, but how should we view the physical presence of the Congress leader Kapil Sibal as an advocate for Zahira Sheikh in the Supreme Court in Delhi? Kapil Sibal is a professional lawyer and his fee for a single appearance is Rs 50,000. Is it possible that Zahira Sheikh could have afforded to pay this high fee to him? But, nowadays, Kapil Sibal is seen as a spokesman of the Congress rather than as a lawyer. What is more, he is now contesting the Lok Sabha elections as a Congress candidate from Chandni Chowk. Certainly, the reason of advocating for Zahira Sheikh must have been some personal gain, apart from the party. The fate of a candidate depends upon the large number of Muslim voters in Chandni Chowk. By advocating for Zahira Sheikh, he has certainly tried to woo the Muslim voters...

What is extremely painful is that one does not get even a whiff of objectivity from the verdict of Justice Pasayat. The judgment said that when innocent children and helpless women were being burned inside the Best Bakery, today's Nero was looking elsewhere, perhaps deliberately. It sounds more like political language than legal. Its aim is clear. The media has aptly replaced the Roman Emperor, Nero's name with that of Gujarat Chief Minister, Narendra Modi. But Narendra Modi is unable to reply to this attack as the author of this verdict is wearing the protective armour of 'contempt of court'.

Even the support of Mahatma Gandhi's name has been taken in the verdict. 'On Mahatma Gandhi's land, vicious killings were taking place, because of which a pertinent question raises its head— whether some people had become so bankrupt with their ideology that they turned away from all those things which he stood for?'

Use of Mahatma Gandhi's name and views certainly makes it emotional but does not seem in accordance with history. Perhaps, the respected judges ignored the fact that Gujarat has a long history of communal violence. During Gandhi's life itself, Gujarat had burnt in such violence. His pain at the 1924 riots of Ahmedabad is visible in his complete works; since Independence sparks of violence have been spreading in the Muslim-dominated areas of Godhra and Ahmedabad; Mohammad Ghaznavi was extended invitation to again prevent the reconstruction of Somnath temple, which caused unbearable pain to Gandhi. Gujarat has had a long history of riots during the Congress regime that called itself the sole inheritor of Gandhi's legacy even after his death. In 1969, during Gandhian Hitendra Desai's rule as Chief Minister, Ahmedabad witnessed communal frenzy, in which more than 3,000 people were killed, i.e. much more than those killed in the riots of 2002. Hence, instead of getting caught in the quagmire of ideology, it is necessary to probe into the causes of this endless chain of communal riots in the state.

Public Faith should not be Shaken

Man is an integral part of the society. Today, the society is facing the serious issue of not finding men of upright character, and this is reflected in every sphere. The person holding the post of a judge also comes from the same society and represents the character of the entire Indian society. It would not be proper to say that the judges of a state are different from those of the other states. If the impartiality and credibility of a judge sitting in the Supreme Court can be questioned, then people can be audacious enough to point their accusing finger at the Supreme Court one day. After all, the judges in the Supreme Court too reach this high post through the High Courts. Recently, Ram Jethmalani had levelled serious charges of corruption and misuse of authority against A.S. Anand, the retired Chief Justice of Supreme Court. The same A.S. Anand is now holding the post of Chairman of the Human Rights Commission. During the Emergency of 1975-77, the role of Supreme Court had become an issue of controversy. If public faith in the impartiality and credibility of the judiciary is lost, then even God will not be able to save the Indian democracy. The responsibility of maintaining this credibility has now fallen upon the Supreme Court.

But it seems that the judges, in order to maintain the dignity of their post, prefer to remain away from the people and are dependent on the media for information about the country and the world. Thus, they must be getting influenced by the media too. But today the Indian media, instead of being the mirror for the society, echoes the voice of a handful of Leftists and anti-Hindu forces."

It is worth commenting on a couple of things here. First, the Supreme Court did not even mention the name of Narendra Modi in its judgment. So, the claim that "Narendra Modi was called a 'Nero' by the Supreme Court" is completely false. Second, neither does the Supreme Court say, "Gujarat Government was fiddling when the Bakery was burning." As a matter of fact, neither did the court have the power to do so. And as another matter of fact, the Chief Minister cannot personally save a Bakery from rioters. It has to be done by the police or the Army. At that time, the Army had already arrived in Vadodara. The job of the Court in its 12 April judgment, was simply to decide whether to transfer the case outside Gujarat or not and it had no power to judge anything on any other issue apart from this. The Court did order the transfer and retrial outside Gujarat on the NHRC's plea. When Zaheera Sheikh, the prime witness in the case, turned hostile on 3 November, 2004 and said that she lied all along on Teesta Setalvad's tutoring, it was found that there is no affidavit in the Court filed by her seeking transfer outside Gujarat, it was done by the Human Rights Commission whose *locus standi* in the matter was questioned by some.

For the record, the Supreme Court acted exactly as the National Human Rights Commission pleaded in some cases on this issue since 2003. The then NHRC chief, Justice A.S. Anand was a recently retired Chief Justice of India. The present sitting Supreme Court judges were his personal friends. Justice V.N. Khare, Justice Arijit Pasayat and others were all his erstwhile colleagues. And Justice V.N. Khare and the other judges passed exactly the same orders which the NHRC wanted them to pass in some cases.

The then Chief Justice of India, Justice **V.N. Khare was an allegedly Indira Gandhi-appointed judge** (of the Allahabad High Court on 25th June, 1983). As an Advocate in 1975, **Khare and his uncle, S.C. Khare, represented Indira Gandhi, the then Prime Minister, in her famous case against Raj Narain,** alleging electoral malpractices. He was responsible for advocating the case that got the order of the Allahabad High Court stayed until an appeal could be filed in the Supreme Court. The adverse and ambiguous decision of the Supreme Court led to the imposition of Emergency in India for a period of 19 months from 1975-1977, the only suspension of democracy in India since 1947. When he retired, he said, "I found there was complete collusion between the accused and the prosecution in Gujarat, throwing rule of law to the winds. The Supreme Court had to step in to break the collusion to ensure protection to the victims and the witnesses. I was anguished and pained by the turn of events during the trial of the riot cases but was determined to salvage the criminal justice delivery system". (*Source*: http://www.hindu.com/2004/05/02/stories/2004050202680800.htm).

After his retirement Justice Khare openly revealed his opinion against the prosecution of the Gujarat government. Let it be reminded here that on 26th December 2003, the Gujarat High Court ruled that the acquittal of all 17 people in the Best Bakery case by the trial court on 27th June, 2003 was right. It asked why it took Zaheera Sheikh one month and eight days after her statement in court on 17th May, 2003 to change her statement that all accused are innocent? Also, this writer saw her say in an interview to *Aaj Tak* in early July 2003: *"Hame jaan ki parvah nahi hai kya?"* (Will we not care for our lives?)

which was in a manner which indicated that she was tutored to talk like this. It appeared that a person truly scared for his life would never talk as openly and candidly as Zahira did on *Aaj Tak*.

We had many retired Supreme Court judges openly talking against Narendra Modi, many of whom, like Justice (Retd.) Krishna Iyer said that Narendra Modi should be prosecuted for murder. When such judges pass such horrible comments post-retirement (going purely on media reports and not objectively listening to the other side), one wonders what they must have done while they were sitting judges, using armour 'contempt of court'. The Concerned Citizens Tribunal gave a report after its study in 2002 in which it held the Gujarat Government culpable and it also made a fool of itself by trying to absolve Muslims of the crime of Godhra, by saying that the fire was 'set from inside' and ruled out that any mob torched the train. This CCT team had many retired judges. What impartiality can one expect from judges with such ideological leanings, when they can go to the extent of whitewashing barbaric killers' sins in Godhra, and defending the indefensible and inhuman barbaric roasting of 59 men, women and children? Justice H. Suresh, a retired Bombay High Court Judge, Justice P.B. Sawant, a former Supreme Court Judge, Justice Lone (Retd.) were members of this tribunal and **Justice V.R. Krishna Iyer (Retd.), former Supreme Court Judge was its chief.**

The judges were members of the fact-finding team headed by veteran jurist and former Supreme Court Judge, Justice V.R. Krishna Iyer, which had gone to Gujarat in March-April 2002 after the post- Godhra riots. The report of PTI on 22nd November, 2002 said:

"With less than a month to go for the assembly elections in Gujarat, a tribunal of eminent citizens, including retired Supreme Court judges, on Thursday (21 Nov), held Chief Minister, Narendra Modi and *Sangh Parivar* outfits directly responsible for the post-Godhra violence and said he was 'liable for prosecution for genocide'.

The nine-member 'Concerned Citizens Tribunal, Gujarat 2002', headed by Justice (retd.) Krishna Iyer, also said that the fire in the Sabarmati Express coach that triggered the violence was 'set from inside'.

Releasing its findings at a joint press conference in Ahmedabad, Justice P.B. Sawant and Justice Hosbet Suresh, both retired, and senior advocate K.G.

Kannabiran said Modi, his cabinet colleagues and organizations like the BJP, RSS, VHP and Bajrang Dal are 'directly responsible for the post-Godhra carnage'.

It said the chief minister 'is liable for prosecution for genocide for refusal to take any preventive measure and protect the lives and properties of minorities in the state.' (*Source*: http://www.rediff.com/ election/2002/nov/22guj5.htm).

Notice how these biased retired judges called the riots a 'genocide' ignoring the hundreds of Hindus killed, defended the Godhra carnage by ruling out that any mob attacked the train (and made a fool of themselves by going to this level) and did not pin-point what Narendra Modi did wrong. They also, of course, ignored all the steps taken to control and prevent the violence like 827 preventive arrests, appeal for peace made on 27th February, etc.!

Rediff.com reported later on the same day, quoting PTI: "...the nine-member tribunal, comprising eminent citizens and headed by former Supreme Court Judge, V.R. Krishna Iyer, has **demanded the arrest and prosecution of Chief Minister, Narendra Modi**, saying the large-scale violence that followed the Godhra carnage was directly related to his decision to 'carry Godhra to the whole state instead of containing the issue therein'. Along with Modi, the tribunal held his cabinet colleagues and organisations like the BJP, RSS, VHP and Bajrang Dal also 'directly responsible for the post Godhra carnage'.

Noting that the tribunal has no statutory authority to conduct an inquiry in such a matter, a State Government release said the findings of the panel were 'one-sided and not based on facts established in accordance with constitutionally sanctioned legal processes'.

The release issued by the state home department cautioned people against being 'misled by self-appointed agencies' and await the report of the Gujarat Government-appointed Commission of Inquiry headed by Justice G.R. Nanavati to probe the Godhra carnage and the subsequent violence.

'It is not proper for any other organisation or institution not empowered by law to comment on issues, which are under the purview of the commission,' it said..." (*Source*: http://www.rediff.com/election/2002/nov/22guj4.htm).

These are some of the facts which should not be ignored by anyone.

Now, let us see some other cases which have been completely ignored by everybody. Let us read the report of *The Indian Express* dated 29th March, 2006:

"9 Convicted in Post-Godhra Riots Case (PTI)

Ahmedabad, 28th March: Nine persons, including prime accused, Mustaq Kaniyo, were on Tuesday convicted in a post- Godhra riots case in the Danilimda locality of the city, where a person was shot dead in April 2002.

Additional Sessions Judge, Sonia Gokani sent Mustaq Ahmed Sheikh to 10 years' rigorous imprisonment for opening fire from a private weapon and killing one person and injuring another in a clash between two communities on 12th April, 2002. The court also imposed on Mustaq a fine of Rs. 5,000 or an additional six months' imprisonment.

Eight other accused—Mehtabraza Islam Saiyed, Rahim Ibrahim Tharda, Haroon Younis Ganyavni, Haji Mohammed Karim Chipa, Yakub Musa Patel, Mohammed Ajimkhan Pathan, Khurshid and Sagir Ahmed Ansari—were awarded one-and-a-half years imprisonment and Rs. 3,000 fine (or an additional two months' imprisonment).

'The eight accused were convicted on various charges including rioting, unlawful assembly, and for possessing sharp-edged weapons,' said Nimaben Rajput, an advocate in this case.

Meanwhile, 25 others were acquitted by the court on 'benefit of doubt'".
http://www.expressindia.com/news/fullstory.php?newsid=65065

This is a clear and direct evidence of the lies that are continued to be fabricated on the Gujarat riots. Did these newspapers bother to write editorials on this conviction? Did any of them fight for justice in this case? Or, did any of them even let the country or the world remember that Muslims were also convicted for rioting in post-Godhra riot cases?

To see the one-sided malicious reporting of the Indian media, see the report of *The Indian Express* dated 13th April, 2002, a day after this event in Ahmedabad (for which Muslims were convicted):

"Ahmedabad, 12th April: Just when it seemed like the worst was over, violence erupted in the Danilimda area of Ahmedabad on Friday morning. A petty issue boomeranged, leading to clashes between two groups in Danilimda, where the police had to open fire to disperse rioting mobs.

Seven people were injured in today's violent incidents. Late on Friday, though the situation was well under control, tension was very much in the air.

The Danilimda police also picked up more than 25 people belonging to both the communities on charges of rioting and causing injury.

Combing operations are still being carried out to track down all the accused. Till late Friday, senior police officials, including Joint Commissioner of Police, M.K. Tandon and Deputy Commissioner of police (DCP), B.S. Jebaliya were camping in the area.

Tension mounted at Memon Ni Chali, about 500 metres from Danilimda police station, at around 11:00 a.m., when two groups started fighting over the parking of handcarts in front of shops. The incident snowballed into a major flare-up, which led to stone-pelting by both sides. The driver of an ST bus plying between Dehgam and Ahmedabad was dragged out of the vehicle and beaten up mercilessly.

This led to an attack on other people, both Hindus and Muslims. Some people even tried to set fire to a couple of shops in the area, but timely action by the police prevented this.

'This was a small issue among two to three people over parking handcarts in front of others' shops. All of a sudden, it resulted in violence. We first lobbed tear gas shells to bring the situation under control, but that did not stop the clashes and we had to fire in the air,' DCP (Zone VI), Jebaliya said.

Two cases of rioting were registered by the Danilimda police in connection with the incident. Following the incident, strict *bandobast* was arranged in the nearby areas of Shahalam, Geetamandir, Khadia, Kalupur, Dariapur and Shahpur, so as to prevent any untoward incident. Security in the Gomtipur area was also beefed up.

'Indefinite curfew was imposed in areas under Danilimda police station at 7:30 p.m. on Friday following the violence. Meanwhile, curfew will be relaxed in areas under the Gomtipur police station on Saturday from 7:00 a.m. to 7: p.m.," Commissioner of Police, P.C. Pandey said. Night curfew will continue in areas under the Khadia, Kalupur, Dariapur, Gaekwad Haveli, Karanj and the Vejalpur police stations.

'Curfew will remain clamped during the night in the areas under the Ranip police outpost, Madhavpura, Kagdapith and the Shahpur police stations,' Pandey added.

The Army was called out and it rushed to the riot-affected Danilimda to help police contain the violence. Authorities imposed curfew this evening as violence continued unabated in the area."

See the judgments of the courts convicting nine Muslims for the riots in the Danilimda area. The newspaper reports of the English dailies and of the TV channels should have been reporting the truth. Did *The Indian Express* report so in its report dated 13th April, 2002 on the events of 12th April? This sickening attitude of a section of the media, of condoning acts of murder and violence by the Muslims and painting one-sided malicious picture of the riots, continues till date.

Now, let us see another court judgment as reported by *The Hindu* dated 17th October, 2003:

"Vadodara 16th October. The Vadodara fast-track special court today acquitted two persons including former Deputy Mayor, Nisar Bapu, while sentencing four others, including Bapu's son, Abid Husain, and his brother-in-law, Akram Ahmed Sheikh, to life imprisonment for the murder of Pankaj Chauhan in the post-Godhra riots in the city—UNI."

Let us see the manner of reporting by *The Hindu*. *The Hindu* does not even mention the name of the judge or anything in a conviction that is as huge as imprisonment for life. **Four Muslims were again given life imprisonment for murdering a Hindu in the riots after Godhra**. Again, the entire media almost completely ignored the entire proceedings and *The Hindu* merely reported this without again writing any editorials on it or giving it any prominence. Imagine how *The Hindu* would have reported this, had Hindus been convicted over attacks on Muslims!

But let us see how some other newspapers reported the same verdict. *The Times of India* reported thus:

"Four Get Life Imprisonment

16th October, 2003 1447 hrs.

Vadodara: The Vadodara fast track court of Justice C.K. Solanki on Thursday acquitted former deputy mayor and Congress councillor, Nisarhussein Saiyed alias Nisar Bapu and Maruf Hussein Saiyed in the Lal Akhada case.

Four other accused including Nisar's son, Abidhussein, son- in-law, Akram Sheikh, Mohammed Ishaq, and Arif Sheikh alias Bekhabar were convicted by the court to life imprisonment and a fine of Rs. 2,500, failing which an additional term of three months has been imposed.

The court convicted them under Sections 120 (b), 302 and 34 of the Indian Penal Code. The accused had stabbed to death Pankaj Chauhan who was stabbed to death at Resham Wali Gali near Champaner on 22nd March, 2002.

Following the conviction, the court witnessed a dramatic scene with relatives of the accused breaking down to tears. Hearing the judgment, Abidhussein seemed to be shocked by the judgment and collapsed in the court. His relatives and other authorities in the court later revived him. A total of 23 witnesses were examined in the case, out of which 10 turned hostile..."

(*Source*: http://timesofindia.indiatimes.com//india/Four-get-life- imprisonment/ articleshow/236376.cms%20).

We should look at the newspaper reports of these newspapers dated 23rd March, 2002 to see how one-sided and blatantly false these dailies reported. We should also see the recordings of the TV channels like NDTV-Star News, *Aaj Tak,* etc. to see the role played by these channels. **Did these channels bother to tell us that a Hindu named Pankaj Chauhan was killed by some Muslims in Vadodara's Resham Wali Gali on 22nd March?** Did these channels and the entire media ever bother to tell the nation that such a judgment has been passed against Muslims? Luckily, some newspapers at least reported this. Many others did not. These court judgments have been completely forgotten ever since, quite unlike the Best Bakery case. But I always feel that the Best Bakery case too should be raised and given publicity (not so much as to make the judges convict innocent persons!) as the society needs champions of minorities too.

Now let us see another court judgment. This was reported by *The Times of India* dated 14 May 2006:

"Ahmedabad: A special POTA (Prevention of Terrorism Act) court sentenced five people to 10 years' imprisonment each in connection with the tiffin bomb blasts in Ahmedabad city buses four years ago.

Judge Sonia Gokani, delivering his 362-page judgement, also imposed a fine of Rs. 27,000 on each of the accused under different sections of POTA, the Indian Penal Code, the Explosive Substances Act, the Bombay Police Act and the Damage of Public Property Act.

The judge found five of the 17 accused guilty for the explosions in five city buses on 29th May, 2002, injuring 23 people in an act seeking vengeance against the post-Godhra violence. The crude explosive devices were hidden in the tiffin boxes.

The other 12 were acquitted for want of evidence against them.

Police had registered the complaint in five different police stations in the city after the explosions, but no arrest had taken place for a year after the blasts. It was after the assassination of the former state home minister, Haren Pandya in 2003, that police arrested 23 persons in the tiffin bomb blast case. They later released four, as charges could not be filed against them. Seventeen accused were tried in the POTA court."

The Hindustan Times also reported this and the source is: http://www. hindustantimes.com/POTA-court-convicts-five-in-Ahmedabad-blast-case/ Article1-97222.aspx

This again goes to show that Muslims were on the offensive after Godhra. This was not a direct case of rioting. But some Muslims targeted Hindus in Ahmedabad by trying to put bombs in buses.

Now, let us see another court judgment. This was reported by *Deccan Herald* dated 5 August, 2005:

"The Special POTA Court here on Thursday sentenced two persons to seven years' rigorous imprisonment in the post-Godhra riot cases.

This is the first conviction under POTA in the cases during the post-Godhra riots of 2002 in Gujarat. Judge Sonia Gokani convicted Mohammad Ashraf Ismali Nagroi and Mohammad Tahir Mohammad Arif Bakaswala, both residents of Surat, on the charges of attempt to murder of Hasmukh Lalwala, a VHP supporter, who had been fighting the cases of Hindus allegedly involved in the post-Godhra riots. The judgement was delivered in the high security zone set up in the Sabarmati Jail.

Two motorcyclists fired two rounds on Mr. Lalwala, when he was passing by the Makai pool in Surat on the way to his office on 21st May, 2002. He sustained injuries. His brother, Ganeshchandra Lalwala filed the complaint. The accused have been sentenced to seven years' rigorous imprisonment under

Section 3 (1) of POTA and six years' imprisonment under Section 307 of the IPC. They will undergo the sentence concurrently. Appearing on behalf of the State Government, counsels H.M. Dhruv, Sudhir Brahmbhatt and Umesh Trivedi said the confessional statement of the accused under Section 32 of POTA should be admitted. In the statement, the accused are believed to have confessed to firing on Mr. Lalwala to scare the Hindus." URL:

http://archive.deccanherald.com/Deccanherald/aug52005/national172323200584.asp

This again shows that Muslims were on the offensive in Gujarat. There is another case. Bajrang Dal activist and leading lawyer, Lalit Kumar Jain was murdered in April 2002 in Maharashtra in Bhiwandi. He was a lawyer, who would fight cases of the Hindus accused of rioting in Gujarat free of charge.

Now let us see some parts of an article written by Arvind Lavakare in the weekly *Organiser* dated 7 May, 2006:

"...in its edition of March 19, 2006, *The Sunday Express* carried the following report from Ahmedabad:

'Post-Godhra riot case: 7 get lifer

The city sessions court on Friday convicted seven people in a post-Godhra riot case and sentenced them to life-term for the murder of 35-year-old Mukesh Panchal, a resident of Lambha. He was attacked by the accused and went missing on 7th November, 2003 from Shah- e-Alam Darwaza. His mutilated body was found near the Chandoka Lake on the 11th November. One of the seven accused—Javed Shaukat Ali—meanwhile managed to give the cops a slip and fled from the court.'...

...out of the five convictions so far in *l'affaire* Godhra, the above two rip the blindfold on Godhra that the country was subjected to since March 2002. Those two convictions conclusively prove that even as some Hindus in Vadodara, Ahmedabad and a few other parts of Gujarat were provoked into insane killing, arson and loot by the S6 carnage, the Muslims in that state were hardly the cattle hiding from the slaughter house that they have been made out by the 'secularists' in and outside our national English media. **Do you, for instance, recall reading about the mutilation of Mukesh Panchal's cadaver in any of the English print media? Did you hear a sound byte about it on our TV?"**

Arvind Lavakare is one of the few writers, who have never fallen for the lies on the case of the Gujarat riots. However, it is not clear from *The Sunday Express'* report as to why this case was called a post-Godhra riot case if the date given is 7 November 2003. Either the date mentioned is wrong, or this is not a post- Godhra case. In any case, this is a case worth mentioning by the Indian media. If someone like Mukesh Panchal was brutally killed, it is worth reporting. But it was largely ignored.

In another report, *The Indian Express* said:

"Post-Godhra Riots: DNA Test Nails 4 Killers

Ahmedabad, 18th May: What proved to be the clincher in this case was the DNA test. Four years after they hacked a man to death in the aftermath of Godhra, a fast track court today convicted four men and sentenced them to life imprisonment. Two others, **also accused of butchering Devanand Ambalal Solanki, a surveyor at the sales tax office, were acquitted. (We saw this case mentioned in the article "Dalits suffered heavily in Gujarat riots" in the chapter "Attacks on Hindus").**

Special City Sessions Judge D.T. Soni sentenced the accused— Faqruddin Kamruddin Mirza, Mohammed Zaheer Abdul Aziz Ansari, Zakir Husain Mehboob Husain and Mohammed Afzal Mohammed Taufiq Sheikh—to life imprisonment. In the judgement, the court observed...though awarded imprisonment for life, however, the convicted persons shall be kept in jail till their whole life.

This post-Godhra riot case is the first in Gujarat, where scientific evidence (DNA tests) nailed the guilty. The accused were booked under various sections of IPC 364, 201, 302 and Bombay Police Act. A fine of Rs. 5,000 each was also ordered, failing which the accused would have to undergo another six months imprisonment". (*Source*: http://www.indianexpress.com/news/postgodhra-riots-dna-test- nails-4-killers/4719/).

Now, let us here see another judgment dated 24th November, 2003, as reported by www.rediff.com:

"A court in the Nadiad taluka of Gujarat on Monday convicted 15 persons for the massacre of 14 Muslims during the post-Godhra communal riots in Ghodasar village in Kheda district on 3rd March, 2002. Forty-eight others were, however, acquitted.

Sessions court judge, C.K. Rane pronounced his judgement in the case in which 12 of the accused were charged under Section 302 of IPC and three under Section 324 of IPC.

The 14 persons were slaughtered in an open field by an armed rioting mob on 3rd March when they were fleeing the area following rumours that three persons of the majority community, who had died nearby, were done to death by members of the minority community.

The police had arrested 64 people, of which one died in judicial custody while the case was in progress. Only 12 of the accused were in judicial custody when the judgement was pronounced.

Defence Advocate, T. R. Vajpayee told PTI that the judge would pronounce the sentence on Tuesday (25th November, 2003)". (*Source*: http://www.rediff. com/news/2003/nov/24godhra.htm)

This again clearly shows that the Hindus were also convicted in the post-Godhra riots in Gujarat. This was dated 24 November, 2003, much before the Best Bakery case. The media did not bother to see this conviction of Hindus as an example of the Gujarat government's successful prosecution. As a matter of fact, so hell-bent was it on attacking Narendra Modi at that time that it did not give publicity of this conviction lest Modi's 'Muslim-killer' image take a beating. It wanted Hindus convicted, but not in Gujarat, outside Gujarat.

This was not the only case where the Hindus were convicted in Gujarat. There are many other cases as well. One such conviction was on 30th October, 2007. *The Times of India* reported on 31st October 2007:

"Gujarat Riots: Eight Convicts Get Life Term

Ahmedabad: Eight persons were sentenced to life while three others were awarded three years' imprisonment by a Godhra sessions court in the 2002 Eral massacre case that left seven people dead in the aftermath of the Godhra riots.

However, 29 people were acquitted in the case. Additional Sessions Judge, H.M. Dholakia awarded life sentence to eight people. Three of them were also convicted for having gangraped two minor girls.

Three others were convicted on charges of looting and violence and were sentenced to three years' imprisonment. The police had filed three chargesheets in the case on the complaint of Madinabibi Sheikh, who was also the key witness. The massacre took place on 3rd March, 2002 (this date seems to be 2nd March) when assailants targetted villages, including Eral in the interior of Panchmahal district in Central Gujarat, following the Godhra riots" (*Source*: http:// articles.timesofindia.indiatimes.com/2007-10-30/india/ 27970801 1 godhra-riots-gujarat-riots-life-term).

To lie through the skin of the teeth that "No justice has been served in Gujarat" is utterly false. There have been a record number of convictions. The following cases are as per official records. Where newspaper reports are not mentioned, they are exclusively official records and where the newspaper reports are given, they are records supplemented by newspaper reports.

A brief summary of total convictions will be as follows:

1 - On 7 October 2002- 1 Hindu was convicted in Bharuch district
2 - On 5 March 2003- 1 Hindu was convicted in Junagadh
3 - On 4 August 2003- 1 Muslim convicted in Modasa town in Sabarkantha district
4 - On 15 September 2003- 4 Muslims were convicted in Anand
5 -On 16 October 2003- 4 Muslims were convicted and given life imprisonment
   http://timesofindia.indiatimes.com//india/Four-get-life-imprisonment/articleshow/236376.cms
6 - On 25 November 2003- 15 Hindus were convicted of whom 12 were given life imprisonment
   http://www.rediff.com/news/2003/nov/24godhra.htm – Link for conviction
   http://www.rediff.com/news/2003/nov/25godhra.htm – Link for punishment
7 - On 15 Jan 2004- 1 Hindu convicted in Ahmedabad
8 - On 5 May 2004- 3 Muslims were convicted
9 - On 27 July 2004- 3 Hindus convicted in Ahmedabad
10 - On 30 July 2004- 1 Muslim was convicted in Ahmedabad
11 - On 1 November 2004- 2 Muslims were convicted in Ahmedabad

12 - On 4 November 2004- 2 Muslims were convicted in Bharuch district under Ankleshwar Police Station

13 - On 30 November 2004- 8 Hindus convicted in Bharuch district under Amod Police Station

14 - On 10 December 2004- 8 Muslims were convicted in Bharuch

15 - On 31 December 2004- 3 Hindus were convicted in Bharuch district under Ankleshwar Police Station

16 - On 31 January 2005- 13 Hindus were convicted in Ahmedabad

17 - On 16 February 2005- 9 Hindus were convicted in Sabarkantha district

18 - On 23 February 2005- 3 Hindus were convicted in Ahmedabad

19 - On 24 February 2005- 2 Hindus were convicted in Panchmahal district

20 - On 22 July 2005- 6 Muslims were convicted in Bharuch district in Ankleshwar city

21 - On 28 July 2005- 7 Muslims were convicted in Ahmedabad

22 - On 4 August 2005- 2 confessing Muslims were convicted
This was reported by Deccan Herald the next day, 5 August 2005. The Muslims confessed their crime.
http://archive.deccanherald.com/Deccanherald/aug52005/national172323200584.asp

23 - On 11 October 2005- 27 Hindus convicted in Kalol town in Panchmahal district

24 - On 24 October 2005- 5 Hindus convicted in Panchmahal district

25 - On 7 December 2005- 8 Hindus convicted in Ahmedabad

26 - On 14 December 2005- 14 Hindus were convicted
http://www.rediff.com/news/2005/dec/14godhra.htm

27 - On 24 February 2006- 9 Hindus were convicted (Outside Gujarat)
http://www.rediff.com/news/2006/feb/24gujarat.htm

28 - On 10 March 2006- 3 Hindus were convicted in Bhavnagar

29 - On 18 March 2006- 7 Muslims were convicted
http://cities.expressindia.com/fullstory.php?newsid=174094

30 - On 28 March 2006- 9 Muslims were convicted
http://www.expressindia.com/news/fullstory.php?newsid=65065

31 - On 14 April 2006- 11 Hindus convicted

32 - On 8 May 2006- 4 Muslims convicted in Ahmedabad

33 - On 12 May 2006- 5 Muslims were convicted in Ahmedabad district under Sanand Police Station

34 - On 14 May 2006- 5 Muslims were convicted
http://www.hindustantimes.com/POTA-court-convicts-five-in-Ahmedabad-blast-case/Article1-97222.aspx

35 - On 18 May 2006- 4 Muslims were convicted
http://www.indianexpress.com/news/postgodhra-riots-dna-test-nails-4-killers/4719/

36 - On 29 May 2006- 5 Hindus were convicted in Anand

37 - On 1 June 2006- 11 Hindus were convicted in Gandhinagar district under Adalaj Police Station

38 - On 23 November 2006- 3 Muslims were convicted for blasts on 6 August 2002 in Ahmedabad in which no one was killed but caused panic
http://articles.timesofindia.indiatimes.com/2006-11-23/india/27818103_1_pota-court-pota-case-memco

39 - On 25 January 2007- 33 Hindus were convicted in Mehsana district

40 - On 19 September 2007- 1 Muslim was convicted

41 - On 30 October 2007- 11 Hindus were convicted
http://articles.timesofindia.indiatimes.com/2007-10-30/india/27970801_1_godhra-riots-gujarat-riots-life-term

42 - On 18 January 2008- 12 Hindus were convicted in the famous Bilkis Bano case (outside Gujarat)
http://www.hindu.com/2008/01/22/stories/2008012259991300.htm

43 - On 20 August 2009- 2 Muslims convicted in Sabarkantha district

44 - On 13 July 2011- 6 Hindus were convicted
http://www.hindustantimes.com/India-news/Ahmedabad/Six-convicted-in-post-Godhra-riot-case-after-nine-years/Article1-720552.aspx

45 - On 9 Nov 2011- 31 Hindus were convicted for the Sadarpura case
http://articles.timesofindia.indiatimes.com/2011-11-09/india/30377556_1_riot-case-riot-victims-sardarpura

46 - On 9 April 2012- 23 Hindus were convicted
http://www.dnaindia.com/india/report_gujarat-riots-court-convicts-23-acquits-23-for-ode-massacre_1673458

47 - On 4 May 2012- 9 Hindus were convicted
http://news.in.msn.com/national/article.aspx?cp-documentid=250003912#page=2

48 - On 30 July 2012- 22 Hindus were convicted
http://www.thehindu.com/news/national/article3702882.ece

49 -On 29 August 2012- 32 Hindus were convicted for the Naroda Patiya killings
http://www.thehindu.com/news/states/other-states/article3835078.ece

50 - On 22 Feb 2011- 31 Muslims were convicted for Godhra roasting of karsewaks which was the cause of everything
http://articles.timesofindia.indiatimes.com/2011-03-01/india/28643060_1_haji-billa-godhra-train-rajjak-kurkur

Now adding all those convicted, we get 111 Muslims convicted in all, 31 for Godhra and 80 for post-Godhra. And we have at least 332 Hindus convicted. Total 443 convictions were there, which shows the efficiency of prosecution and sincerity in prosecuting. It is a world record to see so many people convicted. From newspaper reports available to this writer itself we can see 249 convictions, 184 Hindus and 65 Muslims. Here we must remember that for horrible past riots of Gujarat, 1969, 1985, 1990-91-92 in which far more people were killed and which were far more serious than the 2002 riots, hardly three to four convictions took place under the previous Congress governments. In the 1984 riots, where 3,000 Sikhs were killed, no action was taken against the rioters and only about 30 people were convicted till April 2013.

After reading about these world-record 443 convictions some still say that the convictions could be made possible because of the Supreme Court-appointed SIT and in spite of the Gujarat Government. The fact is that the SIT is seeing only a selected few cases. In other cases SIT is not involved at all and yet many have been convicted. Actually there were at least 95 convictions (from newspaper reports only)- 61 Hindus and 34 Muslims before the SIT was even set up. As for the convictions in SIT seen cases, most of the convicted had already been arrested by the Gujarat Police. Most of those arrested by the SIT were acquitted. For example in the Sadarpura case 31 were convicted, 29 had already been arrested by Gujarat police. Only 2 of the 21 arrested by SIT were convicted- i.e. 19 out of 21 arrested by SIT were acquitted. Even in Naroda Patiya case, 21 out of the 32 convicted were already arrested by the Gujarat police.

Out of 443 convicted till now, only 148 have been in SIT seen cases, 117 Hindus and 31 Muslims. And most of the 117 Hindus convicted had already been arrested by the Gujarat Police. This gives 295 convictions in non-SIT seen cases, a record still. 274 of those convictions were under the Gujarat Government's prosecution. Note here that there are a total of around 2000 cases on in the Gujarat riots. They don't mean 2,000 riots but far lesser number of riots, and cases against 2000 odd accused rioters. Earlier the cases were more than 4000, then 2000 were closed. Then those 2000 were re-examined on the SC order, but after review of those cases most of them were found not worth opening under SC monitoring and hardly 53 cases were re-opened. They were cases against 53 individuals, not 53 riots, which were re-opened. And there were 2000 odd cases which were always open, never closed. So, we have till now 443 people convicted out of total 2000 odd accused, a very high conviction rate, with many cases yet to be decided.

But despite this, the truth continues to be suppressed, and has been unable to triumph.

CHAPTER 11

TEHELKA LIES

This book was first penned in May 2007, six months before weekly *Tehelka* broadcast a sting operation on the topic of the 2002 riots. But after the sting operation of *Tehelka*, it has become necessary to write about it. The question often raised is- was the sting operation a genuine attempt to know the truth or was it nothing but an attempt to forcibly crucify Narendra Modi and the Gujarat Government and is of no value at all? This chapter will make clear the answer to this question. That sting operation has caused immense resentment among innocent Muslims, and also other well-meaning people, both in India and abroad.

The website www.rediff.com reported on 25th October, 2007:

"Gujarat Riots a Genocide; Modi Sanctioned It: Tehelka

Onkar Singh in New Delhi

Investigative weekly *Tehelka* on Thursday claimed to have unravelled the truth behind the 2002 Gujarat riots.

Tehelka claimed it had 'irrefutable' evidence that the killings of Muslims post-Godhra train carnage in Gujarat was 'not a spontaneous swell of anger but a genocide' planned and executed by top functionaries of the *Sangh Parivar* and state authorities 'with the sanction' of the Chief Minister, Narendra Modi.

Addressing a press conference in New Delhi, *Tehelka* Editor-in-Chief, Tarun Tejpal claimed that the magazine had carried out a sting operation over the last six months by talking to a number of *Sangh Parivar* leaders, including Godhra BJP MLA, Haresh Bhatt, Shiv Sena leader, Babu Bajrangi, who was earlier in the Vishwa Hindu Parishad, and VHP leaders, Anil Patel and Dhawal Jayanti Patel, to bring out the truth.

'We have evidence that bombs were being made in the VHP office premises,' Harinder Baweja, Editor (Investigations), told rediff.com.

'In *Tehelka*'s ground breaking investigations, for the first time, hear the truth of the genocidal killings from the men who actually did it. In shocking disclosures, Chief Minister, Narendra Modi came and patted the back of the criminals, and told them that they had done a good job,' Baweja said.

The Bharatiya Janata Party has reacted sharply to the magazine's report stating that *Tehelka* was acting as CIA (Congress Investigating Agency) and it was a collusive sting, which could hardly be called investigative journalism. Party spokesman, Prakash Javedekar said the 'dirty tricks department' of the Congress was at work again in view of the assembly elections in Gujarat.

None of the leaders caught on camera in the exposé was available for comments, except Gujarat VHP leader Dhawal Jayanti Patel, who said Bajrangi had not talked to him during the riots and that he had not seen the sting operation.

Bhatt was purportedly caught on tape saying he was present in a meeting in which Modi allegedly gave him three days time 'to do whatever they wanted'. 'After three days, he (Modi) asked to stop and everything came to a halt,' Bhatt said, adding that the Chief Minister thanked them after the Naroda-Patiya massacre.

The magazine claimed that Dhawal Jayanti Patel told its undercover reporter that the VHP activists made lots of bombs in a factory owned by him. A BJP MLA was shown as saying they even made rocket launchers, which were used in the pogrom. It also claimed that it has exposed 'a trail of lies and coercions' that establishes the fire in coach S6 of the Sabarmati Express in Godhra on 27th February, 2002 was a case of spontaneous mob fury and not a pre-meditated conspiracy as stated by the Gujarat Government." (*Source*: http://www.rediff.com/news/2007/oct/25godhra.htm)

Tarun Tejpal, editor of the weekly Tehelka, wrote in *Tehelka Magazine, Vol. 4, Issue 44, Dated 17th November, 2007:*

"…This time—with our investigation into the Gujarat pogrom of 2002—the conspiracy-seekers scaled new heights. While the BJP attacked us for working for the Congress, the Congress spread the word that we were working for the BJP! Clearly we were doing something right. In all this, the battle for the idea of India was left to Laloo Yadav, Mayawati and the Left. The Congress, one presumes, knows the phrase—since its forebears literally coined it—but they can't anymore seem to remember what it means.

It's extraordinary that more than a week after the Gujarat massacre exposé, the Prime Minister (the then Prime Minister of India, Dr Manmohan Singh) and the Home Minister (the then Home Minister, Shivraj Patil) had not made a single statement. For the first time in the history of journalism, mass murderers were on camera telling us how they killed, why they killed, and with whose permission they did it. Nor were these just petty criminals; these were fanatics, ideologically driven, working the most dangerous faultline of the subcontinent, revealing the truth of a perilous rupture fully capable of tearing this country apart. (**Note:** *Tarun Tejpal knows very well that these so-called criminals could well have been indulging in empty boasts, i.e., boastful lies and may not have done anything they claimed to have done on camera, but he is adding spice.* **And if it does not occur to him that these people could have been indulging in empty lies, then he is not fit to be a journalist**). But that was clearly not enough for the good man of the Race Course Road (Manmohan Singh). Had the CII burped loudly, the PMO would have issued a clarification. Had they then organised a seminar on the untimely burp, the Prime Minister would have addressed it.

It may be unfair to pillory the Prime Minister, a man given responsibility without power, the honest man sitting atop a dishonest hillock. Let us then look at the grand strategists of the Congress, who cannot win an election themselves but know the secret of winning elections for the many. On their perverse abacus, exposing Modi's hand in bestial murders and rapes was designed to convince the Gujarati Hindu that this is precisely the kind of leadership it wanted! (**Note:** *Now he says Modi's hand in rapes, again absolute trash! At least some stray accused lied on camera that Modi patted backs of rioters, but there were not even lies about rapes!*) It never struck them that they could use the evidence of violence to shape a stirring dialogue against it.

The fact is the Congress is today run by petty strategists who no longer know what it is to do the right thing. They possess neither the illuminations of history, nor a vision for the future. They fail to see that once great men sutured a hundred fault-lines—of caste, religion, race, language, class—to create the idea of India out of a diverse, colonised, feudal subcontinent. Foolishly they preside over the reopening of these fault-lines, unable to see the chaos that will ensue. They do not know how to wield morality as a weapon in politics, and they lack the courage to walk any high road. At best they are vote accountants who waver between the profit and the loss of various elections.

The present Congress brings grief to the liberal, secular, democratic Indian, who needs a political umbrella under which to wage the civilisational battle for India's soul. By not saying the right thing, by not doing the right thing, it weakens the resolve of the decent Indian, who lacks the stomach for conflict and seeks affirmation of his decency. The vacated space is then colonised by poisonous ideologies based on exclusion and a garbled—pseudo- religious, pseudo-historic—hunt for identity…."

Tarun Tejpal's statement should not let anyone be fooled into thinking that the Congress was not behind the *Tehelka* sting. The Congress could well be behind it, but it is also possible that the party may not have been. But that matter is not of much importance, because the sting operation has to be judged on merit. Even if the Congress had sponsored it, it does not necessarily become fake, nor does it become genuine if the Congress had nothing to do with it.

Tarun Tejpal, in this same article, had bemoaned the legal action taken against *Tehelka* by the erstwhile NDA Government. **If he reads this chapter fully, Tarun Tejpal will thank his stars that the BJP or Narendra Modi or any of the accused on camera did not sue *Tehelka* and him for damages worth crores (Tens of millions) of rupees.**

Now, let us get into the details of the so-called confessions of the people caught on camera. First, we should all remember the context in which this sting operation was conducted. ***Tehelka* reporter Ashish Khetan visited the people he caught on secret camera and presented himself as an author aiming to write a book from the VHP point of view. He talked casually**

to these people on the riots without telling them that the conversations were being recorded. This background will help a lot of people understand how these so-called confessions are boastful lies.

The ethics and morality of this sting operation have been questioned by some. Actually, those caught on camera could have perhaps sued *Tehelka* for violation of privacy, because what was supposed to be a private conversation was made public, through deceit, the correspondent claimed to be an author aiming to write a book on the *Hindutva* school of thought.

However, even assuming that the ethics of this sting operation were all right, let us see the details of the so-called confessions. Here is what Babu Bajrangi, an accused in the riots, said about Narendra Modi:

"10TH AUGUST, 2007

TEHELKA: The day Patiya happened (i.e. 28th February 2002), didn't Modi support you?

Bajrangi: He made everything all right, otherwise who would have had the strength. It was his hand all the way. If he'd told the police to do differently, they would have f****d us...they could have...they had full control....

TEHELKA: They had control?

Bajrangi: They were very much in control all over the city, all over Gujarat.... [But] for two days, Narendrabhai was in control.... from the third day.... a lot of pressure came from the top.... Sonia-wonia and all came here....

...

TEHELKA: Didn't Narendrabhai come to meet you [in jail]?

Bajrangi: If Narendrabhai comes to meet me, he'll be in deep trouble...I didn't expect to see him. Even today, I don't expect it.

TEHELKA: Did he ever talk to you over the phone?

Bajrangi: That way I do get to speak to him...but not just like that. The whole world starts singing....

TEHELKA: But when you were absconding, then he.

Bajrangi: Hmm... I did speak to him twice or thrice....

TEHELKA: He'd encourage you.

Bajrangi: *Marad aadmi hai* [he's a real man], Narendrabhai.... If he were to tell me to tie a bomb to myself and jump....it wouldn't take even a second...I could sling a bomb around me and jump wherever I was asked to...for Hindus. (Our comment: Boastful lies!)

TEHELKA: Had he not been there, then Naroda-Patiya, Gulbarg (Ehsan Jafri case, Chamanpura) etc.

Bajrangi: Wouldn't have happened. Would've been very difficult.

"1ST SEPTEMBER, 2007

TEHELKA: Did Narendrabhai come to Patiya the day of the massacre?

Bajrangi: Narendrabhai came to Patiya. He could not make it to the place of the incidents because there were commando- phamandos with him. But he came to Patiya, saw our enthusiasm and went away. He left behind a really good atmosphere.

TEHELKA: Said you were all blessed.

Bajrangi: Narendrabhai had come to see that things didn't stop the next day. **He went all around Ahmedabad, to all the places where the *miyas***

296

[Muslims] were, to the Hindu areas...told people they'd done well and should do more... (Our comment: Is it possible to believe this? :D)

Bajrangi: [After the massacre] the commissioner issued orders [against me]...I was told to leave my home...I ran away... Narendrabhai kept me at...the Gujarat Bhavan at Mount Abu for four-and-a-half months. After that, [I did] whatever Narendrabhai told me to.... Nobody can do what Narendrabhai has done in Gujarat.... If I did not have the support of Narendrabhai, we would not have been able to avenge [Godhra]... [After it was over,] Narendrabhai was happy, the people were happy, we were happy...I went to jail and came back... and returned to the life I'd led before.

Bajrangi: Narendrabhai got me out of jail. He kept on changing judges. He set it up so as to ensure my release, otherwise I wouldn't have been out yet. The first judge was one Dholakiaji. He said Babu Bajrangi should be hanged—not once, but four-five times, and he flung the file aside. Then came another who stopped just short of saying I should be hanged. Then there was a third one. By then, four-and-a-half months had elapsed in jail; then Narendrabhai sent me a message...saying he would find a way out. Next he posted a judge named Akshay Mehta. He never even looked at the file or anything.... He just said [bail was] granted. And we were all out. We were free. For this, I believe in God. We are ready to die for Hindutva..." (**Our comment:** But those who know law even a bit will know that a Chief Minister cannot change judges!) (*Source:* http://www.tehelka.com/story_main35.asp?filename=Ne031107To_Get.asp).

Now see his statement: "For two days, they were in control". This is a blatantly false statement—a boastful lie. We have seen in this book already that *The Hindu*, the leading most English daily of South India and a bitter critic of Narendra Modi, had reported: "Unlike 28th February when one community was entirely at the receiving end, the minority backlash on 1st March further worsened the situation."

This clearly shows that the Muslims were on the offensive on the second day of the riots. The Hindus were not at all in 'complete control'. His statement that the police did not do anything is another lie. *The Hindu* reported that on 28th February at least 10 people were believed to have been killed in police firing by evening (in Ahmedabad alone)". *India Today* dated 18 March 2002 also said that the police shot dead five people outside Ehsan Jafri's house in the Gulbarga locality on 28th February in Ahmedabad. The police shot 1496 rounds on 28th February including at least 600 in Ahmedabad and arrested 700 people and burst 4297 tear gas shells.

Babu Bajrangi also says that Narendra Modi came to Naroda-Patiya on the day of the massacre, i.e. 28th February. But the official records show that Narendra Modi did not visit that place that day. Weekly *India Today* in the issue dated 12th November, 2007 reported:

"But the impact of the exposé has been diluted to some extent by inaccuracies in the statements of those interviewed in the sting. Two out of the 14 caught speaking on camera say that one day after the Naroda-Patiya massacre in Ahmedabad on 28th February (in which 89 Muslims were killed by a Hindu mob) Modi came to Naroda-Patiya to thank them.

But the statements of Babu Bajrangi and Suresh Richard, the key accused in the case, seem to be boastful lies as the official records show Modi didn't go to Naroda-Patiya on that day."

As a matter of fact, Modi did not visit Naroda-Patiya either on 28 February, or on 1 March. **Was it not the duty of *Tehelka* to cross-check and cross-examine if the statements made by these people, while thinking that they are talking to a man writing a book from the Hindutva point of view, were boastful lies or real truths before making such serious charges on a Chief Minister and for that matter, these people?**

Note that Babu Bajrangi talking about Narendra Modi helping him are **boastful lies. He wants to boast to the *Tehelka* reporter** (thinking him to be a man writing a book from the VHP point of view) **that he (Bajrangi) has access to the big boss Narendra Modi and that he (Bajrangi) is a big enough guy to get direct favours from Narendra Modi. There is absolutely nothing more in this.** *Tehelka* also knows very well that this is the case, that Bajrangi is simply bragging that he is important enough to know and get help from Narendra Modi (while the reality has been clarified by Narendra Modi in his leaked answers to the SIT that he (Modi) does not know Babu Bajrangi at all and heard his name only through the media months later). Actually,

Tehelka also knew that he will indulge in empty boastful lies and so it fed such questions to him.

As a matter of fact, none of these statements made by any of the 14 accused have any significance as evidence in any court of law in India. Confessions made intentionally on camera to police carry no value as evidence— only confessions made in court to a judge are regarded as evidence. **These so-called confessions were made while casually talking to a person, who secretly recorded the proceedings, and they are clearly boastful lies as we have seen the loopholes in them.** Even if there were no inaccuracies, still the statements would have absolutely no value as evidence.

Note here that the *Tehelka* reporter is asking rhetorical questions egging him to speak. The *Tehelka* reporter asks questions like- "Didn't Narendrabhai come to Naroda?" etc to which Bajrangi and most of the accused simply say 'Yes' and add their salt and pepper. **The questions were deliberately framed like this to get the people to lie on the topic which *Tehelka* wanted.**

The statements on Naroda-Patiya are again lies. The police also saved 900 Muslims in Naroda-Patiya since 95 people were killed (after all missing were declared dead) and there were 1,000 Muslims there as reported by *The Times of India* with the mob aiming to kill everyone. *The Times of India* reported that the police escorted 400 Muslims to a safe place in the wee hours of 1 March (Friday) after dispersing the mob in the night of 28 February (Thursday), a number of them to the SRP (State Reserve Police) headquarters in the vicinity. This article also says: "Even as the SRP constables complain about their 48-hour vigil, the wind blows up ashes of a gutted. 'I am here for two days now without a shave and proper food,' an SRP constable complains…. 'The police has gained upper hand over the crowd and situation is under control,' Pravin Gondia, Deputy Commissioner of Police, said".

And all these statements about the judges are all wrong. The Chief Minister cannot change judges. The Supreme Court-appointed SIT has also examined all this and given similar conclusions, which we will see in the next chapter. Now let us see the statements of Ramesh Dave, a VHP activist—

"12TH JUNE, 2007

Ramesh Dave: We went to the [VHP] office that night…the atmosphere was very disturbing. Everybody felt that [we had taken it] for so many years… Narendrabhai gave us great support….

TEHELKA: What was his reaction when he reached Godhra?

Dave: In Godhra, he gave a very strong statement. He was in a rage. He's been with the Sangh from childhood. His anger was such…he didn't come out into the open then, but the police machinery was turned totally ineffective…." (Official site of *Tehelka*)

The statement, "All the police machinery was turned totally ineffective", is another lie, as we have seen details of the police action on 28 Feb, 1st March and 2nd March earlier.

Now let us see the interview with Haresh Bhatt, former Godhra MLA of the BJP: "**1st JUNE, 2007**

TEHELKA: What was Narendra Modi's reaction when the Godhra incident happened?

Haresh Bhatt: I can't tell you this…but I can say it was favourable…because of the understanding we shared at that time….

TEHELKA: Tell me something. Did he?

Bhatt: I can't give a statement. But what he did, no chief minister has ever done….

TEHELKA: I won't quote it anywhere…for that matter…I am not even going to quote you.

Bhatt: He had given us three days…to do whatever we could. He said he would not give us time after that. He said this openly. After three days, he asked us to stop and everything came to a halt.

TEHELKA: It stopped after three days. Even the army was called in.

Bhatt: All the forces came…. We had three days…and did what we had to in those three days….

TEHELKA: Did he say that?

Bhatt: Yes. That is why I am saying he did what no chief minister can do.

TEHELKA: Did he speak to you?

Bhatt: I told you that we were at the meeting.

Bhatt: He had to run the government…the trouble he is facing now…there are several cases being re-opened…people are rebelling against him.

TEHELKA: People in the BJP are revolting against him.

Bhatt: People in the BJP…for whatever he has done, have made him a larger-than-life figure and the other politicians cannot bear to see that…." (Courtesy: Official website of *Tehelka*)

Here again see, his statement "He gave us three days". This is a lie propagated by a large section of the media right since March 2002 and innocent and well-meaning people have fallen for it. There were no three days given. CNN-IBN's Hindi channel also alleged one day after these sting operations that: "There were given three days". But we have seen the truth in Myth 15. We have seen details earlier that the Army reached very quickly ("frantically" called), the then Defence Minister George Fernandes arrived, the police shot dead 98 rioters, fired 5450 rounds and burst 6,500 tear gas shells. This is sufficient to understand that Haresh Bhatt's statements are absolute lies. Moreover,

Haresh Bhatt also claims that he was there at the meeting. **The fact is that Narendra Modi did not meet Haresh Bhatt at Godhra on 27 February. He (Modi) went to Godhra in the evening and returned on the same day to Ahmedabad. Weekly** *India Today* **dated 12th November, 2007 mentions that the official records show that Modi did not meet Bhatt that day in Godhra. Again, Haresh Bhatt is boasting that he was important enough a guy to be present in Narendra Modi's meeting on 27 February in Godhra.**

Now see the statements made by Suresh Richard, an accused in the riots:

"12TH AUGUST, 2007

Suresh Richard: [On the day of the massacre] we did whatever we did till quite late in the evening. **At around 7:30 pm…around 7:15 p.m., our Modibhai came. Right here, outside the house. My sisters garlanded him with roses…**

TEHELKA: Narendrabhai Modi.

Richard: Narendra Modi. He came with black commandos… got down from his Ambassador car and walked up here. All my sisters garlanded him…a big man is a big man after all.

TEHELKA: He came out on the road?

Richard: Here, near this house. Then he went this way. Looked at how things were in Naroda….

TEHELKA: The day the Patiya incident happened.

Richard: The same evening.

TEHELKA: 28th February.

Richard: 28.

TEHELKA: 2002.

Richard: He went around to all the places. He said our tribe was blessed. He said our mothers were blessed [for bearing us].

TEHELKA: He came at about 5 o'clock or at 7?

Richard: Around 7 or 7:30. At that time, there was no electricity… Everything had been burnt to ashes in the riots…

TEHELKA: Now, after that day, when Narendrabhai Modi visited your home, the day of the Naroda-Patiya massacre, has he ever been back here again?

Richard: Never."
http://www.tehelka.com/story_main35.asp?filename=Ne031107We_Were.asp

Now again we have seen that Modi did not visit Naroda-Patiya that day, neither on 28th February nor on 1st March. As per the leaked answers of Narendra Modi to SIT in the questioning on 27th March, 2010, **Narendra Modi was addressing a press conference at Circuit House in Ahmedabad on the evening of 28th February.** It takes just an iota of common sense to know that it is absolutely impossible for Narendra Modi, who was then Chief Minister of Gujarat, to have actually gone to Naroda-Patiya on 28th February evening at 7- 7:30 p.m. and patted the backs of the rioters. Note that no one made this allegation for almost six years, from February 2002 to November 2007 and even after November 2007, no one except for *Tehelka* will believe this. Actually, neither will *Tehelka* believe this, but it will allege this. So, these statements do not have the slightest meaning as evidence. **And *Tehelka* claimed that it had 'irrefutable evidence' of Modi's involvement! On the contrary, there is 'irrefutable evidence' of the so-called confessions being meaningless** and that Modi handled the riots extremely efficiently, managed to stop riots in three days, while it had taken the previous Congress governments six months to stop riots in 1985 and many weeks in 1969 and other occasions. And, on an average, there were three riots in every four days in Gujarat for the decade of 1960s. *India Today* weekly reported in its issue of 12 November 2007:

"There is a clamour among human rights activists for prosecuting Modi following the exposé. But as Nirupam Nanavati, Gujarat's leading criminal lawyer and Congress leader (a party which is a staunch opponent of Narendra Modi) says, "The statement of a co-accused is not admissible as evidence under the Indian Evidence Act.

Modi's prosecution is possible only after Section 10 of the Act is pressed by the investigation agency to facilitate a fresh probe, which can lead to his implication based on evidence that might surface..."
(*Source*:http://indiatoday.intoday.in/site/Story/1716/Gujarat:+The+noose+tightens.html?complete=1).

We are seeing the full texts of all the interviews published by *Tehelka* on its own site. Here is the interview of Arvind Pandya, former counsel for the Gujarat government:

"6TH JUNE, 2007

Arvind Pandya: [The Muslims of Godhra] thought they could get away with it because the Gujarati is mild by nature. In the past, they had beaten the Gujarati, they have even beaten the entire world, and nobody has shown any courage. Nobody had ever resisted them. They thought they'd get away with it just like they always do, but they used to get away with it because there was Congress rule here earlier. To get their votes, the Congress would suppress Gujaratis and Hindus. But this time, they were thrashed. It is Hindu rule now. All of Gujarat is ruled by Hindus, and that too from the VHP and the BJP....

TEHELKA: They miscalculated.

Pandya: No, what would have happened.... If it were a Congress government, then they would have never allowed Hindus to beat Muslims, they would have used their administrative force just to drag the Hindus down. They never stop [Muslims] from violence. They'll tell Hindus to maintain peace but will never do anything to touch them [Muslims]. They would never have done anything, even in cases like [Godhra], but in this case, there was a Hindu-based government and…so, people were ready and the state was also ready. This is a good connivance [sic].

TEHELKA: This was the good fortune of the Hindu community…the entire Hindu *samaj.*

Pandya: And let us say the ruler was also strong in nature because he gave, just take the revenge and I am ready. We must first salute Kalyan Singh because he accepted every kind of liability before the Supreme Court, saying…I did this, I was the party.

TEHELKA: Later on, when he changed the party.

Pandya: He did, but he was the founder person, he just stood before the Supreme Court boldly and said that I am the person.

TEHELKA: Took sole responsibility.

Pandya: Thereafter, the second hero by the name of…**Narendra Modi came and he gave oral instructions to the police to remain with the Hindus, because the entire kingdom is with the Hindus."**

"8TH JUNE, 2007

TEHELKA: Sir, is it true that when Modi went to Godhra on 27th February, the VHP workers attacked him?

Pandya: No, they didn't. It's like this. There are 58 bodies…and it's evening… people are bound to say, what have you done….

TEHELKA: From 8 o'clock in the morning till evening, he didn't land up. So, when things got heated, then Modi ji got angry and he….

Pandya: No it's not like that... Modi's been on our line for a long time. Forget that matter. But he's occupying a post, so naturally there are more limitations...and he has quite a few... It is he who gave all signals in favour of the Hindus. If the ruler is hard, then things can start happening....

TEHELKA: Did you meet...Narendra Modi after he returned from Godhra on the 27th?

Pandya: No, I will not answer queries on this...I shouldn't.

TEHELKA: Sir, I want to know what was his first reaction?

Pandya: When Narendra Modi first heard it over the phone, his blood was boiling. Tell me, what else do I say...I've given you some hints and I can't reveal more than that...nor should I say it...

TEHELKA: I wanted to know this...what his first reaction was...

Pandya: No, his reaction was like this: if he were not a minister, he would have burst bombs. **If he had the capacity and was not a minister, he would have detonated a few bombs in Juhapura [a Muslim-dominated locality in Ahmedabad]."**

Both the important statements made by Pandya have been highlighted. The first that Modi gave 'oral' instructions to the police to remain with Hindus. This is again false because as we have seen by now, there were 98 people shot dead by the police in the first three days alone, majority of whom are Hindus and all details of actions taken to prevent and control riots.

The second statement: if he were not a minister and he had the capacity, he would have detonated bombs in Juhapura, is also irrelevant. No one detonated bombs in Juhapura.

But Pandya has made a stunning charge against *Tehelka*. He claims that he was asked to say all this by Aaj Tak scribe, Dhimant Purohit, who is his friend, after telling him that this is for an audition test! After this exposure, he filed a defamation suit on various charges, which prompted Purohit to seek

anticipatory bail. **Pandya's statement that when Modi went to Godhra, VHP workers did not attack him, is also incorrect.** *The Times of India's* **website reported on 27 February itself that Modi was manhandled by an irate mob of VHP supporters.**
(*Source*: http://articles.timesofindia.indiatimes.com/2002-02-28/ahmedabad/27119372_1_zadaphia-judicial-probe-modi).

Now let us see the interview of Rajendra Vyas, Ahmedabad VHP chief:

"8TH JUNE 2007

TEHELKA: I wanted to know...about Narendra Modi...what were his first words [after the Godhra train incident]? What did he tell all of you?...

Rajendra Vyas: He first said that we would take revenge... the same thing I myself had said publicly... I hadn't even eaten anything then.... Hadn't even had a drop of water...I was in such a rage that so many people had died, tears were flowing from my eyes...but when I started using my strength...started abusing...he [Modi] said, Rajendrabhai, calm yourself, everything will be taken care of. What did he mean when he said that everything would be taken care of?...All those who were meant to understand, understood..."

There is, of course, no evidence to support that Modi said any of this. And there is evidence to show that he did none of this. The records should be checked to show if Modi actually met Vyas that day or not-this itself seems very unlikely as he was very busy that day. Also, Rajendra Vyas himself may not have done anything like this and just indulged in empty talk. That's what seems most likely!

Now let us again see the other statements of people on camera on what they said about the police. To begin with, Babu Bajrangi:

"1ST SEPTEMBER, 2007

Nobody can do what Narendrabhai has done in Gujarat. If I didn't have Narendrabhai's support, we would not have been able to avenge Godhra... because the police was standing right in front of us, seeing all that was happening, but they had shut their eyes and mouths. At that time, had the police wanted, they would never have let us in. There was just one entry, like a housing society has, and then Patiya begins. If they wanted to stop us, there were 50 of them there, they could have stopped us. We had good support from the police...because of Narendrabhai...and that is because whatever happened in Gujarat, happened for the best. We got some relief from these people [the Muslims]...they had got so high and daring....

The Muslims kept making calls to the police, kept running to the police. They had one man called Salem...supposed to be a sort of Naroda-Patiya dada...he got into a police jeep...got right inside...I myself caught him and dragged him out. The cops said, 'Kill him, if he's left alive, he'll testify against us....' He was taken a little way away and finished off right there.... If the bastard had lived, he would have said he'd climbed into a police jeep and was thrown out, things like that....

[By the end, there were about 700-800 bodies.] They were all removed. The Commissioner came that night and said that if there were so many dead at one place, it would create trouble for him. So, he had the corpses picked up and dumped all over Ahmedabad. When they were brought to the Civil Hospital for the post-mortem, they were said to be from this place or that...."

"10TH AUGUST, 2007

At 2:30 that night, I called the police inspector [Mysorewala].... He said, "Don't come here" [to the station]. There were *dekho to* [shoot at sight] orders against me. Wherever Babu Bajrangi was found, he was to be shot. He told me to run away...our Mysorewala. He said he couldn't do a thing for me...I wasn't even to tell anyone he'd called. But even so, he sent a rider to my house...you can imagine how my children felt at that time....

[Four months later] Narendrabhai told me...there was a lot of pressure on him. The media, TV, so much coverage...Babu Bajrangi is a *goonda*. Laloo complained in the Parliament about my not being caught. So, Narendrabhai asked me to surrender... I said, 'Alright *saheb*, if you tell me to, I will give myself up...' (**Our comment:** But Narendra Modi has clarified that he did not know Bajrangi at all and heard his name through the media years later. So these are again lies).I surrendered near Gandhinagar...it was all a big drama... all a drama...the police, the Crime Branch, had been told I would be passing through that area...P.P. Pandey saheb, who was [joint] commissioner in the Crime Branch then, was there too and some 12 or 13 cars came. These people waited on the road from Biloda to Gandhinagar...they checked a few cars...I had to land up...it was part of the act. If I'd gone straight to the Crime Branch, the media and the NGOs would have ripped me apart. It was all a drama... they caught me, tied me up with rope...all drama. They told me they were tying me up just for show..." (*Source*:http://www.tehelka.com/story_main35.asp?filename=Ne03110TheirEyes.asp).

Now, again, all this has little value. Because, as we have seen, his earlier statement that "Modi came to Naroda-Patiya on 28th February" is false. **The statement that 700-800 bodies were there in Naroda, is another lie. This is because only 95 people were killed in the riots in Naroda-Patiya, after all the missing were declared dead.** We have also seen how the police, instead of allowing any killings to take place actually saved 900 Muslims in the episode and escorted 400 Muslims to safety after dispersing the mob. Also, all details of a man named Salem seem to be very suspicious. After the sting, Babu Bajrangi denied having led any mob in Naroda-Patiya, and he may well have been indulging in boastful lies about his own role. His statements on role of the police and Narendra Modi are, of course, lies. There is a saying *"Jo bhaukte hein, vo kaatte nahi"* (Those who bark, do not bite). Those who brag and bluff, are very timid from inside, is what a saying is.

Note here that on this issue, the Gujarat Chief Minister, Narendra Modi has maintained a complete silence. Hence, we have not been able to know many loopholes of this operation. When Bajrangi actually surrendered, at what place, and in what circumstances, needs to be checked thoroughly. **The statement that: "There were 50 policemen but they didn't do anything" seems to be another lie. This is because** *India Today* **reported that:** "At Naroda-Patia, the scene of the worst carnage, there was no police presence worth the name to prevent the mobs from grouping in the morning and going on a rampage. There were, at least, three mobs of 4,000 to 5,000 each attacking Muslims."

We have seen (former police inspector of Naroda) Mr. Mysorewala say that the Naroda police station with 80 policemen was adequate in normal times but the situation on 28 February was unprecedented and was quickly going out of control. He said he had asked for police reinforcement and was given 24 additional SRP men but even that was inadequate, considering the size of the attacking mob, about 17,000 people.

This is what K.K. Mysorewala told the Nanavati Commission on 19th August, 2004. **Also, whether former Bihar Chief Minister and former Indian Railway Minister Lalu Yadav really asked for the arrest of Babu Bajrangi in the Parliament is not known and is most likely untrue.**

Now, see what Suresh Richard said about the role of the police:

"12TH AUGUST, 2007

The police were with us...I can tell you so myself even now... the police. That day was great. They were shooting right in front of us. **They must have killed 70 or 80 or more...didn't even spare women....**

We'd finished burning everything and had come back. That was when the police called us. They said Muslims were hiding in the gutter. Now when we went there, we saw their houses had all been burned down but seven or eight of them had hidden in the drain. We closed the lid on it...if we'd gone in after them, we might have been in danger. We closed the lid and placed big boulders on it. Later on, they found eight or ten corpses in there. They'd hidden to save their lives, but we closed it off and they died of the gases down there. This happened in the evening...the *dhamaal* went on till night, till about 8:30..."

Again this man has spoken boastful lies about Modi's role: these are more lies. When the police were overwhelmingly outnumbered by mobs of the size of 17,000 as we understand by Mysorewala's testimony before the Nanavati Commission as well as *India Today's* report, they certainly did not kill "70 or 80 or more" people & instead escorted 400 Muslims to safety and saved the lives of more than 900 Muslims in this episode. **Nobody has ever alleged, no Muslim survivor of Naroda-Patiya or anyone else that the "Police killed 70 or 80 or more Muslims in Naroda-Patiya".** His inaccuracies actually make it seem that this man may not have been present in Naroda at all on that day!

The Ahmedabad VHP chief, Rajendra Vyas said about the role of the police:

"**Rajendra Vyas:** As Chief Minister, Narendrabhai couldn't say 'Kill all the Muslims', I could say it publicly because I was from the VHP...Pravinbhai Togadia can say it. But he [Modi] can't say it. But it's like how we say it in Gujarati, *"aa khada kaan khada"* [to turn a blind eye]...meaning, he gave us a free run to do whatever we wanted to, since we were already fed up of the Muslims. The police was with us. Please understand what I'm trying to say—the police was on our side, and so was the entire Hindu *samaj*. Bhai [Modi] was careful about that...or else the police would have been on the other side....

TEHELKA: Yes, if it had been a Congress Government.

Vyas: Then the result would have been the opposite.

TEHELKA: But the police are after all Hindu. What I want to know is what stand did they take then?

Vyas: They didn't go near the Muslims...[though] when people would call them up, they'd say they were coming. That's what they did at that time. The other thing they did was tell people that they could do whatever they wanted... they wouldn't do a thing...."

Now these are again lies. But no mentions of the police killing 70 or 80 or more Muslims in Naroda-Patiya! And we have seen details of the police action already.

M.S. University accountant, Dheemant Bhatt said:

"9TH MAY 2007

Some 50 people like myself had special permission from the police commissioner... to move in curfew areas to help... in order to maintain the peace and law and order. That was just an excuse... I am very open...clear [about it]. But how were we to help the Hindus? At that time, there wasn't even a stick of wood in Hindu homes. So what were we to do?... We took iron pipes...three feet each...iron bars, and if there were people from the Bajrang Dal, then trishuls. The Bajrang Dal people had a plan for putting together the *samaan* [weapons] and we went and supplied them to key persons in various localities. It was very necessary...."

These facts need to be investigated. If for argument's sake, we assume what he says is true, did the police give him permission intentionally? And it seems highly unlikely that they did, they seem to be more lies. But if he is guilty, he should be punished.

Dhawal Jayanti Patel said:

"**TEHELKA:** After Godhra, when you made bombs and sent them to Ahmedabad, didn't the police stop you on the way?

Patel: We concealed them from the police...the police would also let us go. If you say Jai Shri Ram, it matters. After all, they were Hindus, they also understood...."

This is again dubious—whether he really made bombs. But if his confession is true, how is this indictment of the police? **He clearly says that he 'hid' the bombs from the police. If the police was involved in the rioting—would he have needed to 'hide' the bombs?**

Now see the statement made by VHP's zilla mantri in the Kalupur area of Ahmedabad, Ramesh Dave:

"**12th JUNE 2007**

The police were very helpful...very helpful. That's why when the human rights people came...when they saw everything...they said the politicians had a role in it all...the police too, in fact, everyone, who belonged to the [Hindu] *samaj*...because, after all, what were the police?...The police were Hindu too. The thing was, they were under pressure from the government. If they wanted to do something, they couldn't....

[SK] Gadvi *saheb* was a new DCP here. Curfew was on and he was patrolling about...I went up to him on my cycle and said namaskar to him.... 'How are you out in curfew hours,' he asked...'I am a *maharaj*,' I said, 'I can go wherever I please....' Uptil then, he didn't know I was from the Vishwa Hindu Parishad. Then he said he wanted to climb to the top of a nearby temple. I asked him what it was he wanted to do there. He said a lot of Muslims from outside were sitting there and he wanted to set them straight....

I said, 'If you want to set them straight, then there's a spot I can take you to. But you have to promise me that you'll kill at least four or five of them there...' He promised.... Then we went to that place. He said he'd been there before... I said, forget whether you've been here or not. There was a house which was locked. I had the key sent for and we went to the terrace. From there, the place was straight ahead. **He started firing from the terrace, and before we knew it, he'd killed five people....**

Gadvi *saheb* would tell us never to take his name anywhere, but all the policemen helped us...they all did. One shouldn't say it, but they even gave us cartridges..." (*Source*: http://www.tehelka.com/ story main35.asp?filename= Ne031107All The Cops.asp).

India Today dated 12 November, 2007 reported:

"Similarly, a VHP activist, Ramesh Dave, told the Tehelka reporter Ashish Khetan on camera that one of the divisional superintendents of police, S.K. Gadhvi, promised him that he would kill five Muslims during the riots and carried out his promise by killing five Muslims in the Dariapur area.

Official records show that Gadhvi was posted in the Dariapur area of Ahmedabad one month after the riots and no such incident took place under his tenure."

This again nails the *Tehelka* and Ramesh Dave's lies. Now, let us see the statements made by Pralhad Raju, an accused in the Gulbarga case:

"8TH SEPTEMBER, 2007

TEHELKA: How did the police behave with you on the day of the Gulbarg incident?

Raju: The police did nothing except watch us....

TEHELKA: They let you do whatever you wanted to?

Raju: They did not arrest a single person that day. Nobody was touched. (**Our comment:** This is rubbish. The police arrested 700 people on that day!)

TEHELKA: They didn't stop anyone?

Raju: They dispersed us after 4:30.

TEHELKA: Till then nobody was stopped?

Raju: When orders came from the higher-ups…we were told to leave.

TEHELKA: They let you do as you wanted till 4:30?

Raju: Yes. The Crime Branch people behaved very nicely with us... We felt completely at home. Our family members used to come to meet us and they were allowed to. We were kept at the Branch for about a week…."

These are again boastful lies, and this testimony makes it seem as if this man was not present at the Gulbarga locality on 28 February at all. This is because Ehsan Jafri fired at the Hindu crowd, as reported by *India Today, Times of India* and *Outlook,* injuring 15. The police shot dead five rioters and saved the lives of more than 180 Muslims in the episode despite being overwhelmingly outnumbered, as reported by *India Today* and *The Times of India.* **Nowhere in its reports online of 28 February, 2002 does *The Times of India* allege any inaction on the part of the police.**

Now, see the interview of Anil Patel, the VHP state *vibhag pramukh*:

"13TH JUNE 2007

Anil Patel: See, there were some areas where we were very concerned about our safety.

TEHELKA: Such as.

Patel: Kalupur…Dariapur…. Hindus live along the edges of these places. For their safety, we sent some *samaan* [weapons] from here.

TEHELKA: Sent from here.

Patel: From time to time… there were some policemen we were in touch with. They would come and take the *samaan* and deliver it safely to the places it was supposed to go. The police here gave us so much support. Some even said, do something…loot them, break them, finish them…I had a fight once with a DSP. One of our brothers cut a Muslim's ear off with a sword and the DSP arrested him. I told the DSP that our people had been burnt to death and that he was corrupt and used to share food with Muslims in Baroda. Later on, he released the guy. DSP N.D. Solanki was very good. He said, 'Release him…'.

TEHELKA: So Solanki lent support?

Patel: Full, full. He gave me complete support. See, when the riots were dying out, when temperatures had started cooling down, someone in the Biloda village said that nothing had happened there…that something should be done. There was a man there called Mansoori…he was a SIMI sympathiser…he had a vegetable shop…. He was hacked to death…. Later on, a co-minister from our area, [VHP leader] Arvindbhai Soni, was arrested. I went to Biloda and, later on, I called the DSP and talked to him…Jayantibhai and I, both went and met him and he said he would release Arvindbhai. Everything was there on paper, in the arrest report, but when Arvindbhai was to be transferred to judicial custody, he was told to go back to the [VHP] *karyalaya*....

TEHELKA: To go to the *karyalaya*.

Patel: He stayed there for a month and a half.

TEHELKA: That's what the DSP said? Who was the DSP?

Patel: N.D. Solanki.

Patel: There was this IB officer, Shreekumar, who sent a fax to the Ahmedabad Police Commissioner, saying the Sabarkantha VHP had supplied weapons to Ahmedabad. The matter was inquired into…our block minister was arrested. The inspector, who came for the inquiry, was associated with the Sangh….

TEHELKA: What was his name?

Patel: I don't know but…after the inquiry was over, he told us that he was with the Jeevan Dal Bhole, our *vibhag pracharak….*"

It is for the investigators to see if the statements made by this man are really true or again lies. But his statement that there was a concern for the safety of the Hindus in the Kalupur and Dariapur areas of Ahmedabad, is absolutely true. The man he indicts is himself and not Modi.

Now, let us see the statements made by Mangilal Jain—an accused in the Ehsan Jafri case:

"8TH SEPTEMBER, 2007

TEHELKA: What was the name of that inspector you were talking about?

Jain: [KG] Erda [Meghaninagar police inspector].

TEHELKA: Erda…what did he do?

Jain: He supported us. Those people kept away from the public that day.

TEHELKA: Kept away from Muslims?

Jain: From the public…from Hindus…they told us that everything should be finished within two or three hours.

TEHELKA: That means they gave you two or three hours.

Jain: To finish.

TEHELKA: To finish everything.

Jain: This was happening across all of Ahmedabad. [It was understood] no outsider would come. **Even reinforcements weren't going to come. The force wouldn't get there till evening. So we were to do all the work.**

TEHELKA: He told you to do it all in two to three hours.

Jain: He said it and the mob went berserk. Some started looting. Others started killing. Someone dragged a man out and hacked him down and burned him. A lot of this kind of stuff happened.

TEHELKA: You were caught after two months?

Jain: I surrendered after two months.

TEHELKA: Did you appear in court?

Jain: Not in court...I appeared before the Crime Branch people. Sadavrati *saheb* was there...I called him home. We had dinner. He told me to surrender. I did as he said.

TEHELKA: Sadavrati cooperated?

Jain: Cooperated...he met me in the evening.

TEHELKA: Was he of help.

Jain: He said that Mangilal's name was there. He told me to surrender.

TEHELKA: At your house?

Jain: At my house. Don't worry [he said], have no fear and produce yourself at 10 o'clock tomorrow morning. All will be well. Your son will be out in a month or two. Now that his name is on record, there's no way out. If his name is there, it means he has to appear. Even a PM or CM can't help it. So I surrendered to the Crime Branch…they took good care of me….

TEHELKA: They took good care of you.

Jain: Yes sir…down there in the lock-up, there were mosquitoes and it's filthy. We were not kept there…there was a room up above their office. We were kept in the office. There were mattresses…food from my home would come for me twice a day. We were there for three days….

TEHELKA: Three days.

Jain: We were produced in court on the first day.

TEHELKA: Where did they record you as being picked up from?

Jain: They said that we were picked up from home.

TEHELKA: They said this.

Jain: Yes, that's what they said. That's what the police are like, they say one thing and do something else. All they want is to keep their own names looking clean.

TEHELKA: But they took good care of you.

Jain: It was good. We got there in the evening…we would get tea twice a day and we could make phone calls. I would get calls from home…we would also make calls…we had full phone facilities. We were in the Crime Branch for three days…we were not even touched…I have to say this…nobody laid a finger on me…They took my statement that day itself. 'What happened… Where were you that day…' [was all they asked.]

TEHELKA: What did you say?

Jain: I said the shop was closed and I had gone there to watch…I was part of the group…I said I was in the group…and my house was at a distance from that place and there was a huge crowd, I didn't recognize anyone who did the killing. That's what I'd say…'Don't know who was doing the killing. Everybody was raising slogans…so was I…' That's what I told them, and then I said that after it all, I got home by 2. That's what I said.

TEHELKA: That's what you said.

Jain: What I said.

TEHELKA: Didn't they try forcing you to tell the truth?

Jain: No, sir…I wasn't even touched…Whatever I said, they noted down.

TEHELKA: Noted just as you said.

Jain: They didn't say anything to me…I was on remand for two days…the remand was over on the first day itself. It was just for name's sake. For two days, I would get my tiffin from home…my family members would come to meet me. I had every convenience.

TEHELKA: Meaning the remand was just a formality…a legal process.

Jain: These people followed full legal process…."

His statement: "Even reinforcements weren't going to come…. The force wouldn't get there till evening…. So we were to do all the work" is wrong since reinforcements did arrive that day, but, by that time, the mob had swelled to 10,000 as per weekly *India Today*. If this man's statements are indeed true, there is no reason why he should not be prosecuted. But these statements will not stand as evidence in any court of law. But does this really indict Modi?

Another interview is that of Madan Chawal, an accused in the Gulberga episode:

"12TH JUNE 2007

Chawal: I was there that day...all day, I ran with them. When they brought Jafri *saheb*, I was standing there itself...they held him down, kicked him in the back... they meant to chop him up.

TEHELKA: Describe it all in detail. Where did it begin?

Chawal: I was at my shop when the VHP people came around 8:30-9 o'clock to get the shops to down shutters. Around 9-9:30, a shop was set ablaze right in front of mine. That's when I realized it had started.

TEHELKA: Was it a Muslim's shop?

Chawal: Yes, it was. People started running once it started. Papa told me to close my shop...even though it was my region, my area, and nobody would have said anything even if my shop had stayed open. Nobody spoke when they told them to close the shops. Then I gestured with my hands to say it wouldn't look nice, it was a matter of religion and, hence, it was all the more important to close the shops. My father said, 'Close it for today, let's go home.' My father, the others, all of us went home. Then around 10:30 or 11 o'clock, I went out. The moment I did so, I joined the mob...the ruckus continued all the time I was with the crowd...it went on for at least two-and-a-half hours.

TEHELKA: Who was leading the mob?

Chawal: Most people had joined the mob. The moment that shop was set on fire, everyone started gathering there.

TEHELKA: Were the VHP people also part of the mob?

Chawal: All of them.

TEHELKA: Who were there from the VHP?

Chawal: At that time, I didn't know all the leaders. I never had any contacts since I'm from a business background and I knew people only from that field... Later, though, when I met Atul *bhai*, I remembered he was there too.

TEHELKA: Atul Vaid was there.

Chawal: Atul Vaid was there, then there's one Bharatbhai Teli, he was also there. These boys...these big ones...they came to get me out of jail, it was then that I met them...they would come to the police station. Although they never came to the Central jail...they would look at me when they would come to the station. That was when I began realising that they were also there. And I used to wonder why I had been arrested while their names were dropped. Why didn't Atul Vaid and Bharat Teli's names come up when mine did?...I didn't give it too much importance, though, since these people could have helped me leave jail or do something else for me. That is why I never opened my mouth, never dropped a word anywhere about these people being there too...nobody ever said anything about it...not even the 40 boys, who were inside jail.

TEHELKA: Everybody knew it.

Chawal: They knew it. We would never talk about what exactly happened. In jail, we would say that we didn't know anything about it...that we'd just been trapped ...I was recorded in the first chargesheet as having used kerosene to lit a fire. In that chargesheet, I had been shot around 5:30-6:00 in the evening, when Erda *saheb* said...

TEHELKA: Who shot you?

Chawal: Erda *saheb* said that…that whole region. Didn't I show you the place?

TEHELKA: Yes.

Chawal: I was just standing around…some eight to 15 people were there near him. We asked, *saheb*, what are you doing, why are you saving them?

TEHELKA: You said this to Erda.

Chawal: The public…we were 8 to 15 people…everyone asked him 'What are you doing?'

TEHELKA: You asked him where he was taking the Muslims?

Chawal: We asked him where he was taking them…then he told us what he was doing.

TEHELKA: What did he say?

Chawal: He said, do this…when the vehicle [in which the Muslims were] comes this way, our constable [accompanying the vehicle] will run away…set the vehicle on fire. The whole episode will end here itself and there will be no question of framing a case against anyone. *Poori picture yahin khatam ho jayegi* [it will be "The End" here itself]. When he said this, the Bagri community thought that they were taking people, who could turn witness…[they feared] that he might get them in trouble. They started pelting stones at Erda *saheb*… and when one of them hit him, I ran away. He took out his revolver…he was behind me…he yelled at me and told me stop. When I tried to pull my nephew along with me while I was escaping, he shot at me.

TEHELKA: Erda *saheb* shot you? Was it by mistake?

Chawal: It was by mistake…it was shot at my hand. My hand was injured but none of the clinics were open, all of them were closed. All the hospitals at that time…. Then I went to the Civil Hospital. I wasn't aware about things like these because I had never been part of anything like this before. That day, I ended up getting my real name written in the hospital records.

TEHELKA: Then how did you kill Jafri that morning?

Chawal: Jafri. Well, it's like when those people caught him, I kicked him in the back and they pulled him away. The moment they pulled him away.

TEHELKA: You kicked Jafri?

Chawal: Kicked him.

TEHELKA: He fell down.

Chawal: *Gira…woh nahi…khaich…unke haath me tha, na…Paanch chheh jan pakad liye the, phir usko jaise pakad ke khada rakha, phir logon mein kisi ne talwar maari…haath kate…haath kaat ke phir pair kaate…phir na sab kaat dala…phir tukde kar ke phir lakda jo lagaye the, lakde uspe rakh ke phir jala daala… zinda jala daala.* [Fell down… not that. He was pulled by his hand. Five or six people held him, then someone struck him with a sword…chopped off his hand, then his legs…chopped off all his organs…after cutting him to pieces, they put him on the wood they'd piled and set it on fire…burnt him alive.]

TEHELKA: So when you people were cutting up Jafri's body, didn't Erda come to save him?

Chawal: No one did anything. At that time, Erda *saheb* wasn't even there. He had gone to Meghaninagar with his vehicle. He didn't know they were chopping Jafri saheb. All this happened around 1 or 1.30.

TEHELKA: But did the rest of Jafri's family manage to escape?

Chawal: No they didn't. His wife was the only one saved. She disguised herself as a Hindu.

TEHELKA: But some of his daughters were saved?

Chawal: Nobody at the place escaped, none of his family. The only ones who did were the ones who weren't there. His wife said that she was a maid...a Hindu, living in the Patrewali Chawl that is behind. Why do you want to kill me [she said], I'm just a servant. She was dressed like a Hindu...well dressed.

TEHELKA: She escaped because you didn't recognise her?

Chawal: I had never met her because there was never a need to go and meet them. I never had any relations with them.

TEHELKA: How big is the Gulbarga society? Do lots of people live there?

Chawal: Lots of them.

TEHELKA: So, have people come back to live at this place?

Chawal: Nobody has come back... it's closed now...it's like a jail. Nobody came back to it.

TEHELKA: But some people were saved there that evening.

Chawal: Some 40 people ran away...some of them had left before.

TEHELKA: So, how did you enter Gulbarga?

Chawal: People got gas cylinders from their homes. They kept them on the society's outer walls...then they got pipes from the bakery, where bread and so on are made and they opened the cylinders with them. Then they went far and made a *khupda* [cloth torch] and threw the cylinders at the wall. The cylinders exploded and the wall broke. Then we got inside.

TEHELKA: Was the wall too high?

Chawal: Too much…it was no two-ft wall. It must have been around 15-20 feet high. On top of it, there was a barbed wire fence too.

TEHELKA: So, the wall broke with just one or two cylinders?

Chawal: Two cylinders…one was thrown there and the other one in the front. The wall would obviously have broken from the cylinders. Cylinders are heavy.

TEHELKA: So, the houses inside caught fire.

Chawal: People used the residents' own things to burn their houses…nobody needed to get anything from outside…their own things were used to burn them.

TEHELKA: The same thing happened in Patiya too.

Chawal: The same happened in Patiya…" URL: http://www. tehelka.com/ story_main35.asp?filename=Ne031107They_hacked.asp

  The statement "Nobody from his family survived, except his wife" is also blatantly false. The fact is that more than 180 Muslims were saved in the episode and **many relatives, who were there—apart from his wife survived. Also there is no suggestion that his wife disguised herself as a Hindu to save herself.** This is completely wrong on facts. Again these statements are clear lies.

  Also, Jafri was not cut to pieces. The post-mortem report shows he died because of bullet injury, according to *The Pioneer*'s MD and Editor Chandan Mitra in an article titled "A sting without venom" in *Outlook* dated 12 Nov 2007. Chawal's details of Jafri's legs being cut, etc. all clearly seem to be boastful lies.

In his interview, Anil Patel, VHP leader, also says that the Congress leaders were also involved in the riots in attacks on Muslims. What does the Congress Party have to say about that? We have seen *The Times of India's* report of 9 August 2003 that 25 Congress leaders accused of attacking Muslims in the riots.

All this was about the interviews of the accused and others. But no one has heard their points of view after the sting operation. What do these people have to say in self-defence?

But the Gujarat Congress leader and ex-Gujarat Chief Minister Shankersinh Vaghela (1940-) said something else on this *Tehelka* operation.

The *Tehelka* exposé on the Gujarat carnage was a 'belated attempt' by the Narendra Modi Government to boost his sagging image among the voters ahead of the forthcoming state assembly elections, Union Textile Minister, Shankersinh Vaghela alleged on Saturday (27 Oct 2007). "This was just an attempt to deflect public attention from the ongoing infighting within the Gujarat unit of the Bharatiya Janata Party," he added.

"It is more like a fake encounter, to build his own image as a hardcore pro-Hindu and trying to revive Hinduism," the minister alleged (*Source*: http://ia.rediff.com/news/2007/oct/27modi.htm).

Sankarshan Thakur of *Tehelka* claimed that Bajrangi had *confessed* that he had cut open a pregnant woman and pulled out the foetus. In fact, Bajrangi had said that *the FIR on him* stated that he had cut open a pregnant woman (transcript does not mention foetus). This makes it the third version of the foetus story (the other version was supplied by none other than Arundhati Roy, when her distraught friend and an eye-witness called her up to narrate the foetus brandishing incident). We have seen how Balbir Punj reacted to this in *Outlook* in Chapter 7: "Concocted Lies and Myths by the Media".

An article on the Internet posted on 27 October, 2007, says: "**What can one say about this?** Chandan Mitra has a column on *The Pioneer* questioning some of the claims of the sting operation, especially the time frame. **Apart from lip-sync issues, it is disturbing that the videos provided contain very small portion of the actual transcript. It is questionable how faithful these transcripts are. We hope *Tehelka* knows what it's doing, because this will surely snowball into a full blown constitutional crisis....**

...suddenly, the whole of *Tehelka* team is acting all indignant and defensive. They even answered allegations against the sting on the *Tehelka* website. One of the editors, Shoma Chaudhary, put the casualty count at 2,500. Remember that Bajrangi was a non-entity before the media made him a legend of Hindu bride reverse-abductions. This has been going on for a while, even *Tehelka* published long articles on him. This clearly proves that they knew very well what they were doing. They want to connect the riots to people as high in the party hierarchy as possible, ultimately leading to Modi.

They didn't just stumble upon evidence and hurriedly released it. The whole thing was likely engineered and meticulously planned. **The questions were very carefully coined well in advance, not a dare devil reporter asking *impromptu* questions, making use of a windfall opportunity. Haresh Bhatt was extensively interviewed about preparations during the Babri Masjid issue. This was seamlessly merged into the post-Godhra riots.** This has naturally spawned conspiracy theories, some by none other than Modi's chief detractor, ex-CM, (Suresh)Mehta.

As a matter of fact, the constant movie references for a purportedly genuine sting is quite disturbing. The men filmed are constantly being referred to as the *cast of characters*, *Tehelka* Editor, Shoma Chaudhury chose a movie reference for the title of her column on HT. You will require some background in order to appreciate her column:

'This and other genuine errors in recounting the details of the violence in Gujarat, in no way, alters the substance of what journalists, fact-finding missions, or writers, like myself, are saying.'

If you are scratching your head, maybe you should not read Shoma Chaudhury's piece. One wonders why she would need to pontificate so much, going way beyond the scope of the sting (and perhaps way beyond her intellectual depth) and questioning everything about our democracy. While steadfastly maintaining the sting was not political and merely investigative journalism aimed at securing justice for the victims, she ends up exhorting Hindus to vote against Modi.

'The real faultline in India today is not between Hindus and Muslims. It is between Hindus and Hindus. If the Hindus of Gujarat are going to re-elect

Modi after being confronted with visual proof of what he stands for, we have to aggressively reclaim what being Hindu means.'

What started as *irrefutable* evidence to nail Modi thus ends up being a moral sermon. No mention of the actual evidence in the tapes or arguments to bolster the case. It's my way or the highway—if you don't believe in the sting, our democracy is flawed or you must be a communal Hindu.

Meanwhile, the sting is steadily making its way into the *jihadi* fables, the ones used to recruit and radicalize impressionable youth to launch deadly terror attacks. If anything, the sting *proved* that the train fire was not an accident, yet the newspapers in the Middle-East and Pakistan are qualifying it, while reporting the other part at face value:

NEW DELHI: The editor of Tehelka magazine said on Wednesday that Muslims in India's western state of Gujarat were being 'hunted like rabbits'. Hindu extremists had killed around 2,000 Muslims in three days after Sabarmati Express, a train carrying Hindu pilgrims, was **allegedly** set on fire by Muslims at the Godhra Railway Station.

...meanwhile, the *Tehelka* team members are now folk heroes and are acting as such, writing columns, appearing on reality TV style shows and giving interviews. You have to read some of the stuff to believe it. The sting has assumed the status of urban legends now. Absent any forensic analysis and, needless to say, a critical examination of the raw unedited footage of indeterminate length, the *Tehelka* folks are laying it on thick and heavy. **For instance, Prof. Bandukwala was mercilessly killed, according to none other than Ashish Khetan** (of *Tehelka*). **Prof. Bandukwala made a mysterious reappearance very recently to accept the Indira Gandhi Award for National Integration!**

Likewise, Bajrangi had stated on the tapes that his FIR alleged that he had cut open a pregnant woman. This gradually became Bajrangi confessing his crime on tape. Finally, we have Bajrangi actually *gloating over a foetus ripped out of a mother's womb* on live video!

This is what passes for truth in this country. Just like the Narmada Dam *movement*, the Gujarat riots has become stuff of urban legends. A complete self-sustaining industry has formed around them. The true victims of the riots will never know the obscene amount of wealth made on their blood and bones by the media and secular vultures.

Shoma Chaudhury and Sankarshan Thakur really need to take it easy. Sample this: "A host of men go on national television and admit they have hacked and burnt and deformed other human beings—wilfully, gleefully and confidently."

Really? They went on TV just like that? Wilfully, gleefully *and* confidently?

'But the eloquent visionary men, who led us then, pulled the country away from the madness of the Hindu fanatic and gifted us a nation that was sane and wise and inclusive. We could have gone another route. We could have been Pakistan.' Oh, thank God for small mercies!

Conspiracy is an idler's kaleidoscope, the more you turn, the more new designs you see.

Keep turning dude, the 'scope is all yours to turn till the cows home'" (*Source*: http://barbarindians.blogspot.com/2007_10_01_archive.html).

This was posted by barbarindian at 8:15 a.m. on 27th October, 2007. There are many more things worth reporting. Haresh Bhatt said after the sting operation: "You know how these sting operations work. **I was talking of something else and it has been construed and shown as something else.** It is a political gimmick of those who are opposing us."

Babu Bajrangi said: **"I don't know who is taking my name and why. I did not lead any mob in Naroda-Patiya. The sting operation shows me saying that I took a sword and cut open a woman's womb. But I was trying to explain that the FIR filed against me accuses me of that act and that I deny it."** (*The Indian Express* dated 26th October, 2007).

So carried away were *Tehelka* and *Aaj Tak* by their Gujarat sting that they suffered the ides of February. B.P. Singhal writes in his article "Gujarat ka sach" in *The Pioneer* dated 29th October, 2007: "*Aaj Tak* harped on the same old refrain that 'Modi did not call the Army until three days had passed'. When the TV channel contacted me on phone to get my response, I told the anchor that the Godhra carnage took place on 27th February, 2002, that the Hindu backlash commenced on 28th February and the Army was doing flag-march on the forenoon of 1st March.... **He cut me short by saying that 'This is** exactly what we had said, no action was taken by Modi on 29th, 30th and 31st, thus giving three clear days to the murderers…' I had to cut him short by reminding him that the date 28th was 28th February, 2002 and there were no 29th, 30th or 31st in that month. The phone was of course disconnected."

Now, after the broadcast of this sting operation, one blogger, who wrote a blog titled, "Why Modi should Go?", says in his blog: "It is also true that most of the rioters haven't directly named Modi—rather, they have implicated themselves. **No doubt, *Tehelka's* claim of "irrefutable proof" must be taken with the pinch of salt and it is quite likely that none of the evidences will stand the test in a court of law."** (*Source*: http://retributions.nationalinterest. in/ why-modi-should-go/).

And this same man advocated the resignation of Narendra Modi. In a strongly anti-Narendra Modi article, he has confessed that *Tehelka's* claim of irrefutable proof must be taken with a pinch of salt.

On the Internet was also posted: "First a look at the actors in the so-called exposé that, the *Tehelka* is claiming, was captured from a spy camera.

Babu Bajrangi—In the entire script of the sting, this guy doesn't implicate anyone but himself in the riots. This guy is considered the most important witness in the sting. With FIRs already filed and Bajrangi identified as a key accused, what is the surprise here?

Rajendra Vyas—Goes into great details of what he did in Godhra, again not a word directly implicating anyone but himself.

Ramesh Dave—Chimes in on incidents on Godhra, implicates Rajendra Vyas and himself, not a word, despite being egged on by the *Tehelka* reporter, on directly attributing anything to Narendra Modi.

Madan Chawal—First says he saw VHP leaders, then says he did not call VHP leaders by name and then claims that, later on, he remembered that he probably saw Atul Vaid, Bharat Teli. Implicates himself in Gulbarga incidents, nothing to say about anybody else.

Prahlad Raju—Implicates himself in Gulbarga incidents. Is egged on by *Tehelka* to implicate VHP and RSS. All he says, "Atul Vaid told me to move together". Nothing more to say on anyone else.

Mangilal Jain—Implicates himself in the Gulbarga incidents. Is egged on by *Tehelka* to implicate Atul Vaid and Bharat Teli, he merely mentions after consistent egging by the interviewer that an Inspector Erda told him he had two to three hours.

Prakash Rathod, Suresh Richard—Implicate themselves in Naroda-Patiya. Not a word implicating anyone else, making passing references to Narendra Modi visiting the site of incidents.

Dhimant Bhatt—The headlines says idea came from Modi, the detailed transcript says it was a meeting of local leaders but gives no names. This guy neither has a direct reference nor a direct statement to say on Modi or anybody else. Implicates himself.

Deepak Shah—Implicates himself and Dhimant, has nothing substantial to say except reeling out names of lawyers on the legal team.

Anil Patel—This guy does even better than the rest of them. Not only does he implicate himself but also implicates Congress workers. His 5-page sting transcript implicates people who are already accused and are out on bail. Has some hearsay conversations to report with Pravin Togadia nothing to suggest a conspiracy to riot, only suggestions on bailing out accused.

All of them are accused and all of them implicated themselves and no one else directly. So, that is *Tehelka* for you! Now, for some more incredible claims—bombs and rocket launchers that were never used.

Haresh Bhatt— Godhra MLA and riot accused makes incredible claims of ordering guns and other weapons from other states. Hard to believe stuff given how many days it takes for any truck to arrive from distant Punjab or Uttar Pradesh. He just goes on adding states to his list—Bihar, MP.

Dhawal Jayanthi Patel—Shows of a dynamite factory, makes tall claims, has nothing to say about even one specific incident where bombs were used.

Anil Patel—This is the most laughable of the transcripts, the interviewer puts words into his mouth with a single question and all he replies is to confirm that yes there are dynamite factories which supply explosives to Ahmedabad.

Lot of sensational drivel about but none confirming a single incident where bombs were actually used. More bravado than anything else, what can one expect in '*Tehelka*'! The rest of the website is sensational drivel, regurgitating bits and pieces extracted from these transcripts with psychedelic fonts and images. Watching the manner in which *Headlines Today* is running this story on live television, it just goes to highlight how out of control and irresponsible the sensationalism of ratings starved news channels has become.

With this coming together of sensational media of which is constantly on the look-out to manufacture headlines and left wing radicals out to push a fictitious version of the truth, the need for a Right of Center Media in India has once again been highlighted" (*Source*: http://offstumped.wordpress.com/2007/10/26/tehelka- expose-on-gujarat-riots-offstumped-reaction/).

On 27 October 2007, Arvind Pandya announced at a press conference that he had resigned as government counsel, and had filed criminal cases against Dhimant Purohit, correspondent of *Aaj Tak*, charging them with cheating, criminal conspiracy, breach of trust, fraud, trespass and breach of communal harmony. He contended that Purohit had offered him a role in a serial, which the TV channel was purportedly producing and that he was captured on a hidden camera when he was reading from what had been given to him as a script for an *audition* test. The immediate result of Pandya's legal action was that Purohit sought anticipatory bail!

Despite knowing that Babu Bajrangi had said: "The FIR says I slit open a pregnant woman's womb", *Tehelka* tried to say that he had said: "I split open her womb". *Tehelka's* claims of having 'irrefutable' evidence are all baseless. It also shows that the intention of *Tehelka* is to try to nail the accused and hold them guilty by hook or by crook and not paint the reality. Now we have the doctor J.S. Kanoria's report which proves that the womb was not ripped open at all! So, even if Bajrangi had indeed boasted that he committed the act, *Tehelka* should have cross-checked if this was indeed true, and the report of Dr. Kanoria would have made it clear that they were boastful lies. Actually, they were not even boastful lies, he was totally denying the crime. What a criminal offence on *Tehelka's* part!

What we have been saying has also been confirmed by the SIT's closure report. The SIT report has some comments on this *Tehelka* sting on pages 273-274. It says on pp 273-274:

"In this connection, it may be added here that Shri Haresh Bhatt, formerly MLA and Babu Bajrangi (accused in Naroda Patiya case) have admitted their voice as also the contents of the CD. **Shri Haresh Bhatt has stated that one Ashish had approached him and informed that he wanted to write a thesis** on Hindutva and wanted him to contribute some spicy material for the same, so that he could succeed in his mission. He has further stated that Ashish visited him at his residence in Ahmedabad City as well as Godhra at least 7-8 times in a month's time and when the reference came to Gujarat riots, he gave an imaginary story as Ashish wanted some spicy material for his thesis. He has stated that the talks about a CBI inquiry, the fact that he owned a gun factory where diesel bombs and pipe bombs were made and distributed to Hindus, the fact about two truckload of swords ordered from Punjab and subsequently distributed amongst Hindus, making of a rocket launcher in his gun factory by filling them with gun powder and lighting a 595 local made bomb to blast were absolutely false and baseless. He has also mentioned that his talk about Shri Narendra Modi having openly said that we had three days to do, whatever we could do and that he would not give us time after that, was an imaginary story and that Shri Modi had never told these things to him.

Shri Babu Bajrangi has stated that Shri Ashish Khetan had given him a script and he simply read out the same and that none of those facts were correct. Further, they were not questioned by Shri Ashish Khetan as to how and when Shri Narendra Modi gave them three days time. The facts about a gun factory owned by Shri Haresh Bhatt and change of judge thrice by Shri Narendra Modi are unacceptable by any stretch of imagination inasmuch as no such gun factory could be unearthed by the police and Shri Modi was not competent to transfer the Judges, as the same is the prerogative of the Gujarat High Court. There are many factual inaccuracies in the recorded statement of Babu Bajrangi inasmuch as he has stated that there were 700-800 dead bodies in Naroda Patiya and that the Commissioner of Police had instructed the policemen to throw it at different places in Ahmedabad City, as it would be difficult to explain the same. This is absolutely incorrect inasmuch as only 84 dead bodies were found at Naroda Patiya and 11 persons were reportedly missing."

On page 287 the SIT also said: "As regards the Sting Operation carried out by Tehelka on Shri Babu Bajrangi, the FSL Jaipur has confirmed that the voice in the Tehelka CD is that of Babu Bajrangi, an accused in Naroda Patiya case...At the best the disclosure made by Shri Babu Bajrangi in the sting operation could be termed as extra-judicial confession. However, there is no corroborative evidence to support the disclosures made by Shri Babu Bajrangi. On the contrary, the claims made by Shri Babu Bajrangi have been found to be false."

But it does not end merely here. *Tehelka* also tried to concoct imaginary 'provocations' for Godhra and tried to say that Godhra was spontaneous, a result of altercations between *karsevaks* and Muslims at the Godhra Railway Station. It also held the Gujarat government guilty for taking the position that Godhra was planned. **It, of course, could not explain why and how 2,000 Muslims could have quickly reached the train at Signal Falia at 8:00 in the morning, having already managed to procure petrol bombs, acid bombs and swords and surround the train from both the sides and prevent the** *karsevaks* **from running away and saving their lives when the train stops at Godhra only for five minutes.**

Even if, for argument's sake, we assume that many of the 'confessions' of the people interviewed are indeed true, how does that show that the Gujarat riots were a 'genocide', which *Tehelka* has claimed? Who killed the 254 Hindus in the Gujarat riots—a figure given by the UPA Government's MoS for Home, Shriprakash Jaiswal in the Parliament on 11th May, 2005?

Having read the whole reports of *Tehelka* on this matter, it is clear that *Tehelka* is not interested in bringing out the truth but interested in maligning the BJP and Narendra Modi. The fact is that even after Godhra, Muslims were equally on the offensive and killed hundreds of Hindus. How does *Tehelka* explain that? The UPA Government has given the figures which assuming all missing are dead—would amount to 1171. **Still, the *Tehelka* magazine's editor claimed that 2,500 Muslims were killed in the riots in the first 3 days! In a population of 5.5 crore, 1,171 deaths of both Hindus & Muslims are no 'pogrom', despite this *Tehelka* continues to call the riots a pogrom. There have been separate convictions of 80 Muslims for rioting and killing Hindus in the post-Godhra riots. The conviction of Muslims proves that Muslims were equally on the offensive. How does Tarun Tejpal call the riots a 'pogrom' when Muslims have been convicted?**

In the entire sting operation, only two cases are discussed: the Ehsan Jafri case and the Naroda-Patiya case, both of which are two cases of real anti-Muslim riots in the state, apart from Sadarpura, Ode and Pandarwada.

Tehelka has called the Gujarat riots a 'genocide' on the basis of only two cases. There have been several other cases of riots—Himmatnagar near Ahmedabad, Danilimda, Sindhi Market, Bhanderi Pole areas of Ahmedabad, and many other riots throughout Gujarat, when Muslims were on the offensive and attacked Hindus. **Has *Tehelka* bothered to investigate that and see the convictions of Muslims in those cases?**

Tarun Tejpal has written a lot about these 'confessions' aka boastful lies. No one has ever given any answers on the points which have been raised in this chapter about the sting operation. For the lies which have been spoken about the Gujarat riots, perhaps the concerned people deserve a jail sentence and a very very heavy fine, to be paid to Narendra Modi, *Sangh Parivar* and Indian security forces, because the lies are converting innocent Muslims into fanatics, besides tarnishing the image of India, and of Narendra Modi and the *Sangh Parivar*.

CHAPTER 12

FINDINGS OF SIT

Zakia Jafri, wife of the late Ehsan Jafri who was killed in the riots on 28 February 2002, had filed a complaint against Narendra Modi and 62 others. On the basis of this complaint, a Special Investigation Team (SIT) was constituted by the Supreme Court of India to inquire into the charges. This SIT, despite intense pressure from the media, the NGOs, and allegedly also the then UPA Government to frame Narendra Modi, gave him a thorough clean chit. The findings of the SIT were also accepted by the lower court of Gujarat in December 2013. The background of the constitution of this SIT with the timeline is given below.

On June 8, 2006, Zakia Jafri, in a letter to the DGP (Director General of Police), sought registration of a FIR (First Information Report) against the then Gujarat Chief Minister Narendra Modi and 62 others for conspiracy behind 2002 riots in Gujarat. The police refused to lodge the complaint. Then on May 1, 2007, Zakia Jafri moved the Gujarat High Court after the DGP (Director General of Police) declined to entertain her complaint. On Nov 2, 2007 Gujarat High Court dismissed her plea. Subsequently Zakia moved the Supreme Court of India.

Then on March 26, 2008, the Supreme Court (SC) ordered the Narendra Modi government to re-investigate nine cases in the 2002 Gujarat riots, including the Gulberg Society incident in which Zakia's husband was killed. The Supreme Court constituted a Special Investigation Team (SIT) headed by former CBI director R K Raghavan to probe the cases afresh. And in March,

2009 the SC asked the SIT to look into Zakia's complaint over the role of chief minister Narendra Modi and others.

The SIT had submitted its report in November 2010, which was seen and reviewed by the Amicus Curiae Raju Ramchandran in January 2011. On March 11, 2011, the SC asked the SIT to look into the doubts raised by amicus curiae Raju Ramchandran. This was also done. On 12 September 2011, the SC ended its monitoring in this issue.

In February 2012, the SIT probing the 2002 violence filed its final report before a local court. The SIT report gave Modi a clean chit in the Gulberg Society massacre. Zakia filed a protest petition against clean chit given to Modi by the SIT. But all the courts rejected Zakia's petitions and upheld the clean chit given to Narendra Modi by the SIT and accepted its closure report.

Many vital and important finds of the SIT in its closure report need to be highlighted as they have been covered up. This chapter aims at revealing some of them.

Zakia Jafri has alleged in her complaint that '2500 people were killed in 5 days' as per the SIT report on page 9. We have of course seen the truth of the death toll earlier in this book. The SIT report also says on page 5 that: "The allegations made in the complaint dated 8-6-2006 (8 June 2006 and not 6 August 2006 as it could mean in some places outside India) of Zakia Nasim were general in nature, mostly based on media reports as well as other documents like affidavits filed by Shri R B Sreekumar about which she had no personal knowledge…"

The SIT says on pages 16-19 that: "Smt. Zakia Nasim was first examined by the local police on 6 March 2002 and her statement recorded under Section 161 CrPC but she never came up with all the details mentioned in her aforesaid complaint (dated 8 June 2006). **In her statement before the local police she had stated that while they were being shifted from the Gulberg Society in jail vans, the mob assembled there would have lynched all of them to death but for the timely action by the police.** Smt. Zakia Nasim then appeared before the Nanavati Commission of Inquiry on 29 August 2003 but did not disclose the facts given by her in her said complaint. In September 2003, Smt. Zakia Nasim filed an affidavit in the Supreme Court of India, but did not mention these facts. **It was for the first time on 8 June 2006,**

i.e. after a lapse of more than four years of the incident, that she came up with the lengthy complaint in question. **Smt. Zakia Nasim was examined by the SIT on 7 November 2008, but she failed to state any of these facts as mentioned in her complaint dated 8 June 2006.** She does not have any personal knowledge about the facts mentioned in the affidavits filed by **Shri R.B. Sreekumar during the years 2002, 2004 and 2005 on his own.** In this complaint the following glaring discrepancies/ errors have been noticed:

A: The allegations are vague, general and stereotyped and nothing specific had been mentioned in respect of the following accused persons ... Accused Nos. 2, 3, 4, 5, 6, 7, 8, 9, 10, 11, 12, 13, 14, 15, 16, 25, 26, 29, 32, 33, 35, 36, 40, 27, 28, 31, 34, 37, 43, 45, 46, 48, 63, 30, 47, 49, 51, 53, 57, 58, 59, 50, 52. (The SIT report gives details of the vagueness and generalized nature of the complaints by quoting the paragraphs in detail of complaints against the accused.)

B: Paras 29 to 57, 77, 79, 80, 81, 82 & 86 of the complaint have been copied out verbatim from the Affidavits No. I, II, III & IV filed by Shri R.B. Sreekumar, formerly Additional DG (Int.) before Nanavati-Shah Commission of Inquiry. The complainant Zakia Nasim has no personal knowledge of the allegations leveled by R.B. Sreekumar in his affidavits.

C: No specific allegations have been made against Accused Nos. 17,18, 19 & 60.

D: **Accused No. 24 Babubhai Rajput is not traceable at the given address and it has come to light that no such person was ever in existence at the relevant point of time.**

E: Accused No. 11 Anil Tribhovandas Patel was not in public life at the time of riots and had joined Bharatiya Janata Party only towards the end of 2002. He was elected as MLA only in December, 2002 and as such he has been wrongly implicated as an accused in the complaint without any specific role.

F: **Accused No. 45 Shri Rahul Sharma and Accused No. 63 Shri Satish Verma have been listed as witnesses as well as accused persons. Smt. Zakia Nasim, Complainant and Ms. Teesta Setalvad, have**

stated that they are witnesses and have been inadvertently listed as accused persons…"

All these facts make it absolutely clear that the complaint is not a genuine one. There are many more inaccuracies, some of which we will see later, but all the above facts show that Zakia Jafri does not have any idea of the complaint, and that it is made for her by others. The extent of this complaint's childish nature can be seen from the fact that Accused No. 24 was never in existence, and that the complainant's own witnesses were named as accused.

The complaint also states that the decision to bring the bodies to Ahmedabad from Godhra was taken 'in spite of the advice of the Godhra Collector, Smt. Jayanti Ravi against it'. The SIT says on page 463 that a meeting was held at the Collectorate in Godhra by the Chief Minister Narendra Modi in his visit to Godhra on 27 February evening, attended by the Ministers Ashok Bhatt, Gordhan Zadaphiya, Bhupendra Lakhawala, Prabhatsinh Chauhan, and Bhupendrasinh Solanki, and the Collector, Godhra, the District Magistrate, Police Officers and Railway Officers. The SIT report further says that the then Collector of Godhra, Smt. Jayanti Ravi has stated to the SIT that in the meeting held at the Collectorate, a unanimous decision was taken that the dead bodies which had been identified should be handed over to their relatives at Godhra itself and those bodies whose legal heirs or guardians had not come, could be sent to Sola Civil Hospital, Ahmedabad, since the deceased passengers were heading towards Ahmedabad. The report says on pages 463-464 that the decision to send the bodies to Sola Civil Hospital was taken in view of the fact that it was situated on the outskirts of Ahmedabad City and thus away from the crowded area for security reasons, and that 4 identified bodies were handed to legal guardians/ heirs at Godhra itself.

Thus the claim that the Collector of Godhra advised against transporting the bodies to Ahmedabad is also proved false, as she herself stated that the decision was unanimous. The SIT report says on page 64: **"The allegation that the dead bodies were transported to Ahmedabad against the wishes of Smt. Jayanti Ravi is proved to be incorrect."**

Suspended IPS (Indian Police Service) officer Sanjiv Bhatt claimed in 2011 that he was present in the 27 Feb late night crucial meeting and he also claimed that Narendra Modi ordered police to 'allow Hindus to vent their anger the next day i.e. 28 February'. The claim of Zakia Jafri that Narendra Modi told police officers to 'allow Hindus to vent their anger' in the crucial 27 February night meeting has been seen by us in Myth 19 of Chapter 7 already. The SIT also said that this claim is not established and also debunked Sanjiv Bhatt's claim of being present in that 27 Feb meeting. Here we will examine **Sanjiv Bhatt's claim** in detail.

After the initial report by SIT, Amicus Curiae Raju Ramachandran gave some of his observations which included a statement that it may not be correct to rule out the presence of Sanjiv Bhat in that 27 February meeting. After this, the SIT did another thorough investigation and gave its conclusions.

The SIT interviewed all the people who were indeed present at that 27 February meeting, namely S.K. Varma, the then acting Chief Secretary, Ashok Narayan, the then ACS (Home), P.K. Mishra, the then Principal Secretary to CM (Narendra Modi), K Chakravarthi, the then DGP, P.C. Pandey, the then Commissioner of Police, Ahmedabad City, Anil Mukim, the then Additional PS to CM, K Nityanandam, the then Secretary (Home) and Prakash Shah, the then Additional Secretary (law and order). On pages 393 to 397 of the closure report, their statements are given. S K Varma stated that she could not remember if Sanjiv Bhat was present or not, **but dismissed his allegation that Modi said anything** about balancing action against Hindus or Muslims, or that Muslims be taught a lesson or Hindus be allowed to vent their anger. ALL other participants denied the presence of Sanjiv Bhat, and also any Minister, and categorically denied the claim that Modi made any statement of the type alleged by Sanjiv Bhat. The participants have said that no one opposed the decision to bring bodies to Ahmedabad, and that discussions were made to maintain law and order the next day i.e. 28 February in view of the call for bandh and the serious nature of the Godhra carnage.

Sanjiv Bhat claimed to have attended the meeting and also claimed that he opposed the bringing of bodies to Ahmedabad. On pages 30-31 of the SIT closure report, the SIT says that Sanjiv Bhat has also claimed to be present at Narendra Modi's second meeting at his (Modi's) residence (i.e. in Gandhinagar, away from Ahmedabad) on the morning of 28 February at 10:30 AM. The SIT has mentioned this fact on page 400 as well, and stated that:

"Interestingly, the call details of his government mobile phone of Shri Sanjiv Bhatt show that he was in Ahmedabad till 1057 hrs on 28 February 2002". Sanjiv Bhat also claimed that the then Ministers the late Ashok Bhat and I K Jadeja were present at this meeting. The SIT report says on pages 44 and 45:

"The call detail records of the government mobile phone number allotted to Sanjiv Bhat show that on 27 February 2002, Shri Sanjiv Bhat remained at Ahmedabad till 11:20 hours and returned to Ahmedabad at 19:25 hours. He attended to various calls till 20:40, and thereafter, there is no record of any call made or received by him. **Further, on 28 February 2002, he remained at Ahmedabad till 10:57 hours** and then returned to Ahmedabad at 20:56 hours. **The claim of Sanjiv Bhat that he had attended a meeting at CM's residence on 28-02-2002 at 1030 hours is proved to be false and incorrect.** CM's residence is at Gandhinagar, more than 25 KMs from Ahmedabad, and normally takes 30 to 45 minutes to reach there. **His further claim that he had seen the late Ashok Bhat and Shri I K Jadeja, the then Ministers in the DGPs office at 11:00 hours on 28-02-2002, is also belied from the call detail records in as much as the location of the mobile phone of Shri Sanjiv Bhat was at Prerna Tower, Vastrapur-I, Ahmedabad, which happened to be at a distance of 1.5 Kms approximately from his residence and Shri Bhat could not have reached Police Bhavan, Gandhinagar before 11:30 hrs by any stretch of imagination** (page 44)...

(Page 45) **The claim of Sanjiv Bhat that he attended the said meeting at 1030 hours at CM's location is proved to be false from the location of his mobile phone,** which was at Prerna Tower, Vastrapur-I, Ahmedabad City at 10:57: 43 hrs. Moreover, his contention that the aforesaid two ministers (Bhat and Jadeja) were present in the said meeting is proved to be false from the statement of Ashok Narayan, the then ACS (Home) categorically stated that they were not present in the said meeting."

This shows that Sanjiv Bhat also wrongly claimed to have been present at the 28 February morning meeting. We can also see that on 27 February 2002, his call location is not Gandhinagar from 8:40 PM. He reached Ahmedabad at 7:25 PM and his last call record is 8:40 PM at Ahmedabad with not the slightest indication of Gandhinagar. If he attended the 27 February meeting held at 10:30-10:45 PM at Gandhinagar, at least at some time his mobile location would have been shown to be Gandhinagar, post 8:40 PM. Instead the mobile location is shown to be Ahmedabad at 10:57 AM the next day.

The SIT report says on pages 423-428:

"Government of Gujarat vide its letter dated 22-6-2011 forwarded a set of emails exchanged between Shri Sanjiv Bhatt, DIG, Gujarat Police and certain individuals during April & May 2011. It was mentioned in the above letter that during the course of an inquiry instituted against Shri Sanjiv Bhatt, IPS by DG (Civil Defence), Gujarat regarding misuse of official resources, some revelations have been made having direct bearing on the cases monitored by SIT. The material forwarded by Govt. of Gujarat has been scrutinized and the salient features of the same are summarized as below:

(1) **That top Congress leaders of Gujarat namely Shri Shaktisinh Gohil, Leader of Opposition in Gujarat Legislative Assembly and Shri Arjun Modhvadhia, President of the Gujarat Pradesh Congress Committee are in constant touch with Shri Sanjiv Bhatt, DIG. They are providing him "Packages", certain materials and also legal assistance. Further, on 28-04-2011, Shri Sanjiv Bhatt exchanged mails with Shri Shaktisinh Gohil and the former gave points for arguments in Hon'ble Supreme Court matter, allegations to be made against the members of SIT** and to establish that the burning of a coach of Sabarmati Express at Godhra Railway Station was not a conspiracy. From the emails, it appears that **Shri Sanjiv Bhatt was holding personal meetings with senior Congress leaders as well.** In one of the emails, he even mentions that he was "under exploited" by the lawyer representing Congress before Nanavati Commission of Inquiry.

(2) That Shri Sanjiv Bhatt had been persuading various NGOs and other interested groups to influence the Ld. Amicus Curiae and the Hon'ble Supreme Court of India by using "Media Card" and "Pressure Groups".

(3) Shri Sanjiv Bhatt had been exchanging emails with one Nasir Chippa and in the email dated 11-05-2011 Shri Bhatt has stated that he (Nasir

Chippa) should try to mobilize support/pressure-groups in Delhi to influence Ld. Amicus Curiae Raju Ramchandran in a very subtle manner. In another email dated 18-05-2011, Shri Sanjiv Bhatt had requested Shri Nasir Chippa to influence Home Minister Shri P. Chidambaram through pressure groups in US. It is believed that Shri Nasir Chippa has strong US connections and his family stays there.

(4) That Shri Sanjiv Bhatt arranged an appeal from Shri M Hasan Jowher, who runs a so-called NGO titled SPRAT (Society for Promoting Rationality) to Amicus Curiae on 13-05-2011, to call Shri Sanjiv Bhatt, IPS, Shri Rajnish Rai, IPS, Shri Satish Verma, IPS, Shri Kuldeep Sharma, IPS and Shri Rahul Sharma, IPS (all police officers of Gujarat) to tender their version of the Gujarat story. **It may be mentioned here that the draft for the said appeal was sent by Shri Sanjiv Bhatt himself to Shri Jowher.** Further, a copy of this mail was circulated by Shri Sanjiv Bhatt to **Ms. Shabnam Hashmi, Ms. Teesta Setalwad, Shri Himanshu Thakker, journalist, Shri Leo Saldana, Journalist and Shri Nasir Chippa** to encourage prominent persons/ organisation to write to Amicus Curiae on the similar lines so as to pressurize him.

(5) In emails exchanged on June 1, 2011 between Shri Sanjiv Bhatt and Shri M.H. Jowher, it was proposed that a PIL may be filed through a lawyer named Shri K Vakharia (a Sr. Advocate and Chairman of Legal Cell of Congress Party in Gujarat) in the Gujarat High Court for providing security to Shri Sanjiv Bhatt. It was also proposed that another complaint may be filed with the Commissioner of Police, Ahmedabad City against Shri Narendra Modi & others for his alleged involvement in 2002 riots which would be taken to appropriate judicial forums in due course.

(6) That Ms. Teesta Setalwad, her lawyer Shri Mihir Desai and Journalist Shri Manoj Mitta of Times of India were in constant touch with Shri Sanjiv Bhatt, IPS and were instrumental in arranging/drafting of the affidavit for filing the same in the Hon'ble Supreme Court. Vide email dated 10-04-2011, Shri Bhatt solicited "Co-ordinates" from Ms. Teesta Setalwad, who had also arranged for a meeting with her lawyer Shri Mihir Desai at Ellisbridge Gymkhana, Ahmedabad. Shri Sanjiv Bhatt sent the first draft of his proposed affidavit to Shri Manoj Mitta on 13-04-2011, after meeting Shri Mihir Desai, Advocate and invited his suggestions. **Shri Manoj Mitta advised Shri Sanjiv Bhatt to incorporate a few more paragraphs drafted by him which were incorporated by Shri Sanjiv Bhatt in his final affidavit sent to Hon'ble Supreme Court of India as suggested by Mitta.**

(7) That Shri Sanjiv Bhatt was instrumental in arranging an affidavit of one Shri Shubhranshu Chaudhary, a journalist, to corroborate his claim that he had gone to attend a meeting called by the Chief Minister at his residence in the night of 27-02-2002. **Significantly, Shri Bhatt had sent his mobile phone details of 27-02-2002 to Shri Shubhranshu Chaudhary and he had also suggested the probable timings of his meeting to Shri Shubhranshu Chaudhary on 15-05-2011. Simultaneously, these details were sent to Ms. Teesta Setalwad on 16-05-2011, for drafting the document, presumably the affidavit to be filed by Shri Shubhranshu Chaudhary.** Shri Sanjiv Bhatt sent an email to Shri Shubhranshu Chaudhary that the said affidavit could be leaked out to the print media which would force the Amicus Curiae and Hon'ble Supreme Court to take notice of the same. **Shri Sanjiv Bhatt also sent another email to Shri Shubhranshu Chaudhary, in which he has stated that they should play the "Media Trick" so that affidavit is taken seriously by Amicus Curiae and the Hon'ble Supreme Court.**

(8) That Shri Sanjiv Bhat had been exchanging emails with one Leo Saldana, a Narmada Bachao Andolan activist, with a view to mobilize public opinion in their favour. On 01-05-2011, Shri Sanjiv Bhatt had sent an email to the latter to the effect that what they needed to do at this stage was to create a situation where it would be difficult for three judges Supreme Court Bench to disregard the shortcomings of SIT under stewardship of Mr. Raghavan and that the Pressure groups and opinion makers in Delhi could be of great help in forwarding the cause. He has further stated in the mail that he was hopeful that things

would start turning around from the next hearing, if proper pressure was maintained at National level.

(9) **That Shri Sanjiv Bhatt was trying to contact Shri K.S. Subramanyam, a retired IPS officer,** through Shri Nasir Chippa to make an affidavit supporting his stand with a view to convince the Amicus Curiae and through him the Hon'ble Supreme Court of India that Shri K. Chakravarthi, former DGP of Gujarat, was a liar.

(10) That Shri Sanjiv Bhatt had been taking advice of Ms. Teesta Setalwad in connection with his evidence before Nanavati Commission of Inquiry. **He had also been in touch with various journalists, NGOs and had been forwarding his representations, applications and other documents through email, whereas on the other side he had been claiming privilege that being an Intelligence Officer he was duty bound not to disclose anything unless,** he was legally compelled to do so.

(11) That Shri Sanjiv Bhatt has been maintaining a close contact with Shri Rahul Sharma, DIG of Gujarat Police and had been getting his mobile phone calls analyzed with a view to ascertain his own movements of 27-02-2002. **This shows that Bhatt does not recollect his movements on that day. He has also been trying to ascertain the movements of Late Haren Pandya, the then Minister of State for Revenue on 27-02-2002, with a view to introduce him as a participant of the meeting of 27-02-2002 held at CM's residence, but could not do so, as Shri Rahul Sharma had informed him after the analysis that there was absolutely no question of Late Haren Pandya being at Gandhinagar on 27-02-2002 night.**

From the study of emails, it appears that certain vested interests including Shri Sanjiv Bhatt, different NGOs and some political leaders were trying to use Hon'ble Supreme Court/SIT as a forum for settling their scores. This would also go to show that Shri Sanjiv Bhatt had been colluding with the persons with vested interests to see that some kind of charge-sheet is filed against Shri Narendra Modi and others."

This makes things absolutely clear and also shows that many people were involved in this fraud, who knew that Sanjiv Bhatt was not present at the 27 February 2002 meeting, but far from bringing out the truth to the investigators, were helping in this false claim.

Haren Pandya (murdered in March 2003) of course, was not present in that meeting so his testimony does not have the slightest value. The SIT report also says on page 56 that Haren Pandya's mobile records show that he was in Ahmedabad on 27 Feb 2002 at 22:52 hours, meaning that it was impossible for him to attend the meeting in Gandhinagar at 10:30 PM on 27 Feb. As we saw in Myth 19 in Chapter 7, he could not even name correctly the people present in the meeting.

This shows that Sanjiv Bhatt was not present at all in the meeting, and he did not even know basic facts about the meeting. It is known since August 2002 (when Haren Pandya's errors in naming people in the meeting were admitted by him to *Outlook* and by the magazine itself, or at least after his murder in March 2003 after which *Outlook* reported that minister giving the information was indeed Haren Pandya) that **Haren Pandya was by no means present in the meeting. But Sanjiv Bhatt did not even know this and hence first asked Rahul Sharma to find out if Haren Pandya could be introduced as a witness**-a participant in that meeting.

Most importantly, this shows that Sanjiv Bhatt was not present at all. **If Sanjiv Bhatt was present in the meeting, wouldn't he know if Haren Pandya was present or not? Why would he need to ask Rahul Sharma to find the call details?** This also shows that Rahul Sharma also knew the truth, that Sanjiv Bhatt was not present, but did not tell the investigators.

Sanjiv Bhat claimed that he left the 27 February meeting half-way after taking leave from Shri K Chakravarthi, the then DGP. The SIT report says on pages 399-400:

"Shri Sanjiv Bhatt stated that he took leave thereafter from Shri K Chakravarthi, the then DGP, and returned to the State IB office in order to send alert messages and instructions to the concerned police/intelligence units. Subsequent to the aforesaid (27 Feb night) meeting at CM's residence, Shri Bhatt has claimed to have issued several messages to the Police units as well as the field units of the IB with respect to the developing situation including the possibility of wide spread communal violence during the Gujarat bandh and wherein, he reiterated to different CsP (The author thinks it means Commissioners of Police) and SsP (The author thinks it means Superintendents of Police) to take all possible measures to prevent untoward incidents in their respective jurisdiction. **Surprisingly, he informed everyone about it but did not inform his own Head of the Department i.e. Shri G. C. Raiger whom he had allegedly represented in the meeting** and whose presence in the station was very much in his knowledge. He has denied to have contacted Shri G. C. Raiger over phone in the night of the 27-02-2002 and has stated that he briefed Shri Raiger about the said meeting and the deliberations that had taken place, when he had attended office the next day, i.e. 28-02-2002 morning, at about 1000 hrs, **which has been denied by Shri Raiger. Interestingly, the call details of Govt. mobile phone of Shri Sanjiv Bhatt show that he was at Ahmedabad till 1057 hrs on 28-02-2002.**"

Sanjiv Bhat also claimed to be present in a meeting of the Chief Minister at his residence on **28 Feb afternoon** where the decision to call the Army was formally taken. The SIT report says about this on pages 402-403:

"Shri Sanjiv Bhat has gone to the extent of claiming that the Chief Minister took him aside after the meeting and informed him that he had learnt that Late Ahesan Jafri had opened fire on Hindus during earlier communal riots. According to Shri Sanjiv Bhatt, the Chief Minister asked him to dig out all the facts pertaining to earlier instances, wherein Late Ahesan Jafri had opened fire during the past communal riots. Shri Bhatt claimed that he conveyed these facts to Shri G.C. Raiger, the then Additional DG (Int.). However, Shri Bhatt has stated that he could not check/collect this information as he remained busy with certain urgent matters connected with the riots. Shri Sanjiv Bhatt has denied having submitted any report in this regard to his department and claimed that he attended this meeting as a Staff Officer to the DGP or Addl. DG (Int.), **which is incorrect as there was no post of Staff Officer to Addl. DG (Int.).**"

There is the major issue of why it took Sanjiv Bhatt so many years to claim that he was present in that meeting, if indeed he was. On this topic, the SIT report continues on page 403:

"On being questioned, as to why he did not appear as a witness in response to a public notice issued by SIT on 11-03-2008, he claimed that he did not disclose the same to anyone, as it would not have been appropriate on his part to divulge any information that he was privy to as an Intelligence Officer unless he was under a legal obligation to do so. He has also stated that he did not file any affidavit or appeared before any commission or any other body enquiring into the communal riots of 2002, because he was not asked by the Government of Gujarat, DGP, or Addl. DG (Int.) to do so. He has denied knowledge as to whether the alleged instructions given by the Chief Minister were passed on to the field units by any of the officers, who had attended the said meeting on 27-02-2002. The stand taken by Sanjiv Bhatt is not acceptable on account of the fact that it was essentially a law and order meeting, in which many civilian officers were present and there was nothing secret about it. **Furthermore, Shri Bhatt had various opportunities and legal obligations to disclose these facts,** if true, firstly to Shri R.B. Sreekumar, the then Addl. DG (Int.), who had asked him to provide any oral and documentary relevant fact to be included in his affidavit relating to riots incidents on behalf of State IB required to be filed before Nanavati Commission. Secondly, Nanavati Commission, a legally constituted body under Commission of Inquiry Act had issued a public notice calling upon any one having knowledge about the incident of issues involved before it, to file an affidavit and furnish information, but Shri Sanjiv Bhat did not file any affidavit. Thirdly, the SIT, legally constituted by the Hon'ble Supreme Court of India had also issued a public notice on 11.04.2008 calling upon the people to come forward and give information relating to the riots, but Shri Sanjiv Bhat conveniently did not come forward. Fourthly, another opportunity was given to him in November, 2009, to make a statement during the course of inquiry ordered by the Hon'ble Supreme Court of India, but Shri Sanjiv Bhatt took the plea that it would not be professionally appropriate on his part to divulge the exact nature of discussion that took place during the said meeting, unless he was duty bound to disclose the same under legal obligation.

Shri Sanjiv Bhatt, on his own and without being summoned appeared before the IO on 25-03-2011, i.e. two days after the recording of his statement, along with one constable named Shri K.D. Panth and requested that his (Bhatt's) further statement should be recorded..."

348

Meaning that the SIT has said that there was nothing secret about the 27 Feb meeting that prevented Sanjiv Bhatt from disclosing about it to anyone for 9 years, and he could have easily done that. Secondly, the SIT also said that **he was indeed under legal obligation to disclose them on many occasions but did not do so.** And thirdly, he came up and made the claims to the SIT in March 2011, more than 9 years after the incident, all on his own, and without any summons, then by whom and how was the secrecy waived?

Sanjiv Bhatt had claimed that P.C. Pandey, the then Ahmedabad Police Commissioner and K Chakravarthi, the then DGP had opposed the bringing of bodies to Ahmedabad from Godhra. But both of them have dismissed this claim and stated that the decision was unanimous. The SIT report says on pages 406-407:

"Shri K. Chakravarthi, the then DGP has clearly stated that the decision of the Govt. to bring the dead bodies of Godhra victims at Ahmedabad City, was not opposed by anyone on the ground that a large number of victims belonged to Ahmedabad and nearby places, which were easily approachable from Ahmedabad. **This would go to show that Shri Sanjiv Bhatt was giving an imaginary account of the deliberations of the meeting and he did not know as to what exactly transpired there.** Further, it has been contended by Shri Sanjiv Bhatt that both DGP and CP, Ahmedabad City (i.e. Chakravarthi and P. C. Pandey) had tried to impress upon the Chief Minister that the bandh call given by the VHP on 28-02-2002, which was supported by the ruling party BJP was not a good idea as far as the Law and order situation of the State was concerned and that the Chief Minister was not convinced by their arguments. In this regard, **Shri K. Chakravarthi, the then DGP has stated that in the night of 27-02-2002, he did not know that the bandh call given by the VHP was supported by the ruling BJP and as such there was no question of any such opposition by him. Shri P. C. Pandey has also stated that on 27-02-2002, he did not know that the bandh was supported by the BJP and came to know about it only on 28-02-2002, through newspaper reports.** All the participants of the meeting have stated that the Chief Minister had expressed apprehension that the Godhra incident was very serious and bound to affect the public at large, as a result of which there could be repercussions and therefore, adequate bandobast was needed to avoid any untoward incident.

Sanjiv Bhatt has claimed that he mentioned the fact of having attended the said meeting on 27-02-2002 night in his movement diary. **However, the State IB has reported that no such diary was being submitted by Shri Sanjiv Bhatt.** Shri G.C. Raiger, the then Addl. DG (Int.) has stated that there was no such system of submitting any monthly movement diary by DCI and that Shri Sanjiv Bhatt had never submitted any such diary."

The report continues on pages 407-408:

"In this connection (his excuse for the delay in claiming to be present), it would not be out of place to mention here that assuming for the time being that Shri Sanjiv Bhatt attended the alleged meeting of 27.02.2002, the same was essentially **a law & order meeting** attended by the various officials of State Administration and therefore the question of **oath of secrecy or application of the Official Secrets Act does not arise** because it was neither a secret meeting nor would the revelation of the contents of the said meeting jeopardize the public interest. **Shri Sanjiv Bhatt has used the weapon of the Official Secrets Act only as a pretext with a view to justify a long delay of nine years and just because an official of the intelligence unit attended a law & order meeting, the same does not become a secret meeting for which a privilege of secrecy is being claimed by Shri Sanjiv Bhatt.** In any case, Nanavati Commission and SIT have been set up under the provisions of law of the land and all the citizens/ officials **are legally bound to divulge the information** available with them which are relevant to the terms of reference/ crimes of the Commission being investigated by SIT.

In view of this, the explanation put forward by Shri Sanjiv Bhatt does not hold good."

On page 419, the SIT has completely debunked the claim of "Office of Secrecy". The report says:

"However, on 21/22-03-2011, when he made a statement u/s 161 Cr.PC before the SIT, **it is not understood as to by whom and how the claimed secrecy was waived.** His silence for a period of more than nine years without any proper explanation appears to be suspicious and gives an impression that he is trying to manipulate the things to his personal advantage to settle his service matters."

The report continues on page 409:

"Shri Sanjiv Bhatt has further contended that in view of the fact that Late Ahesan Jafri, Ex-MP was residing in Gulberg Society, he had telephonically conveyed the details directly to the Chief Minister either on landline or on the mobile phone of Shri O.P. Singh, PA to CM. However, he has not been able to specify on which telephone he rang up the Chief Minister. **Shri O.P. Singh has denied that he received any call from Shri Sanjiv Bhatt.** The call details of Gandhinagar tower are not available as the same had not been requisitioned by Shri Rahul Sharma, the then SP, during investigation of the riot cases. Notably, there is no practice in Gujarat of SP level officers speaking directly to CM over phone. **Further, Shri G.C. Raiger, the then Addl. DG (Int.), who was very much in office on 28.02.2002, has stated that this was totally false and that Shri Sanjiv Bhatt had never informed him about it."**

Sanjiv Bhatt claimed to have two witnesses to support his claim of being present in that 27 Feb meeting. The SIT report continues on pages 412-414:

"Shri Sanjiv Bhatt, the then DCI (Security) has named two AIOs namely Shri K.D. Panth and Shri Shailesh Raval, who used to accompany him in such meetings along with the files. After Shri Sanjiv Bhatt's further statement was recorded at his own request on 25-03-2011 (His first was recorded on 22-03-2011), he insisted that Shri K.D. Panth, who was accompanying him and was waiting outside, should also be examined. **He stressed that Shri Panth should be examined in his presence. However, Shri Bhatt was informed that Shri K.D. Panth would be called on a date convenient to the IO and examined.** Accordingly, Shri Panth was informed on 04-04-2011, to attend SIT office on 05-04-2011, for his examination.

Shri K.D. Panth in his examination has stated that he was on casual leave on 27-02-2002. Further, he has denied that he followed Shri Sanjiv Bhatt, the then DCI (Security) to CM's residence on 27-02-2002 night. However, he has stated that Shri Sanjiv Bhatt had called him to his residence on 24-03-2011 night and informed that he was going to make a statement before the SIT that he (K.D. Panth) had gone to attend a meeting at CM's residence on 27-02-2002 night, and that he (Panth) had been called at State IB office and be ready with the files for the said meeting. Shri Sanjiv Bhatt further informed Shri Panth that he should accompany him to SIT office on 25-03-2011, and make a statement on these lines.

During his examination, Shri Panth further stated that he had contacted Shri Sanjiv Bhatt over his landline telephone no. 27455117 from mobile no. 8140657775 (belonging to one of his friends) after he was called for examination scheduled for 05-04-2011. Shri Sanjiv Bhatt called him at his residence on 04-04-2011 at 2030 hrs. At his residence, Shri Sanjiv Bhatt informed Shri Panth that he has made a statement to the SIT that he (Bhatt) had accompanied DGP Shri K. Chakravarthi in his official car to CM's office from DGP's office on 27-02-2002 night and that he (Shri Panth) had followed him in his (Shri Sanjiv Bhatt's) staff car along with the files. Shri Sanjiv Bhatt asked Shri Panth to make a statement accordingly.

Subsequently, Shri K.D. Panth lodged a complaint against Shri Sanjiv Bhatt with the local police to the effect that Shri Sanjiv Bhatt had influenced, threatened, detained, put severe pressure and compelled him to sign an affidavit containing false/wrong and incorrect facts, in pursuance of which a case no. I CR No. 149/2011 was registered u/s 189, 193, 195, 341, 342 IPC with Ghatlodia police station, Ahmedabad City, Gujarat State. Shri Sanjiv Bhatt has since been arrested in this case and the matter is under investigation. In view of this, no reliance can be placed upon the version of Shri Sanjiv Bhatt.

This conduct of Shri Sanjiv Bhatt in arranging, prompting and controlling the witness to corroborate his statement is highly suspicious and undesirable. Shri Sanjiv Bhatt also contacted Shri Shailesh Raval on 28-03-2011/29-03-2011, over mobile phone number 9825688223 of one Shri N.J. Chauhan, a clerk in CM's Security and informed him that he would be called by SIT for his examination. Shri Sanjiv Bhatt also asked Shri Shailesh Raval (to testify) that he had worked with him in Security Branch for a long time and was aware that he (Sanjiv Bhatt) used to attend meetings, to which Shri Raval reacted by saying that he had accompanied him in Border Security Nodal Committee meetings, which used to deal with the Border Security only. **Shri Raval also informed Shri Sanjiv Bhatt that he never worked in the Communal Branch and was not aware of anything about it.** Shri Sanjiv

Bhat thereafter disconnected the phone. Shri Shailesh Raval, PI later sent a complaint in writing to the Chairman, SIT that he feared reprisal from Shri Sanjiv Bhatt as he had refused to support the false claims of Shri Bhatt. **This is yet another attempt on the part of Shri Sanjiv Bhatt to tutor a witness to depose in a particular manner so as to support the statement made by him, which further makes his claim of having attended the meeting at CM's residence on 27-02-2002, false.**"

Even R. Sreekumar, who has leveled a similar allegation against Narendra Modi and is a staunch anti-Modi person today, ever after he was denied promotion, is quoted by SIT as saying something else. On page 417, the SIT report says:

"Shri R.B. Sreekumar formerly ADGP Intelligence, in his interview given to Star Hindi news Channel at 12.35 hrs on 22.04.2011 has stated that Shri Sanjiv Bhatt, DCI (Security)had never informed him about having attended a meeting at CM's residence on 27.02.2002. He has further stated that at the time of filing an affidavit before Nanavati Shah Commission, he had asked all officers of State IB to provide him with the relevant information and documents in respect of Godhra riots but Shri Sanjiv Bhatt did not give him any information about the said meeting. According to Shri Sreekumar, Shri Sanjiv Bhatt was handling security portfolio and communal portfolio was being looked after by another officer. Shri Sreekumar has also stated in the interview that it was a normal procedure that if a junior officer had attended a meeting on behalf of senior, he was required to submit a report to his superior and that Shri G.C. Raiger, the then ADGP (Int.) should be asked about it. As already stated above, Shri Raiger has denied having received any information/report from Shri Sanjiv Bhatt in this regard."

This is overwhelming evidence that Sanjiv Bhatt was not present in the 27 February meeting. What we said in Myth 19, Chapter 7 has been vindicated by the SIT's investigations. This is not all. The SIT has pointed out some other facts as well, which disprove Sanjiv Bhatt's claims of being present in the 27 February meeting and also some other of his false claims.

Then comes the issue of state action to prevent riots. The SIT report gives the versions of various officials interviewed on the steps taken by the government to prevent and control violence immediately after Godhra. On pages 445-450 the SIT report says, after giving various facts:

"There is evidence available on record to show that immediately (after Godhra which occurred between 7:47 to 8:20 AM on 27 Feb) the State machinery was put on the high alert and this was communicated to all District authorities and Commissioners of Police. The first alert message of 27-02-2002 from the Home Department covered the need to take precautionary measures including adequate police bandobast and preventive measures including issuance of prohibitory orders depending upon the local situation. **It was instructed that anti-social and hardcore communal elements should be dealt with firmly...** (Page 445)

The alert message of 27-02-2002 was followed by another message from Home Department on 28-02-2002 to all concerned to round up anti-social and known communal elements under the preventive laws. It was further instructed that mobile patrolling should be intensified and adequate protection should also be provided at places of worship and that effective action should be taken to disperse unruly mob, unlawful assemblies, using whatever force necessary. It was also made clear that anti-social elements indulging in violence and bent upon jeopardizing communal harmony must be controlled firmly. Another message dated 28-02-2002, impressed upon all concerned officers to maintain adequate bandobast for 01-03-2002, being Friday and the day of Namaz for the Muslims. Adequate bandobast was directed to be provided to all sensitive areas and curfew was ordered to be strictly enforced... (Page 446)

...It was understood that withdrawing the Army at such critical juncture when war like situation existed with the neighbour needed a high level decision at the Centre. This decision to withdraw the Army and deploy in Gujarat was immediately taken at the highest level in the Centre at the request of Gujarat Govt.... (Page 447)

...The State Govt. had also made a request on 28-02-2002, to the neighbouring States of Maharashtra, Rajasthan and Madhya Pradesh to spare the services of their Armed Reserve Police companies. However, only Maharashtra responded by sending 2 Coys of SRP, whereas the Govt. of Rajasthan and Madhya Pradesh expressed their inability to spare any police force due to the internal commitments. **It may thus be seen that there was**

no delay, whatsoever in requisitioning the Army and its deployment by the State as and when they realized on 28-02-2002 afternoon that the situation was going beyond control. Significantly, Union Defence Minister arrived at Ahmedabad on 28.02.2002 night to ensure that Army formations take their positions without delay.

Shri G. Subba Rao, the then Chief Secretary, who had gone abroad, was recalled and he arrived on 01-03-2002... (Page 448)

...Frantic messages were sent by the Home Department on 01-03-2002 to 06-03-2002 and specific instructions were given to the effect that the riots had to be controlled and all steps should be taken to restore normalcy and peace in the State... (Page 449)

...Further investigation has established that the State Govt. was reasonably vigilant vis-à-vis the developments on the law & order front and immediately responded by bringing to the notice of all District officials, the need to maintain adequate bandobast in view of the Godhra incident on 27-02-2002... (page 450)"

This confirms what we have said in our book. That the Army was called 'frantically', that George Fernandes came immediately, that alert was sounded, police force was requested from neighbouring states, etc.

The SIT quotes the Amicus Curaie, Raju Ramchandran on pages 450-451 as saying that the late Haren Pandya's testimony to the Concerned Citizens Tribunal can be used and that it may not be totally unbelievable that Pandya was present in the 27 Feb meeting. The SIT has dismissed this claim as well. The CCT, which we have seen in Myth 19, Chapter 7, gave its report in November 2002. It was in the form of a book titled "Crime against humanity". The SIT report gives many quotes from that report against the late Haren Pandya himself on his alleged anti-Muslim statements and activities on pages 452-456. The CCT report severally criticized Pandya on Vol. I page 36, page 44, page 48, & Vol. II page 48, page 49, page 52, page 77, page 87. Secondly the SIT report on page 452 quotes Pandya as saying that the then MoS for Home i.e. Gordhan Zadaphiya was present in that 27 Feb meeting and says on page 453 that **there is conclusive evidence to prove that Zadaphiya was in Godhra on 27 February and returned on 28 Feb morning, meaning that there was no way Zadaphiya could have attended the 27 Feb night**

meeting in Gandhinagar, as he was in Godhra. Thus the alleged claim by Pandya that Zadaphiya was present in the meeting is proved false.

Besides, we have seen in Myth 19, Chapter 7 itself that Pandya could not even correctly name the people present in the meeting, wrongly naming people who were abroad on leave as being present in that meeting, so the question of his being present is ruled out. His call records also show that he was present in Ahmedabad till 22:52 hours, so there is no question of him attending the meeting in Gandhinagar at that time. The SIT report also says on page 458 that it appears that the late Haren Pandya had misled the Hon'ble members of the CCT namely, Justice P B Sawant and Justice Hosbet Suresh that he was present in that meeting with a view to increasing his credibility. **Most importantly, the SIT says on page 452 that Pandya's deposition had not been recorded anywhere by the Tribunal (Vindicating what we had said in Myth 19, that CCT has given no proof of Pandya's deposition to it).**

There were allegations that the dead bodies of the killed *karsevaks* were handed over to Jaydeep Patel, the then VHP General Secretary of Gujarat at Godhra. The Amicus Curiae opined that this would have been impossible unless someone high-up in the government gave his consent. The SIT has stated the Amicus Curiae's observation and the facts on pages 463 to 467 of its report. The report concludes on page 467:

"The above facts would go to establish that though a letter had been addressed by Mamalatdar, Godhra to Shri Jaydeep Patel of VHP, yet the dead bodies were **escorted by the police from Godhra to Ahmedabad,** where the same were taken charge of by the hospital authorities, District Administrative and Police Officers and handed over to the kith and kin of deceased persons after taking proper receipt."

54 bodies were sent in 5 trucks from Godhra to Ahmedabad, which left Godhra at around 11:30 pm to 12:00 am and reached Western Ahmedabad's isolated hospital at around 3:30 am on 28 February. The bodies were covered in the trucks and no outsiders could see them, thus care was taken to prevent their seeing by anyone.

It was also alleged in Zakia Jafri's complaint that the then Ministers I K Jadeja and Ashok Bhatt were positioned in the DGP office and the Ahmedabad City Control Room respectively, by the Chief Minister, Narendra Modi.

On page 72, the SIT report says that according to the then DGP Chakravarthi, he (DGP) was informed by the then ACS (Home), Ashok Narayan that it was decided by the government that I K Jadeja would sit in the DGP's office to get information about the law and order situation in the state, as the State Control Room was located in his office. The DGP also said that Ashok Narayan informed him that Ashok Bhatt would similarly sit in the Ahmedabad City Police Control Room, situated in the office of the CP, Ahmedabad City. On this Chakravarthi said that it would be better if the Ministers get the information through Control Room in the Home Department as he was bound to report all the information to the Home Department, but Ashok Narayan told him that no such facility was available in the Home Department and hence the Ministers would visit their offices. The DGP further stated that I K Jadeja sat in his chamber for 15-20 minutes on 28 Feb 2002. The then DGP has said that he could not attend to him much as he was very busy handling calls from other police officers on the riot situation. He thereafter asked someone to shift him to an empty chamber and this was done. **Enquiries conducted by Chakravarthi with his Staff Officer and Officer of the State Control Room revealed that there was no interference by I K Jadeja on the functioning of the State Control Room on that day.**

The SIT report says on page 74 that I K Jadeja has said that the then MoS for Home Gordhan Zadaphiya had requested him to remain present in the DGP's office in Police Bhavan, Gandhinagar to see that in case any information is received in the Control Room about any rioting incident or request is received for extra police force or any other issue of importance then the same should be passed on to the DGP, Home Minister, etc. In view of this, he remained in the office of the DGP for 3-4 hours for the next 3-4 days. He has categorically stated that he did not interfere with the work of the DGP or disturb the police officers in the discharge of their official duties.

On page 75, the report quotes the then Police Commissioner of Ahmedabad P C Pandey as saying that Ashok Bhatt was never deputed to Shahibaug Police Control Room to guide or advise the police officers. Pandey says that on 1st March 2002, Ashok Bhatt came there for 10 minutes to meet George Fernandes. On pages 75-76, Ashok Bhatt is quoted as saying that he does not recollect whether he visited the Control Room on 28 Feb or not, and may have for 5-10 minutes, and that he did visit it on 1st March for 10 minutes to meet George Fernandes, who had gone to the office of the Ahmedabad Police Commissioner. This version of the late Ashok Bhatt is corroborated by the statement of P C Pandey also. On page 76, the report gives details of Ashok Bhatt's call records which show that he did not visit the Control Room on 28 Feb. The SIT says:

"It may thus be seen that these call details would conclusively go to establish that the late Ashok Bhatt did not visit Shahibaug Police Control Room on 28-02-2002."

The report also gives the testimonies of a few more people who were present in the Shahibaug Control Room on that day, which say that Ashok Bhatt did not visit it on 28 Feb 2002.

After these conclusions by the SIT in its original report, the Amicus Curaie disagreed with it. On page 468, the SIT quotes the Amicus Curiae as saying that it is 'obvious that the Chief Minister had placed these 2 Ministers in highly sensitive places which should not have been done.' After this, the SIT did further investigation about it. And its conclusions were same as before, given on page 474. The Amicus Curiae revealed his bias here. When no one ever gave any testimony about the CM positioning either of the two Ministers anywhere, how could he conclude that 'It is obvious that the CM placed these 2 Ministers'? When call records of Ashok Bhatt as well as statements from the people present conclusively prove that Ashok Bhatt did not go to the Shahibaug Control Room at all on 28 Feb, how can any investigation conclude that 'Modi placed him there?'

And I K Jadeja was present not at the State Control Room but in another chamber, and no officer gave any testimony of the slightest interference. Then on what basis can anyone conclude that he 'interfered'? The SIT also says on page 79 (and first line also on page 474) that: "Shri I K Jadeja has taken the plea that it is an established practice in Gujarat State that in case of any natural calamities or serious law & order situation the Ministers of the various departments extend their help in handling the crisis. No material is available to rebut his plea".

On page 78, the SIT quotes the allegation in the complaint of Zakia Jafri that officers Rahul Sharma, Vivek Shrivastava, Himanshu Bhatt, M D Antani,

R B Sreekumar and Satishchandra Verma (all IPS) were given ill-treatment with transfers, so as to facilitate placement of those willing to subvert the system for political and electoral benefits. On pages 79, 80 and 81 the SIT quotes the versions of these officers themselves- Rahul Sharma, Vivek Shrivastava, M D Antani and Satishchandra Verma **none of whom have made the allegation that they were transferred as any punishment.** Shri Satishchandra Verma has said that his transferred new position as Principal, State Reserve Police Training Centre, Junagadh cannot be called an unimportant position. Only R B Sreekumar made some allegations. But, as we have seen, he kept quiet until he was denied promotion in 2005. The SIT has noted several such things, including this very important factor of his silence for a long time, on page 83 and said that Sreekumar's testimony appears to be motivated.

On page 84, the SIT lists the allegation in the complaint of Zakia Jafri that people 'collaborating with the illegal plans of CM/ BJP' were rewarded, namely G Subba Rao, Ashok Narayan, P K Mishra, A K Bhargava, P C Pandey, Kuldeep Sharma (He happened to be their own anti-Modi man!), M K Tandon, Deepak Swaroop, K Nityanandam, Rakesh Asthana, A K Sharma, Shivananda Jha, S K Sinha and D G Vanzara. The SIT has given its investigations on all of them from page 84 to 105 and could not establish such an allegation in case of even a single individual. **On page 94, the SIT notes that on one hand it is alleged in Zakia's complaint that Kuldeep Sharma was 'rewarded for collaborating with illegal plans of CM/BJP' while at the same time it is also alleged that in July 2005 he was transferred 'for not agreeing to book Mallika Sarabhai under a false case' and 'did not oblige to save Prabhatsinh Chauhan, a minister in the Modi Cabinet, in a case of criminal misappropriation'.** The SIT says that these averments are contradictory. Of course they are. The SIT also quotes on page 94 the Concerned Citizens Tribunal praising Kuldeep Sharma in Vol. I, page 185 of its report and 'Communalism Combat' monthly of March-April 2002, edited by Teesta Setalvad and Javed Anand also saying in a piece by Shafibhai Mansuri, ex-President of the Municipal Corporation that Kuldeep Sharma reached within an hour of the incident. **This shows the ridiculous nature of the complaint.**

In late 2013 and early 2014, the war against Narendra Modi launched by the Sharma brothers- Kuldeep Sharma and Pradeep Sharma became open.

And this complaint accuses Kuldeep Sharma himself of being given favors for 'toeing the illegal policies of the CM/ BJP'! Here it is worth reporting the SIT's observations on page 326: "There are material omissions and improvements in the statements made by Shri Kuldeep Sharma and Shri Pradeep Sharma... Further, Shri Kuldeep Sharma has since been charge-sheeted departmentally and has not been promoted, despite being the senior most officer in the IPS cadre of the Gujarat State. On the other hand, a number of criminal cases had been registered against Shri Pradeep Sharma and he remained in jail in 2010 for about 8 months and at present he is in judicial custody in some case since 14.02.2011. In view of these facts both Sharma brothers have an axe to grind against the State Govt. and as such their testimony is not trustworthy [in case of an allegation made by them]."

About A K Bhargava, ex-DGP, Gujarat, the SIT says on page 91 that the first allegation that he was allowed to hold the additional charge of MD, Housing Corporation with a budget of Rs. 200 crores per year **is factually incorrect as he held the additional charge of DGP and main charge of MD, Police Housing Corporation.** The other allegation is that he co-operated with the Govt. and looked after the political interests of the BJP in the matter of review of 2000 odd cases, harassed the officers and agreed with the illegal directives of the Govt. The SIT says on page 91 that 'the same is vague and baseless.' It says: "As regards the review of 2000 odd cases, Shri A K Bhargava has stated that he was directly responsible to the Hon'ble Supreme Court of India and had submitted quarterly progress reports to the Supreme Court, which were duly accepted and never adversely commented upon."

Here we need to mention that in 2004, the Supreme Court ordered re-opening of some 2000-odd riot cases, which were decided to be closed by the Gujarat Government. At that time, many in the media had cried foul over this and claimed that the 'Gujarat government has lost all right to be in power', etc. The reporting was done as if they were cases of 2000 riots. The truth is that they were cases against 2000 odd individuals, i.e. riot-accused. They included Muslims accused of killing Hindus also. The number of riots was far lesser. The Supreme Court, after re-opening the cases, also directed the Gujarat Government to set up a Cell, which would include 7 Range Inspector Generals. The 7 Range Inspector Generals would look into the FIRs, the existing materials in support of the FIRs, any other material found or brought to notice and then decide in connection of each of the 2000 cases whether further investigation was necessary or not. They were to report to 2 Additional Director Generals, who would submit the report to the Director General, who was overall in-charge and reported to the Supreme Court. SC sought the first report on this issue in 90 days. In cases where further investigation was recommended, the same would be done by an independent officer (who had not submitted a summary report in the past) nominated by the Cell. This was reported on page 212 of SIT report.

The SIT report says on page 93:

"Further, as regards the review of 2000-odd cases ordered by the Supreme Court, it may be mentioned that a quarterly progress report was being submitted to the Hon'ble Supreme Court of India and also placed on the website created for this purpose and that the progress reports submitted to the Supreme Court had never been adversely commented upon and were accepted. The review of 2000 odd cases by the Supreme Court included 349 cases pertaining to Ahmedabad City and after sustained investigation only 4/5 were charge-sheeted in the Court."

The SIT report deals with this in more detail on pages 211-216. The SIT quotes P C Pandey as saying that the Riot Cell Committee under the DG and IG of police had directed all committee members to earmark three competent police officers of which one should preferably be a Muslim to help them implement the directions of the SC. Pandey said that extensive publicity was given through press notes as well as through public address systems whenever the committee members visited the site of offences about the exercise being undertaken as per the directives of the Hon'ble SC and people were advised to come forward and register offence and/or give evidence in relation to riot related cases without any fear or pressure. A special website was created for these cases (www.riotcell2002.gujarat.gov.in) and was being updated regularly.

Pandey also said that quarterly reports were being submitted to the SC since November 2004 and till his tenure 11 such reports had been submitted. He also said that till 11 April 2007, 108 applications had been received to the DG for reopening cases which were sent to concerned committee members for necessary action and proper reply to the applicants. He also said that as a test case, 59 cases which were not found worth reopening by the Cell were floated on the website with reasons thereof. But not a single individual, or NGO ever approached any of the Cell members or the DGP against such a decision. Pandey also stated that from the remaining 1958 cases, only 53 cases were converted into charge-sheet.

This shows that the government's decision to close the cases was correct, since even after sustained investigation, Supreme Court monitoring, quarterly reports, very few cases resulted in charge-sheets.

There is also the allegation of Modi using 'Newton's third law'. We have already seen in Myth 13 the truth of this. Here we need to understand that there is a huge difference between saying that: "The riots were a reaction to Godhra" and "Every action has equal and opposite reaction". No one with any common sense can deny that the riots were a spontaneous reaction to the brutal Godhra killings. Not the most diehard BJP-baiter can claim with any honesty that the riots would have occurred even without Godhra. We have seen Vir Sanghvi say on 21 April 2002: "As much as some of us may try and pretend otherwise, nobody with any intellectual honesty can dispute that riots were a response to Godhra."

But the lie concocted from 3rd March 2002 onwards that Modi cited Newton's third law 'Every action has equal and opposite reaction' was carried on for many years. In the immediate days after 3rd March 2002, all of Modi's denials were thrown in the dustbin. After many years when this lie was thoroughly exposed, the desperate people in the media began looking for excuses. They then started criticizing the terming of the riots as a 'reaction' itself, and based on their lies on Newton's 3rd law, managed to create an impression as if calling the riots as a 'reaction to Godhra' (which it undoubtedly was) was something like using Newton's third law. They of course, did not bother to apologize to Narendra Modi for defaming him by falsely alleging that he used Newton's 3rd law, nor did they criticize *The Times of India* for the original defamatory lie and only publishing his denial in a remote corner after many days.

Since the allegation that Modi used Newton's 3rd law could not be made now, they tried to use non-issues like Modi saying *Kriya Pratikriya chal rahi hein. Hum chahte hein kin na kriya ho, na pratikriya ho'* (A chain of action-reaction is going on. We want that neither action, nor reaction happen) to Zee News on 1ˢᵗ March 2002. The SIT reports on page 131 that despite asking Zee News for the CD of this interview, no copy of the CD was made available to SIT. Then how can even the above statement, which is totally harmless, be established? Modi has said to the SIT that he always appealed for peace. We have seen how he did it many times- like first in Godhra on 27 Feb evening, then in an appeal repeatedly broadcast on TV, etc.

The SIT has concluded on page 133 that: "No doubt, during the riots ghastly violent attacks had taken place on Muslims at Gulberg Society, Naroda Patiya and elsewhere by unruly mob, yet the alleged statements made by Chief Minister Narendra Modi appear to have been quoted out of context and therefore, based on these statements, no case is made against him."

The complaint also alleges that there was an undue delay in calling for the Army. The SIT has examined this and dismissed this allegation on pages 135-138. We have seen how *The Hindu* reported that Modi 'frantically' called the Army. This was said by a very anti-Modi paper which launched some of the worst attacks on Modi. Calling the Army 'frantically' means as opposite from 'delaying' as can ever mean.

The complaint also carries the allegation of R Sreekumar that officers at grass-root level were not transferred as per State Intelligence Bureau's recommendation till the arrival of K P S Gill as Advisor to CM (which was on 4ᵗʰ May 2002). The SIT has examined this on pages 145-147 and found this to be completely wrong, and called this allegation as 'without any basis'.

On pages 176-77, the SIT lists the complaint of Zakia that 'No departmental action was taken against Shri Jadeja, the then Superintendent of Police, Dahod District for his misconduct despite recommendation by CBI, who investigated the Bilkis Bano case as per the directions of the Hon'ble Supreme Court.' But it turned out that the CBI had not recommended any departmental action against Jadeja at all! This is **another mistake in the complaint.** Such mistakes were pointed out by the SIT, but it did not recommend any action against the complaint makers, neither Zakia nor Teesta, for making such false complaints against innocent people!

The allegation by Zakia that 'Conducive situation was not created for rehabilitation of riot victims, though a contrary claim was made by the State Administration in its report to NHRC' was examined in detail by the SIT on pages 183-197. The SIT gave details of ex-gratia payments, assistance to the injured, cash doles and assistance for household kits, supply of food grain and other assistance to relief camp inmates, water supply, sanitation, medical and psychological treatment in camps, special care to mothers and children, preventive action (use of purified water etc.), ration to the inmates leaving relief camps and returning home, food grains to BPL families in riot-affected areas, committee to monitor relief camps (which included Congress leaders and others also), special education facilities to students in the relief camps, housing assistance, financial assistance for rebuilding earning assets, rehabilitation of small businesses, assistance to industries/ shops and hotels, interest subsidy on loans to affected units, insurance paid to the affected, rehabilitation of orphaned children and widows, ICDS services to riot-affected children, pregnant and lactating mothers, widows' pension, and trauma counseling.

The SIT concludes on page 197: "In view of the aforesaid measures and steps taken by the government, it cannot be said that the Govt. did not take adequate steps for the rehabilitation of the riot victims".

This is what we had already said in Myth 17, Chapter 7. The SIT investigation has vindicated us.

The complaint alleges, as reported by SIT on page 197, that the survivors of Naroda Patiya and residents of Gulberg Society also made over a hundred distress calls to the then Commissioner of Ahmedabad P C Pandey but his mobile was permanently switched off. On the same page the ridiculous allegation that 36 out of the 40 killed in police firing on 28 February were Muslims is also quoted. On the next few pages the SIT examines this. **On page 204, the SIT report says that call details of P C Pandey's mobile phone reveal that 302 calls were received on or made from his phone between 00:35 hrs and 24:00 hrs on 28 February 2002, and that his mobile was never switched off and that he made calls or received calls every minute or every 2 minutes.** And the complaint said his phone was permanently switched off that day! **The SIT also says that there was only one landline phone of Ehsan Jafri in the Gulberg Society and no other landline or mobile, and**

Jafri himself did not have a mobile phone, and no calls were made to P C Pandey by either Jafri or any other resident of the Gulberg Society. On page 210, the SIT says:

"Enquiries reveal that a total of 182 persons were killed on 28-02-2002 which comprised 31 Hindus and 151 Muslims at Ahmedabad. Further, 17 persons were killed due to police firing on 28-02-2002, out of which 11 were Hindus and 6 Muslims. In view of this the allegation made by Smt. Zakia Nasim that on 28-02-2002, 40 persons were shot dead by the police in Ahmedabad City and/or that out of which 36 were Muslims does not appear to be correct."

The SIT report mentions on page 217 the allegation in Zakia's complaint that a secret meeting was held on 27 Feb 2002 evening in Lunawada village of Sabarkantha district. It alleges that the then Health Minister Ashok Bhatt and the then Transport Minister Prabhatsinh Chauhan were aware of the meeting, and also that a call was made from the house of one Yogesh Pandya of Godhra to Dr. Anil Patel (a member of BJP's Gujarat Doctor's Cell). It also alleges that another call was made to Dr Chandrakant Pandya, Chairman, Police Housing Corporation. One A P Pandya was also alleged to be present in the meeting.

The facts are that Dr Chandrakant Pandya was not the Chairman but the Vice Chairman of the Police Housing Corporation at that time and Lunawada is not a village, but a Taluka headquarters and is situated in Panchmahal district and not in Sabarkantha district. The SIT mentions this on page 225. The SIT has given details of the call records of the Ministers Ashok Bhatt and Prabhatsinh Chauhan and dismissed the possibility of them being in Lunawada, which is 43 km north of Godhra. Ashok Bhatt did not receive any call from Yogesh Pandya or Anil Patel on that day, nor did Prabhatsinh Chauhan. Yogesh Pandya went to Kalol (located 31 km from Godhra in the Southward direction) at 5:30 pm on 27 Feb, according to SIT on page 226. Dr Anil Patel's call records also show that he could not have been in Lunawada. The SIT says on page 226: **"This allegation appears to be a figment of imagination of some interested elements** based on rumours and is, therefore, not established."

We cited this allegation to show the childish nature of the complaint, listing Lunawada as being in 'Sabarkantha district' and absolutely wrong allegations on calls and presence of individuals in Lunawada.

Here, it is worth mentioning the sentences on SIT report page 284: **"It may be mentioned here that the Concerned Citizen Tribunal in their report had leveled an allegation against Shri Prabhatsinh Chauhan having attended a meeting at Lunawada at an undisclosed place late in the evening of 27-02-2002,** where detailed plans were made for the use of kerosene, petrol for arson and other methods of killing. It has been established from the call detail records of Shri Prabhatsinh Chauhan, as well as the evidence of other witnesses that he remained at Godhra and as much could not have attended any such alleged meeting at Lunawada situated at a distance of 43 kms from Godhra."

This also exposes the CCT. How biased, false and inaccurate its report was!

Another allegation mentioned by SIT on pages 226-227 and examined in detail on the next pages alleges that a meeting was held at village Borwai near Pandarwada on 28 Feb 2002 and that 5000-6000 Bajrang Dal members were present with some individuals' names being mentioned, and that the meeting was held to plan attacks on minorities in surrounding areas. Teesta Setalvad has stated that this information was given to her by Mehboob Chauhan of Lunawada and Nasirbhai Sheikh of Pandarwada. The SIT has examined all the people named in the complaint and concluded on pages 236-237:

"There are many inaccuracies and contradictions in the information shared by Shri Mehboob Rasul. After the examination of all the aforesaid persons, it has been reasonably established that no such meeting ever took place at Baliyadev Temple at village Borwai and that Shri Mehboob Rasul had cooked up a false story with a view to settle score with some of these persons known to him. He had an axe to grind against Shri Amrutlal Panchal, who got a painting contract awarded to another painter and had threatened to recover an amount equivalent to ten times the value of the said contract. In view of the aforesaid discussions, the information is devoid of any merit and is, therefore, being discarded."

There was another allegation that Modi visited Godhra on 27 Feb itself but delayed visiting relief camps housing minorities. **The SIT report says on**

page 261 that though Modi was very busy from 28 Feb to 5 March with various meetings and law and order situation, yet he visited riot affected areas along with the then Home Minister of India, L K Advani on 3rd March 2002, as well as independently on 5 and 6 March 2002. It further says that he also visited Godhra, Bhavnagar and Rajkot along with Advani on 3rd and 4th March 2002. The SIT then says:

"Even otherwise he had reviewed the arrangements made for the rehabilitation of the riot victims and also about the compensation and cash doles to be paid to them. He had also supervised for the arrangements made for the medical aid of the affected persons. In view of this it cannot be said that while he visited Godhra on 27 Feb 2002 he neglected the riot victims and had visited riot affected areas on 5 and 6 March 2002. The allegation is, therefore, not established".

The SIT report also says on pages 261-262 that there is no record of any call made by the late Ehsan Jafri to Narendra Modi. Jafri did not have a mobile at that time. We have also dismantled this claim in Myth 11. The Gujarat High Court also made an observation on 22 April 2002 in response to a PIL filed, that reasonable care was taken for the camp inhabitants and the administration took great pains in maintaining the relief camps. The SIT has also mentioned this on page 263.

On page 301, the SIT examines the allegation against Rajendrasinh Rana, the then MP from Bhavnagar. It quotes on page 301 Rana as saying that **it was he who informed Shri Rahul Sharma, the then SP, Bhavnagar telephonically, about 400 students being trapped in a *madarsa* in Bhavnagar on 1st March 2002,** which was surrounded by a mob, bent upon setting fire to it. Rahul Sharma then reached the spot and dispersed the mob and shifted the children to a safer place. The SIT also says that Rana produced a copy of a letter dated 10 Nov 2004 from Master Ahmed of Akwada Madarsa of Bhavnagar, in which he thanked Rana for the timely action taken by Rahul Sharma, SP, at his instance, which could save the lives of innocent children. The SIT also quotes him as saying that **he was not a spokesman of the BJP as alleged and that Shri Nalin Bhatt was the spokesman at that time.**

Kaushik Mehta, the then Gujarat VHP General Secretary has also been listed as an accused by Zakia in the complaint. The SIT says on page 303 that though he has been listed as an accused, yet no allegation has been leveled against him. This shows that not even a vague, generalized allegation was made against Mehta!

We have seen in Myth 20, Chapter 7, that Zakia's complaint wrongly alleged that G Subbarao, the then Chief Secretary was present in the meeting of 27 Feb evening. The SIT report quotes him as saying (on page 312) **that he had gone abroad on 22 Feb 2002 and returned only on 1 March 2002 and as such could not have participated in the 27 Feb night meeting.**

Rakesh Asthana, ex-IGP, Vadodara Range has also been named as an accused in the complaint. The SIT report quotes him on page 328 as saying that the allegation that he was Chief of Vadodara Range in 2002 **was false as he was posted as Spl. IGP, Vadodara Range only after the riots i.e. with effect from 28 April 2003.** Another mistake.

The complaint also alleges that 'mass carnage took place in Mehsana district' during the tenure of A K Sharma as its SP but the SIT report quotes Sharma on page 329 as saying that no mass carnage took place in Mehsana district during his tenure (he took charge on 27 March 2002) inasmuch as only 4 deaths were reported.

The complaint also lists the then Additional CP of Ahmedabad, Shivananda Jha as an accused. But the SIT after examining the facts said on page 350 that in an incident which took place at Sabarmati Police Station on 5 April 2002, lives of 76 Muslims were saved and death of one Hindu in police firing was seen, which 'shows the independence and professional soundness of Shri Jha'. It also says that preventive arrests made by Jha are quite considerable and that it cannot be said that he did not take any preventive action. It further points out that Jha was praised by the late Rafiq Zakaria in his book "Communal Rage in Secular India" and quoted from an article by Namita Bhandare in *The Hindustan Times.*

The complaint also listed D H Brahmbhatt, ex-Collector, Panchmahal district as an accused. **The SIT report on page 351 quotes him as saying that he was posted as Collector on 11 December 2003, i.e. long after the riots.**

Deepak Swaroop, ex- Spl. IGP, Vadodara Range, Gujarat is also named as an accused. The SIT report quotes him on page 352 as saying that on the intervening night of 2 and 3 March, 2000 Muslims were shifted to Dungarwada in Banswada district in Rajasthan and also as saying that the same night, 1500 Muslims from Fatehpura P.S. in Dahod district were shifted to Muslim dominated areas of Galiyakot and Salopad in Banswada District of Rajasthan. He is also quoted as saying that the same night 20 Hindus were shifted from Randikpur in Dahod district to Limkheda. Deepak Swaroop is also quoted as telling about the Bodeli incident (which we saw earlier, reported by *India Today* dated 22 April 2002) in which police saved the Bodeli town after an encounter with the tribals at the only entry point to the town, in which two tribals were shot dead. **Zakia Jafri had alleged that Deepak Swaroop did not depose before the Nanavati Commission, but he had in fact deposed on 22 October 2005 and 29 October 2005 and produced a copy of his deposition to the SIT.**

We saw in Chapter 7, Myth 20 that B S Jebalia was named by Zakia in the complaint as being involved in the Ode massacre as Anand District Police chief. We also saw how this was incorrect on facts. **On page 356, the SIT report also says the same, quotes him as saying that he was posted there as SP from 23 Feb 2004 to 14 Dec 2006 and was not posted there during Feb/March 2002.**

On page 363, the SIT quotes the then Commissioner of Police of Vadodara, D D Tuteja as saying that on 28 Feb 2002, an Islamic Centre in a curfew bound area was attacked, but the police intervened and all 102 children residing there were shifted to a safer place by the police.

Zakia's complaint alleges that Bhagyesh Jha, the then Collector of Vadodara district had not filed any affidavit before Nanavati Shah Commission. **But this turned out to be another lie, and he had filed an affidavit on 15 October 2004, and produced a copy of it to the SIT. This was stated in the report by the SIT on page 366.**

There are even more mistakes in Zakia Jafri's complaint. We have not mentioned all of them. It is astonishing that while the SIT has made observations, recommended departmental action against some individuals accused in the complaint, it has not said anything against the complaint makers for making such blatantly false allegations, naming innocent people in the complaint. Just because one lost close relatives in the riots, this doesn't give anyone the license to make baseless, false allegations on anyone without any evidence, and make massive mistakes in a childish complaint.

Role of Amicus Curiae Raju Ramachandran

Madhu Kishwar, the founder editor of *Manushi- A Journal About Women and Society* and founder president of Manushi Sangathan, an organisation committed to strengthening women's rights and democratic rights in India, has written in her book *"Modi, Muslims and Media"* (Manushi Publications, 2014) on page 216: "Prashant Bhushan and Raju Ramachandran, the two amicus curiae appointed by the Supreme Court at different points, have been close collaborators of Teesta Setalvad."

The SIT had submitted its findings to the Supreme Court on 17 November 2010, and Raju Ramachandran, the Amicus Curiae, had examined it and submitted his observations on 20 Jan 2011. The SIT reports his observations on pages 383-389. In his observations, he had said that it would not be possible for anyone present in the meeting on 27 Feb 2002 to speak against Modi, especially the bureaucracy and the police officials. He also said that it may not be correct to rule out the presence of Sanjiv Bhatt in the meeting, and that Haren Pandya's statements to the CCT be used. He claimed that R Sreekumar's statement cannot be discarded as hearsay in light of Section 6 of the Evidence Act. He also said that 2 Ministers were placed in Control Rooms (Ashok Bhatt and I K Jadeja) and this would be done by the CM. He further said that the allegation that the CM did not visit riot-affected areas of Ahmedabad immediately, though he visited Godhra on the day of the carnage, indicates that the CM had not taken enough steps to ensure that riots in Ahmedabad City were immediately controlled by his direct intervention. And most importantly, Ramachandran claimed that Modi's interview to Zee News on 1st March 2002 indicates an attempt to justify violence against the minority community.

These observations (along with some others) were further investigated by the SIT. After Ramachandran's first examination and opinion given on 20 Jan 2011, the SC ordered SIT to conduct further investigation on 15 March 2011, which was done and another report was submitted to the SC on 25 April 2011. The Amicus Curaie examined it and gave his recommendations on 25 July 2011. In this report, he agreed with many SIT observations but disagreed with some.

He agreed that since Haren Pandya could not have been present in the 27 Feb night meeting, his statement may be disregarded. He also agreed that R Sreekumar's statement on K Chakravarthi is hearsay and inadmissible as evidence. He also said that the SIT's conclusion on Narendra Modi's steps to control violence in Ahmedabad may be accepted, as also the SIT's observations on Modi's statement on TV on 1st March 2002.

But, at this stage as well, Raju Ramachandran claimed that prima facie offences under 153-A, 153-B, 166 and 502(2) IPC are made out against Modi. He further said that it would be for the competent court to decide whether Modi should be summoned for these offences or any other offences. This was reported by SIT on page 512. Ramachandran's reasons were based on grounds given on page 513. They included the claim of Sanjiv Bhatt that he was present in the 27 Feb meeting, that Sanjiv Bhatt submitted an affidavit on 17.6.2011 of K D Panth supporting Bhatt's version of going to CM's residence on 27 Feb night. Ramachandran basically says that it's unlikely that Bhatt would make such an allegation on a Chief Minister without any basis. He said that there is no documentary evidence to show that Bhatt was not present on 27 Feb night meeting, only statements of other participants.

The SIT says on pages 515-516 that the recommendations of Ramachandran are based on the sole testimony of Shri Sanjiv Bhatt, the then DCI (Security) who has claimed to have attended the 27 Feb meeting. The SIT says on page 516:

"The Ld. Amicus Curiae has wrongly projected that Shri K.D.Panth, constable has supported the version of Shri Sanjiv Bhatt about the latter's visit to CM's residence on 27.02.2002, in as much as Shri K.D.Panth has lodged a complaint on 17.06.2011, against Shri Sanjiv Bhatt for wrongful confinement and also for getting an affidavit signed from him under duress and threat and a case I CR No. 149/2011 was registered u/s 189, 193, 195, 341, 342 IPC against Sanjiv Bhatt on 22.06.2011 in Ghatlodia P.S., Ahmedabad City. Shri Raju Ramachandran has relied upon a copy of this affidavit which was handed over to him by Shri Sanjiv Bhatt on 17.06.2011. In fact, Shri K.D.Panth had sent a letter to Chairman, SIT in this regard on 17.06.2011 itself along with another affidavit sworn before the Dy. Collector, Gandhinagar to the effect that he was on leave on 27.02.2002 and that his statement made before the

SIT in this regard was correct. **It would not be out of place to mention here that a copy of the said letter along with the affidavit submitted to SIT by Shri K.D.Panth with its English translation were handed over to Shri Raju Ramchandran by Shri Y.C.Modi, Member, SIT and Shri A.K.Malhotra, Member, SIT personally on 21.06.2011, but the same has been conveniently ignored by the Ld. Amicus Curiae."**

The SIT in the next lines says that the then DGP Chakravarthi dismissed Sanjiv Bhatt's claims that Bhatt accompanied him in his staff car to CM's residence on 27 Feb night and that two PSOs to the then DGP (Chakravarthi) and two drivers attached to the DGP have categorically denied that Sanjiv Bhatt ever travelled in DGPs staff car.

The SIT says on page 517:

"It is significant to note that the Ld. Amicus Curiae had admitted that

'I am conscious of the fact that though Shri Sanjiv Bhatt has been contending that he would speak only when under a legal obligation to do so, his conduct after making his statement u/s 161 Cr.PC has not been that of a detached police officer, who is content with giving his version. I am left with no doubt that he is actively "strategizing" and is in touch with those, who would benefit or gain mileage from his testimony.'

The Ld. Amicus Curiae has also mentioned that Shri Rahul Sharma, DIG has submitted an analysis of the call records of senior police officers, which according to Shri Sharma corroborates the statement of Shri Bhatt. Shri Rahul Sharma never said anything like that before the SIT. **Shri Rahul Sharma has not stated that in what manner the call details of the senior officers corroborate the statement of Shri Sanjiv Bhatt."**

On page 518 the SIT continues: **"The view of the Ld. Amicus Curiae that it does not appear very likely that a serving police officer would make such a serious allegation without some basis appears to be erroneous in as much as Shri Sanjiv Bhatt had been all along a delinquent in his career and had been trying to bargain with the government.** The very fact that three departmental enquiries against Shri Sanjiv Bhatt were dropped in 2006-07 and he was given three promotions on a single day would by itself go to show his service career progression. Again, his promotion to the rank of IGP was due for quite some time but he did not get the same because of other departmental enquiries as well as court cases pending against him. The reason by itself is sufficient to bring a motive on part of Sanjiv Bhatt to make a statement against the Chief Minister...**The observation made by the Ld. Amicus Curiae that Shri Sanjiv Bhatt cannot be disbelieved because his statement was motivated and he has an axe to grind against the government over issues concerning his career and also that his statement was not supported by other officers, is absurd...**"

The SIT says on page 519 that Ramachandran's observations that Bhatt's call records do not contradict his claim is baseless as the same do not even support his statement. **And the SIT says that his call records do contradict his claim of being present in the meeting on 28 Feb morning.** On pages 521-22 the SIT quotes Modi's statements urging people to maintain peace and that the culprits of Godhra would be punished. It gives details of the sections claimed by Ramachandran and refutes the claim that any offence can be made out under them.

After careful consideration of the matter, including the Amicus Curiae's views of 25 July 2011 (believing Sanjiv Bhatt and making out offences against Narendra Modi) the SC gave an order on 12 September 2011, ending its monitoring and transferring the case to the lower trial court. The Supreme Court did not agree with the claims of Ramachandran.

This shows the bias of Raju Ramachandran. His initial report on 20 Jan 2011 saying that Sreekumar's claim on Chakravarthi is acceptable, Haren Pandya's claim should be accepted and that Modi 'appeared to justify violence against the minority community' shows the reality-his bias against Modi. He himself accepted the SIT's findings in his later report on the above issues. Sreekumar did not give any evidence of Chakravarthi saying anything to him, and Chakravarthi denied saying so- this is no evidence at all, as even the most amateur knower of law would know. The same is seen with regard to Haren Pandya and also on the Zee News interview, when no CD was made available at all.

The Amicus Curiae's conduct of ignoring Sanjiv Bhatt bringing K.D.Panth to the SIT and insisting Panth's examination in his presence (the deeds of Sanjiv Bhatt were termed by SIT as an attempt to tutor witnesses) and claiming that Panth supported Bhatt's version when he in fact filed a police complaint against Sanjiv Bhatt shows that the Amicus Curiae was heavily biased against Narendra Modi and in favour of Sanjiv Bhatt. **Sanjiv Bhatt's claim of being present in a meeting in Gandhinagar on 28 Feb morning, contradicted by his call records** was also ignored. Rahul Sharma never said that Sanjiv Bhatt's statements have been corroborated by call records of some individuals, **which the Amicus Curiae wrongly claimed**. After examining the claim of Sanjiv Bhatt (by us in Myth 19 as well as by the SIT, particularly the disclosure on emails between Sanjiv Bhatt, Arjun Modhvadhia, Shaktisinh Gohil, Teesta Setalvad, Rahul Sharma), it would have enough evidence to convince any person with an iota of common sense that Sanjiv Bhatt was not present at the meeting, or at least his claim of being present cannot be relied upon. Sanjiv Bhatt asking Rahul Sharma to tell his own call records of 27 Feb and asking him to find out if Haren Pandya was present in the meeting or not based on call records would conclusively show that Sanjiv Bhatt was not present at all.

It seems that the Amicus Curiae desperately wanted some offences to be made out against Narendra Modi. But the extent of his desperate claims became obvious in his statement of 20 January 2011. So after SITs re-investigation, he dropped most of what he claimed on 20 January 2011, accepted many of SIT's findings but still wanted some stick to beat Narendra Modi with.

This writer always knew the ideology of Prashant Bhushan, and his strong anti-BJP views and anti-Narendra Modi views, but he did not know Raju Ramachandran's alleged links with Teesta Setalvad. Madhu Kishwar's book claiming that on page 216 has made things very clear.

It is not that the Amicus Curiae is genuine in his views, he conveniently ignored facts- like the SIT informing him of K.D.Panth's letter and affidavit. The SIT has investigated all the allegations, found most of the allegations to be 'not established' and recommended departmental action against some individuals. The Amicus Curiae is completely wrong in saying that no person present in the 27 Feb meeting would speak against Modi. On the contrary, with a media eager to make anyone talking against Modi a 'hero', rewards from political rivals, NGOs etc, there was a strong cause for any of the participants to do so, but none of them did. And by that logic, he implies that words of people not present in the meeting be considered to judge what happened inside the meeting!

The media has of course, covered up all the mistakes of Zakia Jafri. But this SIT report confirms many of the facts that we said in this book right from 2007. It also exposes most of the mistakes of Zakia Jafri's complaint. The SIT also reveals in its report that some people were trying to influence the Amicus Curiae. The Amicus Curiae had said that though not a single person present in the 27 Feb meeting has supported Sanjiv Bhatt's claim of being present, that though Bhatt had several axes to grind against the Modi Government, still these grounds are not sufficient to disregard his claim. The SIT has exposed the biased Ramachandran by revealing how he conveniently ignored several facts told to him by SIT members.

Here, one feels that there should be accountability. Some action should be taken against Ramachandran for trying to forcibly make out cases against innocent individuals, i.e. Narendra Modi, and for saying that K.D.Panth supported Sanjiv Bhatt's claim when he in fact filed a police complaint.

This shows how much biases can affect the behavior of people in important positions. Ultimately, it was a matter of great fortune that the SIT resisted the temptation of succumbing to pressure from the media, the NGOs, the political opponents, the Amicus Curiae also, and brought out the truth.

CHAPTER 13

THE CAUSES OF THE LIES

By now, throughout this book, we have seen the lies that biased people in the English media and the private television channels have spread and concocted about the Gujarat riots. We have seen the truth of the riots and the contrast of day and night in the versions of the riots as projected by the English media, Indian and also global and the reality of the Gujarat riots. But the question here arises—Why do these people in the media lie? This chapter aims at explaining the causes of those lies.

Many in the *Sangh Parivar* (RSS and allied organizations like VHP, ABVP, BJP etc) believe that 'it is the business' of the English media to condemn and malign the RSS. What does this mean? Another pro-RSS individual, G.C. Asnani (born 1922), has written: "Some politicians and press people are also there to make some money coming from outside India."

In other words, some of them believe that the media is paid to utter these lies by either the foreign Christian nations, or opponents of the *Sangh Parivar* in India such as the CPI (M) and Christian missionaries in India, some of whom are funded from abroad. Some others go to the extent of calling these newspaper editors as 'anti-nationals' and people having no national self-respect.

But this would not be a correct assessment. There is much more to this, than what meets the eye. Alok Tiwari, then one of the editors of the Nagpur-based English daily, *The Hitavada*, wrote in his weekly column in the daily dated 26th February, 2006, "If it (the claim that the English media is funded from abroad) was true, it would be one of the biggest stories in India. Is he (the then RSS chief, K.S. Sudarshan) saying that the media is paid to attack the RSS.... This media has also been very harsh on the Leftists just as much as the RSS in recent times...."

After the then Gujarat Chief Minister Narendra Modi won a huge majority in the Gujarat Assembly elections, *India Today* (30 December 2002) interviewed him. Some parts of that interview were as follows:

"Q. While in Delhi, you were quite popular as the national BJP spokesman. But as the Chief Minister, you emerged as a hate figure for the media. Why?

A. It is a loaded question. A vast section of the media has no problem with me. Yes, there is a section that is critical of me through sheer conviction. I take that in my stride. But there is yet another section that vilifies me only because it will have to down its shutters if it doesn't. Members of this section are rootless people who have no connection with the country's ground realities. I go by a *chopai* (verse) in Tulsidas' *Ramayan*: 'Nindak nikat raakhiye re' (Keep critics close to you)."

Narendra Modi here clearly states that there is a section of the media that is critical of him through sheer conviction. Among the third category of the media that is critical of Narendra Modi simply because it will have to down its shutters if it does not, *Combat Communalism* of Teesta Setalvad and Javed Akhtar could perhaps be one. Teesta Setalvad herself admitted in an interview to SAB TV in December 2004 that *Combat Communalism* was being given donation by the then CPI (M) Government of West Bengal. *Combat Communalism* gave full-page advertisements in English dailies in 1999 before the Lok Sabha polls held in September & October 1999 in India, urging people not to vote for the BJP. When it was asked how it managed to get funds (the ads cost more than one crore rupees), it admitted that Congress, Left, etc. gave them money. (*Source:* http://web.archive.org/web/20021217191815/http://www.humanscapeindia.net/humanscape/hs1199/hs11997t.htm).

As Modi says, members of this section are rootless people, who have no connection with India's ground realities. This section could be one which castigates Modi simply because it has no other source to earn money.

Vir Sanghvi's article

What *The Hindustan Times'* editor, Vir Sanghvi wrote on 28 Feb 2002, reproduced here in Chapter 2 really explains everything on the issue. See his sentences, **"...we are programmed to see Hindu- Muslim relations in simplistic terms: Hindus provoke, Muslims suffer.** When this formula does not work—it is clear now that a well-armed Muslim mob murdered unarmed Hindus—**we simply do not know how to cope."**

We have already made an analysis of that statement. The reason for this 'programming' arises out of the majority-minority divide. **In all over the world, it is the minority which is oppressed by the majority. In India, Muslims are the minority. And, hence, "Hindus oppress Muslims" is assumed.** Instead of looking at the past of how Muslims dealt with the Hindus right since A.D. 636, and seeing that Muslims oppress the Hindus in Pakistan, Bangladesh etc the newspaper editors are lost in a world of their own. They also do not consider one thing—that some Muslims of India can also be communal. And the second reason is—mental slavery of minorities and cowardice.

Origin of 'Secular' Word

This word originated in medieval Europe. In medieval Europe, the Pope and the Church had a large and immoral influence on the king, i.e. the State. Secularism in Europe meant separation of the Church and the State. There were no religious minorities, for whom equal respect meant secularism. It was, in a way, anti-Church, as it wanted to restrict the Church's powers and oppose its corrupt practices.

But in India, there is no Church. Hence, the only institution parallel to it is Hinduism. And, hence, 'anti-Hinduism' became secularism for those people who blindly imitate the West. The weekly *India Today* wrote in its editorial dated 30th December 2002, **"Secularism in practice in India meant romancing the minority and demonizing the majority".**

This one-sided, lack of objective and rational thinking and closed-mindedness continues to haunt the 'secularist' newspaper editors.

In his report in the weekly *India Today* dated 8th April, 2002, Swapan Dasgupta wrote: "On May 14, 1970, initiating a discussion on the Bhiwandi riots in Maharashtra, Atal Bihari Vajpayee delivered a speech, that could well be a replication of what the Gujarat Chief Minister, Narendra Modi is professing today. **He cited a Home Ministry report that blamed Muslims for starting 23 of the 24 riots between 1968 and 1970.** "We must understand two things," he went on to say, "Our Muslim brethren are getting more and more communal, and as a reaction, Hindus are getting more and more aggressive.... Hindus will no more take a beating in this country." On the face of it, nothing has really changed in 32 years. The same charges of Muslim aggression, RSS instigation, official blundering and police partisanship, that followed every communal clash in the past, are being repeated."

The truth again is that Muslims started 23 out of the 24 riots in between 1968 and 1970. This was again as per the report of the Union Home Ministry of the Congress Party. But this remained largely ignored.

And as we have seen earlier, the media tried to concoct imaginary provocations for the Godhra massacre. But the important thing noticed by S.K. Modi in his book, *Godhra—The Missing Rage* was:

"...They (the media) forgot to tell us:

1. If it was a conspiracy, it was worse than 9/11.
2. If **it was spontaneous, it was even worse.**"

When it was blatantly clear that it was impossible for Godhra to have been anything but planned, the 'secularists' blamed the Ayodhya movement for it. *The Hindu* said: "This said, one cannot but pin- point the harsh reality that events such as the horror of Godhra were tragically predictable as a result of the wounding and aggressive communal campaign of the VHP." It was far from it. Godhra was by no means a predictable event. If Godhra was 'predictable', because of the Ayodhya movement, then was not the Ayodhya movement predictable, because of the slaughter of so many innocent Hindus in the past by foreign Muslims, especially for the Ayodhya temple? **Were not the post-Godhra riots predictable because of the aggressive communal murders of**

Hindus in Godhra by Muslims? At that time, all 'predictability' came to an end, and the riots were called as 'state-sponsored riots'.

To think that the gruesome murder of 59 innocent people including 40 women and children in a horrifying manner, not allowing a single person to escape from the coach, and watching 15 children burn to death in a ghastly manner by the mob outside, is predictable, is nothing but mental bankruptcy, which is an integral part of a section of the media.

See This Mentality on other Incidents

In January 1999, violent clashes took place between Hindu tribals and Christians in Gujarat's tribal belts, i.e. Dangs district. Instead of opening their eyes and seeing what happened, they immediately closed their eyes and the moment they saw clashes, they blamed the Hindus and took side of the Christians. They, needless to say, at random, blamed the *Sangh Parivar*, Hindu organisations like the RSS, the VHP, the Bajrang Dal, etc. and the BJP Government of the State. The opposition party, Congress demanded the resignation of the State BJP Government for the clashes, in which not a single person died and not even a single bone was broken.

The hue-and-cry raised by some organisations and the self-styled secularists was amusing. The minority group allegedly started the trouble (and violence) by stoning the meeting of the tribals, who had gathered there to protect their religion, following reckless conversion of Hindus in that area. The tribals then retaliated by stoning back at the group, who then cried, "Communalism, Communalism!" The newspaper editors and writers, who are partisan as from Vir Sanghvi's piece, then immediately blamed the Hindus editorially and otherwise, and condemned the RSS, the VHP, the Bajrang Dal, and the BJP Government of the State, ignoring the basic cause of violence. The violence against anyone, be it minorities or the majority should be reported, as violence in any form is condemnable. But the full truth also should be reported on the merit of the question, on who started the trouble.

Acharya Giriraj Kishore (1920-2014) gave a statement released in New Delhi on 2 January 1999, carried by the weekly *Organiser* dated 10 January 1999. *Organiser* reported: "The senior VHP leader termed the allegations as a part of a well-calculated global conspiracy to lower the BJP and the VHP in the eyes of the world. The VHP leader said that in recent incidents, Christian youths attacked a peaceful public meeting and insulted several Hindu saints. **He quoted a report carried by** *The Asian Age* **on 26 December, 1998, that, 'about 35 Christian youths mounted an attack on a 3,000-odd Hindu public meeting in the Ahwa town. Swami Ramdasji and Amar Singhji, Maharaj of Surat, were hurt, and eight persons were injured'.** Likewise, *Gujarat Samachar* carried news of this incident on 25th December and wrote that arson and pilferage were carried out in a Hanuman temple near Ahwa. Mainly similar news-items ignored; a mispropaganda was also carried out and the aggressors were projected as the victims and they have been masquerading as such, he said..."

Some parts of these statements could be exaggerations.

If some people could dare to blame Godhra on VHP and the *karsevaks* by concocting provocations and misbehaviour, in an event where everyone could see the reality, then what must they have done and what must they be doing in events not so clear? This is made clearer by Vir Sanghvi's statement, "When everybody can see that a trainload of Hindus was massacred by a Muslim mob, you gain nothing by blaming the murders on the VHP or arguing that the dead men and women had it coming to them." So, perhaps if everybody could not see that a trainload of Hindus was massacred by a Muslim mob, then it would have been understandable to blame the murders on the VHP or by arguing that the dead men and women (and children) had it coming.

In most of the clashes in India, things are not so clear. The case of Dangs quoted above is the perfect example. The statement—"If you report the truth, then you will inflame Hindu sentiments..." also reveals their mentality. And that is, Hindu sufferings should not be reported; Hindu suffering is of no consequence. These people have somehow managed to convince themselves this— because of the 'fear' of inflaming Hindus. That is one reason why they reported like this on Godhra and have ignored many attacks on Hindus by Muslims and others in India. Four RSS officials were kidnapped in Tripura (on 6 August 1999), held captive for over one year and then brutally killed—an event unnoticed by the media. There are many more such instances.

And the reality is exactly the opposite. Hindu sufferings should be reported because Hindus hardly ever retaliate. And the media has inflamed Muslim sentiments through its lies on the Gujarat riots.

Afghanistan's Death Penalty

In March 2006, the first Muslim in Afghanistan who had converted to Christianity, Abdul Rahman, was given death penalty for it. This was legal in a country supposedly rescued by liberals from the fanatical Taliban.

What were its reactions in India? Absolutely none. No newspaper editor bothered about this. The self-styled secularists remained quiet. The TV channels also were silent. No angry editorials appeared in the English dailies condemning the blatant violation of freedom of religion. Only Swaminathan Aiyar wrote in his weekly column in *The Times of India* dated 2 April 2006 about this. He also condemned the others of his fellow-secularist brigade for their silence. He wrote:

"The Sad Silence Over Abdul Rahman

If the Rashtriya Swayamsevak Sangh proposed that any Hindu who converted to Islam or Christianity should be hanged, there would be a hue and cry. Political parties ranging from the Congress to the Samajwadi Party to the Left Front, would condemn the shameful bigotry of the RSS, and rightly so. I would be at the forefront of the chorus of condemnation. Although I am an atheist, I believe that to kill a man for changing his religious beliefs is appalling. It is a throwback to the ghastly ancient Catholic custom of burning heretics at the stake.

So, I am aghast at the virtual silence in India over the proposed execution of Abdul Rahman of Afghanistan for what his country's legal system regards as the capital offence of having converted to Christianity.

But I hear no outcry from moderate Muslims, or Hindu intellectuals, who normally wave the secular flag. None of the major secular parties seems interested in deploring the horror. They would rather bury their heads in the sand and emerge only when Hindu communalism is the issue. I always knew that Afghanistan's new Constitution made it an Islamic state. But I had no idea that its laws called for the execution of any Muslim, who converts to another religion. Needless to say, the law happily permits Christians or Hindus to convert to Islam. **This is not a case of some Islamic extremist saying crazy things. This is not a law in some state ruled by mad *mullahs*. It is the law in a country supposedly rescued by liberals from the religious extremism of the Taliban. It is the law in a country that India hails as secular, and as an old friend**. For that reason, intellectuals and political parties that never hesitated to condemn the excesses of the Taliban, are silent today. To me, this reeks of hypocrisy.

Abdul Rahman's troubles began with a divorce suit. He attempted to gain custody of his children, but his wife told the court that Rahman was unfit to get custody since he had converted to Christianity 16 years earlier. An alert prosecutor promptly charged Rahman with apostasy, punishable by death.

The prosecution had widespread public support. Rahman had to be kept in a high-security cell for fear that other prison inmates would kill him. Apparently, his 'crime' was enough to enrage even the hardened criminals.

Most people would have quickly repudiated their conversion to escape death. But Rahman refused to budge. Go ahead and kill me, he said, but I will remain true to my faith.

This was politically inconvenient for the Afghan President, Hamid Karzai, who had come to power with American assistance. Instead of amending the obnoxious law, he has (with the connivance of courts) resorted to the stratagem of pretending that Rahman is insane and unfit to stand trial.

Probably, Rahman will be given asylum in some foreign country. Some would say that a man, who prefers death to religious opportunism, is indeed insane. I say that a person willing to die for his religious beliefs, without threatening violence or retribution, is a hero. My fellow secularists will argue: Why raise a fuss about Abdul Rahman? He is going to be sent out of Afghanistan, and will not die. Indeed, sundry Christian associations will hail and support him wherever he goes. **To me, this is moral cowardice parading as pragmatism.** Religious bigotry, whether of the Hindu or Islamic variety, is a curse, an evil. If it is not attacked wherever it exists, it will spread.

I have fought most of my life against Hindu religious bigotry, and castigated the Rashtriya Swayamsevak Sangh as a threat to the social fabric of multi-cultural India. **I have viewed Indian Muslim communalism as a minor threat, and sometimes, no more than a reaction to Hindu bigotry.** But international Muslim communalism today is a rising threat to all of us, as evidenced by foreign religious soldiers in Kashmir, and bomb blasts in Indian cities.

A milder but still disturbing form of international communalism is the lack of protests in Muslim countries over Abdul Rahman's prosecution. It bodes ill for the future. We need to fight all religious bigotry—Muslim, Hindu or Christian. We must not gloss over the shocking Afghan law placing religious converts at par with murderers, worthy of execution.

I use the word 'we', yet I do not know how many people are with me on this issue. **I hear mainly silence from the Islamic countries. I hear mainly silence from supposed secularists in India. Hardly anybody wants to rock the boat for something as minor as principle.**

All my life, I have sought a brotherhood of man. But if some fellow humans say I can be killed for my beliefs, will they ever be my brothers? Is there any future for this vision of brotherhood?"

There is no need to explain anything after this self-confessed article by Aiyar. The only point that we should analyze is "I have viewed Indian Muslim communalism as a minor threat, and sometimes, no more than a reaction to Hindu bigotry." The reality is the opposite. It is Hindu communalism which is a minor threat to India, and it is at times only a reaction to Islamic communalism. Aiyar and his ilk are blind to the stunning de-Hinduisation in India, Pakistan and Bangladesh, right since 1947. Hindu and Sikh population in Pakistan has reduced from around 22 per cent in 1947 to just 1 per cent now, in Bangladesh it has reduced from 29 per cent in 1947 to just 10 per cent in 2001, and in India, it has declined from more than 85 per cent in 1951 to just 80.5 per cent in 2001. For undivided India, the Hindu population was 79 per cent in 1881, while the Muslim population was 19% or so. In 1991, i.e. within 110 years, the Hindu population reduced to 67% while the Muslim population was 29.9 per cent. In 2001, the Muslim population crossed 30 per cent in the sub continent. And by some estimates, Hindus will become a minority in 2047 in the subcontinent. Of course, for some of our self-proclaimed secularists in the media, even destruction of Hinduism is not a bad thing, since Hindus are 'medieval, casteist people' in their opinion. But for a mutli-cultural, plural world, doesn't it also need a Hindu homeland? A prominent individual when asked by a reporter in the 1960s 'Is India only for Hindus?' had replied: 'Only India is for Hindus'.

It is the habit of this section of the media to rationalize anything wrong that any Muslim does. But what rationalization can any objective person give of the Abdul Rahman case?

Contempt for Tradition

These elite media men, who are self- proclaimed 'secularists' and 'champions of minorities' and 'guardians of humanity' and 'conscience—keepers' have contempt for tradition.

They are basically English speaking people and have contempt for their own native things. **Veteran columnist, M.V. Kamath (1921- 9 October 2014) once wrote in weekly *Organiser*, "Strange though it may sound, there are no other people in the world who derive as much pleasure from** condemning their countrymen, maligning their country as Indians, and who have as much contempt for their country's glorious past and achievements and traditions as Indian secularists". They have no pride in the country's glorious past, and no desire to safeguard ancient treasures of knowledge of this country. Gurcharan Das, a self-styled secularist himself wrote in *The Times of India* in May 2003, "I was reading an ancient book when a friend came and said seeing me read the ancient book, 'You haven't embraced Hindutva, have you?' I was left wondering—Is reading an ancient book 'communal'?" Gurcharan Das has, on many occasions, criticized his fellow pseudo-secularists' false ideas of 'secularism' and cited examples such as opposition to teaching of *Ramayana* and *Mahabharata* to schoolchildren by headmasters for fear of being called 'communal'.

What Gurcharan says for his friends is true for all self-styled secularists. Can you ever imagine Prannoy Roy, Rajdeep Sardesai, Barkha Dutt, Vir

Sanghvi, Vinod Sharma, Yogendra Yadav, Pankaj Pachouri, Shekhar Gupta, etc. reading our ancient books like Vedas, Ramayana, etc.? Can you ever imagine them donating money for such organisations working to protect our ancient literature? Do these people seem to have any affection to Sanskrit as an ancient language, which needs to be protected?

The answer to all these questions is 'No'. Reading the blogs of some of these journalists of TV channels like CNN-IBN on its website, it is clear that for them it is mandatory to attack VHP before doing anything to prove their 'secularism'. This media is completely Westernized, with contempt for anything cultural and traditional. This media has been harsh on Narendra Modi (like schoolchildren angry with a teacher for scolding them, without looking at the story in whole) and not only that, but also on anyone who has not attacked Modi. This media has criticized George Fernandes, Mayawati and all those who backed Narendra Modi in 2002. This media was livid with so-called secular NDA allies like Trinamool Congress, TDP, JD(U), DMK, MDMK, PMK, etc. for not supporting the dismissal of the Modi Government in May 2002.

But Arun Jaitley, General Secretary of the BJP, was one of the strongest advocates of Modi. He defended Modi rigorously all along right from March 2002. Not only that, he attacked anti-Modi people like NHRC. But despite this, the media loves Arun Jaitley. This is because he is fluent English-speaking, suave, urban and modern. The same was true also for the late Pramod Mahajan.

But Uma Bharti, Narendra Modi, Kalyan Singh and Rajnath Singh are not fluent in speaking English and are ideologically very firm. Hence, they are not the media's favorites. **If Arun Jaitley had been the Chief Minister of Gujarat during Godhra and the post-Godhra riots, the media may have painted the truth and lauded him for saving 24,000 Muslims, and controlling the riots within three days.**

Reactions after Danish Cartoons Episode

In February 2006, some European newspapers published objectionable cartoons on the Prophet Muhammad. They were originally drawn by a Danish cartoonist and published in a newspaper in Denmark.

After that unfortunate incident, many Muslims from all over the world came to the streets, resulting in the deaths of at least 32 people. India too was affected by these Muslim protests. Violence was seen at many places. Frank and outright condemnation of the violence was not done by everybody. A few journalists did say that the offended people should: "Protest, but peacefully". Vir Sanghvi had the courage to call a spade a spade. He wrote on 11 February, 2006 in *The Hindustan Times*, the following:

"I am sorry if you feel you have had enough of the latest religion vs. freedom of expression controversy: the fuss over the Danish cartoons that featured the Prophet Mohammed. And yes, I am also sorry that my own position mirrors familiar liberal arguments—so, no surprises there. But I do think that much of what has been said or written about the issue misses the point. So, bear with me this Sunday.

The first distinction that I think is blurred, is the difference between causing offence and losing the right to freedom of expression. All of us accept that religion is a sensitive subject. We recognize that men who will forgive jokes about their looks, their jobs, or their wives, will suddenly lose their tempers when you make the slightest reference to their faiths. Thus, even if we make ethnic jokes, we will laugh at the community, not at the religion. It may be okay to crack a Sardarji joke (though these days, even that seems less acceptable) but you never ever say anything jokey about Guru Govind Singh or Guru Nanak.

So, we refrain from offending people about their religions; we exercise some internal restraint. But do we lose the right to focus on religion—in a critical or satirical way—only because we know it may cause offence?

The philosophical distinction is an important one. We have no right to make defamatory or slanderous statements about people. All of us also accept that the right to free speech can be curtailed on grounds of national security. But there are good reasons for these limitations. To reveal defence secrets may compromise the security of the state. To defame somebody harms their reputations and affects how they are perceived in the eyes of the public.

Do statements that cause religious offence, fall in the same category? To argue that they do, we would have to prove that they caused damage to the safety of the religious faith (the national security parallel) or that they affected the way the faith was perceived by society, or even lowered its standing. But surely none of the people, who complain about insults to religion, accept that the slights can have these consequences? Is the safety of Islam threatened because a Danish newspaper carries a cartoon? Is Islam so weak a religion that a couple of cartoons can cause the world or society in general to think less of it?

Clearly not. So, I'm not sure on what grounds we could abridge the right to free speech when it comes to religion. The only argument you are left with is the "it has caused offence" line. And nearly all of the big ban-this-book, burn-this-cartoon, destroy-this-painting kind of demands have rested on the we-are-offended argument.

But just because something offends you, it does not follow that you have the right to stop me from saying it. For instance, I am deeply offended by the insistence of the more reactionary elements in the Catholic Church that the only way to get to heaven is to swear allegiance to the Vatican. But I wouldn't dream of banning anybody— let alone the current Panzer Pope—from saying it. I am also offended by the Muslim fundamentalist position that a woman who wears make-up is loose and, therefore, condemned to eternal damnation. But I would not arrest or assault any loony cleric, who took this position.

The problem with the people who think that their sense of offence gives them the right to curb your or my freedom of expression is that the basis of their value system is illiberal. I am quite prepared to believe that many Muslims find *The Satanic Verses* offensive. But my solution to their anger is simple enough: don't read the damn thing—that way you won't be offended. They have no business to curtail my right to read the book.

Similarly, I am prepared to believe that members of the VHP find M.F. Husain's portrayals of the goddess Saraswati offensive. But given that the VHP is not a body that is known for its love of fine art, the solution there is also simple enough: don't go to a gallery and see the paintings. But do not deny an artist the right to create art. And do not deny me my right to view it.

Of course, we should be sensitive to religious sentiments. Of course, we should try and avoid giving offence. But these are not absolute rules. If we do cause offence, then we are still within our rights as citizens of a free society to do so. And the people who are offended should simply avert their gaze. In no liberal society does the causing of offence automatically give those who are offended the right to demand bans.

The second important point that is blurred in this debate is that many of the people who protest the loudest have not actually been offended at all. Syed Shahbuddin had not even read *The Satanic Verses* when he demanded a ban on the book. **The international Muslims, who are calling for action against the Danish paper that carried the offending cartoons, have not even seen the cartoons.** The so-called Indian Muslim leader, who demanded that we expel the Danish ambassador, had never glanced at the offending cartoons.

It is instructive that the agitation against the Danish cartoons began three months after their publication. In many cases—dare one say, in nearly every case?—the outrage is manufactured by religious and political leaders, who whip a frenzy among ignorant followers. Let's stick with *The Satanic Verses*. **Ayatollah Khomeini placed the fatwa on Salman Rushdie's head only because he heard about demonstrations in the Indian subcontinent. He never read the book and nor did any of his assassins.**

After the rabble-rousers have manufactured the outrage, they incite their followers to violence. The argument then placed before governments is straightforward blackmail: if you do not ban the book/ film/play/newspaper, etc. then there will be a riot and people will die.

Governments are expected to say, surely no cartoon is worth the lives of innocent people, and to promptly declare a ban.

It is to the credit of Western societies that they rarely give in to this blackmail. In India, unfortunately, we surrender at the slightest provocation. And so every nasty, unpleasant political grouping has a readymade strategy: protest against a book on Shivaji, an art exhibition, a novel or a movie. The threat of violence (and, in many cases, the violence itself) will cause the state to impose a ban and the political grouping will seem important and powerful. That is how the unit of *Water* was driven out of India and that is how the Shiv Sena has hounded M.F. Hussain.

India is not to become a soft state, then we must stand up for liberal principles. We must stand up to the rioters, arrest those who foment violence and never, ever, give in to the blackmail.

The third point is one that I am always reluctant to make because I know it will be misused by right-wing fanatics and extremists. But I think I am going to make it anyway. All of us who espouse the secular cause follow—to some degree—a double standard when it comes to comparing Muslim anger to Hindu outrage. I first noticed this during *The Satanic Verses* controversy when perfect liberals—men who railed against Hindu fundamentalism day after day—suddenly abandoned their liberal values and began supporting a ban on the book on the grounds that minority sentiments were at stake.

We see this now on a regular basis. All of us are outraged when the VHP or the Shiv Sena objects to Hussain's portrayals of Hindu goddesses and argue that, as an artist, he has perfect right to paint what he likes. **But would we take the same position if his paintings offended Muslims?**

The sad truth is that we are much more mindful of offending the sentiments of Muslims than we are of Hindus, Sikhs or Christians.

We claim we do this because we know that Muslims are a minority. **But the real reason is because we know that Muslims tend to protest more loudly than Hindus; because these protests can be unreasonable; and because so few liberal Muslims stand up to the extremists in their community.** When the VHP goes on the rampage, it is the liberal Hindus who issue the loudest condemnation. When the lunatic fringe of the Muslim community gets agitated about the length of Sania Mirza's skirt or about a cartoon in an European paper, few moderate Muslim voices are heard.

In the process, it has become easy for the Hindu zealots to caricature the entire Muslim community as comprising fanatics, fundamentalists and lunatics. As the joke goes: Islam is a peaceful religion and, if you don't accept that, they start sending you death threats.

I have waited many years for liberal Muslims to break this conspiracy of silence. And while I do hear some voices, these are people on the fringes of their community. Muslim liberals are still as shamefully silent as they were when students at Jamia assaulted the gentle and scholarly Mushirul Hassan for saying that while he found *The Satanic Verses* deeply offensive, he did not believe in the principle of banning books.

The time has now come, I think, for us to stop waiting for moderate Muslims to speak up. Liberal Hindus must end the double standard of the secular mindset and speak out as loudly against Muslim fundamentalism as they do against Hindu extremism.

If we do not do that, we discredit the whole concept of secularism. More important, we admit that our liberalism is not an absolute value but a convenient stick to beat Hindu extremists with while making shameful and unnecessary compromises with minority intolerance."

Does this not reveal all the problems of our self-styled secularists?

The statement from Vir Sanghvi that **"But the real reason is because we know that Muslims tend to protest more loudly than Hindus; because these protests can be unreasonable; and because so few liberal Muslims stand up to the extremists in their community",** again gives the game up.

M.F. Hussain (1915-2011) had not painted objectionable paintings of Hindu Goddesses only once in his life. He had wounded Hindu sentiments many times. This is because he did that to deliberately spite the Hindu community. His intention was more to spite the Hindu society than to exhibit his skill. When the Bajrang Dal activists demonstrated against that, they did not kill anyone. No bones were broken, only windowpanes were. The reaction was genuine and controlled one. We make it clear here that we are against even the slightest form of violence, including breaking of windowpanes, and feel that any paintings which are not violations of law should be allowed. Those offended should fight their cause only legally.

And yet, the newspaper editors turned a blind eye to all that and castigated the Bajrang Dal and called it 'Hindu Taliban'. But bomb blasts in Indian cities like Mumbai, Ahmedabad were rationalized and blamed on 'Gujarat riots'. This shows that they rationalize Muslim acts of murder as a result of some provocation; while they do not rationalize Hindu acts of breaking windowpanes despite huge provocations. On the contrary, they call these minor acts of breaking windowpanes as 'Talibanism'!

These newspaper editors and other elite media men, who call themselves 'secularists', have never stopped to think what the impact of their lies is having on the nation, and the Muslim minds. They have lied through the skin of their teeth on the Gujarat riots and painted only Muslims as victims. This has been used by Muslim radicals all over the world to incite innocent Muslims to terrorism. Not only that, many well-meaning Hindus have also fallen prey to it. When the BJP campaigned for Muslim votes in the 2004 Lok Sabha polls, the party was embarrassed because of repeated raising of the Gujarat riots. The BJP did not have the capacity to blast the media myths on the Gujarat riots.

Instead of satisfying their short-sighted goal of demonizing BJP and the Sangh Parivar, the biased section of the media should learn to look at things in totality. While serving the media's aim of maligning the BJP and the Sangh Parivar, the lies of Gujarat riots have caused far more trouble to India. In September 2002, the then President of Pakistan, General Pervez Musharraf made many charges against India at the United Nations. Among them one was the Gujarat riots. The Indian media was debating back home, "Vajpayee will respond to all allegations made by the General. But what answer will he give on Gujarat?" The answer he gave was, "We don't need sermons on secularism from anyone". What could he have done? Could he have condemned the Indian media for lying on the Gujarat riots from the United Nations?

Occasional truths and self-confessed articles by people like Vir Sanghvi, Gurcharan Das and Swaminathan Aiyar result in nothing substantial. It only exposes the truth of the situation, but does nothing to change it. The society undoubtedly needs people to raise the causes of the Muslims as well. The BJP and its ideological allies also need a critic. But the extent should always be in limit.

The case of the Gujarat riots is just the tip of the iceberg. There are so many cases where the truth has lost and lies have triumphed. All attempts should be made to bring out the truth fearlessly. Among the many other cases, some prominent ones are—The Ayodhya movement—Babri demolition, the rape of the nuns in Jhabua, and many others. The case of the death of Netaji Subhash Chandra Bose is another one in point. Did the government of India try to suppress the truth?

In these cases, however, the national motto of the country 'Satyameva Jayate' (Truth alone triumphs) is not true in the least. Facts are hidden from the public, either deliberately or unintentionally. In all such cases, only one thing needs to be remembered:

"Facts do not cease to exist just because they are ignored".

NOTES AND REFERENCES

Bharatiya Vidya Bhavan published "The History and Culture of Indian People"
Chief Editor: R C Majumdar

1	R C Majumdar:	The History and Culture of Indian people;	Vol. 3, p 167
2	RCM	ibid	Vol. 3, p 169
3	RCM	ibid	Vol. 3, p 169
4	RCM	ibid	Vol. 3, p 169
5	RCM	ibid	Vol. 3, p 167
6	RCM	ibid	Vol. 3, p 168
7	RCM	ibid	Vol. 3, p 168
8	RCM	ibid	Vol. 3, p 170
9	RCM	ibid	Vol. 3, pp 172-73
10	RCM	The History and Culture of Indian People	Vol. 4, p 99
11	RCM	ibid	Vol. 4, p 99
12	RCM	The History and Culture of Indian People	Vol. 5, p 2
13	RCM	ibid	Vol. 5, pp 2-5
14	RCM	ibid	Vol. 5, pp 5-22
15	RCM	ibid	Vol. 5, p 6
16	RCM	ibid	Vol. 5, p 6

17	RCM	ibid	Vol. 5, p 7
18	RCM	ibid	Vol. 5, p 8
19	RCM	ibid	Vol. 5, p 8
20	RCM	ibid	ibid
21	RCM	ibid	Vol. 5, pp 8-9
22	RCM	ibid	Vol. 5, p 10
23	RCM	ibid	Vol. 5, p 10
24	RCM	ibid	Vol. 5, p 10
25	RCM	ibid	Vol. 5, p 10
26	RCM	ibid	Vol. 5, p 11
27	RCM	ibid	Vol. 5, p 12
28	RCM	ibid	Vol. 5, p 12
29	RCM	ibid	Vol. 5, p 13
30	RCM	ibid	Vol. 5, pp 13-14
31	RCM	ibid	Vol. 5, p 14
32	RCM	ibid	Vol. 5, p 14
33	RCM	ibid	Vol. 5, p 15
34	RCM	ibid	Vol. 5, p 15
35	RCM	ibid	Vol. 5, p 15
36	RCM	ibid	Vol. 5, p 16
37	RCM	ibid	Vol. 5, p 17
38	RCM	ibid	Vol. 5, pp 17-18
39	RCM	ibid	Vol. 5, p 18
40	RCM	ibid	Vol. 5, p 18
41	RCM	ibid	Vol. 5, p 18
42	RCM	ibid	Vol. 5, p 19
43	RCM	ibid	Vol. 5, p 20
44	RCM	ibid	Vol. 5, pp 21-22
45	RCM	ibid	Vol. 5, p 61
46	RCM	ibid	Vol. 5, p 93
47	RCM	ibid	Vol. 5, p 78
48	RCM	ibid	Vol. 5, p 110
49	RCM	ibid	Vol. 5, p 112
50	RCM	ibid	Vol. 5, p 54

[51]	RCM	ibid	Vol. 5, p 120
[52]	RCM	ibid	Vol. 5, p 120
[53]	RCM	ibid	Vol. 5, p 121
[54]	RCM	ibid	Vol. 5, p 188
[55]	RCM	ibid	Vol. 5, p 123
[56]	RCM	ibid	Vol. 5, p 124
[57]	RCM	ibid	Vol. 5, p 71
[58]	RCM	The History and Culture of Indian People	Vol. 6, pp 15-16
[59]	RCM	ibid	Vol. 6, pp 23-25
[60]	RCM	ibid	Vol. 6, p 29
[61]	RCM	ibid	Vol. 6, pp 33-34
[62]	RCM	ibid	Vol. 6, pp 35-36
[63]	RCM	ibid	Vol. 6, p 63
[64]	RCM	ibid	Vol. 6, pp 76-77
[65]	RCM	ibid	Vol. 6, pp 92-93
[66]	RCM	ibid	Vol. 6, p 252
[67]	RCM	ibid	Vol. 6, pp 162-166
[68]	RCM	ibid	Vol. 6, p 163
[69]	RCM	ibid	Vol. 6, p 163
[70]	RCM	ibid	Vol. 6, p 164
[71]	RCM	ibid	Vol. 6, p 165
[72]	RCM	The History and Culture of Indian People	Vol. 7, p 36
[73]	RCM	ibid	Vol. 7, p 37
[74]	RCM	ibid	Vol. 7, pp 414-415
[75]	RCM	ibid	Vol. 7, p 334
[76]	RCM	ibid	Vol. 7, p 460
[77]	RCM	ibid	Vol. 7, p 235
[78]	RCM	ibid	Vol. 7, p 235
[79]	RCM	ibid	Vol. 7, p 235
[80]	RCM	ibid	Vol. 7, p 321
[81]	RCM	ibid	Vol. 7, pp 322-323

[82]	RCM	The History and Culture of Indian People	Vol. 8, p 127
[83]	RCM	ibid	Vol. 8, p 127
[84]	RCM	ibid	Vol. 8, p 93
[85]	RCM	ibid	Vol. 8, p 123
[86]	RCM	ibid	Vol. 8, p 124
[87]	RCM	ibid	Vol. 8, p 124
[88]	RCM	ibid	Vol. 8, p 124
[89]	RCM	ibid	Vol. 8, p 125
[90]	RCM	ibid	Vol. 8, p 125
[91]	RCM	ibid	Vol. 8, p 125
[92]	RCM	ibid	Vol. 8, p 125
[93]	RCM	ibid	Vol. 11, pp 360-361
[94]	RCM	ibid	Vol. 11, p 436
[95]	RCM	ibid	Vol. 11, p 748

ENDORSEMENTS

"The Gujarat riots of 2002 have made headlines, but of the sort that generates more heat than light. International commotion has ensued, resulting in a hate campaign against Narendra Modi, who suffered the ignominy of being denied a US entry visa even though he was the most successful Chief Minister in India. That Barack Obama was forced to rescind this ban and stand in line for a meeting with Modi, now Prime Minister, was due to changed power equations, not to a correction of the prevalent understanding of the 2002 riots. It has fallen to M D Deshpande to do the laborious job of collecting all the primary data and setting the record straight, both on the riots themselves and on the ensuing campaign by some partisan NGO's and a section of the media. This work does all that, and brings out the truth leaving no doubt." –Dr Koenraad Elst, Belgian Indologist

Funny

"An honest investigator tries to get at the truth by marshalling strong evidence. As an author M D Deshpande has done this job in a forceful manner to present the complete picture of the 2002 Gujarat riots in this book by doing painstaking research. The 2002 episode will forever remain an important chapter in Indian history. The reason: from it rose the phenomenon called Narendra Modi who looks set to rule this nation for quite some time to come. 2002 is the starting point of the Modi story and gives a deep insight as to how and why a majority of Indians saw Modi as the 'wronged' person in the 2002 episode and caused the sympathy factor in his favour. Those who want to know the 2002 episode deeper will find this book very interesting." - Uday Mahurkar, Senior Editor, *India Today*